The Meaning of Others

The
Meaning
of Others

Narrative Studies of Relationships

Edited by
**Ruthellen Josselson, Amia Lieblich,
and Dan P. McAdams**

American Psychological Association
Washington, DC

Published by
American Psychological Association
750 First Street, NE
Washington, DC 20002
www.apa.org

To order
APA Order Department
P.O. Box 92984
Washington, DC 20090-2984
Tel: (800) 374-2721; Direct: (202) 336-5510
Fax: (202) 336-5502; TDD/TTY: (202) 336-6123
Online: www.apa.org/books/
E-mail: order@apa.org

In the U.K., Europe, Africa, and the Middle East, copies may be ordered from
American Psychological Association
3 Henrietta Street
Covent Garden, London
WC2E 8LU England

Typeset in Goudy by Stephen McDougal, Mechanicsville, MD

Printer: Book-mart Press, Inc., North Bergen, NJ
Cover Designer: Naylor Design, Washington, DC
Technical/Production Editor: Devon Bourexis

The opinions and statements published are the responsibility of the authors, and such opinions and statements do not necessarily represent the policies of the American Psychological Association.

Library of Congress Cataloging-in-Publication Data

The meaning of others : narrative studies of relationships / edited by Ruthellen Josselson, Amia Lieblich, and Dan P. McAdams.
   p. cm.
  Includes index.
  ISBN-13: 978-1-59147-816-4
  ISBN-10: 1-59147-816-2
  1. Interpersonal relations. 2. Social interaction. I. Josselson, Ruthellen. II. Lieblich, Amia, 1939- III. McAdams, Dan P.

HM1106.M43 2007
305.072'2—dc22
                                         2006034811

British Library Cataloguing-in-Publication Data
A CIP record is available from the British Library.

Printed in the United States of America
First Edition

CONTENTS

CONTRIBUTORS

Jonathan M. Adler, Northwestern University, Evanston, IL

Nancy L. Deutsch, University of Virginia, Charlottesville

Jennifer F. Dobbins, City University of New York, New York

Mark Freeman, College of the Holy Cross, Worcester, MA

Ruthellen Josselson, Fielding Graduate University, Baltimore, MD

Amia Lieblich, The Hebrew University of Jerusalem, Jerusalem, Israel

Dan P. McAdams, Northwestern University, Evanston, IL

Valory Mitchell, California School of Professional Psychology at Alliant University, San Francisco

Ron Nasim, The Hebrew University of Jerusalem, Jerusalem, Israel

Tracie O'Neill, Saint Martin's University, Lacey, WA

Danna Pessach-Ramati, The Hebrew University of Jerusalem, Jerusalem, Israel

Alon Raz, University of Haifa, Haifa, Israel

Annie G. Rogers, Hampshire College, Amherst, MA

Brian Schiff, Saint Martin's University, Lacey, WA

Ruth Sharabany, University of Haifa, Haifa, Israel

Kazumi Sugimura, Nagoya University, Nagoya, Japan

Hadas Wiseman, University of Haifa, Haifa, Israel

ACKNOWLEDGMENTS

The editors would like to thank the many people who reviewed manuscripts for this volume: Jim Anderson, Michael Bamberg, Jaimie Baron, Donald R. Brown, Lisa Dorner, Michelle Fine, Gary Gregg, Joshua Gunn, Sherry Hatcher, Ravenna Helson, Jane Kroger, Tamar Kron, Ofra Mayseless, Kate McLean, Robert Neimeyer, Suzanne Ouellette, Jefferson Singer, and Rivkah Tuval-Mashiach. We also wish to thank the Foley Family Foundation for their support of our book series titled *The Narrative Study of Lives*.

THE NARRATIVE STUDY OF LIVES ADVISORY BOARD

Richard L. Ochberg, *Boston, MA*

June H. Price, Nursing, *Fairleigh Dickinson University*

Gabriele Rosenthal, Sociology, *Gesamthochschule Kassel, Germany*

George C. Rosenwald, Psychology, *University of Michigan*

William McKinley Runyan, School of Social Service, *University of California, Berkeley*

Abigail J. Stewart, Psychology and Women's Studies, *University of Michigan*

George E. Vaillant, Psychiatry, *Dartmouth Medical Center*

Guy Widdershoven, Philosophy, *University of Limburg, the Netherlands*

The Meaning of Others

INTRODUCTION

Relationships are central, from the very beginning of and throughout life, to the constitution and expression of the self. The enigmas of distinguishing self from other and understanding the ways in which the self creates the other and the other creates the self have challenged philosophers and social scientists. In general, psychology has attended more to the self and its development into separateness and autonomy than to the experience of relatedness to others. This has been, in part, because the agency and actions of the self are more visible and more accessible to language than is the interpenetrating flux of experience that is denoted linguistically as *relationship* between and among people. While we can witness the products of a person's doings in the world, we need narratives to access the relational meanings that may create, direct, or sustain these activities.

There are more pervasive reasons as well for the privileging of agency over communion. Our late editorial board member, David Bakan, who named this duality, pointed out that it is in the nature of the agentic side of human nature to separate itself, often forcefully, from its communion aspect (Bakan, 1966). An agentic framing of human experience that stresses self-expression, individuality, and control must often disown the communion side which, by its nature, endeavors to overcome separateness. A theory told from the agentic viewpoint in agentic language stresses developmental movement toward action, competence, and individuation. Such a theory cannot illuminate compassion or care or the capacity to love, which are states not of doing but of being-with. Theory told from a communion standpoint would detail differentiated forms of making contact with each other, trace the growth of self-in-relation (Miller, 1976), postulate individuation toward greater belonging and sharing, and would see the trajectory of development as moving toward increasingly complex relatedness. This volume, for example, is a physical entity that presents in written form the (agentic) work and ideas of a number of people. It is a product of cognition, of effort, and of expertise. And it is also a product of relationship, relationship that would ordinarily remain in the background. True, most writers express their gratitude to others for supporting or inspiring them. They say things such as "Without the help of so-and-so, this work would not be possible." And we readers may be interested (vaguely) in just how so-and-so made the work possible, but we are not told and, anyway, we got the book to read the work.

This is the fifth (or eleventh) volume of a series called *The Narrative Study of Lives*. It is the fifth published by the American Psychological Association; six earlier volumes were published by Sage Publications. The series began as a product of a friendship formed through shared intellectual interests between Amia Lieblich and myself. But saying this tells little about what the friendship has been like or what it means in our lives. This story is what gets omitted from accounts. We could tell it only as a narrative, a long one, and then we probably still couldn't fully capture its essential qualities and meanings. Some 8 years into our joint work editing this series, we invited Dan McAdams to join us. We liked his work, and we also liked him, and we thought he could bring another point of view as well as be interesting and fun to work with. The past five volumes have been the product of the complex relational dynamics among us. What readers do not see is how we make and shift alliances as we agree and disagree over what is and is not "good" work. We have different sensibilities, the three of us, and we all change as a result of our interchanges. We enliven and enlighten each other and also weary (and sometimes annoy) each other. But we cannot, if we are reflective, separate the work from the vagaries of the relationships among us. We have created clearly defined roles that make it possible to carry out the tasks (I, for example, have been "coordinating editor" for this volume) but who we are as people for one another is equally important for how the work gets done. And each of us would narrate the relationship(s) differently.

This volume is an effort to cast a wide net in order to bring the meanings of others to the forefront of psychological investigation, to illuminate what is an often obscured background. Efforts to measure relationships, although they have produced large bodies of research studies, inevitably simplify and decontextualize relationship. Relationships require narrative to evoke the empathy and multilayered attention necessary for one person to have some sense of the nature of someone else's relational experience.

Along with the "narrative turn" in the social sciences has come a "relational turn" in the understanding of human lives. The late 20th-century critique of the social science depiction of human beings as (desirably) autonomous, individuated, and self-reliant has given way to a view of people as interrelated, interdependent, and mutually constructive of one another. Where psychological development was construed as a process of movement from merger to separation, theorists have added a developmental story of growth being a process of increasing—and increasingly complex—connections to others.

That the narrative and relational turns overlap is more than coincidental. Narrative approaches to understanding human lives have made possible the empirical investigation of relational experiences that are inaccessible to psychometric scales or experimentation. But *how* people represent others and their relationship to them brings social science to the edge of the ineffable. Language more comfortably yields to the linear description of the lone, well-bounded self—self-confident, self-reliant, oriented to personally defined goals—than it does to the self imperfectly delineated from others, whose proclivities are experienced as a mass of voices and influences, whose actions in the world are meaningful to the extent that they have meaning to others. Issues of what belongs to self and what belongs to other fade to the background when psychology considers the interpenetration of selves that is mutually constructive. Human relationships, because they have (always shifting) meaning at unconscious and affective, as well as cognitive, levels, become exceedingly challenging to render in language, let alone with the precision of terminology required by science.

The language of relationship in contemporary culture tends to be sparse or polysemous. Thus, it is difficult to describe other than a narrow range or vague sense of what seems to be occurring between others or even between oneself and another. There does not exist enough language to encompass what people know about the nuances of relationship and emotional connection, and psychology therefore often relies on rough indicators or gross concepts of relationship—for example, are they "good" or "bad," whatever this may mean.

In Plato's *Symposium,* Diotima, the "wise woman" friend of Socrates, explained that "one part of love is separated off and receives the name of the whole" (Hamilton & Cairns, 1961, p. 539), which is, I think, the current situation in psychological research. Up until about 20 years ago, love was understood in psychoanalytic terms to be synonymous with passionate love, sexual union, and libidinal fulfillment. Within psychoanalysis, all love was reductionistically subsumed under forms and transformations of libidinal investment—eros transmogrified into various forms of expression. More recently, the attachment concept has been separated off, in Diotima's terms, and theorists have made valiant efforts to rethink love as forms and transformations of attachment—internal working models of the predicted responsiveness of others with a sense of attachment security coming to stand for love in its various manifestations.

Narrative accounts of emotionally important relationships promise to expand psychology's lexicon and understanding of the ways in which relationship to others structures, sustains, and transforms a life. Studying people's narrations about significant aspects of their relational life allows us to assess proportion and depth and meaning of relationship in a life. In such approaches, we can go beyond trying to name or classify or evaluate; we can aim to investigate process and construction of relational experience in the context of the experience of self.

INQUIRY IN A NARRATIVE FRAMEWORK

The authors of the chapters in this volume use a range of narrative modes of inquiry to describe and then conceptualize significant aspects of interpersonal experience. All begin with some sort of text that expresses textured aspects of human relationship and then initiate a conversation between the contextualized phenomenological account and a psychological understanding. As editors, we continue to resist a compilation of narrative approaches into a cookbook of methods, but rather value reflective epistemologies suited to the research questions being explored. We join Norman Denzin and Yvonna Lincoln (2000) in regarding the qualitative researcher as a "bricoleur," who uses or invents interpretive tools that are fitted to the particular complexities of the situation. In this volume, we showcase the application of a range of creative means of gathering and analyzing narrative data. The chapters in this volume span approaches that involve inductive interpretation of novels and biographies (see chaps. 1–3), coding of structured interviews (see chaps. 6 and 10), and discourse analysis of an Internet forum (see chap. 9). The other chapters involve authors' carefully detailed thematic readings of interview-derived texts to arrive at some higher level of abstraction or understanding within a theoretical framework.

Discussion of a text becomes yet another text, speaking from its specific location in time and culture. Although we encourage our authors to place themselves in the narration of their texts rather than trying to recount others' stories from the point of view of disembodied observers, our authors vary in the way they take up their reflexivity. Textbooks about the theory and practice of narrative research always extol the importance of the researcher locating him- or herself in the text. There is, within a hermeneutic epistemology, no objective place to stand. With this statement, we think all of our authors would agree, yet researchers, when actually doing narrative research, position themselves differently in terms of how much they think telling the reader about their sociocultural positioning is appropriate or useful. Those who work with living participants also vary in how much they tell the reader about the context and dynamics of the relationship between interviewer and interviewee. Some more or less take for granted that their participants are revealing preexisting internal structures; others recognize that multilayered motivations underlie a cocreated narrative with a particular researcher on a particular occasion. We think there is much for readers to learn from this variation; it is an opportunity to reflect on what degree or kind of authorial self-positioning adds to the meaning available to the reader. Here, too, we encourage reflexivity but eschew dogma.

Whether an author is self-consciously and overtly self-reflexive or not, the manner of presentation of narrative material inevitably repackages stories into the container of an author's sociocultural, ideological, intellectual, and (perhaps even) psychodynamic window on the world. As a narrative researcher moves from being listener (or reader) to storyteller, representational choices mark how the narrative is to be evaluated and interpreted. For each chapter, we could imagine an equally lengthy chapter focused just on how choices were made about what is detailed and what omitted; what that may mean about the researcher, the participant, and the interaction; and what these choices imply about the epistemological assumptions, the culture in which these assumptions are embedded, the texts that the presentation is in dialogue with, and so on. There is always another level of analysis within (and around) this work that, in our view, is to be regarded as a heuristic strength rather than an omission.

A book on narrative and relationship is essentially dialogic. Our authors are in dialogue with their subject-texts about their experiences of relationship to others. The focus of these inquiries is on the space between self and other, the tension between the subjectivity of desire and the press of social necessity represented by the desire of the other. The result of the inquiries is equally dialogic as the authors of these chapters enter into conversation with readers who bring their own frameworks and questions, their own desires into relationship with the authors.

Many texts explicate procedures for carrying out narrative research but fewer provide examples of researchers less self-consciously using these tools. In the main, the authors of this volume are oriented to exploring what they can learn about relationships through narratives. Narratives here are the data that offer the possibility to refine, extend, or contradict theory.

AN OVERVIEW OF THE CHAPTERS

We begin by exploring the dilemmas of locating and representing relationships in the narrative of a life. The volume opens with Mark Freeman detailing the philosophical foundations for the place of the other in the story of the self. Drawing primarily on the work of Martin Buber and using Tolstoy's Ivan Ilych as an example, Freeman builds an argument for the centrality of others not only to the life narrative but also to the very constitution of the self. Being, as Freeman illustrates, is being-with. A person's life story is always a narrative of relationship to what is other-than-self.

The next two chapters are studies of intense relationships between creative people that are not easily labeled in conventional terms. My (Josselson's) contribution, chapter 2, is a contrast of parallel biographies, one of Henry Murray, the other of Christiana Morgan—two people in a complex relationship with one another—and my aim is to analyze the ways in which this relationship has been narrated (and thereby constructed) by the biographers. When relationships structure or center a life, they become supremely difficult to narrate, in part because shaping a narrative that appropriately balances and contains the complexities of meanings both within the relationship and within the larger social context becomes a monumental challenge. The "story" can be told many ways; the relationship can be seen kaleidoscopically: It shifts its shape, its texture, its colors as the narrative contexts change. I raise the issue of the relational "Third," the context within which relationships are constituted and viewed, and the dialectic between relational experience inside a relationship and its construction by the social order.

In a related but quite different approach in chapter 3, Annie G. Rogers grapples from a Lacanian perspective with the relationship between Auguste Rodin and Camille Claudel. In Lacanian theory, all relationship is constituted by *lack*, which exists outside symbolic language. Rogers gives voice through poetry to Lacanian concepts that may shed light on this complex (and painful) relationship and demonstrates the ways in which the unconscious is implicated in all interpretation. In publishing this chapter, we join the growing effort in the qualitative research field to investigate performative means of presentation of findings that cannot be adequately represented in traditional linear forms.

Relationship and identity are intertwined in complex ways, and the next group of chapters closely examines their mutual interplay. In chapter 4, Nancy L. Deutsch describes the experience of a young African American man whose involvement in a community program mitigated an early history of relational disruption. This program embedded him in a chain of relationships, a community of support that created a sense of relational interdependence that was a foundation for his identity. Deutsch offers an argument for the importance of attending to "what is missing when the individual is prioritized over ties to others" in our social programming.

In a similar vein in chapter 5, also by looking intently at the narrative of a single individual, Valory Mitchell details the transformation in one woman from insecure attachment to an "earned secure" position. She demonstrates how a person can fundamentally alter her inner working model of the self and relationships, thus shedding light on what has been an enigma in attachment research. Through an analysis of this woman's narrative of her life, Mitchell describes and conceptualizes the slow process of change through learning in relationships.

Although identity researchers are well aware of the influence of relationships on identity, few have examined narratives of identity construction to understand just how such influence occurs. In chapter 6, Kazumi Sugimura, studying transitions in the process of identity formation among Japanese female adolescents, demonstrates stages in how others' wishes and viewpoints are incorporated and integrated in a young person's life decision-making. There are differences in how adolescents make use of others: some just "go along" with other people, and some balance ideas of others and learn about the self in the process. Cultural attitudes about the role of relationships influence the ways in which others have impact on identity choices.

Even racial identity has its roots in relational experience. In chapter 7, looking at the narratives of two biracial young women, Brian Schiff and Tracie O'Neill trace the ways in which internal relatedness to a parent is reflected in the racial position a daughter adopts. Both of these women could "pass" for White in the dominant White majority culture, yet chose to emphasize their biraciality as a way of expressing a particular sense of relatedness to a parent who was racially identified with a nondominant culture.

Relationships are constructed in culture, which creates the conditions under which relational possibilities and enactments are defined. Moving between cultures involves shifts in relational expectations that can be challenging and disruptive. Danna Pessach-Ramati and I present chapter 8, which investigates the relational experience of a group of young Ethiopian immigrants to Israel and focuses on the ways in which their needs for secure holding color their efforts to adapt to a very different society. The social dislocation of their parents compromises parental authority and impedes their ability to provide adequate "holding" for their adolescent children.

A close look at relational experience implies thick description of particular relationships that are enacted under specific conditions. In chapter 9, Jennifer F. Dobbins is concerned with how the relational role of caregiver is constructed by stories. She monitored an online support group to analyze how caregivers bring their life experiences online and thereby revise their life stories and their understanding of themselves as caregivers. Using positioning theory to explore the caregiver narrative, she extends our understanding of caregiving as a series of interrelationships.

We need narratives of relationships to understand them precisely because relationships have idiosyncratic meanings in a life. Jonathan M. Adler and Dan P. McAdams looked at one of the best-researched and documented relationships within psychology—that of the psychotherapy relationship—and investigated the different ways in which this relationship is retrospectively narrated by different groups of people. They discovered that people high in ego development but low in well-being featured the therapeutic relationship prominently in their stories whereas those at high levels of both deemphasized the role of their therapist in their narratives. In chapter 10, the authors raise questions about the narrative patterns of relational dynamics that support different constellations of current functioning.

Relationships can figure prominently in a life by their absence as well as their presence. Alon Raz, Hadas Wiseman, and Ruth Sharabany studied the relational narratives of people in their 20s who have been unable to form satisfying long-term romantic relationships, and they try to understand what relational assumptions or needs may be common among them. Chapter 11 shows that such people demonstrate acute sensitivity to rejection as well as a proclivity to reject others who don't meet their internal expectations, which leaves them both frustrated and alone.

Finally, in chapter 12, Ron Nasim engages the debate in bereavement theory about continuing bonds with the deceased. Is it better to let go of those who have died or find ways of continuing a sense of relationship? Using intensive interviews with young people who lost a parent in childhood, Nasim shows a range of ways that his participants kept their relationship with their deceased parent alive in the service of their own growth and development. Through recounting their deceased parent's life story, the young people formed complex representations of the deceased, aspects of which these surviving children may choose to draw on at different stages in their lives.

Thus, the participants in the relationships studied in this volume range from lovers to caregivers to psychotherapy patients to adolescents on the cusp of different cultures. Yet all offer windows for conceptualizing how relationships are constructed and narrated and are formative in life history. We think this volume will be of interest to all who seek a more complex understanding of the experience of relationship in human development as well as to life history researchers. Those who work with people—counselors, therapists, and educators—can profit from the insight these authors provide into the multilayered aspects of human interaction. Students of developmental, personality, and clinical psychology would do well to use these presentations to reflect on the location of human relationship in context and in its many narratively structured possibilities for meaning.

Ruthellen Josselson
In collaboration with Amia Lieblich and Dan P. McAdams

REFERENCES

Bakan, D. (1966). *The duality of human existence*. Boston: Beacon Press.

Denzin, N. K., & Lincoln, Y. S. (Eds.). (2000). *Handbook of qualitative research* (2nd ed.). Thousand Oaks, CA: Sage.

Hamilton, E., & Cairns, H. (Eds.). (1961). *The collected dialogues of Plato* (M. Joyce, Trans.). Princeton, NJ: Princeton University Press.

Miller, J. B. (1976). *Toward a new psychology of women*. Boston: Beacon Press.

1

NARRATIVE AND RELATION: THE PLACE OF THE OTHER IN THE STORY OF THE SELF

MARK FREEMAN

One of the central purposes of this chapter is to see in the idea of relationship a vitally important vehicle for opening up lines of narrative inquiry that are often left unexplored. I do not mean to suggest that drawing on the idea of relationship in thinking about narrative is an entirely new project. From Gergen and Gergen's (1988) early work in this area, through the work of Hermans and Kempen (e.g., 1993) and others, this idea has had considerable currency in the field, particularly among those who wish to think beyond the sovereign *I*, cordoned off from others. At the same time, the radical potential of relational thinking for refiguring some significant dimensions of narrative inquiry has yet to fully be realized. Among the many reasons for this situation is the very legacy of Western modernity itself, with its persistent privileging of the individuated, "monological" self, carving out its own singular path in the course of its own realization. Relational thinking seeks to shift the angle of vision and thereby open up new, more fully human ways of figuring human lives. This aim is its great challenge and its great promise.

In the pages to follow, I draw significantly on the work of Martin Buber, who, along with such thinkers as Levinas (e.g., 1969, 1996, 1999), Marcel (e.g., 1950, 1973), and Rosenzweig (e.g., 1970, 1999), offers a concerted effort to rethink the very nature of the human condition along what might be termed "ex-centric" rather than "ego-centric" lines (see Freeman, 2004). In each of their perspectives, albeit in different ways, the sovereign self is displaced. In some cases (e.g., Levinas), the *Other* has priority. In Buber's case especially, however, what is most fundamental is that which exists *between* self and Other—namely, relation itself. Indeed, "The genuineness and adequacy of the self cannot stand the test in self-commerce, but only in communication with the whole of otherness" (1965, p. 178). As such, "Only when we try to understand the human person in his whole situation, in the possibilities of his relation to all that is not himself, do we understand man" (p. 181). The narrative study of lives represents exactly such an effort at understanding, the somewhat paradoxical implication here being that the self receives its inspiration, even its very being, from its relation to what is irrevocably Other-than-self. By following Buber's thinking, along with that of several others, I hope to shed some new light not only on narrative but also on those relational spheres of the human condition that figure prominently in the stories people tell about their lives.

THE THREE SPHERES OF RELATION

According to Buber (1970), there are three basic spheres in which the world of relation arises, and one can only bring one's nature to "full reality . . . if all [these] living relations become essential" (p. 177). He fleshed out this "threefold living relation" by referring to

> first, his relation to the world and to things, second, his relation to men—both to individuals and to the many—third, his relation to the mystery of being—which is dimly apparent through all this but infinitely transcends it—which the philosopher calls the Absolute and the believer calls God, and which cannot in fact be eliminated from the situation even by a man who rejects both designations. (p. 177)

The first two of these spheres seem fairly straightforward: As human beings, we are in relation, or potential relation, not only with other people but with both the beings and things that are found in the animate and inanimate world. Notice already, then, that for Buber the Other extends beyond the human, alone. Another distinctive feature of Buber's perspective is his insistence that we also exist in relation to the spiritual, broadly conceived; and this is so, he has asserted, even for the philosophically or theologically faithless. If Buber is right about this, it has profound implications for narrative inquiry. For it suggests that life narratives, insofar as they are oriented toward fundamental questions of meaning and value, are inextricably linked to ultimate human concerns.

It should be emphasized that, for Buber, an important distinction is to be made between what he termed "I–It" relations and "I–You" relations, arguing essentially that our adoption of one or the other mode of relating to the world is in large measure a function of our own attitude, our own comportment toward whatever it is we encounter (Buber, 1970): Whereas the former attitude is problematically objectifying, such that the Other is dealt with in a predominantly instrumental way, the latter attitude is rooted in respect and reciprocity and therefore embodies a much more authentically relational mode of being in the world.

To my mind, there may be no better example of the threefold relation of which Buber spoke, as well as the distinction between I–It and I–You attitudes, than Tolstoy's harrowing novella, *The Death of Ivan Ilych* (1960). In terms of the first sphere, Ilych was described as "a capable, cheerful, good-natured, and sociable man, though strict in the fulfillment of what he considered to be his duty: and he considered his duty to be what was so considered by those in authority." He was particularly "attracted to people of high station, as a fly is drawn to the light, assimilating their ways and views of life." He would buy clothes at "the fashionable tailor," eat at a "first-class restaurant," and gather whatever else he needed at "the best shops" around. Ilych's relation to the world of work told much the same story. Having become an examining magistrate, he felt that "everyone without exception . . . was in his power"; and though he "never abused his power, . . . the consciousness of it and of the possibility of softening its effect, supplied the chief interest and attraction of his office." Regarding his work itself, he had adopted a method of

> eliminating all considerations irrelevant to the legal aspect of the case and reducing even the most complicated case to a form in which it would be presented on paper only in its externals, completely excluding his personal opinion of the matter, while above all observing every prescribed formality. (p. 103)

As for the "charming" home he would eventually own, "it was just what is usually seen in the houses of people of moderate means who want to appear rich, and therefore succeed only in resembling others like themselves" (p. 114).

The sphere of personal relations was largely an extension of this basic attitude. He would meet his wife-to-be, "who was the most attractive, clever, and brilliant girl of the set in which he moved," and when she fell in love with him, the next step was an obvious one: "Really, why shouldn't I marry?" he had asked himself. And so he did. All went well until his wife's pregnancy, which brought with it "something new, unpleasant, depressing, and unseemly, and from which there was no way of escape." As a result, "He now realized that matrimony . . . was not always conducive to the pleasures and amenities of life, but on the contrary often infringed both comfort and propriety" (p. 107)—hence the need "to entrench himself against such infringement [and for] securing for himself an existence outside his family life." Ilych was largely successful in this effort, his attitude toward home life rendering him "almost impervious" to the demands it made on him. "He only required of it those conveniences—dinner at home, housewife, and bed—which it could give him, and above all that propriety of external forms required by public opinion." And "if he met with antagonism and querulousness," he could always retreat into "his separate fenced-off world of official duties." Indeed, "his new duties, their importance, the possibility of indicting and imprisoning anyone he chose, the publicity his speeches received, and the success he had in all these things, made his work still more attractive" (p. 108).

As a result, "The whole interest of his life now centred in the official world [and] continued to flow as he considered it should do—pleasantly and properly" (p. 109). Indeed, in the context of Buber's third sphere of relation, which deals essentially with the meaning of life itself, "everything progressed and progressed and approached the ideal he had set himself: even when things were only half completed they exceeded his expectations" (p. 113). And although "he occasionally became irritable" maintaining his home, "on the whole his life ran its course as he believed it should do: easily, pleasantly, and decorously" (p. 115). "Everything," therefore, "was as it should be" (p. 116), his life corresponding neatly to his own dearly held images of how things ought to be, what they ought to look like, what kind of story ought to be told.

An accident Ilych suffered while doing some home decorating disturbed all this. And faced with the prospect of his own imminent death, he found the need to entertain a most disturbing and painful possibility. "'Maybe I did not live as I ought to have done,' it suddenly occurred to him. 'But how could that be, when I did everything properly?'" (p. 145). At first, it was simply inconceivable that his life, which had seemed so thoroughly correct, had in fact been misguided and wrong. "'An explanation would be possible if it could be said that I have not lived as I ought to,'" Ilych had tried to convince himself. "'But it is impossible to say that,' and he remembered all the legality, correctitude, and propriety of his life" (p. 147). Some 2 weeks later, however, he found himself facing squarely the possibility in question: "'What if my whole life has really been wrong?'"

> It occurred to him that what had appeared perfectly impossible before, namely that he had not spent his life as he should have done, might after all be true. It occurred to him that his scarcely perceptible attempts to struggle against what was considered good by the most highly placed people, those scarcely noticeable impulses which he had immediately suppressed, might have been the real thing, and all the rest false. He tried to defend all those things to himself and suddenly felt the weakness of what he was defending. There was nothing to defend. (p. 148)

Ilych's past had suddenly been reconfigured, and "he began to pass his life in review in quite a new way," such that its "awful truth" was revealed to him for the first time. He had mistaken for real that which "was not real at all, but a terrible and huge deception which had hidden both life and death" (p. 149). The result was that death, the end point of his lifelong lie, became that much more terrifying. After he struggled for 3 solid days "as a man condemned to death struggles in the hands of the executioner" (p. 151), a mysterious force came upon him, and he was freed from his awful terror and torment. Having "caught sight of the light, . . . it was revealed to him that though his life had not been what it should have been, this could still be rectified" (p. 151). For the first time, he felt sympathy for his wife and son, and they him. He would no longer hurt them; he would avow the utter corruption that had been his life and, through that avowal, would live his final moments with a measure of care.

Tolstoy has done well to underscore the significance of our relations to "the world and to things," to other people, and to broader issues of meaning, including that sort of ultimate meaning generally associated with the religious. Moreover, he has done well to consider the link between these relations and narrative. Only in the face of his awful demise—the "ending," as it were—could Ilych begin to see the threefold error of his earlier ways. All there had been, he came to realize, were I–It relationships: in which work had merely been a vehicle for his own self-aggrandizement; in which people had been objectified and used, occluded by his own egocentric wishes and fantasies; in which the very meaning of his life had been a function mainly of his stature and his approval by others. The result was that he could tell only a kind of frozen myth about his life: Judging by appearances, Ivan Ilych had

> performed his official tasks, made his career, and at the same time amused himself pleasantly and decorously. . . . It was all done with clean hands, in clean linen, with French phrases, and above all among people of the best society and consequently with the approval of people of rank. (p. 104)

But his 11th-hour recognition of the terrible poverty of all three spheres of relation, indeed of his very life, would ultimately dissolve the mythic story he had told himself and lead him in the direction of a more truthful account. In true dialectical fashion, it was precisely this more truthful account that would lead to authentic engagement with the world, particularly his relationships with others.

NARRATIVE INTEGRITY

In the sphere of human relations, Buber wrote, "Every means is an obstacle. Only where all means have disintegrated encounters occur" (1970, p. 63). He did offer a qualification in this context:

To be sure, some men who in the world of things make do with experiencing and using have constructed for themselves an idea annex or superstructure in which they find refuge and reassurance in the face of intimations of nothingness. At the threshold they take off the clothes of the ugly weekday, shroud themselves in clean garments, and feel restored as they contemplate primal being or what ought to be—something in which their life has no share. It may also make them feel good to proclaim it.

But the It-humanity that some imagine, postulate, and advertise has nothing in common with the bodily humanity to which a human being can truly say You. The noblest fiction is a fetish, the most sublime fictitious sentiment is a vice. (p. 65)

The convergence between Buber's and Tolstoy's ideas is quite remarkable. Especially significant is their joint suggestion of a deep connection between the quality and depth of one's relationship to others and what might be termed the "integrity" of one's narrative (see Freeman, 1997; Freeman & Brockmeier, 2001). In a basic sense, this notion of narrative integrity has to do with how well expectations line up with actualities, whether they are realized or thwarted in the course of one's life. In this sense, the idea is about the relationship of the projected and perhaps hoped-for future to the life one ultimately leads. If, on the one hand, there is a good measure of congruence between expectations and actualities, one will likely have achieved a sense of integrity. If, on the other hand, there is a marked lack of congruence, one may very well come to experience despair: The life one had imagined living will have given way to a different one, a lesser one, altogether. There is another sense, however, in which this idea is about the very nature of both expectations and actualities. As the story of Ivan Ilych shows with painful clarity, the actualities of one's life may be perfectly congruent with one's expectations without any sense of integrity at all emerging: It all depends on the depth and magnitude of the expectations one has and the life one ultimately lives.

Narrative integrity, therefore, refers "not only to harmony of proportion or beauty of form as principles of narrative composition but to the coherence and depth of one's ethical commitments, as evidenced by the shape of one's life" (Freeman & Brockmeier, 2001, p. 76; see also Freeman, 1997). Nearing death, Ilych had a revelation: He saw his ignorance and superficiality as well as the fact that he had been uncaring and unkind, that he had been so caught up in the niceties of his own small world that others had been relegated to the status of things, objects, *Its*, there to bolster his ever-needy ego. He therefore came to see the utter impoverishment of the first two spheres of relation identified by Buber. Also significant, however, was his utter failure to find "devotional objects" outside himself that would orient his life meaningfully. These objects are themselves embodiments of the Other, and, according to Buber, they are profoundly important for the ongoing work of narrative. So it is that he spoke of the importance of "the life in which the individual . . . is essentially related to something other than himself" (1965, p. 166).

Charles Taylor's (1989, 1991) work is important in this context as well, for what he too suggested was the existence of the need to be related to *something*—if not a "being" per se then a principle, an ideal, a *good*—that draws the self beyond its own borders and thereby orients the life in question. Indeed, Taylor argued that the need to be connected to the good—to what can be considered "of crucial importance, or of fundamental value"—is "one of the most basic aspirations of human beings" (1989, p. 42); it is a "craving," one that is "ineradicable from human life" (p. 44). What's more, human beings' relationship to the good should be understood "not just as a matter of more or less but as a question of yes or no." That is to say, it concerns "not how near or far we are from what we see as the good, but rather the direction of our lives, towards or away from it, or the source of motivations in regard to it" (p. 45). It is here that narrative enters the picture, for "this sense of the good has to be woven into my life as an unfolding story" (p. 47). As Taylor went on to argue,

> Making sense of my present action, when we are not dealing with such trivial questions as where I shall go in the next five minutes but with the issue of my place relative to the good, requires a narrative understanding of my life, a sense of what I have become which can only be given in a story. And as I project my life forward and endorse the existing direction or give it a new one, I project a future story, not just a state of the momentary future but a bent for my whole life to come. (p. 48)

This process of endorsing the existing direction of one's life or giving it a new one is intimately tied to the narrative integrity, or lack thereof, of the life in question.

According to Buber, the measure of one's narrative integrity is largely a function of the integrity of one's relationship with other people. This is the relational sphere of spheres, as it were; it is primary, coming before any and all others. Buber's own reflections on this sphere, it should be noted, extend well beyond the kinds of face-to-face relations that are generally associated with the interpersonal realm, all the way to social institutions, cultural expressions, and, most fundamentally, community. But his message about these larger arenas of interpersonal or "interhuman" relatedness (see Buber, 1998) is much the same. Put in simple terms, here too, in this larger arena of human relations, the integrity of one's story, as an individual, is a function of the integrity—the ethical and spiritual soundness—of one's relationship to others. "Egos appear by setting themselves apart from other egos," Buber (1970) asserted. "Persons," however, "appear by entering into relation with other persons" (p. 112). The ego, he continued, "wallows in his being-that-way— or rather for the most part in the fiction of his being-that-way—a fiction that he has devised for himself. For at bottom self-knowledge usually means to him the fabrication of an effective apparition of the self that has the power to deceive him ever more thoroughly." The person, however, "beholds his self . . . , becomes conscious of himself as participating in being, as being-with, and thus as a being" (pp. 114–115). In this very being-with, therefore, the person is able to devise not only more person-oriented stories but more truthful ones, with a greater measure of existential solidity.

The view being advanced herein underscores the importance of personal relationships in conceptualizing narrative inquiry. In addition, it underscores the relational moment of narrative itself. Following Buber, in speaking of the relational, I consider the entire realm of otherness to which we as humans are related. There remains a tendency, within psychology especially, to see this realm as being ancillary to narrative. There is a reason for this. In a basic and obvious sense, narratives issue from a self, an individual: The story of my life is thus irrevocably *mine*. This statement says nothing whatsoever, though, about the ultimate sources of my story, about the driving forces that propel it forward, giving it meaning and substance. These forces cannot, and do not, derive from the self. Rather, they derive from the Other-than-self, distributed throughout the various spheres of relation that I have considered in this chapter. Perhaps we can say, therefore, that while the proximal source of personal narrative is the self, the distal source is the Other. Indeed, along the lines that have been drawn here, it might also be said— cautiously—that the Other is the distal source of selfhood itself. *Relationship*, to the Other, is what moves the self to speak, and narrative is its native language.

REFERENCES

Buber, M. (1965). *Between man and man*. New York: Macmillan.

Buber, M. (1970). *I and thou*. New York: Scribner.

Buber, M. (1998). *The knowledge of man*. Amherst, NY: Humanity Books.

Freeman, M. (1997). Death, narrative integrity, and the radical challenge of self-understanding: A reading of Tolstoy's *Death of Ivan Ilych*. *Ageing & Society, 17*, 373–398.

Freeman, M. (2004). The priority of the Other: Mysticism's challenge to the legacy of the self. In J. Belzen & A. Geels (Eds.), *Mysticism: A variety of psychological approaches* (pp. 213–234). Amsterdam: Rodopi.

Freeman, M., & Brockmeier, J. (2001). Narrative integrity: Autobiographical identity and the meaning of the "good life." In J. Brockmeier & D. Carbaugh (Eds.), *Narrative and identity* (pp. 75–99). Amsterdam: John Benjamins.

Gergen, K. J., & Gergen, M. (1988). Narrative and the self as relationship. In L. Berkowitz (Ed.), *Advances in experimental social psychology* (Vol. 21, pp. 17–56). New York: Academic Press.

Hermans, H. J. M., & Kempen, H. J. G. (1993). *The dialogic self: Meaning as movement*. New York: Academic Press.

Levinas, E. (1969). *Totality and infinity*. Pittsburgh, PA: Duquesne University Press.

Levinas, E. (1996). Substitution. In A. T. Peperzak, S. Critchley, & R. Bernasconi (Eds.), *Emmanuel Levinas: Basic philosophical writings* (pp. 80–95). Bloomington: Indiana University Press.

Levinas, E. (1999). *Alterity and transcendence*. New York: Columbia University Press.

Marcel, G. (1950). *The mystery of being: Vol. 1. Reflection and mystery*. Chicago: Henry Regnery.

Marcel, G. (1973). *Tragic wisdom and beyond*. Evanston, IL: Northwestern University Press.

Rosenzweig, F. (1970). *The star of redemption*. New York: Holt, Rinehart & Winston.

Rosenzweig, F. (1999). *Understanding the sick and the healthy: A view of world, man, and God*. Cambridge, MA: Harvard University Press.

Taylor, C. (1989). *Sources of the self: The making of modern identity*. Cambridge, MA: Harvard University Press.

Taylor, C. (1991). *The ethics of authenticity*. Cambridge, MA: Harvard University Press.

Tolstoy, L. (1960). *The death of Ivan Ilych*. New York: Signet Classic.

2

LOVE IN THE NARRATIVE CONTEXT: THE RELATIONSHIP BETWEEN HENRY MURRAY AND CHRISTIANA MORGAN

RUTHELLEN JOSSELSON

Relationships between two people are always triadic.[1] Two people are experiencing, behaving, and interpreting their meanings to one another, and this always exists within some social context (the "Third") that gives it significance. How the relationship is named and expressed in language presupposes this context; the semiotic code anchors it in the shared meanings of culture and forms the point from which one can get a perspective on it (Muller, 1999).[2] Narrating a relationship between two other people always brings some wider context to bear: What the observer describes about the nature of the connection, represented through (socially constructed) language, constitutes the meanings interpreted (or interpolated) between the two people under scrutiny.

I am grateful to Jim Anderson, Alan Elms, Annie Rogers, and Irvin Yalom for their helpful comments on drafts of this chapter.

[1]I am indebted to Ed Shapiro for helping me to clarify this point. His insightful application of this idea to families and organizations is found in Shapiro and Carr (1991).
[2]These are essentially Lacanian ideas.

To explore the narrative contexts of relationships, I compare, in this chapter, the representation of a relationship in two excellent, related biographies: one of Christiana Morgan, written by a woman, Claire Douglas, a Jungian analyst, and one of Henry (Harry) Murray, written by a man, Forrest Robinson, an American studies scholar. Harry Murray and Christiana Morgan, both brilliant, creative, articulate, and insightful people, both by profession devoted to understanding the human psyche, had an intense and unconventional 40-year relationship that meant so much to them that one cannot reasonably tell one's biography without telling the other's. I do not yet name what kind of relationship it was because the aim of this chapter is to demonstrate the challenges posed by this as-yet-unnamed relationship to those who would try to contain it narratively.

The biographies were published within 2 years of each other, so the historical context of the telling remains constant. The biographers worked from similar archival and interview material although Robinson heard the story directly from Murray (over many years) as well. They cite each other's work. Neither seems to have had "factual" information the other did not, so the differences between the narratives are a matter of interpretation and viewpoint rather than "fact." (I have not read the primary sources as I am interested in comparing these biographical narratives, not in creating my own.)

Christiana and Harry, if I may refer to them this way, especially when focusing on their more private selves, struggled throughout their time together to represent and contextualize what was occurring between them. They left voluminous letters, notes, journals, dialogues, and draft chapters of unpublished books that detail the nature, events, and history of their relationship and what meanings they made of it. For them as well as for their biographers, the problem lay in finding language (or metaphor) adequate to the complex, intense, and transmuting feelings they had for one another. To say that they were in love or loved one another communicates little about the nature of this experience, for such a statement presumes some shared, agreed-on understanding of love. Love often, or perhaps always, contains irrational elements that defy logical or even psycho-logical categorization. Christiana and Harry, both psychologists who contributed significantly to depth psychology, in part saw their life work as articulating in some communicable way the nature of the kind of love they created together.

Their effort was "to discover and represent the truth of the human heart" (Robinson, 1992, p. 261).[3] They understood that love is both an overcoming of self and an enlargement of self. Christiana wrote, "The moment we met I

---

[3]All Robinson (1992) quotations cited throughout this chapter were reprinted by permission of the publisher from *Love's Story Told: A Life of Henry A. Murray*, by Forrest Robinson, pp. 102, 112, 113, 115, 121, 156, 157, 158, 169, 170, 172, 193, 195, 204, 208, 248, 249, 252, 255, 256, 261, 265, 302, 323, 324, 330, 354, Cambridge, MA: Harvard University Press, Copyright © by the President and Fellows of Harvard College.

knew that we were one. . . . The feel of his body before he even spoke—was an answer of joy and power" (p. 323). Harry wrote at the same time that what was between them was "synergy—taking into oneself the highest potential of the other and giving to it" (p. 324). Their story was one of a particular and unique experience of union and can be told in very different ways as I shift the context to try to make sense of it. I offer first a fairly detailed reading of the two biographies because I want to highlight the biographers' use of language and viewpoint in narrating this relationship, in full recognition that there is here no correct reading, only interpretive stances.

THE BEGINNING

The story began straightforwardly enough. Harry Murray, a 30-year-old upper-class patrician New Yorker, Harvard-educated biologist, physiologist, and physician, married father of a daughter, met the 26-year-old Christiana Morgan, a Boston-bred, upper-class, restless, largely self-educated, married mother of a son, at a concert in 1923, a meeting he remembered sharply but that made little impression on her. The crucial moment occurred a few months later when, seated next to him at a dinner party, she asked him if he preferred Jung or Freud. He had read neither, but subsequently did so. This question changed both of their lives.

Here the biographical renderings begin to diverge. Robinson chooses to first narrate this period of Harry's life as an intellectual biography, tracing the origin and unfolding of his fascination with the unconscious, represented in the works of Melville and Jung, as developments seemingly independent of Christiana. In Robinson's story, the intellectual metamorphosis in Harry induced by Melville and Jung occurs before Christiana is introduced as a character in his life, although it becomes clear that Harry's intellectual excitement, from the dinner party through the next 40 years, was inseparable from Christiana. "There was no separating work and love, for depth psychology and Christiana Morgan were intertwined in Harry's thinking" (p. 112). Yet, to tell their story, both biographers narratively separate work from love, if only to try to examine which is which and how they interconnect.

Robinson's version has Harry and Christiana falling in love before they go to England a year later, joined by their interest in Jung. But how to characterize and describe the nature of this love? He describes the early period as "an affair of the mind" (p. 102)—but says that those around them saw "what was happening" and their spouses suffered because of it. "They both recognized that something powerful had them in their grip." Mike, Harry's younger brother, "was also fascinated with Christiana." It was on the ship sailing to England, where Christiana was to join him, that Harry first read *Moby Dick* and allowed Melville (as well as Jung) to lead him to a lifetime effort to understand the depths of the human psyche.

On the surface, then, Robinson tells this story as the familiar drama of two married people struggling against their attraction for one another to preserve the social order. But in psychological terms, Robinson's understanding of this early period was that "their powerful attraction for each other" had its mysterious origins "in the unconscious recesses of their fullest selves." His reading is that they were each breaking free of the "libidinal bond with the devouring parent . . . to rise toward the expression of his or her full creative potential . . . a way to sanity and health" (p. 103). Robinson uses Jungian terms to paint them as "opposites that attract, anima and animus, incomplete beings made whole by union." Robinson initially describes Harry as finding in Christiana a

> gateway to the unconscious; she gave him access to the submerged human terrain that he was setting himself to explore. Thus between them they were a whole world. The united subject and object of passionate inquiry. Christiana was his love and work; he hers. (pp. 112–113)

She offered him "resurrection . . . the promise of . . . a new, fully individuated self" (p. 115).

The surrounding social climate that Robinson describes is one of "probity"—Harry's intense attraction to Christiana "so ran against the grain of what he had been trained to expect of himself" (p. 106). He worried about the immorality of adultery (although he had had previous extramarital sexual relationships and had struggled with impotence) and the possible sacrifice of the security and social standing he had achieved through his marriage to Jo Rantoul, his practical, outgoing, socially perfect match.

Douglas (1993) tells a related but different story about the beginning of the relationship. In her portrait, Christiana is an intense woman who wants to lose herself in feeling and was always attracted to idealistic men. She was prone to depression and moodiness. Her marriage to Will, "a perfectly dear boy," (p. 63)[4] fulfilled her neither emotionally nor physically. Bored, Christiana had had affairs with a number of men, including Chaim Weitzman—and, according to Douglas, also with Harry's younger brother, Mike. In Douglas's reading, Christiana showed no very special interest in Harry before they all went to England. In contrast to the staid, repressive Victorian social climate that Robinson details, the social surround that Douglas describes was one of bohemianism and sexual experimentation that was relatively open and accepted (in Bloomsbury fashion). When she began her affair with Harry, presumably this relationship was open as well. Christiana was, at the time, in a close friendship with Jo and with Mike's wife as well.[5]

---

[4]All Douglas (1993) quotations cited throughout this chapter are from *Translate This Darkness: The Life of Christiana Morgan, The Veiled Woman in Jung's Circle*, by C. Douglas, 1993, New York: Simon & Schuster. Copyright 1993 by Claire Douglas.
[5]The matter of Mike is one "factual" contradiction in the two stories that may or may not be important. Evidently its documentation, unlike all that happened after, is less clear. But it seems to me

While the whole group (Harry and Jo, Christiana and Will, Mike and his wife) was occupied with exploration of the ideas of Melville and Jung, pondering the mysteries of the inner life and the unconscious plumbed by both, the intellectual fervor belonged primarily to Harry and Christiana. Douglas explains that for Christiana, through the discussions with Harry about Melville and Jung, "attraction grew into passionate fascination" (p. 122).

> At this stage, when Harry and Christiana were merely talking about the *idea* of erotic love, they expressed their unclear feelings by comparing them to what they were reading. This added a complicated literary overtone to their infatuation, in which Jung's ideas and Melville's literary parallels merged to become the instruments by which they opened up their world and their psyches. (Douglas, 1993, p. 123)

Thus, there was a social context in which Christiana and Harry were intensely interconnected with each other and with ideas that featured exploration of the unknowable but seductive unconscious. The social context, depending on the version, either allowed or prohibited extramarital sexual involvements. Eros, and what it meant, was, however, very much present in both experience and inquiry—and, it seems, in the group context.

In terms of the psychological context, both biographers' versions stress the idea of merger as a context for understanding the deepening of feeling between Harry and Christiana. Douglas writes, "Part of the joy of their discussion lay in the fact that they responded as if they were one person, Harry having the formed thoughts that Christiana could admire and Christiana making the leaps of imagination that transported Harry" (p. 125). But Douglas at this point adds a Narcissus metaphor to their bond: "Typologically brother and sister, they each gazed at the other's face in the pool, failing to perceive that they were attracted to their own reflection" (p. 125). Interpreting further, she adds that Christiana embodied for Harry "an unknown but injured aspect of himself" (p. 126). In Melvillian terms that Robinson echoes throughout his work, Douglas writes that Christiana "called" him the way, in Melville's work, Isabel called Pierre and the whale called Ahab (p. 128).

Thus, both biographers use Romantic and Jungian lexicons as well as Melvillian literary parallels to name the "call" that Harry and Christiana heard from one another. This vocabulary of attraction, which existed in the context of passionate connection to ideas, includes terms and metaphors of union, excitement and being stirred, narcissistic reflection, healing of internal wounds and lacks, life-giving energy, and creative self-expansion.

---

to make a difference in how Harry and Christiana may have experienced their connection. In Douglas's version, Mike went with them to England in a special relationship with Christiana that must have been apparent, if not acknowledged, to Harry. In Robinson's version, Mike fell hopelessly in love with Christiana while they were in England and Europe. (The meaning of the role of "others" in this relationship lies relatively unexamined by both biographers throughout.)

In both versions, Harry, in part prompted by his confusion over and fear of his intense feelings for Christiana, visits Jung, who discourses on the importance of the anima embodied by a particular woman. Jung offers his own situation of open involvement with both his wife and Toni Wolff as a model for Harry.

Harry returns to the group filled with enthusiasm and insight gained from Jung and proposes a similar arrangement for himself, Jo, and Christiana. In Douglas's version, this proposal is explicit and discussed among the two couples and initially, neither Jo nor Christiana accepted the idea. Douglas explains that Christiana hesitated because she wanted him to "recognize her for herself and not just as his inspirer; nevertheless, she felt attracted by the extra energy his idealization gave her" (p. 133). In Robinson's version, Jung's suggestion to Harry is never openly discussed.

Eventually, while the group was on holiday together, Harry climbs onto Christiana's balcony and they make love for the first time, according to Robinson. Douglas is less clear that they had sexual intercourse. Robinson takes their physical lovemaking from here on as evident, but Douglas notes that Christiana was frustrated by Harry's sexual reticence and his not making love to her physically. Christiana, in Douglas's version, understood his need for her as an anima and felt his demand for her responsiveness to his ideas and her offering of her own, but was confused and distressed by his lack of physical passion. Douglas's reading of Christiana's journals led her to conclude that Christiana was worried that Harry treated her like an imaginary idea rather than a physical woman. Still, Christiana was entranced by finding herself in him, intensified and empowered. Douglas quotes from Christiana's journal: "There seemed to be only the slightest definitely focused sexual feeling—only a great live awareness when we were together" (p. 137). "I felt that—I was a divine goddess to him . . . but he fled from my lips" (p. 138). Robinson also notes Harry recoiling from the "sexual as from a descent into the pit" (p. 158) and his "hesitation to take fire sexually" as a concern to Christiana.

The role of sexuality in this relationship was, then, still very much in process between Harry and Christiana at this point. That their connection was erotic and passionate was clear, but not in the usual paradigms of sexual experimentation or intense physical attraction. It was not a simple "affair" in contemporary terms: The nature of the connection they felt was precisely what they set out to discover.

THE RELATIONSHIP MATURES

One challenge to the biographers was to understand Jung's role in the evolving relationship, for he and his theories were more and more becoming the grounding framework for Christiana and Harry's understanding of what was happening between them. Jung had given them a context for their feelings for one another, as well as a model, by naming the role that Christiana was to occupy—that of *anima*. From the time of Christiana's analysis with Jung, beginning in 1926, the meanings the biographers assign to the unfolding relationship begin to diverge. Douglas is critical of Jung for trying to help Christiana take on the role of inspiring Harry—becoming his anima, his *femme inspiratrice*, rather than helping her to develop her own talents. Jung's instruction to her was to create Harry rather than herself. Christiana's intense visions, which captivated Jung (and formed his *Vision Seminars*), led to an explosion of passion in Harry. "The trances fertilized their lovemaking" (Douglas, 1993, p. 162). Jung had unleashed her eroticism and sexuality and she, in turn, liberated Harry. "Harry had the imaginative capacity and erotic resourcefulness to meet Christiana in both her worlds while helping her to keep one foot strongly in reality" (p. 162). In her visions, Harry found the embodiment of his own, their shared, and the universal unconscious that so entranced him. Douglas is never at peace with Christiana serving as anima for Harry; Robinson embraces this role for her but doesn't think she did a very good job.

Just after beginning her analysis with Jung, in response to Jung's urging, Christiana wrote Harry a crucial, lyrical letter wondering whether they could give themselves to one another in the context of an open relationship with their spouses—and telling him she intended to talk to Will about it, suggesting Harry show her letter to Jo. In Robinson's version, both Harry and Jo as well as Will come to Zurich later that year, and Jung and Toni Wolff try to explain to the spouses the nature of Harry and Christiana's needs for the other; both acquiesce to the arrangement. (In Douglas's version, Jo and Jung meet only briefly many years later.) Thus, Jung, both in his theoretical context and his living arrangement, provides a contextualization for Harry and Christiana's relationship, but it is unclear how much active involvement he had. Christiana understood from Jung the need to synthesize body and soul, feeling and thought, sexuality and spirit. Her hope was that she and Harry would pursue this journey together, following Melville. "Let's do it, Harry!" she wrote. "To go on with what Jung has begun would be the biggest thing that could be done at the present time. Is there a bigger whale or a whiter whale than the chains of the outworn attitudes which fetter and hinder the spirit?" (Robinson, 1992, p. 156).

Robinson, who at this point begins to see Christiana as a force threatening to distract Harry from his "important" work, starts to depict her as the impetus for a quest to create an example for the world in their relationship, taking a lead she insisted that Harry follow: "It is fair to say that she was the more adventurous of the two, if we add that an admixture of desperation on her side was a good part of the difference between them" (p. 157). Christiana was more willing to plunge into the darkness and chaos within. In Robinson's version, Harry hesitated while they were apart.

At a distance of several thousand miles, he had begun to waver, most especially out of concern for Jo and Will. But he was also determined to protect his new career, both from distraction and from . . . scandal—divorce and kindred personal embarrassments—that had cost others at Harvard and elsewhere their jobs. (p. 157)

But in Douglas's version, Harry used social concerns to mask his competition with Christiana's inner life. Harry described them as "two whirlpools" in a power struggle "for dominance and centrality" (p. 188).

Once at Harvard, in 1927 they became work partners at the Harvard Psychological Clinic and lovers with their own apartment nearby for clandestine meetings that were nevertheless an open secret. But their relationship still could not be classified in the usual categories of man and mistress. For Harry, Christiana's visions embodied the unconscious and his fascination with Melville, the pivotal wellsprings of his intellectual work. Here Robinson calls on the word *enthralled* (i.e., in thrall to, in servitude to) to describe Harry's connection to the inner resources he found in Christiana (or in the spaces they created together). In 1927, in words quoted by both biographers, Harry acknowledged that her trances

"represent, express, order our love. Thus they are central. We cannot go ahead without them. They are our language. . . . Our purpose is the creation of a trance epic. . . . I do not know of anything as big as this ever being attempted, but I feel fully capable of doing it *with you*." (Robinson, 1992, p. 169)

Both were committed to this project, but who was more committed at any given time seemed to vary. In Robinson's version, Christiana soon after gives Harry an ultimatum in which he has to choose between his commitment to her and their project in regard to her visions and his commitment to the Harvard Psychological Clinic and to Melville. According to Robinson, Christiana faulted him because "too much of his time and energy was going to the Clinic and to Melville; not enough to her truth as it unfolded in their relationship" (p. 169). Robinson seems to grow increasingly unsympathetic to Harry's investment in his passion for Christiana and their creation of what they believed was a unique relationship, although he dutifully cites from Harry's letters:

"You are the center of my world and the compass of all my hopes. . . . Your center is spiritual and your truths soul-truths, so you must determine the climate for our life, and be the leading principle of our life. . . . Keep me at the center." (p. 170)

From any reading of their letters and journals, it is clear that they believed the story of their union would transform the world. "They had been called as a couple to take a leading role in the history of the human spirit" (p. 170).

In Robinson's recounting, it was Christiana who named them Wona and Mansol, special mystical and mythical names that embodied the larger meanings of who they felt they were for one another. In Douglas's telling, they did it together. As his story progresses, Robinson starts to intensify his portrait of Christiana as a woman who engaged suffering for its own sake, who regarded herself as having a tragic destiny, full of "pain," "panic," and "desperation." Harry, in Robinson's version, although "he had a certain penchant for darkness," was "surely the much brighter hemisphere of the dyad" (p. 171). "It was her part . . . to suffer . . . Harry's to heal." "Sex was the rapturous sequel to pain"—Christiana's pain. "He worked; she waited. He called; she dropped everything to be with him. . . . When Harry was with her alone, she flourished, but when he was gone, . . . it was all emptiness and waiting" (p. 172).

Douglas, however, goes to great lengths to document Christiana's involvement in and contribution to the Clinic, stressing that she did not demand credit for her ideas, ideas that were claimed by others. The central example is the Thematic Apperception Test, for which Christiana was initially listed as the first author but her name was later omitted altogether from the test; Murray has generally received all the credit. In telling about the evolution of the relationship, Douglas wrote,

> Murray would imbue their romance with almost archetypal grandeur in an effort to increase its power over him. . . . When they were together, their love flourished and was often filled with intense passion and drama, but it lacked consistency. The nature of their love and the amount of time they spent together changed with the tide of Murray's enthusiasms. . . . Christiana, always preferring ecstatic intensity, grew to equate the strength of their brief peak moments and of her yearning loneliness with deepening love. (p. 207)

Douglas grows impatient with Christiana waiting for Harry, spending her time writing about their relationship, and wants her to claim her own agency and to realize her unique talents in the world. Perhaps Christiana, she suggests, began to feel exploited and used, like any other mistress, and perhaps the archetypes, the anima role, their plan to write the *Proposition* which would offer their relationship as a kind of salvation to a repressive, shallow world, were just empty and hollow props.

As time went on, the relationship became increasingly filled with intricate rituals and ceremonies that celebrated aspects of their meaning for one another. In Robinson's voice,

> The elaborate naming and ritualizing and recording were to become more and more characteristic of Christiana. She viewed herself as the inspiration for the dyad, the agent through which its forms emerged, and its holy scribe. Her passion for ceremony and record-keeping was at once the measure of her spiritual involvement with Harry and of her fear that

the high romantic life she longed and grasped for was falling away. It was symptomatic of the frailty of her ecstatic dream that it required constant refabrication. . . . For Christiana, quivering intensity itself, almost regardless of its source, was increasingly the goal. Harry played along side her in the drama of the dyad. He believed, as she did, that they were bearers of a precious message. He was Mansol just as surely as she was Wona. . . . But Harry had several parts to play, while Christiana had but one. (p. 193)

Robinson depicts their relationship over the next years as a "pattern of crisis and reconciliation. . . . They theorized their relationship in terms of repeating cycles of stability and instability, permanence and change" (p. 195). But Robinson theorizes their relationship in a different register:

they made a virtue of painful necessity. . . . Christiana was in love with the idea of herself as anguished inspiratrice; Harry was in love with the unconscious. The objects of their loves met and coalesced in the anima. Thus, by the brilliant, lethal economy of the dyad, she suffered, he explored and they called it love. And love it was, of course. They made a world and a life of it. (p. 195)

Here, it seems to me that Robinson has moved into irony as a response perhaps to the difficulty of languaging the passionate, elaborate, ritualized, mystical other-worldliness of this relationship. And, he seems to be saying that he finds it hard to believe their conviction that what they were doing with one another falls within a definition (that he could accept) of love. Perhaps they loved something else; perhaps the intensity itself was "lethal."

Although the biographers' reports are not clear about the dates, around 1930 Harry had a brief infatuation and affair with another woman at the Clinic and he seemed to break with Christiana for about a year; this new involvement, in Douglas's version, led Christiana to have a "nervous breakdown" and stay away from her work at the Clinic. Later, the couple has an intense reconciliation and recommitment to their relationship as part of which Harry proposed to build a Tower (like Jung's) on Christiana's land to commemorate their relationship, express her visions, and create a retreat for contemplation and creative work. They begin a volume of quotations and poems to illustrate their history together.

In Robinson's view (Robinson still wishing Harry would write his Melville biography), Harry returns to Christiana to reclaim "the first and only living source of inspiration available to him . . . in hopes that she could awaken in him the energy and eloquence to write what they both knew about Melville and love" (p. 204). "They agreed to think of the dyad as having three phases—*vision, synergy* (the living unity of two in one) and the *proposition* [italics added] (the representation of their love in words)" (p. 205). Citing Christiana's writings, Robinson notes that this was also a time of strongly reemerging sexual energy and activity.

Throughout his biography, Robinson refers to Harry and Christiana as "the dyad," which appears to be a term Murray used. Douglas never uses it. Robinson says that Christiana avoided the term, disliking "its binary emphasis, and stressed instead the unifying absorption and interpenetration of their lives" (p. 323). Douglas often refers to their relationship as an "affair," a term that I doubt that they would have found suitable. This was a relationship without a satisfactory name, for to name it would be either to sunder the union that formed "two into one" or to try to place this union in a social context that did not exist but that Harry and Christiana hoped to create in the written work (the *Proposition*) they envisioned together. The goal of the *Proposition*, as Harry phrased it, was to try to represent their love in words.

Both biographers tried to capture the process of this relationship, for it was never static. In Robinson's words,

> They never lost sight of their creative, passionate, mutually reinforcing, life-affirmative ideal. . . . They recognized that their task was not to arrive at some fixed point but rather to keep moving and adapting and experimenting. . . . There would be painful changes and bitter sacrifices along the way. Nietzsche's yoking of creativity and destruction was axiomatic with them. (p. 208)

The imaginative worlds of Melville, Nietzsche, and Jung provided soil from which Harry and Christiana drew inspiration and in which they felt they could locate their shared experience of one another. Their concern for the larger social context in which they actually lived becomes increasingly less important in both biographies as they struggle with how to describe and name their own context. Robinson persists in depicting Harry as a man of traditional moral scruples who felt very guilty about his relationship with Christiana. Each had other sexual relationships that seem to have been examined in the context of their meanings to their own relationship—jealousy and possession were idiosyncratically constructed. Christiana, though, had the unfortunate penchant for taking lovers who could not bear her terms and there were at least two suicides among them.

Christiana's husband, Will, died in 1934, leaving her free to move into the Tower that she and Harry had built. But, as she grew older, Christiana

> had more and more difficulty accepting the ebb and flow of Murray's attention. . . . She wrote and spoke of how tired she was of the perpetual pendulum swing of his affection. Yet the very absences, the dizzying peaks and valleys of their affair, lent a frenzied intensity to their lives that both of them craved. (Douglas, 1993, p. 216)

In their Tower, in which every architectural and decorative detail—carved, painted, and sculpted largely by Christiana—symbolized some aspect of their relationship, they established a secret life of "creative intensity." In their identities of Wona and Mansol, they "invented laws, contracts, didactic formulations, rituals, celebrations and feasts for a multilayered fantasy realm—a play world imbued with lusty eroticism" (p. 223). Harry would write there, with Christiana lying nearby, trying "to concretize the subtle alchemy that sometimes plays between creator and inspiration" (p. 226). Christiana took Harry's failure to create his Melville book as her failure to properly inspire him, although she dedicated herself exclusively to this effort. But, in Douglas's reading, she felt that "Harry's expectations of her were impossible for anyone to live out and made her feel sad, submerged, frightened, and broken" (p. 230). Robinson, however, says that Harry abandoned the biography "to save the dyad" (p. 248).

This period, characterized by words such as *passion*, *intensity*, and *energy*, coincided with the flowering of public creativity in the Clinic, work shared and engendered by Harry and Christiana, as well as in the private creativity of the Tower. *Explorations in Personality*, the Harvard Psychological Clinic group's major work, for which authorship has often been attributed (in citations) solely to Murray, but to which Christiana also made significant contributions, was published during this time.[6]

THE FAR REACHES OF SEXUALITY

As the intensity and exploration in this relationship increased, both biographers had to struggle with how to contextualize Christiana and Harry's "increasingly complex and idiosyncratic" (Robinson, 1992, p. 252) sexual relations that featured the introduction of pain into their sexual expression. Some summarizers of these biographical works have simply said that they were "into sadomasochism" as though that describes or explains. The biographers, however, worked much harder than this. According to Robinson,

> [The dyad] . . . took them to the endurable limit of contradiction and intensity, pain, passion, narcissism, and joy. . . . Their sexuality blazed as never before; but it became more complex and more violent as its fires reached their peak. (p. 249)

Douglas introduced this aspect of their life together in terms of their "daring to explore the darker sides of their sexuality. . . . The rituals they invented for this search condoned violence as well as excess" (pp. 260–261).

Harry and Christiana left a detailed record of their sexual activities, but the biographers could not depict these activities without implicit interpretation. According to Robinson, Christiana took Harry's willingness to inflict pain as "the sign that he had passed beyond good and evil" (p. 249) and,

---

[6]Authorship is attributed to "the workers of the Harvard Psychological Clinic" with Murray listed as first author. The next authors are a group of six. Only two of the six do not have doctoral degrees: Christiana Morgan and Erik Homberger (later Erikson).

because it heightened their sexual pleasure, it was also an aspect of her control over him. His need for her to whip him was a sign of his submission to her superior force. All of this was chronicled in mythic terms, part of Christiana's hope that he would write their story. She wanted him to articulate her visions, to translate the irrationality that mesmerized them both into language. Harry writes about wanting to let the world know of "the dark and ultimate love between man and woman." (p. 255)

Douglas saw these activities as a way for the lovers to charge up the intensity in a relationship that was cooling, an interpretation that Robinson seems to share. Douglas's view, though, is a bit more physical, less mythical. She writes,

> Both enjoyed living on the crest, for drama, intensity and peak experiences, yet both had difficulty attaining this orgasmically—Murray having problems with potency and Morgan, after her sympathectomy, with normal sexual response. (p. 262)

THE WAR YEARS AND AFTER

During the war, Harry was away most of the time. Christiana underwent a radical sympathectomy and had bouts of depression and despair. During this time, her love relationships with Alfred North Whitehead and Lewis Mumford, both of whose work she inspired in anima fashion, intensified and comforted her, but did not touch the regions that she and Harry shared. According to Douglas (1993), she became during this time increasingly enslaved to Harry as he became increasingly disengaged from her. After the war, Christiana reclaimed her power, demanding that Harry refocus his attentions on her as master, which seemed briefly to restoke his passion, but he then spent more time away from her while demanding that she write their *Proposition*, the history of their relationship. Alternations between periods of intense closeness and tense distance marked their later years together.

Christiana devoted herself to carvings and artwork that would represent the relationship in embodied form in the Tower. Robinson (1992) wrote, "The building was conceived as an allegorical construction, a harmonious composite of the elements—mind, body and spirit—that Harry and Christiana sought to develop and integrate in their union" (p. 256). Their quest together was for human wholeness. Christiana titled the story of their union *What Joy!*

Neither the Melville biography nor the *Proposition* was ever completed. Christiana increasingly struggled with alcoholism; she and Harry both drank quite a bit, together and separately, but she had difficulties with control. Jo died in 1962 but Harry and Christiana never married. While on holiday with Harry in 1967, Christiana drowned in 2 feet of water. At the time Harry was involved with another woman whom he later married. By Harry's account, his last words to Christiana, finding her in an intoxicated state, were "You're disgusting." There is no way to know if her death was an accident or suicide.

THE BIOGRAPHERS' STANCES

All biographers develop complex emotional relationships with their subjects (Schepeler, 1990) and both Robinson and Douglas seem to have been fairly transparent in their stances and feelings about their subjects. Like two therapists treating members of a married couple, the biographers absorbed the dynamics of the relationship itself. Both admired, even venerated, their own biographical subjects, though grew impatient with what they considered to be their relational excesses, and were annoyed at the "other" and sometimes at the relationship itself. Both wished their subject had achieved more and (subtly or sometimes overtly) blamed the other member of the couple for holding their subject back. Douglas believed that Christiana Morgan, like many women, contributed much, much more to the achievements of her partner than has been acknowledged, and was outraged about this (as well as at Jung's treatment of her). She tried to redress this by detailing Christiana's independent contributions to psychology. In her feminist reading of Christiana's life, she concludes that "Morgan channeled her creativity into a relationship with a mercurial and inconstant though brilliant man and never developed her self-reliance or her own inner resources" (p. 303).

Both noticed that Harry was the more ambivalent of the two, the more likely to provoke the separations and distance. Douglas, taking Christiana's side, saw Harry as unable to fully commit himself to her vision, to her depths; he held on to his rationality. Robinson, however, thought Harry allowed himself too much irrationality where Christiana was concerned. Douglas worried that Harry may have been exploiting Christiana in the ways men have always exploited women as mistresses and was never as fully committed to the relational project as was Christiana. Robinson (sometimes) regarded Christiana as a grasping, demanding, insatiable woman, a seductress drawing Harry away from his family and his serious work which, because Robinson came to Harry's work through a shared interest in Melville, he saw as primarily the completion of the Melville biography. Robinson also seems to me to be more conventional than Douglas in his grounding, more protective of the social order, liking Harry best when he was the "great man" the public saw or the good family man sharing comfortable, companionable moments with Jo. Douglas, as a Jungian, seemed to resonate more with Christiana's visions as an entrée to the unconscious.

After considering and weighing massive quantities of material, each biographer organized a narrative that in his or her view best represented the material. Both wrote, to my mind, in evocative, lyrical, and psychologically sophisticated terms, quoting widely from their subjects but adding their own interpretation of the documents at hand.[7] Neither could tell the story of his or her own subject without telling the other story as well, so enmeshed were Christiana's and Harry's lives. Both biographers ended their work with a summarizing chapter, offering their own view of the meanings of the relationship in the life of their particular subject.

Robinson and Douglas had somewhat different starting points and agendas and worked from somewhat different viewpoints on the material. Robinson, an American studies scholar with an interest in Melville, had a 10-year relationship with Murray in which he conducted more than 100 interviews with his subject. When he first approached Murray about doing a biography, Murray told him that "there was little to tell . . . except for a secret love affair of more than forty years." Robinson titled his biography *Love's Story Told*; his project was to portray the interplay between the private and public Murray, the lover and the scholar. Robinson wrote,

> As the life gradually fell open, it became clear that the secret love affair was the key to it all. It everywhere energized and informed the public career; it was the hidden center, the focus, the source of inspiration and direction. . . . Love had revolutionized his life. (p. viii)

From this beginning in the energizing core of love, Robinson, by the end, moves to seeing the love relationship as essentially destructive and crippling, bordering on madness. "From the beginning, Harry and Christiana took to tragic models. . . . They knew they were in for trouble—indeed, they cultivated the trouble" (p. 383).

Douglas came to the project as a Jungian analyst, wishing to bring out of the shadows the woman who had had a powerful effect on Jung. She began with Christiana's contributions to Jung through her drawings and visions and notes the way in which women's creativity had for so long been appropriated by men who failed to nourish them in return. "She remains a footnote in other people's history" (p. 12), Douglas said of Christiana, who allowed her work to be unattributed, jumbled into Murray's.

> Her lifelong struggle to find a way to put all her talents to use thrust her into a conflict between what she felt and what her culture, as well as Jung, told her she should be feeling. . . . The subtext of this biography concerns male and female relationships and what befalls a woman who strives to create a life of her own while remaining in thrall to the idea of Romantic love. (p. 15)

Douglas maintains this stance throughout the biography and, as her narrative proceeds, seems to grow increasingly angry at Harry for subduing, sub-

---

[7]In my opinion, both are superb works, and I would be unable to recommend one over the other.

verting, and abusing Christiana. Although she recognizes and details Christiana's life project to experience and document the new form for relationship she believed she and Harry were creating, Douglas concludes that the experiment was a failure. As her summary progresses, her criticism and outrage grow:

> Their attempt at a creative relationship ended in a tragedy littered with corpses: Will Morgan, Jo Murray, other lovers, two abandoned children who suffered profoundly. . . . And finally, Harry, an honest and creative man with eleven aborted books, and Christiana, her visions veiled and unlived, dead by drowning so Harry could try again with a younger, more rational, saltier woman. (p. 317)

So both conclude, in their own ways, the relationship to be a destructive misadventure even as it organized both lives. Both biographers, however, seemed to me to have taken on the project their subjects left unfinished (but with the pieces preserved), which was to try to find a social and narrative context for this relationship.

THE MEANINGS AND CONTEXT

No language is available to position this relationship in socially recognized terms, which was Harry and Christiana's struggle as well. They seemed to be reaching for a Jungian understanding of their experience, to interpret and present it in archetypal terms, subverting the usual categories of gender as they traded masculine and feminine clothing and roles; exploring the intersection between love and power, surrender and autonomy; stretching the limits of sexual experience by experimenting with the extremes of dominance and submission; and undergoing pain to understand its relationship to pleasure, all the while trying to find language for the intensities of feeling and aliveness that engulfed them.

If they thought of their union as a critique of the alienation of modern society and a restoration of spirituality and personal creativity, then it had larger meaning. But these are very rational terms for something that had at its core so much that was not rational. That was their whole aim—to explore the unconscious, which defies logic or linearity. Once, Harry complained to Christiana that if she lost faith in their project "then the Synergy is the greatest Love Affair of all time but it is *not* the salvation of man." Their relationship might become nothing more than "closeness," Harry worried (Robinson, p. 302). Thus, Harry tells us that even if we contemporary readers and psychologists were willing to view this as "the greatest love affair of all time," he would think we had missed the point.

Robinson found Harry's most direct published references to his relationship with Christiana in his paper "Vicissitudes of Creativity." There, Harry tries to describe "two interdependent regions of imagination operating as a single system" that relies on sexuality and "exchanges of nourishing, gutty thoughts or feelings . . . [and] complete emotional expression" (Robinson, p. 354). Douglas quotes from an outline for the *Proposition* Harry wrote in 1949. In it, Harry described their relationship as unequaled "in the history of mankind" and "attributed the success of their relationship to its endurance, its intensity and its fecundity." He described it as having no quarrels (ignoring its volatility). He used words such as "serene, stable and trustful" and said it fulfilled their basic needs including "succor, nurturance, religion, domination, submission, aggression and above all, erotic affection" (1993, p. 256). Harry stressed that they had "shared aims, tastes, values and sentiments" and that they "trusted the relationship" and expected it to endure throughout their lives. He saw as the chief causes for the strength of "their relationship their religious commitment to the union's creativity; the trances; Jung's example of his life with his wife and Toni Wolff"; their use of Jung's "concept of animus and anima; their shared profession; their freedom from conventionality; their separation, which intensified their relationship and kept it fresh; Murray's wealth, which permitted their isolation; building the Tower" and their apartment in the city; "and their ability to put their synergy first as their highest philosophy" (pp. 256–257). Christiana, in her effort in *What Joy!* to describe the relationship, stresses the "generative power of the unconscious" and the "pleasures of creativity of all kinds." At the same time, Christiana rues their "limited literary powers" (Robinson, p. 330, quoting from *What Joy!*) that, in the end, she felt could not manage the task of languaging their experience.

Harry and Christiana believed that they had created something life-affirming and energizing, something to do with creativity and spirit, emotional and sexual freedom, something enlarging despite its travails and pain. But Douglas, having read through the mass of drafts and notes detailing their effort to contextualize their relationship, wrote that "when the chapters [focus] on the universal and messianic meaning of their life together, they elude or irritate the reader with their inflated pomposity" (p. 260). Harry and Christiana were struggling for a larger, public meaning—a name—for their experience, but what was it? And is there a context in which we as psychologists can understand it?

THE NARRATIVE CONTEXTS OF RELATIONSHIP

I now turn to consider the possible narrative contexts that underlie the biographers' presentation of the relationship. Through these accounts one finds implicit narrative framings that alternate among the case history of pathology, the social critique, and more elusively, the intersubjective.

Pathology As a Narrative Context

Any relationship that exists outside of canonical forms invites
pathologizing as a first response. In colloquial terms, people are quick to say
(or think) "That's sick" when hearing about surprising events in others' relationships. In conceptual terms, psychoanalysis offers a range of possibilities
for reducing adult relational experience to its infantile or irrational roots.

Both biographers are psychoanalytically informed and offer interpretations based in object relations theory. One can analyze this relationship from
a psychoanalytically reductionistic point of view, noting, for example, the
ways in which their sadomasochistic rituals allowed them each to live out
and master early childhood traumas: Harry's experience with his dominating
mother and his helpless rage at the hands of his overstimulating and cruel
sister; Christiana's early punishments, locked in a dark closet, for being too
rebellious. As they played at being master and slave, the repetition compulsion
allowed them each to try to heal childhood wounds. Both biographers offer
this and other such analysis. This form of analysis is reassuring for it grounds
this story in the familiar idea that love provides an opportunity to relive and to
better resolve the painful experiences of the past. But does this fully explain
the nature of their experience in the relationship—the intense yearning and
need, the fulfillment and vitality they found in one another, and the fact
that it lasted 40 years? An analysis like this cannot account for the mystical,
intense realms of experience that these people were trying to reach.

Douglas also ventures into the diagnostic:

> Technically each had what psychologists once referred to as an "as-if"
> personality; this narcissistic personality disorder demanded that they pose
> as iconoclastic rebels in a grandiose drama of their own making. . . .
> Playing an anima figure or *femme inspiratrice* precluded true pairing, for
> the woman behind the figure disappears beneath the role, while the man
> who loves his reflection feels he has the right to the reflector as part of
> his own imaginative property. (p. 303)

This analysis of the pathology of the couple is either an astute insight or a
reflection of Douglas's anger at Harry for

> resisting Christiana while demanding that she engulf him, defeating her
> while demanding that she create him, and forcing her to embody his
> ideal at the peril of losing him altogether. He became the admired man
> of the world while she grew more lonely and isolated. (p. 310)

Douglas even suggests that he abused her, physically as well as psychologically.

> Because of her maternally-deprived and punitive childhood, Christiana
> needed an idealized conqueror who would punish and annihilate the needy
> female in his rituals of ecstasy and pain. Despotism, submission, aban-

donment, shame and release swirled unanalyzed in the adult woman's unconscious as they did, in different form, inside her male lover. (p. 310)

Robinson, for his part, offers psychological interpretations based on Harry's unconscious attraction to suffering women whom he felt compelled to try to heal. He is rather unsparing in his view of Christiana as depressed, neurotic, perhaps even mad. But this relationship had so many facets, as each biographer carefully details, that no one interpretation will encompass it.

Both Robinson and Douglas judged their subject to have been creatively unfulfilled, leaving most of their work undone. Each biographer believed that his or her subject somehow wanted the other to take charge of his or her own projects and got caught in cycles of hope and despair, supplication and blame. From this vantage point of unfulfilled promise, one can judge the relationship an impediment, a distraction, a self-destructive obsession based in neurotic conflict.

Another pathologizing strategy is to regard this whole relationship as illusion. If the relationship cannot be anchored in existing terms, it must have been only a form of imagination. In full pathologizing mode, Robinson wrote, "It was symptomatic of the frailty of her ecstatic dream that it required constant refabrication. . . . Little wonder that in shoring up her crumbling Xanadu she sometimes mistook the parched rush of anxiety for the real romantic thing" (p. 193). But all love emanates from the imagination (Person, 1988), and to describe its imaginative elements is not to explain or contextualize the experience. As Nussbaum (1990) points out, the problem is not an illusion on the lover's part—rather it is that the lovers' ways of seeing and valuing are not publicly communicable. The lover endows the other with value that the spectator often cannot find. The "pathology," then, may be in the spectator's blinders or too firm a conviction that one can know the "reality" of relationships. Robinson, however, analyzing, of course, from outside, attributes the "blindness" to them:

> Had they fully recognized the extent to which the dyad rationalized and concealed separate, competing agendas—and thereby fostered endless crises in the name of endless love and made it possible to confuse great pain with great pleasure—they might have thought better of it. . . . They seem to have had a stake in blindness. (Robinson, 1992, p. 195)

Or one can simply dismiss what they were doing as delusion, which is how the psychobiographer Mac Runyan (Schultz, 2001) read Robinson's presentation. Douglas wrote that "their private world began to take on elements of a Romantic *folie-a-deux* pretend world . . . a shared, grandiose delusion" (p. 254). Robinson, coming out a bit from his biographer's stance (in what was my favorite line in both works), concluded, charmingly, "It was folly, of course. But, what a ride!" (p. 383). Perhaps it was folly, perhaps even "folie,"[8] (in

---

[8]According to Harry's account, his analyst, Franz Alexander, regarded the couple as a "narcissism a deux" (Anderson, 1990, p. 320).

whose judgment?) but it was not just that. Christiana, almost as though she were in conversation with this point of view, once wrote that "vulgarity consists in not being able to distinguish between the *ardent* which is always outside the norm and the *sick* which is also outside the norm" (Douglas, 1993, p. 227).

Social Critique As a Narrative Context

Society provides the framework in which people assign significance to their emotional experience (Shapiro & Carr, 1991). Where there is protest against the prescribed forms found at hand in one's social world, one can frame the relationship as social critique. This can be seen not in the language of pathology, but in the language of creative rebellion.

> Christiana and Harry invented private rituals that united them in a way that pushed the limits of traditional rituals. They used ritual to enrich their life and to explore repressed wishes and desires. The two set out to confront what the superego abhorred—all the divine, dangerous, repressed, aggressive, sexual, perverse and/or ecstatically religious impulses that were forbidden in their upbringing. Ritual provided Christiana and Harry with a formalized context in which they could play with, yet try to contain and regulate, the backwaters of the human psyche that fascinated and repelled them or drew their obeisance. . . . Both had the courage to push their fantasies far enough and had imaginations large enough to risk experiencing the demonic side of their natures. (Douglas, 1993, p. 261)

And they had positive rituals as well. "They played at being animals or gods, had dramas they enacted, dances" (p. 263).[9]

Here, the context of play invokes Winnicottian ideas of the transitional space, the place of all creativity where the harsh demands of reality are temporarily set aside in order for something new to emerge. As Wona and Mansol (and they sometimes switched roles), the socially constructed Christiana and Harry could experiment with self-extension in the new, transitional space they were creating and discovering together. The "pretend" world, then, can be cast by the observer as folly (*folie*) or inventiveness, depending, I submit, on the dynamics of the observer. Wona–Mansol created a relationship separate from their outside identities. It was this relationship they were trying to name, articulate, understand, and locate in—and in opposition to—the social world.

Within this context, Harry and Christiana thought of themselves as offering to the world a new model for living; after all, they titled the treatise they were writing about their relationship the *Proposition*, indicating that

---

[9]Muller (1999) points out that without any structuring influence of the Third (the social context), dyads inevitably become prone to intense love–hate vacillations.

they saw themselves as proposing something. They carved on the Tower door the words "The standard of living is ecstasy." But, as Robinson points out, "the more they elaborated their system, the more intensely private it became" (p. 252). It was "a retreat from the world's poverty of spirit," rather than the healing model they wished to generate, and this, perhaps, was their greatest disappointment. But if we regard them from this vantage point, we construct them as failed visionaries or unheard prophets.

Neither biographer could narrate the story from this transitional space. Instead, they narrated from within their own prevailing social frameworks. Robinson, positioned in the social context of achievement, laments Harry's unrealized writing. Douglas, from a feminist stance, decries the normative roles for women that led Christiana to sacrifice her own agency in favor of self-sacrifice to a "doomed, romantic fantasy of relationship" (p. 316). Neither biographer could find a social good in whatever social critique the couple enacted.

Profoundly intimate relationships, because they are intimate, do not include the social world in their activities. Thus, the world has always attempted to regulate the forces of eros, recognizing its power to disrupt the social order by its sheer possibility of creating a private but unshared world (Person, 1988). Harry and Christiana, in their effort to write the *Proposition*, were attempting to define a context for their experiences with one another, to locate it in something beyond their own unconscious yearnings and needs, to provide it with a significance that could be shared by others. They knew what they opposed: In his essay "Vicissitudes of Creativity," Murray wrote that "complete emotional expression" between two members of a dyad was a corrective to "the traditional Christian practice of repression of primitive impulsions" and to "the psychoanalytic notion of the replacement of the id by the ego (rationality), which results so often in a half-gelded, cautious, guarded, conformist, uncreative, and dogmatic way of coping with the world" (Robinson, 1992, p. 345).

Harry and Christiana found their feelings best represented, however implicitly, by Jung and Melville. They felt themselves enlarging on and embodying these ideas in their creation of their relationship, but the contexts were literary and psychological, not social. (Christiana was, for example, occupied about whether or not she was a good enough anima, a question not meaningful in the external social frame.) Feeling they had discovered the life force and held it between them, they wanted to add their creation to the lexicon of stories available in the world which, at the same time, they recognized, was unlikely to understand.

Without such a social context, the relationship cannot have a name. Languaging the relationship places it semiotically within the culture, which is something that Christiana and Harry themselves never found a way to do satisfactorily. The publisher's note to the Douglas book labels Christiana an "erotic muse"; the note to the Robinson book says that he had a "highly erotic and mystical affair" with her; Edwin Schneidman (2001), who worked with Christiana at the Clinic, called her a "mystical companion" (p. 289) and Mac Runyan (1994) referred to her as a "soulmate" (p. 702). Alan Elms (1987), who wrote about Harry before his death, deftly called Christiana Harry's closest professional collaborator and his "femme inspiratrice" (p. 11). These are perhaps acceptable names for what she may have been for him (overlooking what he was for her), but not for the nature of the relationship they created.[10] Anderson (1999), who interviewed Murray at length, described them as having "an intimate emotional, intellectual and sexual relationship" (p. 24)—a good modernist definition (Gergen & Gergen, 1995), but one that eschews the Romantic in omitting the passionate and the erotic which, in its classical meaning (of or pertaining to the god of love, Eros), was central to Harry and Christiana.

Is Romanticism an escape into fantasy or a discovery of a more "real" underpinning of experience (Mitchell, 2002)? Harry and Christiana experienced their relationship within a Romantic frame but set themselves the task of translating their experience into terms that fit the modernist, Enlightenment intellectual tradition of their times. Thus, their struggle to understand their experience reflected a long-standing epistemological dialectic in their society which is, perhaps, another social context.

Intersubjectivity As a Narrative Context

Like all lovers, Christiana and Harry sought and experienced union, a felt restoration of a lost wholeness. But their intellectual and emotional interest in this union went beyond the sense of merger[11] and they attempted to explore the elements of what existed in this "between" that united them.

Because they prized creativity above all and because they felt that they were most creative in what they were evolving together, Harry and Christiana searched for some way of grounding their experience in something sharable outside their twosome. They believed that they "discovered" something in the same way that Melville "discovered" the unconscious and Jung "discovered" the archetypes. Douglas (1993), however, was impatient with this:

> He and Christiana filled their private world with a multiplicity of signs and symbols, each of which took on a significance intelligible only to themselves. The depictions of their life together, at least in the rough drafts of their book, read like minutely detailed yet plotless illustrations of the arcane practices of a lost religion whose central tenets elude the outsider. Neither could allow their pillow talk simply to express the ten-

---

[10]Barenbaum (2006) elided the naming problem in writing about Murray by describing the two as having a "turbulent personal and professional relationship" (p. 173).
[11]Person (1988) observed that the kind of merger experienced in passionate love, which expands the self as it loosens its boundaries, is completely different from the obliteration of the sense of self in psychosis, which leads to terror.

derness between two lovers . . . but forced it to assume the grandiose importance of a new language full of relevance and universal validity and equal to the great religious symbolism of the past. (p. 255)

The notion of religion, which invokes the spiritual foundation of the kind of relationship under consideration here, suggests a contextualizing link to experiences beyond and transcending the self. In psychoanalytic terms that are making their way into the mainstream of developmental psychology, the reference is to the intersubjective, to experiences that emerge in the "we" space between people. The language of individualism makes it difficult to describe or express processes of transitional space, transitional object, or projective identification, all names for contents and processes in the intersubjective space that spin and recombine elements of conscious and unconscious emotional experience in the players, belonging to both but to neither alone (see Josselson, in press). Passionate love is transformative because it offers access into another's subjectivity, and theorists of love have suggested that its preservation depends on the sharing of aspects of self that emanate from the unconscious (Mitchell, 2002; Person, 1988).

Ogden (1994) had a profound effect on the understanding of the analytic relationship by detailing the *analytic third*, which represents the unconscious interplay of subjectivities in the analytic situation. Between two people, internal images and experiences mingle and are transformed and reinternalized in novel ways without any clearly identifiable sense of who has contributed which elements. The creation occurs in this "space between" and disappears if one tries to translate the experience into individualistic terms. In the analytic situation, the analysis itself provides the context for the experience.[12] In the course of life in an individualistic world, however, intersubjectivity goes either unnoticed or disavowed.

From this point of view, we might use two words that to some extent contextualize the intersubjective nature of this relationship. One word that Robinson (1992) borrows from Donne early in the text but then abandons is *interanimate*. This word seems to be a good description of what Christiana and Harry were doing for one another. They animated each other through the vitality of their union; Harry believed that they had surpassed Jung's idea of individuation by finding a process within which two people could evolve together (Douglas, 1993). A second word is one that Harry used to mark their union: *synergy*. The dictionary defines *synergy* as the interaction of two or more agents or forces so that their combined effect is greater than the sum of their individual effects. What captured Harry and Christiana's attention was the energy their relational project engendered.

---

[12]This idea, however, differs from Muller's (1999) concept of the Third, which refers to the anchoring of a dyadic relationship in a context (Aron, 1999). Thus, one can conceptualize Christiana and Harry's struggle as locating the intersubjective space in the external world.

From this interanimated, synergistic stance, I would argue with Douglas's and Robinson's conclusions that the Morgan–Murray relationship was a story of failed achievement. Murray has been lionized precisely because his (their) creation of the Harvard Psychological Clinic inspired and empowered a stellar group of scholars who, because of the sheer energy and excitement of the place, went on to influence the development of psychology in profound and lasting ways. This group became the grand theorists, the teachers, the generative center of the field. From where did this remarkable vitality emanate? Some want to attribute it to Murray, but it seems to me that these biographies make clear that the wellspring was in the relationship between these principals.[13] Christiana created all the physical spaces that the Clinic occupied and attended to the spirit and rhythms of the working environment (according to Douglas, but not to Robinson), and she had a large part in planning the research agenda. In Bion's terms, they formed the pair that unconsciously for the group embodied hope and futurity. The very intensity and aspiration of that pairing may have powered the waves of intellectual passion in the Clinic that reached beyond into the next generations.[14] Douglas alludes to this idea when she writes of the Clinic: "The atmosphere of excitement, even enchantment, and the almost erotic magnetism of the work itself was the outward manifestation of Murray's and Morgan's inner marriage" (p. 193). Robinson cites many noted psychologists commenting on Murray's zest, imagination, and creativity. But Murray himself repeatedly attributed this part of himself to Christiana, telling Jim Anderson that Christiana was part of every aspect of his thinking, his writing, and his speaking (Douglas, 1993, p. 297); she, for her part, saw him as empowering her capacity to have visions and to access the unconscious that led them both.

So how does one narrate a relationship that cannot be contained in available (individualistic) language but is emotionally central and life-structuring for two creative and reflective people and has its (unconscious) effects on others? Doing so would require a language of the intersubjective space, an emergent creation of the unconscious elements of two people. But it requires the difficult task of narrating the invisible because the space between, although feeling full and substantial to those within its boundaries, cannot be located (consciously) by those looking on.

---

[13]Most brief intellectual biographies of Murray simply edit Christiana Morgan out even though those who have looked carefully at the archives say that his notes for nearly all of his works until the time of her death include her writing interspersed with his (Douglas, 1993).

[14]Among those who worked in the Clinic and went on to make significant contributions to psychology were Erik Erikson, Robert White, Jerome Frank, Nevitt Sanford, Donald MacKinnon, and Fredrick Wyatt. Wyatt went on to create the Psychological Clinic at the University of Michigan, where I was among those he trained. I recognize in Robinson's (1992; and others') descriptions of the *esprit* at the Harvard Psychological Clinic the kind of intellectual passion I experienced at the Michigan Clinic (and have never encountered since), which suggests an energy there that could be carried to other places. In any case, I can trace my own intellectual inheritance to the Murray–Morgan alliance.

Passion, because it involves the quest for union in the context of arousal, cannot be conceived just as an aspect of self, although many have noted its role in catalyzing the self (Person, 1988; Viederman, 1988). It is an interanimating intersubjective interconnection that produces its own synergic field that radiates outward in ways we are not schooled to notice. It is easier and more apparent to trace the pain of passion—the inevitable separations, disjunctions, rages, and refusals—because at these moments the individuals reappear. It is in the periods of union, when the two-in-one flowers, that language fails.

Shared Meanings: Speaking in One Voice

Thinking in synergistic terms, however, goes deeply against the grain of intellectual tradition, which is rooted in individualism, and I offer the following example to illustrate this difficulty. In one remarkable contrast between the biographies, Douglas quotes a long document written by Harry as though from Christiana's point of view in which he details her effort to convert him away from his narrow conventionality to her vision and inner world, demanding of him that he be strong enough to overcome her power and force her to submit. In this telling of the history of their relationship, Harry, in Christiana's voice, portrays himself as a conventional, bourgeois, sexually inhibited, spiritually vacant person whom Christiana initiated into the mysteries of the mind and the soul. He credits her for leading him into psychology, for unveiling the realm of the unconscious and teaching him the joys of sexual expression. He recognizes that she had been impatient with his boyishness and intellectualization and documents how she patiently led him, step by step, to the core of experience. She broke down his "deadening rationality" and his "outmoded conscience." She helped him traverse the "vast distance in experience, in depth and sincerity of living" that separated them. Having chosen him, she needed to close the chasm between them or be alone with the anguish and terror of "carrying the life force unaided." She "had to bring him to a realization of the flesh" (Douglas, p. 272). This letter is, then, about as close to a concise psychological developmental summary in accessible language that they offered. Robinson, however, who also quotes extensively from this same document, presents it as though Christiana wrote it (p. 258; Douglas, p. 266). It is my own individualistic bias that wants to correct Robinson, to point out that, according to Douglas, Harry wrote it.

But, on further thought, I find this contradiction illuminating because in some sense the shared consciousness between them seems to be precisely what they were trying to convey through terms such as *synergy* and *two in one*. In synergistic relational thinking, one might say that this document emerged from their shared experience; authorship lies in the relationship. As Robinson said, "The truth is . . . mingled and elusive" (p. 261).

TOWARD A LANGUAGE OF RELATIONSHIP

We cannot narrate the space between in linear language and this fact, I think, leads us as psychologists to turn away from the kaleidoscopic nature, texture, and meanings of relationships in the lives of those we study. While watching the gymnastic dance company Pilobolus, a troupe that makes impossible kinetic sculptures out of the interconnections between human bodies, I had the insight that the pas de deux is the more apt metaphor for dyadic relationships than a linear verbal form. In the pas de deux are intertwinings and interdependencies played off against separations, comings apart, and comings together in new configurations. Dancers are coiled around and cantilevered against one another in shifting shapes. Often, in the forms created by Pilobolus, it was not immediately apparent how the people were balanced against each other; who was holding who and how, if one dancer was doing the holding or allowing him- or herself to be held on to; or which parts of them were bearing the weight. The illusion was that a complex, new being emerged from the interweaving of bodies, a new creation from two making one. Indeed, they concretized Plato's mythical being of two heads, four legs, and four arms, embodying the various forms such a creature could take. Verbal language, though, is the language of self and we tend to describe relationships as being an additive result of two selves rather than a dynamic interconnection and interweaving of selves that meet and move apart and meet again.

We also narrate relationships within the implicit conventions of our culture that offer canonical templates for what relationships ought to be like. This limited range of narrative scripts becomes the horizon of understanding for psychology to interpret the meanings of relationships in people's lives. Because our language and knowledge of the self are so far beyond our language and "scientific" knowledge of relational experience (Josselson, 1992), much of what passes for analysis is conventionality cloaked in the language of psychopathology. We write from the conventions of how we think relationships ought to be, subtly—or not so subtly—critiquing what is outside these bounds. As Ethel Person (1988) points out, academic disciplines, allied with the rationalist tradition, regard love as a dangerous Romantic illusion, and, in allegiance to a modernist view of science, perpetuate a cultural split between feeling and knowing.[15] Furthermore, she points out, contemporary therapists are schooled in a rationalist "commitment" kind of love, stripped of its excesses, based on mutual respect, shared values and common interests, and duty and responsibility rather than emotional pleasure and sexual passion.

The essence of intimate exchange is that it is private and usually beyond outside scrutiny. The documentation of the Murray–Morgan relation-

---

[15]Part of Harry and Christiana's quest was to be able to think and feel at the same time, a Jungian ideal.

ship is highly exceptional as a catalog of relational experience. A look inside what they found compelling and meaningful, beyond whatever anxieties such voyeurism may cause, offers a glimpse of a rarely seen but perhaps not uncommon experience of transcendence. As Nussbaum (1990) put it, "For the lovers, this life has the charms of mystery, secrecy and intimacy; from the outside it is simply mysterious" (p. 344).

Those we interview for our studies are similarly embedded in cultural conventions of language and concept and are often at pains to articulate the meanings of relationships in their lives, so the interview goes on to other, more easily discussed topics: ambitions, achievements, values, activities—those more public aspects of experience for which language is readily available. With both interviewee and researcher operating within such limits, the realm of relational experience becomes the underside or background or hidden arena of our depiction and understanding of human life, shrouded in silence, apparent only when disruptions, betrayals, disappointments, or losses make it manifest. Or it gets subsumed into notions of security and attachment. Relationship then comes to be constructed within a discourse of safety and satisfaction, predictability, and convention. We now have a better understanding of love when it supports a life, but not when it forms the structure of, or vitalizes, a life. Passionate love, in its erotic, life-creating sense, is accorded to the province of opera and literature.

Yet love is often the central organizing force in adult life. For Christiana and Harry (and for how many others?), it was the wellspring of their feeling of aliveness. "All real living is meeting," said Buber (1958, p. 25), although the distinction between adequate adjustment and "real living" has eluded much of psychological theory. Longitudinal studies and studies of mature adults show that when people look back on their lives, their relationships loom largest in terms of meaning and gratification (e.g., Holahan, 1994; Josselson, 2000). But these relationships are not given or found. What creates their meaning is the dynamic, developmental process people engage in as they try to work out what others will or will not be for them and the qualities of desire and responsiveness they can expect from—and offer to—others. Love, because it is a complex way of being with another person that evolves over time, requires a story that includes its denial and its yielding, its tensions, illusions, and excitement—and the special terms in which it is idiosyncratically cast. It can be grasped only in narrative form because only narrative can allow a view of subjectivity (and intersubjectivity). It may even require a polyphonic, multivocal narrative. From a postmodern point of view, in which the coconstruction of a world and a "we" can be understood apart from a preexisting order (Gergen & Gergen, 1995), the power of language can bring new things into being. What is needed is a language with which to narrate the intersubjective.

The challenge to narrative psychology is the same as that faced by Harry and Christiana and by most people, though for the latter perhaps in less dramatic and intense terms: how to narrate the eros of relational experience that structures and enlivens a life and may create an intersubjectivity that itself has effects in the world.

> Life without love is load; and time stands still.
> What we refuse to him, to death we give;
> And then, then only, when we love, we live.
> —*Congreve*
> (Engraved over the Tower door; from Robinson, 1992, p. 324)

REFERENCES

Anderson, J. (1990). The life of Henry A. Murray: 1893–1988. In A. I. Rabin, R. A. Zucker, R. Emmons, & S. Frank (Eds.), *Studying persons and lives* (pp. 304–334). New York: Springer Publishing Company.

Anderson, J. (1999). Henry A. Murray and the creation of the Thematic Apperception Test. In L. Gieser & M. I. Stein (Eds.), *Evocative images: The Thematic Apperception Test and the art of projection* (pp. 23–38). Washington, DC: American Psychological Association.

Aron, L. (1999). Clinical choices and the relational matrix. *Psychoanalytic Dialogues, 9*, 1–29.

Barenbaum, N. B. (2006). Henry A. Murray: Personology as biography, science, and art. In D. A. Dewsbury, L. T. Benjamin, & M. Wertheimer (Eds.), *Portraits of pioneers in psychology* (Vol. VI, pp. 169–187). Washington, DC: American Psychological Association.

Buber, M. (1958). *I and thou.* New York: Scribner.

Douglas, C. (1993). *Translate this darkness: The life of Christiana Morgan, the veiled woman in Jung's circle.* New York: Simon & Schuster.

Elms, A. (1987). The personalities of Henry A. Murray. *Perspectives in Personality, 2*, 1–14.

Gergen, M. M., & Gergen, K. J. (1995). What is this thing called love? Emotional scenarios in historical perspective. *Journal of Narrative and Life History, 5*, 221–237.

Holahan, C. K. (1994). Women's goal orientations across the life cycle: Findings from the Terman Study of the Gifted. In B. F. Turner & L. E. Troll (Eds.), *Women growing older: Psychological perspectives* (pp. 35–67). Thousand Oaks, CA: Sage.

Josselson, R. (1992). *The space between us: Exploring the dimensions of human relationship.* San Francisco: Jossey-Bass.

Josselson, R. (2000). Relationship and connection in women's identity from college to midlife. In M. E. Miller & A. N. West (Eds.), *Spirituality, ethics and relationship in adulthood: Clinical and theoretical explorations* (pp. 113–146). Madison, CT: Psychosocial Press.

Josselson, R. (in press). *Playing pygmalion. How people create one another*. New York: Jason Aronson.

Mitchell, S. (2002). *Can love last? The fate of romance over time*. New York: Norton.

Muller, J. T. (1999). The Third as holding the dyad. *Psychoanalytic Dialogues, 9*, 471–480.

Nussbaum, M. (1990). *Love's knowledge*. New York: Oxford University Press.

Ogden, T. (1994). The analytic third: Working with intersubjective clinical facts. *International Journal of Psychoanalysis, 75*, 3–20.

Person, E. S. (1988). *Dreams of love and fateful encounters: The power of romantic passion*. New York: Norton.

Robinson, F. (1992). *Love's story told: A life of Henry A. Murray*. Cambridge, MA: Harvard University Press.

Runyan, W. M. (1994). Coming to terms with the life, loves, and work of Henry A. Murray. *Contemporary Psychology, 39*, 701–704.

Schepeler, E. (1990). The biographer's transference: A chapter in psychobiographical epistemology. *Biography, 15*, 111–129.

Schneidman, E. S. (2001). My visit with Christiana Morgan. *History of Psychology, 4*, 289–296.

Schultz, W. T. (2001, December). Psychobiography and the study of lives: Interview with William McKinley Runyan. *Clio's Psyche: A Psychohistorical Forum*, pp. 105–112.

Shapiro, E. R., & Carr, A. W. (1991). *Lost in familiar places*. New Haven, CT: Yale University Press.

Viederman, M. (1988). The nature of passionate love. In W. Gaylin & E. Person (Eds.), *Passionate attachments* (pp. 1–15). New York: Free Press.

3

CAMILLE CLAUDEL AND AUGUSTE RODIN: TOWARD A LACANIAN POETICS

ANNIE G. ROGERS

Last June, while in Québec City studying Lacanian psychoanalysis,[1] I went to see an exhibit in the art museum. *A Fateful Encounter* was riveting: It was composed of five rooms of Auguste Rodin's sculptures accompanied by work from an artist I knew nothing about—Camille Claudel. I bypassed the headsets narrating their lives and walked about in silence, room by room, entranced. In one section of the exhibit it was not possible to distinguish their work: little heads, half-scaled to life, were lined up without the artists' names. Then Rodin's figures grew bolder, larger, more artful, and impossible to translate into words. And I saw Claudel's work become small, smaller, falter, hover at an edge of anguish, and stop. I learned that she spent the last 30 years of her life in an insane asylum, and that they'd once been lovers. She was 17 when she came to Paris and met Rodin as his pupil. He was 41. What had happened that allowed them both to flourish for a time? How had each construed the other? What led to her madness and to his success? I was not

---

[1] I was entering my 4th year of studying Lacanian psychoanalysis at the Freudian School of Québec, attending the summer seminar.

much interested in their love affair because it was too easily a story of a hero and heroine, or worse, a villain and his victim. I was not interested in the art world's critique of particular works, except to place Claudel and Rodin in a wider social context. It was enough to know that each had been prolific and original.

I wakened the next morning from a dream that I'd acquired an old property and a little black cat. The house was set high on a hill with a view; it was an old house with an open studio space and lots of light. It came with two big animals, a hippo and a buffalo, which had to be walked for an hour and a half daily. Keeping this routine seemed impossible. Also, I had to get Lacan's papers and letters to acquire the property, which would require speaking. I was reluctant, but knew I must do this or the cat would be killed.

In my associations to this dream, the cat reminded me of Claudel, the old studio reminded me of Rodin, and the two big animals reminded me of some task related to both. The required papers indicated that I needed to read the seminars of Jacques Lacan, especially the later ones (some only recently translated), and to speak. Later in the day I considered a way to speak in the voice of each sculptor: through poetry. And then the weeks flew by, and I did nothing.

In mid-August I had another dream, a dream I couldn't recall. But I wakened with Camille's voice in my mind: "It is dark now and quiet and cool . . . and walls of stone close in on my narrow asylum bed." I got up and wrote down these words. In 2 weeks I had six poems, an unprecedented output after several years of writing no poetry at all. Why was I compelled to write poetry again? What was it about that exhibit that haunted me for 2 months without my knowing it? I can't answer either of those questions, though they were at work in the formation of both the dreams and the poems.

Through the poems I've brought to life a fantasy. My construction of Claudel and Rodin, particularly the ways they construed one another, is an effect of that fantasy. As characters they've been shaped by things I can articulate only up to a point: the images of the exhibit, biographies I read later, and ideas pertaining to Lacan and my teachers in Quebec that have become part of me, part of my thinking. In the most central way, as imagined characters they reach into my own history, my conscious and unconscious use of language. Claudel and Rodin's relationship emerged for me alongside the possibilities and constraints involved in solving artistic problems in each of the poems. In this chapter, I want to bring readers with me into some understanding of the ideas I brought to bear when creating my vision of this relationship. In my analysis of their relationship I reveal them as subjects through Lacan's theory of psychic structures. In the poems I also create a poetics that is distinctively Lacanian. But first, let me situate this odd endeavor in the world of qualitative inquiry and the relatively recent turn to a poetics in the social sciences.

POETICS, PERFORMATIVE TEXTS, AND POETRY

The only place to begin a discussion of poetics is where it all started, with Aristotle's influential 4th-century BC essay on the nature and structure of tragic drama. In this treatise he proposed six parts of drama: plot, character, thought or theme, language or diction, music, and spectacle. He discussed each part in detail to formulate an aesthetics as an interpretive framework (Halliwell, 1998). In the contemporary world of scholarship, literary critics understand and use the term *poetics* to denote any system that explains the terms, tools, and functions of expression. In the realm of qualitative inquiry, some social scientists, mainly anthropologists and sociologists, have broken new ground in arguing for the use of expressive writing and poetry as methods of inquiry (Richardson, 1997, 2000). Some scholars of this tradition situated expressive writing, poetry, and ethnography in postmodern or poststructuralist ideas (Denzin & Lincoln, 2002), whereas others appeared to focus on more stable, constructed ideas about self and identity that reflect a modernist approach (Krieger, 1991). In light of the interest in poetry and poetics in the social sciences, it is surprising that psychologists (to my knowledge) seldom invoke a poetics or explore its possibilities in relation to narrative psychology or the interpretation of texts.

Despite the absence of discussion about poetics in psychology, social scientists working in a narrative tradition continue to define and push the boundaries concerning the scope of a poetics to theorize autoethnography and performative texts as forms of interpretation (Brady, 1991; Denzin, 2003; Jones, 2002; Spry, 2001). Autoethnography refers to locating the individual researcher as a presence in the field or in the research process by combining autobiography with ethnography. Performative texts refer to shifting dramatic performances in writing in relation to changing audiences. Such texts range from short fictive scenes to dialogues to poems, all used in a process of writing qualitative inquiry. Some scholars explicitly advocate the use of poetry as a genre in qualitative inquiry. Ivan Brady (2004), for instance, argued that

> poetry is another way to encode and share the foundations of experience; poetry can ground theories of the world that actually involve our interactions with it, not just abstractions from it. Thus, a more robust entrance point for modern ethnography may be best centered on some combination of humanistic and scientific design as artful-science. (p. 622)

I situate myself with Brady and others in the creation of an "artful-science" in two ways. First of all, I have worked to create and modify a method of textual analysis, an interpretive poetics, to interpret tacit, negated, ambiguous, and often unconscious layers of knowledge in relation to psychological research questions (Rogers, 2004; Rogers et al., 1999). I have also used lyrical prose and poetry to construct knowledge in psychological texts precisely because this use of language highlights ambiguity and defers any possibility of a final meaning to readers. In psychological analyses poetry evokes and creates effects, rather than simply explains and theorizes research (Rogers, 1993, 1995). Though I've never called these articles and books "performative," they seem to fit this genre of qualitative inquiry.

However, my effort to bring Claudel and Rodin to readers through poems adds another layer to the performative aspect of writing. I bring theory to bear on a creative process, and at the end of this chapter, I also explore a Lacanian poetics in relation to the poetry I've written. I draw on my clinical training in Lacanian psychoanalysis as well as the work of two literary critics: Lacanian readings of fiction by James Mellard in *Using Lacan, Reading Fiction* (1991) and the Lacanian poetics outlined by Ellie Ragland-Sullivan (1984). I explain these ideas more fully after I introduce my two principles, and turn next to the sources I used to construct Claudel and Rodin as characters in the context in which they worked and lived and met one another.

LIFE STORIES AND THE SHAPING OF CHARACTERS

I am going to begin by speaking in an impressionist way about the lives of Claudel and Rodin and the relationship between them. Almost as soon as I began reading about them, I gathered pieces I wanted to use to build them as characters in the poems. As I perused biographies and exhibition books (Ayral-Clause, 2002; Butler, 1993; Grunfeld, 1987; Musée national des beaux-arts du Québec/Musée Rodin, Paris, 2005), I was particularly interested in their childhoods and their relationships with their parents and siblings, long before they met one another. What was the tenor of life in the family for each of them? Had either experienced a trauma that might affect who they later became, and how they later construed one another? When and how did each begin to sculpt, and with what response from their families?

Camille Claudel was born in 1864, the daughter of Louise-Athanaïse Cerveaux (from a bourgeoisie family) and Louis Proper Claudel, who worked as a registrar in Fére en Tardenois, a town in rural France. In the summers, the family went to the town of Villeneuve, the home of the Claudel family for generations. Claudel's grandfather made ceramic tiles and had a working kiln in a geographic area rich with red clay. The young Claudel used etchings and prints from her grandfather's library to make her first pieces of sculpture, enlisting her brother and sister (Paul and Louise) to help her get clay, and when they refused, ordering a servant girl to help her. Near the village was a place of legend where Claudel and her siblings played and explored. It was called Hotteé du Diable, roughly "the devil's basket." Local lore had it that the devil ran off in a panic and spilled a big basket of animals and mythical beings, frozen as massive stones.

I was surprised to learn that her parents had lost a child just 2 years before Claudel's birth, a son. I marked this loss as important: She was not the firstborn. When she was born, was she meant to replace this lost son, or perhaps resented because she wasn't another boy? It was hard to learn anything much about this. However, the biographies I read were clear that Claudel's relationship with her mother had been strained since childhood. Her father, however, saw his daughter as gifted and tried to support and protect her. Her mother felt this daughter controlled the family, and resented her alliance with her father. These tensions in the family only worsened over time.

Even as a child, Claudel sculpted objects and drew with skill. When Claudel was 13, the family moved to Nogent-sur-Seine, where she met the sculptor Alfred Boucher and made her first two human figures: David and Goliath. These sculptures were very accomplished, with robust muscles and strong profiles. Just a few years later, Claudel moved to Paris with her mother, sister, and brother. Though she took formal lessons at Académie Colarossi, Boucher continued to work with her as his student. It was during this time, when Claudel was just 17, that Rodin began to teach Boucher's pupils. Before I say much more about how they met and what ensued, I want to sketch out Rodin's early life.

Auguste Rodin was born in Paris in 1840 to Jean Baptist Rodin, a warden with the Paris police, and Marie Cheffer, from a family of weavers. When Rodin was born, he had a 2-year-old sister, Marie-Louise, called Maria to distinguish her from her mother. As a child Rodin became nearsighted. He loved to touch things, to play with things he held, and had unusually large hands. I was amused and moved by a story his mother related about Rodin making a little dough-man on a bread-making day, as though this incident and the glee it inspired led to Rodin's choice to become a sculptor. In fact, he had access to formal schooling only up to age 14. Although he took art classes and drew incessantly, he was not accepted into the major art school in Paris. As a result, he apprenticed as a decorative sculptor (a tradesman) and worked on other men's projects in their studios in France and in Brussels, until he was nearly 40.

Rodin's sister, Maria, entered a convent when she was 24 years old (the best way for a woman of her class to obtain an education). After only 6 months she contracted an illness and came home to die. Rodin was just 22 then, and, in an effort to assuage his grief, entered a seminary himself. This foray lasted just about 1 year, however. It registered with me that Rodin went against his artistic inclinations (he drew and sculpted avidly before he went into the seminary) to cope with the loss of his sister.

In 1864, when Rodin was 24, he met Rose Beuret, a seamstress working in Paris. She became pregnant and bore a son she named Auguste. Rodin and Beuret lived in poverty for many years, in close, cold quarters, sometimes with little food. She served as his model and took care of his sculptures, keeping them damp and intact when he went to work in Brussels. He did not forget these years. But theirs was not a conventional arrangement. Rodin never claimed their son as his own. And although Rodin claimed to love Beuret and would not leave her, he did not marry her until they were both very old, just 2 weeks before she died.

When Rodin began to exhibit his work, it was so realistic and fine that established sculptors claimed he was casting his figures from life, rather than sculpting. Although accused of "falsifying," he became known, especially among younger sculptors, as a genius with his hands. But it wasn't until 1880, when Rodin was commissioned by the French government to make *The Gates of Hell*, that he had his own studio and the means to pay assistants to help him for the first time. It was in this context that he began to teach Claudel, and around this time her name first showed up in records of assistants working in his studio. It was unusual to have a woman in such a role, let alone two women: Jessie Liscomb, a young English woman, was also listed as an assistant. She was Claudel's friend, sharing Claudel's studio with her at the time.

Rodin and Claudel fell in love and became lovers very quickly, certainly within the 1st year of their acquaintance. In this 1st year, too, Rodin made a sculpture of Claudel's head: *Camille With Short Hair*. Later, she would make a plaster, then a bronze, of his head. In the 10 years of their relationship, fraught with intense longing on Rodin's part and intermittent flights from her mentor and lover on Claudel's part, Liscomb played a central role in mediating their difficulties. Despite the tumult in their relationship, Rodin and Claudel deeply influenced and inspired one another as sculptors. Rodin spotted Claudel's talent and gave her the most difficult and trusted modeling tasks: shaping hands and feet. Others observed that he consulted her about every artistic choice. Claudel soaked in his teaching and example; though she was much younger and less experienced, each artist drew inspiration from the other.

It's clear from the biographies and letters (Musée national des beaux-arts du Québec/Musée Rodin, Paris, 2005) that from time to time Claudel fled Rodin, sometimes as far as England, to Liscomb's home in Peterborough, or to the Isle of Wight. When Claudel fled, Rodin was frantic to see her and found that he was so distressed he was unable to sculpt. He wrote pleas for her return, sometimes addressed to Liscomb. Rodin even traveled to England to see his lover, but she refused to meet him. If the triangle of Rodin, Claudel, and Liscomb mediated the relationship between the lovers, the second triangle in their relationship eventually led to its deterioration. Claudel deeply resented Rose Beuret and sent Rodin a series of drawings depicting her as a hag, including a grotesque, even obscene drawing of the couple naked and glued together at the rear, each pulling in opposite directions. Claudel became pregnant by Rodin and had at least one (and probably more than one) abortion. Even during the time they were lovers, Claudel was tempestuous, suspicious, and at times paranoid. When she returned from England she drew up a contract stipulating exactly what Rodin was to do to see her. He was to have no pupil but Claudel, promote and advance her in the art world, and marry her. In turn, she agreed to see him four times a month. But the terms of the contract were never filled. In fact, shortly afterward Rodin moved into a new house in Bellevue, outside Paris, with Beuret.

But perhaps Claudel suffered most in relation to Rodin when the art critics viewed her exhibited work as a copy of his style—and she blamed him for this. Later, she accused him of stealing her ideas to make his works. She left him, and broke off all association with him in the end because she couldn't bear being seen as part of him, and seeking to erase his influence, made her own sculptures small, calling them "scenes from nature."

After the relationship ended, Rodin found Claudel a studio, and through friends supported her financially for many years. Claudel became increasingly isolated, spent days and weeks alone, speaking to no one. During the 10 years after their affair ended, she began to cast her suspicions as accusations, most of all against Rodin. She also broke off her association with Liscomb. Her father's support, and Rodin's efforts behind the scenes, made it possible for Claudel to obtain just enough income to rent her studio and eat. Her mother and sister refused to have her in the house with them, so she also lived in her studio in another part of the city. Her brother, Paul, who'd become a diplomat through Rodin's intercession, lived and worked abroad, and took little interest in his sister's life.

In her last months in Paris Claudel spent the days making new sculptures only to hammer them to pieces at night; these cycles of creation and destruction were enacted each day. When her father died (Claudel was not told of his death and didn't attend the funeral), her mother, with the consent of her siblings, had her committed to the mental asylum at Ville-Évrard in 1913. Claudel accused Rodin of having had her committed so as to get his hands on her works. Despite her family's opposition, however, Rodin sent money to Claudel. During the war, she was transferred to the asylum at Montdevergues, far from Paris, and though she begged to be moved closer to Paris, she remained at Montdevergues until her death in 1943.

Little is known about her life inside the asylum. Paul seldom visited; years elapsed between his visits. He predicted repeatedly that she would die soon, but she didn't die for a very long time. Her sister, Louise, never came to see her. Her mother never came to see her. In short, Claudel was sequestered for 30 years. By family order, she was allowed no visitors, and no letters went out or came in for her. Worst of all, she didn't know what was happening to her letters. The only one to break through was the friend of her youth, Liscomb, who came to see Claudel as an old woman. Liscomb concluded that her friend was not mad at all.

Rodin's work soared in the years beyond the breakup with Claudel. Many fine biographies and art books record his life and works. What interested me most was that he never forgot Claudel: He continued to sculpt her head in various ways, to depict abstract ideas. From her head he created *Thought* and

The Farewell. These are, in my view, among his most eloquent pieces. And they are haunting in the way they evoke a young girl, someone lost to Rodin.

FORMATIONS OF THE SUBJECT

In this section, I review some concepts from Lacanian psychoanalysis to create a foundation for understanding the emergence of the human child as a speaking subject. I first discuss Lacan's idea that as human beings we are created through language (Lacan, 1977) and traumatized by language (Apollon, Bergeron, & Cantin, 2002); then I introduce Lacan's mirror stage and his revision of Freud's Oedipal crisis, which explains the emergence of distinctive psychic structures, particularly neurosis and psychosis (Miller, 1997). These ideas were foundational to the way I created Claudel and Rodin in the poems, as I discuss later. It is difficult to summarize Lacanian theory briefly without sacrificing a great deal of its complexity because his concepts are deeply entwined. In the interest of clarity, I have created a gloss that belies the reach, power, and sophistication of Lacan's language.

Lacan's most fundamental position is that we as humans are all born into language. Language creates us as subjects, and creates trauma in the human psyche (for a succinct discussion, see Cantin, 2002). We are each given a name, born into a line of names that have already affected our parents, and assigned a place in language, even before we are born. We have to fit ourselves into language, which alienates us from ourselves from the very beginning. Language creates a trauma, a split in the human being, which carries over from one generation to the next generation. Willy Apollon, Danielle Begeron, and Lucie Cantin (Appollon et al., 2002) linked the trauma of language with *jouissance*. Jouissance was an excess for Lacan, not merely a pleasure. The first experience of jouissance comes from something imposed on a child. Something that was unbearable for the parents directly affects the child's body and psychic life. For example, a parent may have grown up with the feeling that a sibling was "allowed to get away with murder." Unable to protest the situation in the original context, the parent as a mother may create a situation in which her child grows up with no limits, but the child feels her mother's unspoken resentment every time that child misbehaves and gets away with it. The jouissance involved in this kind of repetition is unconscious on the part of both parents and children. Children are far from passive in the process, but in fact become subjects through a distinctively intersubjective process.

In Lacanian theory, the emergence of the human being as a subject depends on two developmental moments: the mirror stage (between 6 and 18 months) and the Oedipal crisis (between 3 and 5 years), which I explain in some detail because it is the foundation for the construction of Claudel and Rodin in the poems.

Prior to the mirror stage, the infant is little more than a body in bits and pieces, unable to clearly separate *I* and *other*, and wholly dependent for its survival (for a length of time unique in the animal kingdom) on its first nurturers. The body is felt and known in parts—in zones, sensations, needs, and impulses—rather than as an integrated totality. The infant knows only whatever body part comes into her[2] field of vision. The fist or arm or foot remains there only as long as the infant can see it, and then disappears. The infant, confused about corporeal boundaries, sees her own hand and another's finger and does not know to whom each belongs. She can magically summon another person, and when the other comes, can incorporate parts of the other's body into her own body. She has no idea of her own wholeness or separateness.

The infant experiences herself and the world initially through what Lacan calls the register of the Real, which has nothing to do with reality. It is the realm of experience in which things are not represented, or assimilated—because this realm has no borders, divisions, or oppositions. In the 1st weeks and months of life the infant forms a primal, corporeal unity with the first nurturer (usually the mother). The infant cannot take absence into account. For example, if the breast or bottle is missing, she will suck, and sucking evokes the feeling of contentment without milk (up to a point of organic hunger).

The infant's recognition of an absence is a pivotal moment that ushers in the mirror stage. Into the circuit of need and magical satisfaction comes an absence recognized as absence. For example, the mother leaves the room and the child cannot summon her mother back—she is other and beyond magical control. The child, seeing this, loses the unity of the Real and is positioned to enter the Imaginary—the order of images, doubles, and others.

Lacan comments on infantile transitivity as that phenomenon that occurs when the infant behaves as though her body and the bodies of others are interchangeable. This phenomenon is at its height in the early part of the mirror stage. The problem the infant struggles with is the separability of bodies. During this time, she learns to recognize her own image in the mirror, before she is able to speak or have complete control over her motor skills. But the infant does not come into immediate possession of a clear relation between the image in the mirror and a model of herself. When she first sees herself in the mirror, she usually does not recognize her image as a virtual image. When she sees her mother in the mirror, she first assumes a double of her mother, holding another child!

When the child first spots herself in the mirror (usually through a gesture), she has a visual image that is whole and complete, and a kinesthesis of the body as partial and located in another place. She must learn that the image of herself is not herself (because she is here, where she feels herself to

---

[2]I use feminine pronouns in this discussion of development to counter the view that Lacan's theory best fits boys and men; it applies equally to both sexes.

be). She must also learn that at the very place she feels herself to be, any external witness sees her as she sees the image in the mirror. Lacan called this capacity *autoscopy*, the external perception of the self, as a totality, that can be seen or watched by others.

When the infant identifies herself in a mirror, she is fascinated and delighted with an image of herself in a whole body, fixed in space. Yet the infant must come to terms with the reflection as a virtual image, not identical to herself. This realization ironically marks the child's entry into an imaginary illusion about the *self*: I (as a whole body) am like the one in the mirror, and that is who I *want to be*, not a body-in-pieces, but a whole, coherent body who can master the body-in-pieces. In other words, I am where I (as a body-in-pieces) am not!

Lacan's mirror stage delineates a human subject decentered from her own body. As I have said, at first the recognition of her body as a gestalt whole brings the child great pleasure. For Lacan, this *affairement jubilatoire* is a testimony to how, in the recognition of its mirror image, the child is having its first anticipation of itself as a unified individual. For Lacan, this intense pleasure is also an ensnarement; the child is captivated by her specular double, and this captivation gives rise to identification, the logic of Imaginary relations. The mirror image provides a condition for a body image, a socially created body. During the mirror stage, the infant learns to recognize herself and other people as separate others. When the child first formulates some idea of self or *I* identified with its own *other* in the mirror stage, then she enters what Lacan calls the Imaginary order. The new ego or *I* vacillates between two poles—pleasure and frustration—which leads to aggression. Why aggression? Because the new ego can't settle anywhere, but is continually changing and frustrated. The *I* is split—as unified and in-pieces, the one who watches and the one who is watched. This splitting produces what Lacan called *paranoiac knowledge*—a vacillation between self-aggrandizement and fear—a point I discuss later in relation to psychosis.

The early identifications of other with self and self with other become thoroughly entwined, and in Lacanian psychoanalysis the ego is the product of this internalization of alterity (otherness). Yet the actual experience of *I* increasingly becomes an experience of being a separate, whole, and autonomous being. In other words the *I* is the narcissistic ego, and as such is an illusion. People create an "imaginary anatomy" composed of imaginary identifications with others and then mistaken for the self. Our earlier experience of being a body-in-pieces, dislocated in space, remains with us, however, and we can see this disorganized body experience in dreams, myths, art, and psychosis—wherever the human body appears with extra, missing, or extraordinary parts (animal, machine) or parts rearranged in space in impossible ways. In other words, the body is "fragilized" along pre-Oedipal and premirror stage lines, regardless of gender—with organs and parts appearing in odd places and in unusual arrangements.

A second shift in psychic development happens when the child constructs others in the form Lacan called the big Other. For most people, this happens usually with the mother first. The Other is, in Lacan's terminology, "unbarred" initially. Imagine that you are a young child again. As you learn to speak, you realize that you cannot predict your mother, you cannot please her, and your life depends on knowing what is required. So you create an idea of your mother, and this is never who she actually is. Because you have to go through her for the satisfaction of your demands, and she isn't predictable (you can't know her response before it happens), you have to go through the requirements of her demand of you. When your mother's demand is spoken, you are not entirely lost. But you also sense that your mother wants more than she says. "What does she want?" is a crucial question, and it's powerful precisely because it refers to an unspoken thing, a lack.

What is lacking, for Lacan, gives rise to desire. Desire isn't about sexual lust, or about wanting this or that object. Desire pushes toward something impossible, something always receding. In contrast to a demand, in which a child asks for something specific and may, in fact, receive a momentary recognition of what she wants—a fleeting sense of being loved—the *desire* for love can't be filled through words or another person's particular, momentary response. So the child is forced beyond the specific requests inherent in a demand into a realm of seeking something lacking, always receding. It is a paradox that when one has what one desires, desire itself disappears. But desire comes alive in the face of a lack.

How does a little child respond to her mother's lack? (I use the pronoun *she*, but this process pertains equally to boys.) She tries to guess what's required of her to be loved; she tries to be the one who perfectly fills the lack in her mother: the corporeal, actual epitome of her mother's unspoken desire. For instance, she might attempt to be a stiff, eerily quiet child in response to her mother's unspoken desire to be reunited with a child who has died. Or the child may become a violent little girl who hurts her little brother in response to her mother's unconscious desire to create suffering in relation to her own brother, who was the apple of his mother's eye, while she felt neglected and unseen.

The subjectivity of the child is created in the crucible of the parent's lack and the child's reading of a demand. Whatever the child tries to be for her mother, she has to go through the jouissance of the Other. Lacan refers to an old definition of *jouissance* as the use of something a person owns and therefore has a right to use. Parents unconsciously often have children to fill an anguished lack in their lives. And though it's rare to consciously use a child as an object in this way, parents' unconscious use escapes them. But, nevertheless, the child feels the jouissance of the Other, experienced as an excess of anxiety, terror, or pain imposed on her, at the moment she is overwhelmed by something unspoken. This is the price of the child's guessing her mother's desire. Small children try to make themselves an object of an impossible, unspoken desire, and because their survival is at stake, they are often uncannily accurate.

Escape from the jouissance of the mother, and the possibility of another kind of subjectivity, depend theoretically on the father, who has a central role to play in a child's development. This is particularly the case during the Oedipal period, when the child is approximately 3 to 5 years of age. The biological father, when he is present, plays the crucial role of a catalyst for creating a psychological separation between mother and child in the family. If he isn't present, any third party, even the "Third" of society itself, can fill the paternal function. For Lacan, it is critical to clarify the difference between the biological father and "the paternal metaphor." The paternal metaphor is the "no" of a third party (outside the mother–child duality). In French, *nom du père* and *non du père* refer to *the name* and to *no!*, respectively. The paternal function says "no" to the child—no, you cannot be the desire of your mother, you cannot fill her lack, because it's impossible. The paternal function works through the discourse of the mother. It is she who must remind the child that her lack cannot be filled—so, in short: Give up trying. The child must experience this impossibility from the mother. The child then theoretically enters the symbolic realm of language, a world in which desire itself is symbolic and out of reach, a world of limits that apply to all people, in which no one can fully be the desire of another.

But what happens if the message of *no* carried to the child isn't quite clear enough? This is a linchpin question in Lacanian theory. When the paternal metaphor isn't quite strong enough, the child becomes neurotic. The child, repressing the full force of his or her original desire, accepts the *no* resentfully and secretly clings to the possibility of perfectly filling the unconscious lack in the mother, or in someone else. When the paternal metaphor doesn't even enter the mother's speech, when she does nothing to represent any limit on her whim or power to the child, then her child remains subject to her jouissance, and becomes psychotic, though the symptoms may not emerge immediately.

For Lacan these structures are not necessarily linked to psychopathology; more fundamentally, they describe one's position in relation to three registers of human experience: the Real, the Imaginary, and the Symbolic. In Lacanian theory there are three registers through which persons experience the world. The Real is the primordial unity with the mother, but it is also continuously what is there but cannot be imagined or symbolized. In Lacanian psychoanalysis the Real impinges on the person only for brief, shocking periods because it lies beyond language and recognition. For instance, consider a moment in which you register something in a glance and your body responds with a startle; in that moment before words or even the clarity of an image, you are facing the Real. The Symbolic order is the register that relies on a logic of mediation through a third; it is the order of values and exchanges, the basis for the norms and rules of any society. Full entry into the symbolic entails an acceptance of a lack in all human subjectivity, and also an awareness that language cannot commute all of internal experience. The Imaginary is the place where the Symbolic is experienced as literal, the register of images, doubles, and illusions. It is also the register in which illusions are misrecognized as reality. The Imaginary, at its base, is the result of the mirror stage, the false sense of a unified self. The subject with a neurotic structure lives largely in a Symbolic world, but her (this also applies to boys and men) perceptions cannot be divorced from the Imaginary and the Real. She fails to see that the Symbolic contains a gap or a lack—something that would show how she stakes her life on flimsy constructions. For example, she may love a man who overlooks her desire, intent on becoming his desire. The subject with a psychotic structure lives largely in the Imaginary and creates a logical coherence from impingements of the Real (experienced as a kind of invasion or persecution from outside). Mistaking the Imaginary for reality, the subject construes these elements of experience as actual, threatening sources of danger, or perceives them as forces of rescue from imminent danger. The Symbolic is foreclosed and cannot be used to mediate these perceptions. In both structures, the subject is haunted, but differently. What is most haunting to the individual with a neurotic structure is the gap or lack that can't be named or known—the trade-off for entering the Symbolic is a loss—and desire pushes toward finding what was lost. What is most haunting to the individual with a psychotic structure is jouissance itself—the experience of being used without limit—recast as a delusional system that explains the immediacy of experiences of impingement, entrapment, and dread.

I hope that through this foray into Lacan's theory, you will be able to glimpse how I've made Rodin and Claudel. I've created Rodin as a neurotic structure. As a price of entering the Symbolic, I propose that he was continually searching for some aspect of a lost mother. When his sister Maria died, his original loss was doubled. Rodin attempted to fill the gap in the Symbolic that he couldn't fully accept by finding particular characteristics of his mother in Beuret. But he also wanted Claudel as a lover. She filled another gap or lack, and Rodin treated her as if she were his older sister, though she was some 24 years younger than he. When it became clear that he couldn't have both women in his life, he kept using Claudel's face as a form to hold the place for an unbearable lack.

Claudel, however, wasn't obsessed with Rodin as a place to fill a lack. Rodin became the original mother of infancy, the mother who renders the world through words, shapes, and images, and eroticizes the child's body through her touch. And Rodin became and remained this mother in her unbarred aspect. She was also all-seeing, all-encompassing, and impinged on Claudel's life with caprice and without limit. Claudel, I believe, felt this acutely with Rodin, and only later did the feeling of impingement crystallize into a delusion. There was crucial truth in her delusion: Claudel's mother later turned on her daughter, took her creative life from her, and had her committed. She did not come to see her child, not once, and she refused Claudel all other visitors, save her brother who visited very rarely. But, from Claudel's point of view, it was Rodin who stole her ideas by incorporating her shapes into his sculptures, and Rodin was a danger to her because he wanted her put away.

Claudel and Rodin misrecognized each other even when they were lovers, and certainly after the affair was over. I gave Jessie Liscomb a voice for their misrecognition because she could know things that Rodin and Claudel couldn't know or speak. First of all, Liscomb knew that Rodin saw her and relied on her as a Third, and she was the one to mediate the terms of his seeing Claudel. And second, Liscomb knew that Claudel sought escape from being overwhelmed by the intensity of Rodin's love by fleeing to her. But there were limits to what Liscomb could know and bear, too. And for this reason, it is possible to read more than she knows in each of the poems written in her voice.

I wanted to make each voice distinctive. In the poems in Claudel's voice, I attempted to capture the sense of being dominated by the register of the Imaginary. I began with her recollection of herself as a child in relation to her apprehension of shapes that shifted, repeating movements of her mother's body, as viewed by the child from her bed in the dark. The shapes repeat in the first poem in the series and are intended to erase a clear boundary between inner and outer reality, between Claudel's anguish and the answer she created for herself through sculpture. Claudel's voice isn't mad but (in her own terms) is absolutely logical. Though she feels rage toward Beuret and wants Rodin as hers alone, her torment has its source in her inability to free herself of a jouissance imposed on her originally, a terror that reappears everywhere in her life. It took a longer time to find a voice for Rodin, and in a strange way, I felt as though the true timbre of his voice came to me in only two poems in this series. In each, Rodin struggles with the loss of an illusion. In "Petersborough, England" he is caught up in an anguish he can't escape and the illusion that his only rescue is through Claudel. In "The Farewell," he shatters the illusion that love can keep him alive, a realization so disturbing that it undercuts the Symbolic ordering of his life and leaves him alone, utterly alone, with dread and the nearness of death. In this poem, he is closest to the "reality" Claudel has known all her life.

As I created Claudel and Rodin in the poems, I included not only Lacan's neurotic and psychotic structures but also his ideas of jouissance, the Other, and the three registers of human experience, as well as desire (and lack) as key to subjectivity. But the poems themselves are little puzzles; in each I posed a problem to be solved in language within the structure of contemporary free verse. In this sense, they are grounded in an aesthetics.

As I guide you through the poems, I hope you will see how a Lacanian understanding of psychic structures influenced my invention. I am reluctant to explain the poems in detail, however, in part because I do not presume I can explicate them accurately; the narrator as an ego speaking about the poems is, after all, full of illusions, according to Lacan. What's more, I assume that each of you will read something different into an ambiguous text, and poetry heightens naturally occurring ambiguities with the intention of making words say more than they can say otherwise. My remarks therefore are brief, and are not intended to explain away the joy of reading.

CLAUDEL AND RODIN: THE POEMS

In the first poem, I wanted to create a sense of being trapped in the Imaginary in a way that was also very logical. "Double" begins the series of poems in Claudel's voice. In this poem, Claudel has just arrived at the asylum and she remembers her childhood as a way of preserving her history. She was 48 years old then, and I challenged myself to make the poem 48 lines long. I created Claudel's voice in relation to the uncanny, the sense of being haunted by her beginnings in a particular way. In the poem, Claudel filters the world through images, and she identifies with each thing she sees. In this way she creates a world of doubles. What cannot be symbolized returns in her experience of the Real, in the form of voices, hallucinations. Here I bring Claudel to life in the process of animating the double of the rooster on the steeple in precisely this way: making it alive, able to make a sound, to speak to another weathervane and to Claudel. She is compelled to find a shape, and image, for this experience of the uncanny. For me, this experience of the uncanny is the basis for her subjectivity and her creativity.

Double

It is dark now, and quiet and cool. The last light
    seeps under rude floorboards, and walls of stone
close in on my narrow asylum bed. I am a child
    in Villeneuve again, near sleep, near waking,
and bent over my bed is a shape: now rooster
    now horse, now Angel, now haystack, falling,
now Devil, now Mother, her arm, her broad
    back, her imposed silhouettes, changing. I am

ten years old, bent over red soil, a battered tin
    cup in my left hand spilling with water, to make
clay! With my stick and a cracked bowl, I gather
    my portion, while all around me my grandfather's
workers take theirs, to make roof tiles. Imagine it!
    Twenty-five thousand shapes to go into his kiln,
each alike, each with a mar or nick to mark it off
    as his, as his, as his! And then begin again. I make

little crabs with giant claws, the tapered beak of a
    thin ibis, so like a steeple, and a human arm, its elbow,

hinged—shapes like a covey of nightmares
        out of the Devil's Basket. I've gone there,
where the fallen Angel dropped his massive stones
        in fright, hearing a rooster crow before dawn. I take
my forms from etchings in a book. From my hands,
        they're borne, and once here, they're mine. I give

orders for making plaster to Paul and Louise
        and sometimes our servant girl, Eugenie. None
of them like to work for me, but then the men
        do not like my Grandfather's work. Paul
and Louise escape sometimes, to sit under lime
        trees in the town square, vying in a game with
walnuts, enclosed by houses all around, and
        sleeping with their eyes wide open. I look

up at the church, its imposing silhouette
        a dark triangle on the ground, sharp, then fading.
My brother and sister don't see the clouds
        pressed down like a giant hand on their
heads. When it rains, the wind makes the rooster
        on the steeple go round around, as if it could sail
straight off. The weathervane on our house begins
        screeching, screeching to its double. I hear

that sound fly back and forth between them.
        Shrill and melodic, a new shape comes
into my mind. Tomorrow I'll find it in the fine
        red clay, and fire it to fastness, and keep it
as a souvenir. David and Goliath, Jacob
        and the Angel. You can picture them after
their night of wrestling is over; they stand
        as dancers, heads inclined, eyes shut, resting.

In the Imaginary, the subject merges with imagoes or identifications, but in the Symbolic, there is a third to mediate meaning. In the next three poems, I created the voice of Jessie Liscomb to reveal how Claudel and Rodin misrecognize one another as a result of their different relations to jouissance and the Other (which I explained most clearly in the second poem in this series). I sought a form for three-ness, and thinking about an artistic form led me to the visual convention of the triptych, a tableau composed of three panels. I began with one scene, a monoscene of unity, in which Liscomb imagines that Rodin is a stand-in for Claudel's mother. The poem opens as Liscomb's letter comes into Claudel's hands (just weeks before she arrives on a visit), when both sculptors are old women. Liscomb's letter is a reminder of their youth, of course, and it carries not only her affection for Claudel but also Liscomb's horror of the human body seen in profiles, broken down into pieces. Although Liscomb says this horror has nothing to do with being a mother herself, an infant reduces the mother's body to pieces and parts. A negation can unconsciously be an affirmation, and the poem ends by intimating that no one escapes the Real of the body in pieces.

I. Monoscene: Mother and Children

"You may not recognize me," you write, but I'm
an old woman now, too. And I've not forgotten.

You sit on your little chair. You sit for hours,
molding your lump into a hand
or a foot. Sometimes you look up,
in those blue eyes an intent
look, then back to the foot before you. Ten, twelve
hours you sit, a girl really, just seventeen, just

hours old, seeing for the first time. He was a mother
first, a mother, teaching us to see! Do you remember
how he made us walk around Pierre Wissant, to see,
turn and see him, learn to sculpt in profiles, walk
and see and sculpt a body in pieces, turn again, move
around him? You loved that slanted, interrupted looking,
and then his look, his answer. You demanded love

and he loved you, our mother hardening to a man.
Back in England, for years I saw like that. I'd turn
and see bodies everywhere. One bright May morning
white shirts boiled in a vat. An arm surfaced,
then the neck, next the broad blister of back. I didn't
sculpt for seven years. It had nothing to do with
children coming, or with being a mother, myself.

In the second poem in the series, I created the equivalent of a visual diptych, but rather than pairing mother and child, I paired father and child. The poem is intended to be read first in columns, then across in rows. The form shows how a second duality is created when the father (as a third mediating term) does not enter the speech of the mother. Here Jessie sees and records more than she knows, because she narrates each column and does not think to make the nonsense of reading across the columns tell of Claudel's horror. But I wanted to convey Claudel's sense of being buried alive under Rodin's influence (her experience of jouissance in relation to the Other), even as he tried to save her. I used the little heads in the exhibit that I could not tell apart, Claudel's flight to the Isle of Wight, and a newspaper story about a child buried in a sand dune as sources for Jessie's narrative in each column.

II. Diptych: Father and Child

He made The Head	On the Isle of Wight
of Avarice, you made	I saw a girl of five or six

The Head of a Slave;
He shaped The Cry, you
shaped Laughing Man;
He formed Crouching
Woman, Crouching
Woman you formed.
He turned a torso.
You turned one too.
They said you copied
his; I saw that
he consulted you
on everything; only
when you agreed
would he make up
his mind. And yours.
Your little heads,
half-scaled to life,
turned and moved.
They sucked in air,
their mouths, his
and yours,
opened, laughed
cried out, called.

somersault against a sky,
make her skirt a bell
turning over. She rolled
onto the Dune, gathered
sand, crouched in a spin,
she formed a ball,
her torso turned to
sand, collapsing. Sand
buried her alive, as
her father stood below
gaping, just feet between
them. He dug. But
sand collapsed on sand.
Twice he leapt back,
so as not to drown in it.
When we finally dug
his child out, the eyes
closed, lashes studded
with sand, the mouth
open and filled, red
dress whorled with gold
rolled up to her neck. She
held a little fist of sand.

In the final poem in Liscomb's voice, I used the triptych as a form to show what happens when the Name of the Father as a third term is foreclosed, as it is in the psychotic structure. Read across, the words form a narrative about Claudel's capture in the m(Other)'s jouissance. The tools of sculpting come from the mother's use of the child, a use that has no limit and later transfers to Claudel's relationships to both Rodin and Liscomb. Reading the words down each column makes sense only if you are willing to let each word slip into idiosyncratic meanings, a kind of sense-making foreign to Liscomb but probably not to Claudel. For the psychotic subject, signifiers slip away from key points of signification, creating meanings in nonsense.

III. Triptych: Mother-Child-Sculpting

Necessary	sculpting	tools
mother	her	desire
to	make	you
hers	alone	unleashed
voices	listen	now
raucous	gulls	screech
headdress	of	nurses
you	cast	me
away	I	left
you	fled	him
he	sought	you

in	plaster	caught
your	head	seams
lined	with	blame
the	wrong	one
used	without	limit.

In the next poem, the jouissance that originated with Claudel's mother transfers to Rodin; I believe that Claudel created him as the Other of an unbarred and dangerous jouissance. But how did I imagine him creating her? The price of entering the Symbolic is the loss of whatever one desired to *be* for one's mother—and yet one goes on searching for that which is already irredeemably lost. It's clear from his letters to both Claudel and Liscomb that Rodin's desire came alive most acutely when Claudel fled him. Then he searched for her frantically. It is precisely because she prohibited him from seeing her that he was driven into excess, into his own original experience of jouissance, a "sick guesswork" about a woman's desire—which he must address to someone else, not to the one he actually desired. In the following poem, the first in his voice, Rodin is prohibited from seeing Claudel, and in her absence, he invokes a "glance" from her. This glance is aggressive (a blow, as well as a look), but it is better than being ignored and effaced (literally, wasted away). In this poem Rodin intimates his nearness to death and dissolution as he confronts the imagined loss of his lover.

Peterborough, England

Advancing by sick guesswork
Jessie, I write to you instead.
Because she's fled to this far
foreign city, I sink my feet
in paths of sand, more silver
than grass. I'm losing

ground. My greatcoat hangs
on sticks, my beard's untrimmed.
I await her glimmering
scissors' slice into me, altering
my form, my very aspect
reformed by her

as you read. That little face
closes; she will not admit
me to pass, trespass. Yet I'm
here, a famous man made
to wait. Her face effaces
an old man. The evening's air

becomes an ear. The trees' light
green's a treachery. I'm a comet
crossing the Channel—come,

dissolving, gone, So near
I hear a hinge that speaks, a door
on an ordinary evening, I see

her head turn, her hair's a light
cap I long to caress. She strides
the room, frowns and tears
the letter she holds.
It comes as a blow across the air;
I'm here, I'm there

taking the glance.

The scope of this chapter does not permit me to explore the poems I wrote about the changes in their relationship, so I come now to the last poems in the series, one in each of their voices. In "The Farewell," Rodin is an old man speaking to Claudel, though he knows that she cannot really hear him because she's living in the mental asylum at Montdevergues. In this poem he talks fondly of Beuret and their life together (he married her just a few weeks before she died), telling a little story about a hen. He says he is nearing 77 years of age—but for him, Claudel is still 17. The images in the poem sum up the changes of a lifetime and adumbrate the nearness of death, but what remains constant for Rodin is Claudel's imagined presence through his image of her as a girl, the image he has sculpted and titled *The Farewell*.

The Farewell

The hen's cornered in a narrow
path. She comes at the same
hour each day, and the black cat
stalks her. It's only a game; you
can see the hen laughing. We call her
"Clara," the cat "le Chat." *Wintering
with Clara* is a story we tell, how
the hen comes in on a freezing night
to roost on our basket of logs
by the stove; four chicks emerge. But
the cat pounces, tears her feathers,

and everything changes; faces
hover over a crib, enthralled, laughing,
pleased, gone. Fingernails grow;
their clippings new moons scattered
on the floor. We place them against
the window up in the sky, watch them
wax to fullness. Sheets on the line
billow out, pegged sails crack in a strong
wind tonight. The arc of a nave
cracks too. Centuries old, the cathedral
leans to ground, sinks down in one

corner. Light, energy, atoms, stars
sing a requiem only you can hear.
Your fingers rise up from your lap,
touch air, arrive at your lips, stay.
You are still seventeen. Rose is
gone now, and I'm seventy-seven
this November. I wake in the night
to feel the cosmos leaning in. My skin
cracks. When I roll over, the sheets
grab me and won't let go. It's only
a game now. A new moon rises
in the window. In the morning
I find a tiny fingernail on the sill.

I followed this poem, which ends with Rodin's perception of the moon as a tiny nail on the sill, with three poems in Claudel's voice about her windowsill at Montdevergues. Linking the poems in this chronology allowed me to imagine that Claudel knew something about Rodin's windowsill experience, because her voice continues his. In this instance, I take an impossible juxtaposition of chance perceptions to give Claudel access to an impossible knowledge. I also remembered Liscomb's perception that her friend was "not mad at all," and wanted to show Lacan's idea that a person with psychosis may break down in a crisis (where there is no access to the Symbolic) but is not always insane—far from it! In the first poem, Claudel's sill is a projection screen for realistic memory; in the second it records the movement of life indifferently; and in the third the light on the sill becomes a metaphor for transcendence. The three poems, brief as they are, undercut the reader's pity for Claudel and show her, even in the end, as a subject creating a world of her own.

Sill, Montdevergues

I.

Early morning trees
lift their arms
to the first light of day;
on my windowsill
the faint crossing paths
of the streets of Paris
appear. I can smell
warm bread
from the shops.

II.

Birds, clouds
a flash of fish,
tidal movements
cross the sill. Swift shadows

still to slowness
the hours
stop to watch.
The hours
have come
and gone
to no effect.

III.
I surface
from a nightmare. Light
still takes the same path
across my windowsill
each day; a tiny dot,
then a triangle, its vertices
widening, opening over
the whole white-lit surface,
until the liquid light
recedes,
runs off.

TOWARD A LACANIAN POETICS

I hope my explanations have not entirely encumbered your experience of reading the poems. And furthermore, although you (as subjects who have been reading) are "barred" from entering my text as I read it, I trust that your own unconscious fantasy about Claudel and Rodin has guided your experience of reading. I say this sincerely, on the basis of the notion that an experience of reading involves an unconscious process. Fantasy in Lacanian terms is not a daydream or a representation of whatever people imagine. Rather "the subject is its object in the writing of the fantasme" (Harari, 2004, p. 10). In other words, the cause of a fantasy (and also an unconscious reading) is the inscription of our position as subjects in language. Meanings we read into a text are not fixed but deferred and elusive, determined by the limits of language and our position in language. There is no language, no conceptual frame, outside the limits of language itself that divides us into unconscious as well as conscious speakers, readers, and writers. This is an unusual point of view for social scientists to consider.

In Lacanian terms, the text becomes the Other of each reader's unconscious, a place where language opens into unconscious truths. Why should this understanding of reading interest narrative psychology as a field? One reason is because narrative psychology produces rich and original accounts of lives, written in voices that intend to carry more than scientific discourse can ordinarily convey. Lacanian theory offers a system for reading lives, and reading our accounts of lives, by taking the unconscious into account.

A Lacanian poetics opens the possibility of exploring the interface of "reader-as-text and text as textual-Other" (Mellard, 1991, p. 44). Such a poetics articulates laws of language that join "visible language and invisible effects" (Ragland-Sullivan, 1984, p. 382) of the structure of language itself. Lacan provided a theory through which it is possible to explore signification through the chaining of signifiers in the metonymic and metaphoric axes of language. Lacan showed how the unconscious plays through language and provided a framework for an exploration of writing and reading. But there is a limit to what we as human subjects can say. What falls away is fantasy; what stays is a gap in knowing, the lack that becomes an invocation to know, to go beyond this or that word. In the end Rodin and Claudel and Liscomb are the phantoms of a fantasy, souvenirs of my unconscious in words, signifying things I know in only a very limited way, even though I can articulate how I drew from biographies, artworks, their letters, and Lacanian theory to create them. Interpretation is also borne of fantasy, and by this I mean that any attempt to create meaning involves the unconscious in ways we as human beings subjected to the unconscious can't know or name. For example, I have told you a little about the biographies I've read and about the Lacanian ideas that shaped my understanding of Rodin and Claudel, and I have referred to my dreams and experience of the exhibit of their works that presaged the poems. But, what can I say about the elements of writing that relied on my projections, my own illusions, or a lack in myself, unacknowledged? Of these aspects of interpretation and creation, I can say nothing. And this is humbling because it shows that I'm quite flawed as an interpreter; there are real limits to how I might question what I have done here.

In summary, whatever we as psychologists or as narrative researchers say about one another (or about relationships) with certainty is sure to hold a gap, a lack. And whatever we say in language is left amorphous, ambiguous, its meaning(s) deferred. This richness in any text creates fugitive meanings that are impossible for us to grasp and to know fully. A poetics grounded in the unconscious invites a distinct mode of inquiry—one that is wary of its own interpretive stance as it portrays what Ivan Brady called an "artful-science."

REFERENCES

Apollon, W., Bergeron, D., & Cantin, L. (2002). *After Lacan: Clinical practice and the subject of the unconscious*. Albany: State University of New York.

Ayral-Clause, O. (2002). *Camille Claudel: A life*. New York: Harry N. Abrams.

Brady, I. (1991). Harmony and argument: Bringing forth the artful-science. In I. Brady (Ed.), *Anthropological poetics* (pp. 3–30). Savage, MD: Rowman & Littlefield.

Brady, I. (2004). In defense of the sensual: Meaning construction in ethnography and poetics. *Qualitative Inquiry, 10*, 622–644.

Butler, R. (1993). *The shape of genius*. New Haven, CT: Yale University Press.

Cantin, L. (2002). The trauma of language. In R. Hughes & K. R. Malone (Eds.), *After Lacan: Clinical practice and the subject of the unconscious* (pp. 35–48). Albany: State University of New York.

Denzin, N. K. (2003). *Performance ethnography: Critical pedagogy and the politics of culture*. Thousand Oaks, CA: Sage.

Denzin, N. K., & Lincoln, Y. S. (Eds.). (2002). *The qualitative inquiry reader*. Thousand Oaks, CA: Sage.

Grunfeld, F. (1987). *Rodin: A biography*. London: Hutchinson.

Halliwell, S. (1998). *Aristotle's poetics* (2nd ed.). Chicago: University of Chicago Press.

Harari, R. (2004). *Lacan's four fundamental concepts of psychoanalysis: An introduction*. New York: Other Press.

Jones, J. L. (2002). Performance ethnography: The role of embodiment in cultural authenticity. *Theatre Topics, 12*, 1–16.

Krieger, S. (1991). *Social science and the self: Personal essays on an art form*. Brunswick, NJ: Rutgers University Press.

Lacan, J. (1977). *Écrits: A selection* (A. Sheridan, Trans.). London: Tavistock.

Mellard, J. (1991). *Using Lacan, reading fiction*. Chicago: University of Illinois Press.

Miller, J.-A. (Ed.). (1997). *The seminar of Jacques Lacan: Book III. The psychoses, 1955–1956* (R. Grigg, Trans.). New York: Norton.

Musée national des beaux-arts du Québec/Musée Rodin, Paris. (2005). *Claudel and Rodin: Fateful encounter*. Paris: Hazan.

Ragland-Sullivan, E. (1984). The magnetism between reader and text: Prolegomena to a Lacanian poetics. *Poetics, 13*, 381–406.

Richardson, L. (1997). *Fields of play: Constructing an academic life*. New Brunswick, NJ: Rutgers University Press.

Richardson, L. (2000). Writing: A method of inquiry. In N. K. Denzin & Y. S. Lincoln (Eds.), *Handbook of qualitative research* (2nd ed., pp. 923–948). Thousand Oaks, CA: Sage.

Rogers, A. (1993). Voice, play and a practice of ordinary courage in girls' and women's lives. *Harvard Educational Review, 63*, 265–295.

Rogers, A. (1995). *A shining affliction: A story of harm and healing in psychotherapy*. New York: Penguin.

Rogers, A. (2004). Interviewing children using an interpretive poetics. In S. Greene & D. Hogan (Eds.), *Researching children's experiences: Approaches and methods* (pp. 158–174). London: Sage.

Rogers, A., Casey, M., Holland, J., Ekert, J., Nakkula, V., & Sheinberg, N. (1999). An interpretive poetics: Languages of the unsayable. In R. Josselson & A. Lieblich (Eds.), *The narrative study of lives* (Vol. 6, pp. 77–106). Chicago: Sage.

Spry, T. (2001). Performing autoethnography: An embodied methodological praxis. *Qualitative Inquiry, 7*, 706–732.

4

FROM ISLAND TO ARCHIPELAGO: NARRATIVES OF RELATEDNESS IN AN URBAN YOUTH ORGANIZATION

NANCY L. DEUTSCH

Respectful [is my most important trait]. I like to treat others as others will treat me.
                                    —*Lorenzo, 17-year-old Boys & Girls Club member*

I am a rock, I am an island.
                                    —*Paul Simon, American musician*

Despite Paul Simon's claim, humans are not isolated lumps of granite. We are, rather, interdependent individuals living and growing within complex ecosystems. The human baby, requiring 9 months of gestation and years of close protection and care, is a hint of what is to follow in the average life. From an evolutionary standpoint, group identity may be a more basic need than individual identity; human survival has historically relied on interdependence (Lerner, Brentano, Dowling, & Anderson, 2002; Newman & Newman, 2001). Yet the American narrative of strong character, hard work, and individual triumph, of "pulling oneself up by one's bootstraps," has influenced how Westerners position identity as a developmental task.

Early theorists recognized that the self is created in dialogue with the social world. They used the "looking glass self" and the "generalized other" as

I am grateful to Ruthellen Josselson for her helpful comments on drafts of this chapter as well as to Bart Hirsch and Dan McAdams for their support and insights into this work.

To protect the anonymity of study participants, all names of people and places have been changed. Youth chose their own pseudonyms during their interviews.

models to describe how we infuse the views of others into our self-concepts (Cooley, 1902; James, 1890/1981; Mead, 1934). Although self is distinct from identity, the two are linked. Erik Erikson drew on early self-theorists in creating his stages of individual identity development. To Erikson, the task of identity integration is in part the struggle of the individual to find a place for him- or herself in society (Erikson, 1959, 1968). Whereas the self is influenced by the social world but exists solely within individual heads, identity exists within both the world and the individual psyche.

It is during adolescence that the issues and tasks associated with identity construction take on the greatest salience. Although researchers recognize that identity is developed psychosocially, relationships have tended to serve as a backdrop to the process of separation in developmental theory, with the focus being on how adolescents individuate from their families, explore possible future roles, and develop integrated identities (Adams & Marshall, 1996; Erikson, 1959, 1968; Harter, 1999; Steinberg, 1990). Connection and autonomy have been pitted against each other rather than considered as complementary modes of development (Josselson, 1992). The prevalence of measuring identity status as an outcome (Marcia, 1980) has veiled the more nuanced paths by which adolescents arrive at these statuses. Psychologists tend to assume that individuation, not relatedness, is key to reaching an achieved identity status (Josselson, 1989).

Yet this focus on separation may be an artifact of the Western emphasis on individualism. Cross-cultural research reveals differences in the process of separation. Adolescents in some Eastern cultures report strong interdependence and greater happiness with their families (Larson & Wilson, 2004). Research on women and girls suggests that female identity is often more situated in interpersonal relationships (Gilligan, 1982; Josselson, 1989, 1992; Miller, 1976). There is evidence that independent and interdependent self-construals coexist as distinct dimensions rather than as wholly different constructions of self (Singelis, 1994). Human psyches are designed for connections with others (S. E. Cross & Madson, 1997; Tice & Baumeister, 2001). Close personal relationships provide a powerful context for and influence on the self, often becoming incorporated into the self-concept (Aron & McLaughlin-Volpe, 2001; Tice & Baumeister, 2001). Some have suggested that relatedness is one of three basic human needs along with competence and autonomy, pointing out that relationships and autonomy are not mutually exclusive (Ryan & Deci, 2000; Ryan, Deci, & Grolnick, 1995).

Community and family-tied selves have been part of American identity, but primarily considered in relation to women and ethnic populations (di Leonardo, 1999). In African American culture, supportive communities are seen as fostering strength and independence (DeFrancisco & Chatham-Carpenter, 2000). The image of the village in the oft-repeated African proverb symbolizes the interrelatedness of the numerous people who are invested in the development and support of individual children (McAdoo, 2002).

Interpersonal relationships have been written about extensively in relation to women's sense of self and identity (Gilligan, 1982; Josselson, 1989, 1992; Miller, 1976). Yet emerging research on boys suggests that relationships are also key to their development. Relationships may help boys to resist, rather than internalize, others' negative views or expectations of them (Chu, 2004). African American boys may have more intimate and self-disclosing friendships than do their White peers (DuBois & Hirsch, 1990; Way, 2004). The context of development may have an influence because of the valuing of interdependence in African American and Hispanic cultures, the pressures of racism, and, for some, the necessities of surviving on dangerous streets (Ferguson, 2000; Franklin, 2004).

One researcher who has helped expand relatedness beyond the dichotomous model is Ruthellen Josselson (1992, 1994), who suggested that part of all individual development is the integration of relational contexts and cultivation of "increasingly complex forms of relatedness" (1992, p. 16). She proposed eight dimensions of relatedness: holding, attachment, passionate experience, eye-to-eye validation, idealization and identification, mutuality, embeddedness, and tending and care (see Josselson, 1992). These dimensions are not emphasized equally in all of our lives, but all people develop along relational pathways that highlight some of these dimensions. Many dimensions are linked to primary developmental needs. Josselson melded these into a model of the person in relation throughout the life span. She suggested that adolescent identity achievement is a matter of balancing individuation and relatedness, not eschewing one for the other (Josselson, 1989).

It is clear that the cast of characters and relationships that populate our lives serves as more than a backdrop to our individual development. We come to know ourselves through our relationships with others; through knowing ourselves, we form better relationships (Josselson, 1992, 1994). Our relationships with other people, and the ways in which we build those relationships into our life stories, shape our very identity. The narrative tradition of analysis suggests that an individual's life story both constitutes the self and provides a window into development (McAdams, 1993, 2001; Pratt, Arnold, & Mackey, 2001). Examining the ways in which relationships are woven into life stories may explicate both the content and process of identity in adolescence. Studying such stories can help dispel the myth that adolescence is only about separation. The narratives of adolescents demonstrate the ways in which relationships buttress the development of an identity that is both autonomous and connected. Studying the stories of ethnic and racial minority adolescents and those living in poverty, youth whose narratives are often missing from research, allows psychologists to consider more deeply the role of context, including race, in the development of relational identities.[1]

---

[1]There is increasing research focusing on social categories such as race, gender, and social class as contexts of human development (Coll et al., 1996; Eccles, 2001; Quintana, 2004; Quintana & Segura-Herrera, 2003).

In this chapter, I use the narrative of Lorenzo, a 17-year-old African American young man, to illuminate the ways in which relationships influence adolescent identity. Using a life story approach to self-construction (McAdams, 1993, 2001), I examine how this teen infused his narrative with interpersonal relationships. I came to Lorenzo's story through an interest in how the contexts of today's adolescents promote or inhibit relational selves. I sought to look at the environments of youth deemed "at risk"[2] because of the disjuncture I felt between the portrayal of urban teens as hedonistic and irresponsible and my experiences with inner-city after-school programs, in which I met adolescents who felt deep connections to others. Furthermore, I was not satisfied with much of the literature on relatedness and identity, which focused on how girls develop differently from boys, suggesting that the process of relatedness was important only for half of the population. Because adolescence has been constructed as a time of separation, researchers have not explored the ways in which teens seek out dimensions of relatedness and incorporate them into their own identities. Psychologists have largely ignored both the relational needs of teens and the opportunities for self-discovery that relationships with others provide.

In the remainder of this chapter I examine how Lorenzo came to integrate relationships into his identity. Through the relationships he formed at an after-school program, Lorenzo developed a narrative of self that emphasized his ties to other people. Lorenzo's story highlights a number of Josselson's (1992, 1994) eight dimensions of relatedness. His story shows both how these dimensions are important to adolescent identity development and how an after-school program can help nurture complex forms of relatedness and meet basic relational needs.

LORENZO AND THE EAST SIDE BOYS & GIRLS CLUB: THE CONSTRUCTION OF A CONNECTED SELF

Lorenzo's story is drawn from a larger study of the construction of self among adolescents at the East Side Boys & Girls Club (Deutsch, 2005b). The club, located in a large, midwestern city, serves primarily Black and Hispanic youth from a public housing project. I spent 4 years there as a participant observer. During that time I talked with youth and staff, participated in activities, and conducted interviews, focus groups, and photography projects with 17 club members between the ages of 12 and 18. Lorenzo's story is a

---

[2]I use the term *at risk* with trepidation. It is common practice to use the phrase as a marker for particular sociodemographic factors. I believe that researchers have a responsibility to define their terms and the factors that serve as stand-ins for more specific features. The term *urban* has also become a signifier for racial or ethnic minority, poverty, teen parenthood, and gangbanging (Olsen, 1996; Tolman, 1996; Way, 1998). I use these phrases as shortcuts, as markers for poverty and racial minority status, but do not always agree with their implications.

poignant example of how youth construct narratives of relatedness and develop senses of self tied to those around them.

Lorenzo is a 17-year-old African American young man who joined the East Side Boys & Girls Club at age 13, when he moved to the nearby projects. He is dark-skinned, broad, and tall with cornrowed hair that hangs down to the bottom of his neck. Usually sporting t-shirts and loose pants or athletic clothes, he tends to don a serious facial expression. A small tattoo peeks out from the blue sweatband that always graces his right wrist. When I first met Lorenzo he seemed a serious, somewhat intimidating figure. His height, athleticism, and stoic demeanor give off a sense of sternness which, as one gets to know him, fades into quiet reflection and an exterior hardened by life. As he once told me, sometimes he just doesn't have anything to smile about.

Lorenzo was in 12th grade when I interviewed him. For 4 years he had lived with his aunt and her children in the local housing project. He moved in with them at his mother's request. Although he would have preferred to stay with his mother and younger siblings, he chose to respect his mother's wish. At age 14 he took care of his younger siblings for a few months while his mother was away. Lorenzo felt "misused," as if his childhood "was took from [him]."

Lorenzo appears somewhat aloof to outsiders, but enjoys playing the clown to younger club members. When he spoke in interviews and focus groups he was serious and seemed to give his honest thoughts. His expression tends towards indifference but he breaks into a smile when something strikes him as funny. Lorenzo is articulate and thoughtful and speaks a lot about being responsible and respectful. In both the focus group and his interviews he discussed being a role model for younger kids at the club, a theme that I explore in depth later.

Lorenzo's narrative demonstrates how East Side provided needed dimensions of relatedness that Lorenzo worked into his identity. The club served as a space in which he experienced holding, a sense of security and safety, which is a basic, human relational need (Josselson, 1992, 1994). This is especially important because holding was largely missing from Lorenzo's early life, as he had little consistent adult caretaking as a child. But the club went beyond this, offering opportunities for more complex forms of relatedness such as idealization and identification (seeing possible selves in others), embeddedness (a sense of belonging), eye-to-eye validation (discovering that one has meaning to others), and tending and care (sustaining and enhancing relationships with others; Josselson, 1992, 1994). At the club Lorenzo experienced the mutuality of relationships. He derived meaning from his experiences of being relationally important to other people, and this meaning informed his sense of self and identity.

It must be noted that the context of this research, the Boys & Girls Club, was a relationship-rich environment, which may have influenced Lorenzo's narrative. My observations of Lorenzo took place in a space, the

Boys & Girls Club, in which a variety of adult and youth relationships were available to Lorenzo. The interviews were conducted within the club, within the emotional space of those relationships. Thus, the relational elements of his story may be more salient because Lorenzo constructed and told his narrative inside the club. It is possible that the relational aspects would have receded had the research taken place in an environment such as school, where Lorenzo did not report having relationships as rich. Yet this does not detract from the importance of his narrative but reveals the need for relationally rich spaces in the lives of youth.

LORENZO'S SENSE OF SELF

Despite an early history that could have made it difficult for Lorenzo to form close relationships, Lorenzo constructed himself as someone with important connections to other people. He prided himself on being respectful and responsible. When asked, as part of this project, to take pictures of an adult to whom he was close and people who were important to him, he photographed adult staff at the club. He said he chose them because they care about and help him. He also took pictures of younger club members who looked up to him, talking of his relationships with these kids with fondness and a sense of responsibility.[3] At the same time, Lorenzo was proud of his individual talents. He described himself as nice, caring, respectful, honest, and "very talented." When asked for the five words that describe him the best, Lorenzo replied with the following: honest, respectful, dependable, responsible, and athletic. Four of these are words that I have termed *connected* characteristics. They refer to his relations with other people.[4] Thus, being respectful means being respectful toward someone else. Its meaning relies on the relational space between people. Athletic, however, can be enacted individually. It makes no reference to connections with another human.[5] The prevalence of connected words in Lorenzo's self-description is not atypical for youth at East Side. Their identities are in part rooted in how they relate to and are seen by others (Deutsch, 2005a).

---

[3]As part of the research, I gave youth disposable cameras. I provided a list of things to photograph, such as close adult, five things in the club, something that represents what you'd like to be when you grow up, and so on. The rest of the film (about half the exposures) could be used for anything they felt would "tell me more about who you are." Youth were given a set of photos and a photo album to take home.

[4]I coded the self-descriptive words as individuated or connected. A set of self-descriptions was given to a second coder for reliability. Kappas were .88 to .89. Connected words refer to youths' relationships with others. Individual words describe a trait that is independent of connections with others. All words were coded within the context of the individual's descriptions of what the words meant to him or her. Therefore, some words may be coded differently for different youth.

[5]An exception would be if he had defined himself as a "team player," which would be a connected trait because it relies on relations with other people for its existence and definition.

Like most of his peers, Lorenzo prized both his relational characteristics and his individual skills. His talents, especially in the area of sports, were important to him because they were "his whole life" and represented what he wanted to do when he grew up. Yet he felt that his most important quality was "respectful" because he liked "to treat others as others will treat me." He also liked people to be able to trust him and that people could, he said, "rely on me to get the job done."

Lorenzo did not think that he would be the same person he was without East Side. East Side was the group that had had the most influence on him, making him "more active, more concerned, more open minded":

> Volunteering with the kids [at the club influenced what I want to be in the future]. To reach out to people and see different prospects of how people see life. Charles [a staff member] . . . has been like a father to me. He talks to me. He cheers me up. At the same time we have fun. He taught me everything I know about basketball. . . . The club teaches me. I know kids look up to me and I like to set a positive vibe for them. . . . [If I hadn't come to the club] I feel I wouldn't be open. People wouldn't understand how I feel.

Lorenzo felt that his responsibility, respectfulness, and honesty, traits important to his sense of self, were encouraged and appreciated at the club. This was not just rhetoric. Conversations with staff and observations of Lorenzo supported his view of East Side as a place where these qualities were nurtured. Sean, the club's program director, initially thought that he could not trust Lorenzo but was proven wrong. He worked to get Lorenzo into a leadership role. "You know, he used to be the one who wanted to make all the moves and be the star of the game. But in a leadership role he's still getting attention and it's positive." Lorenzo's role in the club, particularly as a role model for younger kids, was an important dimension of his identity and a role that I discuss in depth later.

All but one of the youths I interviewed were Black or Hispanic and nearly all lived in a public housing project. Black and Hispanic communities have privileged interdependence more so than does the White culture (McAdoo, 2002; Way, 2004). Economic positioning may also change the salience of independence. Racial minority boys have not experienced the same benefits of individualism as have White male adolescents and, therefore, may be less committed to that model of masculine identity (Way, 2004). Furthermore, the presence of gangs, police harassment, and racist "microaggressions" make interdependence a mechanism for survival (Franklin, 2004; Way, 2004). Thus, the very context of Lorenzo's development, including his race and class positioning, may have primed him for the construction of a self-narrative in which interpersonal relationships are privileged.

In line with his connected sense of self, Lorenzo reported having close relationships with his aunt and cousins, as well as his best friend. He credited his aunt with always having been there for him when he needed her, having taken care of him for "my whole life. She is my mother and my aunt." Lorenzo liked to hang out with his friends. He was popular at the club and in the neighborhood. He had a best friend with whom he shared an interest in basketball. They "have faith in each other," each knowing that the other could do anything to which he set his mind. Lorenzo said that he tried "to stay positive and do whatever it takes to keep our friendship good." Although such close friendships run counter to the popular image of male adolescents, research on African American male friendships reveals that although attempts at close friendships are often thwarted by a lack of trust, boys desire intimate friendships based on depth and communication (DuBois & Hirsch, 1990; Way, 1998). Such friendships may help boys validate their own sense of self and "be who they want to be" (Chu, 2004). For African American men these relationships can be an important source of self-esteem, confirming identity in the face of a majority White culture in which one may be often misread or ignored (Franklin, 2004).

Lorenzo's definitions of success reflected his commitment to relatedness as a vital aspect of identity. He described a successful man as "smart, intelligent, responsible, works, takes care of responsibility." A successful woman is "independent . . . can also take care of herself, raise a family on her own." Independence was prized as a female trait, which is not surprising given that Lorenzo's father left his family; Lorenzo was raised by himself, his mother, and his aunt. But independence, in Lorenzo's description, includes taking care of others. It is an independence that exists within a network of relationships. This corresponds with African American history and culture, in which women have been more economically independent, with female strength often celebrated as existing within community (DeFrancisco & Chatham-Carpenter, 2000).

Likewise, being a successful man means living up to one's responsibilities to others. This is important given Lorenzo's life story. He did not live with either of his parents. His family life was fraught with separation. Lorenzo mentioned numerous times that he did not have a childhood and had to "grow up fast." He described himself as an angry, misused, unloved, and worthless child. He said, "[I] never had a bond with my mother or father." He did not want to be like his father, who "don't take care of his responsibilities." Lorenzo privileged a "manhood" in which one is evaluated not only by his individual achievements but also by his caring for others (Franklin, 2004).

Many people have discussed the importance of spaces in which Black individuals can come together and "be themselves" (W. E. Cross & Strauss, 1998; Franklin, 2004; hooks, 1990). These spaces, in which individual selves are validated within a community of others, may also serve as places in which relatedness is nurtured. By listening to Lorenzo's story, one can see how such a community, in which Lorenzo felt that he belonged, allows for dimensions of relatedness to emerge.

HOLDING AND EMBEDDEDNESS

It was at East Side that Lorenzo experienced being held, the sense of safety that is important to an adolescent's ability to embark on his own journey of self-discovery (Josselson, 1994). It was through Lorenzo's relationships with the adult staff at East Side that this holding was both nurtured and modeled. Over time, Lorenzo came to hold others, as he developed relationships with younger kids who looked up to him. His affective experiences of both being held and giving back through holding others appear to have influenced his sense of self.

The adults at East Side provided Lorenzo with an environment in which he began to learn that he could trust others to be there for him. Lorenzo developed a relationship with Charles, the physical education director, whom he described as being like both a big brother and a father to him. The club director demonstrated to Lorenzo that there is always "someone out there to give you a helping hand." In contrast to his home life, where he was thrust into an adult role at an early age, East Side provided Lorenzo with needed assistance. He was able to open up to people and "receive opinions and help, ask people for help." Lorenzo said, "I can rely on people." The club director showed him "that there's always someone out there who can help you, give you a helping hand." He took a picture of a female staff member as an adult to whom he was close because she cared about how he felt: "I'm comfortable around her. I can tell her anything." Lorenzo said that she was like a mother to him and that he could go to her if he was down or needed something. "You can tell one of the staff a problem and they can help you with it. . . . They can influence me," he said.

Lorenzo appeared to have learned a sense of interdependence at the club. He learned to ask for help. This ability to ask for help should not be underestimated in its importance to youth development. Adolescents must learn to balance their desires for independence with their needs for adult support (Grotevant & Cooper, 1998; Youniss & Smollar, 1985). In light of Lorenzo's history, it was important for him to find a space in which he felt he could ask for and receive help from adults. To move on to more complex modes of relatedness he had to first experience the holding that was missing from other environments of his life. He had cared for others before, but never within such a web of support as he experienced at East Side. As he began to see how he fit into the relational network at the club, he experienced a type of affective reciprocity that was not readily available to him in other contexts of his life.

Through his relationships at East Side Lorenzo began to see himself as a responsible member of the community. He contributed to it, serving as a role model to younger club members. Lorenzo was both part of East Side's community and a recognized contributor to it (Franklin, 2004). He learned what it means to be embedded in a community of care. As I show later, the holding that Lorenzo experienced helped embed him further in the club, providing a sense of belonging and opportunities to both meet and nurture his need to hold and tend to others.

TENDING, CARE, AND VALIDATION THROUGH ROLE MODELING

Lorenzo made the following statement during a focus group: "I just learned it just got brought to my attention that some things you do you have to watch out for your actions. I never thought that actually little kids would look up to someone like [me]." By the time of his interviews, a year later, Lorenzo had incorporated this role into his identity. Nearly every day I was at East Side, Lorenzo was in the gym with Charles, playing with or coaching younger boys.

Lorenzo's relationship with Charles is a nice example of the trilevel role modeling that is possible at such multi-age after-school programs. This process involves three levels of role modeling: adult to teen, teen to younger child, and adult to younger child. It allows teens to model themselves on adults both as individual achievers and as examples to others (Deutsch, 2005b). Behavior modeling can be viewed as individually based, with little attention paid to the affective link between the model and the learner. This stems from Bandura's (1977; Schultz & Schultz, 1994) approach to social learning, which focuses on individuals modeling behavior on the actions of observed others. The role modeling I observed at East Side was a more relationally based process. It relied on a sense of social embeddedness as the context in which role modeling, particularly around tending and care, takes place (Josselson, 1992, 1994). This involves not just observation, retention, and repetition of behaviors (Bandura, 1977; Schultz & Schultz, 1994) but a sense of support that leads to a desire to sustain relationships in part through caring for other youth. Furthermore, it differs from traditional notions of social learning because it rests on the affective meaning of the social interactions in which the modeling and repetition occur. This process is elucidated later in the chapter.

Lorenzo said, "[Charles] has been like a father to me. He talks to me, he cheers me up." He referred to Charles in the two interviews as both the "big brother I never had" and a father: "When I was down he always wanted to know why I was down. He always influenced me to want to do new stuff, to never give up. He's a big reason why I still play ball." Lorenzo and Charles had fun together and Lorenzo credited Charles for teaching him all he knew about basketball. Lorenzo also said that Charles gave him more motivation to focus on school: "[Charles] told me I had to be more serious than just sports cause there's no guarantee that I'm going to make it or whatever, but, actually to put sports behind education."

Charles was a role model for Lorenzo, influencing him and teaching him that "life is worth living." There was an aspect of idealization and identification in Lorenzo's relationship with Charles. Lorenzo saw in Charles a possible future self. Helping Charles with the kids made him think about what he wanted to do in the future. While Charles was serving as a role model for Lorenzo, Lorenzo came to realize that he could also be a role model for the younger kids. This realization was rooted in part in the relational tie that Lorenzo felt with Charles and other staff. This socioemotional aspect of their role modeling relationship differentiates it from researchers' traditional ideas of role modeling and social learning, which focus less on the emotional ties between people and more on observation and repetition of actions and behaviors.

> I feel that when I'm here I got to, like, act like a role model 'cause I know like the staff they like probably expect more of me cause I been here so long and they work with me for long so I just try to . . . be a good example for the little kids and all that.

Through his relationship with Charles and other staff Lorenzo became embedded in the community and saw himself as having an important role within it. He did not simply mimic the behavior of the adults at East Side; rather, he experienced a sense of relatedness with them that he wanted to maintain. Sustaining these relationships required him to live up to their expectations and act in ways that were in line with the club's norms. For the teens, these norms and expectations involved serving as positive role models and caretakers to the younger club members. In light of Lorenzo's comments about his own position as a role model to younger club members, this role had relational meaning to him. It helped him regulate his own behavior. But it also made him feel relationally meaningful to other people. Just as he allowed Charles and other staff to support him, he could serve that function for other kids. This process is more than social learning; it is relational learning, discovering the personal, emotional benefits of interdependence.

The back-and-forth between Charles, Lorenzo, and the younger members is illustrated by a softball game during which Charles and Lorenzo played with the younger kids. The interactions between Charles and Lorenzo, as well as Charles and the younger players and Lorenzo and the kids, demonstrate the ways in which these relationships mirrored each other.

> Lorenzo hit a home run and kissed his two fingers, touched his chest with them, and then pointed up to the basketball basket. He looked at Charles and grinned. Charles laughed. . . . Lorenzo stood at the sidelines now and then, shuffling his feet back and forth, doing a little dance, and grinning at the boy who was running the scoreboard. He clapped a lot when his team made a good play and also teased [a young girl]. [The girl] smiled at him and ran to hit him with the bat when he teased her. Lorenzo grinned and hid behind a large mat that was propped up against the wall. They

went back and forth like this for a while, with him teasing her while she was up to bat and her running after him threatening to hit him with the bat. Charles joked around with the players and smiled when people made good plays. He made faces when he was up to bat. There was a lot of laughter and good humor overall in the game.

During this game Lorenzo interacted with Charles as a mentee, showing off when he made a good play and receiving validation from Charles. He also acted as a mentor, mimicking Charles's style of friendly interaction with the kids, encouraging them and making them laugh. At other times, Lorenzo acted as the coach for the younger boys' teams, giving instruction and calling players in and out of the game. The younger kids benefited from both these relationships, as well as from their own interaction with Charles. They observed Lorenzo's relationship with Charles and the part he played within the club, seeing a possible future role for themselves at East Side. Being modeled were both embeddedness and tending, important dimensions of relatedness (Josselson, 1992, 1994). Furthermore, Lorenzo was recognized, by both the kids and adults, for his role at the club. Such recognition is an important factor in helping African American men overcome what has been termed "the invisibility syndrome" (Franklin, 2004). Lorenzo saw another Black man (Charles) who had a valued role in relation to others. He learned to enact similar relationships himself and, in doing so, became a role model for younger male adolescents in the club. Lorenzo discovered that he had meaning to others, both the younger kids and adult staff.

It took time for Lorenzo to come into his then-current role as a positive, social leader. At first he was more focused on showcasing his individual prowess in sports. Over time, Lorenzo demonstrated more prosocial modes of interaction. Sean, the program director, responded, helping move Lorenzo into his leadership role with Charles. Lorenzo recognized this effort. He took a photograph of Sean and some younger boys as important people in his life. In describing why they were important Lorenzo said that Sean gave him chances when no one else would and that the boys looked up to him. Lorenzo recognized both his responsibility as a role model and the respect that was given to him by club staff in terms of allowing him to prove himself beyond first impressions. Furthermore, he emphasized the affective meaning of these roles to him. Lorenzo's narrative demonstrates that he had incorporated the image of himself as a role model into his identity. This may be an individual trait, one that focuses on oneself as the central figure ("They look up to *me*"). But it also demonstrates how Lorenzo was embedded in the community. It was within East Side that Lorenzo saw himself as a role model. This individual role existed because of the attachments he had formed within the club. He did not talk about being a role model in terms of basketball skills, something with which he could be concerned. Instead, he embedded his narrative of being a role model in conversations about feeling understood at East

Side, of learning to be open and in connection to other people. His sense of social belonging was tied to his position as role model, not distinct from it.

East Side gave youth adult support in dealing with the stressors in their lives. It was a place where they could forget about their troubles and experience the freedom and frivolity of childhood (Hirsch, 2005). Yet staff also expected teens to be role models for the younger kids. In doing so, the club recognized the dual nature of adolescence: children becoming adults and needing aspects of both worlds to support their development. Youth are having their primary holding needs met while simultaneously learning to enact tending toward others (Josselson, 1992, 1994).

This type of relational context is rare. It requires a level of community and trust that is sadly absent from many schools and neighborhoods in America today. Although trust has been cited as an important factor in effective schools (Bryk & Schneider, 2002), such relational reciprocity is not the norm for high schools, especially large urban schools such as the one Lorenzo attended. Lorenzo felt that at school he was "always trying to adjust." At East Side, however, "it's a relief to get back to your regular [self]." People understood him there. It is also likely that he felt more respected and trusted at East Side. The only mention Lorenzo made of his teachers was in a story of when one used a racial epithet in an argument with him. In fact, Lorenzo had a problematic relationship with school, periodically dropping out and then returning when encouraged by Charles.

East Side helped Lorenzo to balance his need for validation as a talented individual with his need for group affiliation. He found a respected role to play within the social environment of the club. Such provision of meaningful social roles for youth has been found to be a common characteristic of successful youth organizations (Halpern, Barker, & Mollard, 2000; McLaughlin, Irby, & Langman, 1994). Lorenzo moved from individual attention-seeking to more prosocial behavior through role modeling for and tending to younger youth. East Side provided Lorenzo with adult support and mentoring, which was lacking in his life outside the club. Lorenzo simultaneously received respect for his own abilities and responsibility as a maturing, young adult, helping him develop an identity that emphasized traits valued in society.

CONCLUSION

Lorenzo's early experiences of relationships were isolating and difficult. Although he took care of others, he did so without reciprocity, leaving him feeling "misused." As an adolescent, Lorenzo found support at East Side, an environment in which he learned to ask for help and came to see himself as embedded in a community where he was held, tended to others, and was recognized and validated for his social role. No longer an island, Lorenzo was part of an archipelago. He was embedded in a chain of relationships, a community of support. These relationships played an integral role in his life story, not only providing a context for the development of his identity but also becoming part of his narrative of self. Lorenzo valued his relational traits and made them an important aspect of his identity. It is to society's benefit to recognize what Lorenzo's story suggests. Having an environment that encourages the construction of narratives centered on interpersonal relationships is important. Adolescents need settings that both meet their primary relatedness needs and nurture more complex dimensions of relatedness. This point is particularly poignant today. In a time when the United States models ideals of individual responsibility over collective care, it feels all the more important to nurture a sense of relatedness in American teens. As conservative politicians push for an increasingly privatized state, in which the autonomy of individual citizens is emphasized, Lorenzo's story is a reminder of what is missing when the individual is prioritized over ties to others. If we, as reasearchers, psychologists, and cititzens, do not cultivate relationally rich environments, we may find ourselves adrift in a sea of islands, without any sense of our interdependence and ecological overlap.

REFERENCES

Adams, G. R., & Marshall, S. K. (1996). A developmental social psychology of identity: Understanding the person-in-context. *Journal of Adolescence, 19*, 429–442.

Aron, A., & McLaughlin-Volpe, T. (2001). Including others in the self: Extension to own and partner's group memberships. In C. Sedikides & M. Brewer (Eds.), *Individual self, relational self, collective self* (pp. 89–108). Philadelphia: Psychology Press.

Bandura, A. (1977). *Social learning theory.* Englewood Cliffs, NJ: Prentice-Hall.

Bryk, A. S., & Schneider, B. (2002). *Trust in schools: A core resource for improvement.* New York: Russell Sage Foundation.

Chu, J. Y. (2004). A relational perspective on adolescent boys' identity development. In N. Way & J. Y. Chu (Eds.), *Adolescent boys: Exploring diverse cultures of boyhood* (pp. 78–104). New York: New York University Press.

Coll, C. G., Lamberty, G., Jenkins, R., McAdoo, H. P., Crnic, K., Wasik, B. H., & Vasquez Garcia, H. (1996). An integrative model for the study of developmental competencies in minority children. *Child Development, 67*, 1891–1914.

Cooley, C. H. (1902). *Human nature and the social order.* New York: Schocken.

Cross, S. E., & Madson, L. (1997). Models of the self: Self-construals and gender. *Psychological Bulletin, 122*, 5–37.

Cross, W. E., & Strauss, L. (1998). The everyday functions of African American identity. In J. K. Swim & C. Stangor (Eds.), *Prejudice: The target's perspective* (pp. 267–279). San Diego: Academic Press.

DeFrancisco, V. L., & Chatham-Carpenter, A. (2000). Self in community: African American women's views of self-esteem. *The Howard Journal of Communications, 11*, 73–92.

Deutsch, N. L. (2005a). "I like to treat others as others would treat me": The development of prosocial selves in an urban youth organization. In D. B. Fink (Ed.), *New directions for youth development: Vol. 108. Doing the right thing: Ethical development across diverse environments* (pp. 89–105). San Francisco: Jossey-Bass.

Deutsch, N. L. (2005b). There are birds in the projects: The construction of self in an urban youth organization. *Dissertation Abstracts International 65*(12), 6706B. (UMI No. AAT 3156573)

di Leonardo, M. (1999). "Why can't they be like our grandparents?" and other racial fairy tales. In J. A. Reed (Ed.), *Without justice for all: The new liberalism and our retreat from racial equality* (pp. 29–64). Boulder, CO: Westview Press.

DuBois, D., & Hirsch, B. (1990). School and neighborhood friendship patterns of blacks and whites in early adolescence. *Child Development, 61*, 524–536.

Eccles, J. (2001, March). *Gender and ethnicity as developmental contexts.* Paper presented at the meeting of the Society for Research in Child Development, Minneapolis, MN.

Erikson, E. (1959). *Identity and the life cycle.* New York: Norton.

Erikson, E. (1968). *Identity, youth and crisis.* New York: Norton.

Ferguson, A. A. (2000). *Bad boys: Public schools in the making of black masculinity.* Ann Arbor: University of Michigan Press.

Franklin, A. J. (2004). *From brotherhood to manhood: How black men rescue their relationships and dreams from the invisibility syndrome.* Hoboken, NJ: Wiley.

Gilligan, C. (1982). *In a different voice.* Cambridge, MA: Harvard University Press.

Grotevant, H. D., & Cooper, C. R. (1998). Individuality and connectedness in adolescent development: Review and prospects for research on identity, relationships, and context. In E. E. A. Skoe & A. L. von der Lippe (Eds.), *Personality development in adolescence: A cross national and life span perspective* (pp. 3–37). London: Routledge.

Halpern, R., Barker, G., & Mollard, W. (2000). Youth programs as alternative spaces to be: A study of neighborhood youth programs in Chicago's west town. *Youth & Society, 31*, 469–506.

Harter, S. (1999). *The construction of the self: A developmental perspective.* New York: Guilford Press.

Hirsch, B. (2005). *A place to call home: Community based after-school programs for urban youth.* Washington, DC: American Psychological Association.

hooks, b. (1990). *Yearning: Race, gender, and cultural politics.* Boston: South End Press.

James, W. (1981). *The principles of psychology.* Cambridge, MA: Harvard University Press. (Original work published 1890)

Josselson, R. (1989). Identity formation in adolescence: Implications for young adulthood. In S. C. Feinstein & A. H. Esman (Eds.), *Adolescent psychiatry: Develop-*

mental and clinical studies (Vol. 16, pp. 142–154). Chicago: University of Chicago Press.

Josselson, R. (1992). *The space between us: Exploring the dimensions of human relationships*. San Francisco: Jossey-Bass.

Josselson, R. (1994). Identity and relatedness in the lifecycle. In H. A. Bosma, T. L. G. Graafsma, H. D. Grotevant, and D. J. De Levita (Eds.), *Identity and development: An interdisciplinary approach*. Thousand Oaks, CA: Sage.

Larson, R., & Wilson, S. (2004). Adolescence across place and time: Globalization and the changing pathways to adulthood. In R. M. Lerner & L. Steinberg (Eds.), *Handbook of adolescent psychology* (2nd ed., pp. 299–330). Hoboken, NJ: Wiley.

Lerner, R. M., Brentano, C., Dowling, E. M., & Anderson, P. M. (2002). Positive youth development: Thriving as the basis of personhood and civil society. In G. Noam (Series Ed.), R. M. Lerner, C. S. Taylor, & A. von Eye (Vol. Eds.), *New directions for youth development: Vol. 95. Theory, practice and research: Pathways to positive youth development among diverse youth* (pp. 11–33). San Francisco: Jossey-Bass.

Marcia, J. E. (1980). Identity in adolescence. In J. Adelson (Ed.), *Handbook of adolescent psychology* (pp. 159–187). New York: Wiley.

McAdams, D. P. (1993). *The stories we live by: Personal myths and the making of the self*. New York: Morrow.

McAdams, D. P. (2001). The psychology of life stories. *Review of General Psychology, 5*, 100–122.

McAdoo, H. P. (2002). The village talks: Racial socialization of our children. In H. P. McAdoo (Ed.), *Black children: Social, emotional, and parental environments* (2nd ed., pp. 47–55). Thousand Oaks, CA: Sage.

McLaughlin, M., Irby, M., & Langman, J. (1994). *Urban sanctuaries: Neighborhood organizations in the lives and futures of inner city youth*. San Francisco: Jossey-Bass.

Mead, G. H. (1934). *Mind, self, and society from the standpoint of a social behaviorist*. Chicago: University of Chicago Press.

Miller, J. B. (1976). *Toward a new psychology of women*. Boston: Beacon Press.

Newman, B. M., & Newman, P. R. (2001). Group identity and alienation: Giving the we its due. *Journal of Youth and Adolescence, 30*, 515–538.

Olsen, C. S. (1996). African-American adolescent women: Perceptions of gender, race, and class. *Marriage & Family Review, 24*, 105–121.

Pratt, M. W., Arnold, M. L., & Mackey, K. (2001). Adolescents' representations of the parent voice in stories of personal turning points. In D. P. McAdams, R. Josselson, & A. Lieblich (Eds.), *Turns in the road: Narrative studies of lives in transition* (pp. 227–252). Washington, DC: American Psychological Association.

Quintana, S. M. (2004). Race, ethnicity, and culture in child development. *Child Development, 75*, v–vi.

Quintana, S. M., & Segura-Herrera, T. A. (2003). Developmental transformations of self and identity in the context of oppression. *Self and Identity, 2*, 269–285.

Ryan, R. M., & Deci, E. L. (2000). The darker and brighter sides of human existence: Basic psychological needs as a unifying concept. *Psychological Inquiry, 11*, 319–338.

Ryan, R. M., Deci, E. L., & Grolnick, W. S. (1995). Autonomy, relatedness, and the self: Their relation to development and psychopathology. In D. Cicchetti & D. J. Cohen (Eds.), *Developmental psychopathology: Vol 1. Theory and methods* (pp. 618–655). Oxford, England: Wiley.

Schultz, D., & Schultz, S. E. (1994). *Theories of personality.* Pacific Grove, CA: Brooks/Cole.

Singelis, T. M. (1994). The measurement of independent and interdependent self-construals. *Personality and Social Psychology Bulletin, 20*, 580–591.

Steinberg, L. (1990). Autonomy, conflict, and harmony in the family relationship. In S. S. Feldman & G. R. Elliott (Eds.), *At the threshold: The developing adolescent* (pp. 255–276). Cambridge, MA: Harvard University Press.

Tice, D. M., & Baumeister, R. F. (2001). Primacy of the interpersonal self. In C. Sedikides & M. Brewer (Eds.), *Individual self, relational self, collective self* (pp. 71–88). Philadelphia: Psychology Press.

Tolman, D. L. (1996). Adolescent girls' sexuality: Debunking the myth of the urban girl. In B. Leadbeater & N. Way (Eds.), *Urban girls: Resisting stereotypes, creating identities* (pp. 255–271). New York: New York University Press.

Way, N. (1998). *Everyday courage: The lives and stories of urban teenagers.* New York: New York University Press.

Way, N. (2004). Intimacy, desire, and distrust in the friendships of adolescent boys. In N. Way & J. Y. Chu (Eds.), *Adolescent boys: Exploring diverse cultures of boyhood* (pp. 167–196). New York: New York University Press.

Youniss, J., & Smollar, J. (1985). *Adolescent relations with mothers, fathers, and friends.* Chicago: University of Chicago Press.

5

EARNING A SECURE ATTACHMENT STYLE: A NARRATIVE OF PERSONALITY CHANGE IN ADULTHOOD

VALORY MITCHELL

PROLOGUE

The student of personality development can easily become captivated by a longitudinal data archive. Only there, following "lives through time" (Block, 1971), can the answers, the antecedents and consequences, truly emerge. In the linear chronology of longitudinal work a narrative cannot help but unfold, as each round of data collection whispers "and *then?*"

For 48 years (since 1958), a woman I call Ann[1] has been a participant in a longitudinal study of personality development in women (e.g., Helson,

I would like to thank Ravenna Helson for creating and maintaining the longitudinal study from which this chapter could emerge and for her perspective on and suggestions about this chapter from start to finish. I would also like to thank Carol George for bringing her expertise in developmental attachment to verify and extend the understanding of Ann's story.

[1]To preserve her privacy, "Ann" has chosen this pseudonym, and I have altered or masked specific information that might reveal her identity.

Mitchell, & Moane, 1984; Helson & Soto, 2005). Ann had been among the first to be studied, as a college senior. At the next contact, 6 years later, she had gotten a teaching credential, married, moved back and forth across the United States, and was pregnant with her second child.

I first met her (or rather, her paper-and-pencil self-report data) 15 years after that, when I was in graduate school. She was 43, a divorced professional with teenage children; it was 1980. By then, the project had evolved from research on women's creativity and leadership potential (a startling topic for research at that time) into a study of adult development.

I was immersed in the lives and the psychological patterns of the nearly 100 women who had described their experience of the past 15 years. One part of my work was to write a summary of each woman's personality change using profiles generated by the California Psychological Inventory (CPI; Gough & Bradley, 1996), which Ann had taken at ages 21, 27, and 43.[2] I remember sitting in a Berkeley backyard on balmy summer days, flicking my long brown hair off the notebook paper as I wrote. A summary was sent to each woman in appreciation of the many hours of work she had contributed to the project. The summaries of Ann's personality change are included in this chapter.

It is 26 years later now, 2006. While on sabbatical, I return to the archive. Two more rounds of data have been gathered (when the women were ages 52 and 61). As I walk the long corridor of the psychology building to view the videotape of Ann's interview, I brush past the doorways and ghosts of my teachers, my peers, myself, 25 years gone. My hair is short now, and entirely white. When I actually see Ann for the first time (on videotape), she is 63 (or was; the interview and tape are 7 years old).

The life story she told at age 63 was different from the ones she had told before. She had let her secrets out, over the years. What I am about has also changed. Twenty-six years ago I would not have written this; neither narrative theory nor attachment theory would have yet offered the theoretical rationale for this study. And you are implicated too; your attention was elsewhere. Had I written it, would you have read it? Perhaps all of us have let our secrets out, over the years. As feminist and postmodern methodologists (Gergen, 1990) have noted, we are all participant observers.

This statement is powerfully and poignantly true of the life-span developmentalist who works on a longitudinal project. What shades of meaning are recast when we consider that the principal investigator, who launched the project shortly after her 30th birthday, turned 80 last year? Or that I am nearing 60? Not only the interviewee but the researchers, too, look back across the decades, look out at the world from their present vantage point,

---

[2]Data were collected when the women in the sample were, on average, ages 21, 27, 43, 52, and 61. Ann was one of the first, and therefore older, participants, and thus a little over the average age at the time of each wave of data collection. In the text, I have used the average age.

and consider what is important now. Ann, you and I, and also the field of psychology and the culture in which we are all embedded have changed, perhaps have even developed. It is to that topic I now turn.

THE CENTRALITY OF ATTACHMENT AND THE POSSIBILITY OF DEVELOPMENT

Out of the accrued experience with our parents in infancy and childhood, we fashion a sense of self, a sense of other, and an orientation to the interpersonal world. So says attachment theory (Bowlby, 1969, 1973, 1988; and others who have followed him, e.g., Fonagy, 1999; Kraemer, 1992; Sroufe & Fleeson, 1986), and researchers have amassed a great deal of robust research to support and elaborate on this premise (see Cassidy & Shaver, 1999).

Though there is evidence for the stability of attachment status across time, cross-sectional and longitudinal studies have also found instances of patterned change in attachment status (Rothbart & Shaver, 1994; Sroufe, Egeland, Carlson, & Collins, 2005; Waters, Merrick, Treboux, Crowell, & Albersheim, 2000). Those whom attachment theorists call "the earned secure" (Main, Kaplan, & Cassidy, 1985) have emerged from childhood with a working model of insecure attachment; in some way, they transcend fears, anxieties, and defenses, and fundamentally alter their inner working model of the self. How is this possible?

This study portrays such a transformation in one woman. I begin with Ann's narrative of her childhood, recounted in an interview at age 61. Here she describes the experiences from which she first constructed her internal working models of attachment. A second interview segment tells the story of how she changed her fundamental premises. Finally, her narrative reveals the subjective experience of living in a secure self, and its implications for development in several domains. In the interpretive sections, I supplement Ann's narrative with additional data from the longitudinal study: personality profiles as well as selections from other interviews and from her open-ended written responses to questionnaires.

Uses of This Chapter

This chapter may prove useful in several ways. First, looking at this narrative through the lens of attachment offers a way to conceptualize the self. The narrative shows what it is like to be a particular kind of self, looking out through a particular worldview. Second, for those of us who were unable to start off with a secure attachment, it is heartening to hope that it might be attained later in life. Contemporary clinical theorists increasingly posit this transformation of self-in-relation (Jordan, 1991) as the central goal of psychotherapy (Holmes, 1996; Wallin, 2002). This chapter shows how a self, which was constructed out of real-life events, can also be transformed in the process of living.

Finally, this project offers a glimpse of what may occur, for some, as they experience the pull to consider their life in full. At these times, the life span itself may become a numinous backdrop against which the formal properties of a life and life story—coherence (Main, 1991) and meaning—take shape as they have not before (Erikson, 1960; Loevinger, 1976). Ann may reflect this in what she chooses, now, to say. The researchers may reflect it in what they choose, now, to ask; as well, it may be reflected in the extensive narrative space that the researchers have made available to contain the scope of Ann's response.[3] In this way, narrative work allows access to fundamental parameters of the psychological life span.

What Is Attachment?

The attachment system, like the immune system, is presumed to have evolved because it improves the likelihood of survival: We mammals are less vulnerable when we are able to maintain proximity to those who care about us. Our attachment figures rise to our defense (against both literal and symbolic predators), comfort us and help us heal from injury or illness (physical or psychological), and provide for our basic (physical and psychological) needs. The complement to the child's attachment system is the parent's caregiving system, which equips attachment figures with a predisposition for attention and attunement to their young, and to others in the group for whom they care (George & Solomon, 1999).

Attachment Status

An attachment event happens when an internal or external threat activates the attachment system, so that the individual seeks proximity to an attachment figure. These episodes and their outcomes accumulate, over time, to create an internal working model, described as an attachment status.

Across cultures, Ainsworth (Ainsworth, Blehar, Waters, & Wall, 1978) and many who followed have been able to reliably classify infants according to the status of attachment they manifest. The largest group of infants is securely attached; when distressed, secure infants use their voice, their gaze, and their capacity for movement, without hesitation or ambivalence, to directly seek proximity to their attachment figures. Proximity to (even contact with) and comfort by a responsive caregiver create a sense of safety—a *secure base*—and the infant is therefore able to resume an attitude of curiosity and exploration (Ainsworth et al., 1978; Bowlby, 1988).

Other infant–caregiver dyads, however, manifest one of several insecure patterns of attachment behavior. These infants are not able to use direct

---

[3]For a discussion of the holistic content approach to using the single case study in research, see Lieblich, Tuval-Mashiach, and Zilber (1998).

and effective ways to obtain a modicum of security in relation to a caregiver who is anxious, confused, misattuned, inattentive, frightening, rejecting, or an unpredictable blend of these. Because these infants experience the caregiver as a limited or erratic source of security, they remain in limbo, and are slow or sometimes unable to return to an attitude of curiosity, exploration, or openness to their environment (George & Solomon, 1999; Main & Solomon, 1986). Children with insecure attachment can be classified into three broad categories: avoidant, ambivalent, and unable to organize a consistent status because they are frightened and unable to seek the attachment figure as a solution to their fear (Main & Hesse, 1990; Main & Solomon, 1986). These patterns are paralleled in adults and labeled dismissing of attachment, preoccupied with attachment, and disorganized/fearful (Main et al., 1985).

Attachment Status Becomes Personality Style

Over time, these patterns of attachment are internalized into the psyche as a generalized template, or working model, for interpersonal life (Bowlby, 1969, 1988; Bretherton & Munholland, 1999). Once consolidated, they are difficult (but not impossible) to change.

Different views of self and other characterize adults in the different attachment statuses. Securely attached individuals have a positive sense of the self and the other. They see themselves as competent, strong, relaxed, warm, cooperative, and playful; they approach others with expectations of a trusting, sensitive, and affectionate relationship (Klohnen & John, 1998). All insecure individuals have some form of negative view of self, but people of dismissive, preoccupied, and disorganized/fearful statuses express and defend against it differently. Dismissive individuals see themselves in a positive light, but defensively so. They are independent, self-reliant, and calm, but expect little from others, so they may come across as unemotional and even indifferent. In contrast, preoccupied individuals flip back and forth between a positive and negative self and other representation, consistent with their defense of cognitive disconnection. Those with disorganized/fearful attachment experience the self as vulnerable, anxious, or frightened when attachment is activated; at other times they may show a pseudo-strength (George & West, 1999).

The Interview

Ann's narrative emerged in response to the questions of the Adult Attachment Interview protocol (George, Kaplan, & Main, 1985). The question-and-answer format of this interview does not allow one to tell a story uninterrupted, all in one piece. I have taken Ann's responses and sewn them together to approximate a continuous story. Her actual responses are unedited (except for material in brackets).

Ann was asked about her family relationships during childhood, and about how she felt these relationships may have influenced her. As she addressed this last question, she elected to tell how she had been able to undo, in significant measure, the enormous influence of these early experiences and to reveal the subjective experience of her developmental shift. Ann was extraordinarily clear and articulate in this interview; these formal properties of her narrative are telling manifestations of secure attachment status and the intrapsychic representational structure that goes with it.

ANN TELLS THE STORY OF HER CHILDHOOD

I was born to a family that was Christian Science. So (after my birth), my mother was taken to a Christian Science maternity home. My mother had tuberculosis when she was 16, then recovered with a sort of miraculous Christian Science healing. She was never supposed to have children; she'd had a portion of her lung gone. She had me, and then had a hard recovery from the birth. So my father brought me back, and to my grandmother's house, and my grandfather's.

My mother had a recurrence of tuberculosis when I was about 3 or 4, and it got more and more severe. My mother, father, and I all moved into my grandmother and grandfather's house, and then she died when I was 6, and I continued living with my father, grandmother, and grandfather until my dad remarried when I was about 8. So that's kind of the basic family constellation.

"Because It Was Such a Marvelous Thing to Have Her"

It's really hard for me to differentiate how much I've romanticized my mother. When a mother dies young, you know, she becomes. . . . So I have a lot of questions about how that was. I remember hanging out with her when she was cooking and I was learning the ABCs. . . . I have this sort of warm, soft sense of the world being safe and wanting very much to please her. I remember mostly her touch, because when she was in bed in the last 2 years of her life, at least the 1st year that she was in bed, she was able to brush my hair. In the morning, my treat was I would go in and she would brush my hair. I had curly hair and if you wound it around your fingers it would stay in ringlets. I really looked forward to that, because it was such a marvelous thing to have her. And when she died, the worst thing I could think of, it's going to have to be grandma who would do my hair, and grandma was rough, and she pulled and she put water on it. She was just trying to get it done.

My mother certainly raised me until I was 4, and my father. And then definitely, at some point, my grandmother phased in as my mother phased out. My grandma, who really did all the unseen, sturdy, hard work to keep a family together—with a woman she was nursing who was dying, and (her own) husband who was losing some capacities (he had difficulty walking), and an uppity kid, in a two-bedroom house—was very influential. She wasn't affectionate; she was just a very pragmatic, small German woman who *did* things.

My grandfather had some—I don't know if it was arthritis or what—but he had diminished capacity for walking, so he used to sit in a rocking chair a lot. He was not very old when I was little, but he had something wrong with his legs. Since we were Christian Science, you never really knew what was wrong with anybody—basically nothing! But he taught me to read. When I was about 4, he sat me in his lap and we rocked a lot, and he would read the sports section, which was green, so you had the green part of the newspaper, and he would read the King James Bible, in a big beautiful onion-skin leather gorgeous book. I learned to read baseball scores and golf games and King James English. Grandpa was really a very nurturing man.

My dad was . . . I loved to sit next to him and read. He would read to me the Oz stories, one chapter a night. He loved them; he loved all the characters. . . . We had this whole world together. We were very close when I was little . . . dad's-coming-home-from-work close. But when we moved to my grandmother's house, he got increasingly worried. My biggest worry was that I wouldn't pray hard enough and my mother would die, and she did.

"And That Was Enough Discipline Right There"

My mother's death was—hideous—and available to me. . . . I watched her throw up blood in the toilet and not be able to walk. . . . [During her last years,] the rules inside the house were very clear, and there was just no fooling, and I didn't *want* to fool around with them.[4] Death was threatening, and that was enough discipline right there. You had to be quiet, children weren't allowed in; I could color and I could read, and we were cramped. But outside, nobody cared. You could go out and come back at six for dinner. So I roller skated, and snuck off with kids, and slid down the sand dunes. I would ride the bus anywhere I wanted.

Obedience was where it was at, and I was a "good girl." I didn't need a lot of controlling, but I was strong-minded and I had my way of coping, which was mainly to escape and do my own thing. . . . Under the circumstances, I preferred neglect to attention. It was *fine*.

"And He Wouldn't Have Anything to Do With Me"

And then she died, and I was brought in to be told that she had died, although I knew very well that she was dead. It was the big dramatic moment

---

[4]Italics indicate the speaker's emphasis.

for the family to tell her daughter. . . . At that point, my dad put his head down and wouldn't look at me, and I wanted to sit in his lap, and he wouldn't have anything to do with me. My grandpa said, "Your dad really can't do this right now, come and [sit] with me." I didn't want to do that, but he was the only one available, so I went [to] my grandpa.

And then my dad and I just really didn't have a relationship for a very long time. Although he began to recover about a year later and took me on bike rides . . . early, before church. But he was dating my stepmother, so sometimes he would call it off, and sometimes he would go. And that was the only contact I had with him.

"In a Way, I Think That Was More Traumatic"

[*Interviewer: I wonder if you could tell me, which of the people who raised you . . . do you feel closest to?*] It would have been my mother when I was really young, and I kept that closeness even after she was gone. My dad pulled away. I might have felt close to him. In a way, I think that was more traumatic to me than my mother's death, because he was still around. I don't know if it was more, but it ranks up there. I just think . . . something inside of me closed.

You know, I think I raised myself after my mother died. I think a part of me closed off very firmly, and I don't think I've let people get close to me until the last 10 to 15 years, and even then it's with some reserve. I think there's a part of me that just has never opened up. My father died, my grandmother died, my grandfather died, and I really haven't felt a huge sense of loss. A little sadness, but I didn't cry.

[*Interviewer: Do you remember any time when you were hurt, ill, or upset, someone holding you or comforting you?*] That was not allowed. I don't know if you know about Christian Science; it's really quite an elaborate system. [They believe] if you go against it, if you respond to the pain, you are making it more real. So it's a paradox: to respond in that way is to make it more lively, so you don't do that. No, people did not hold me. I did a lot of therapy and finally realized I was just touch starved, really touch starved. Life has been, it's really wonderful. You get to reverse things [*laughs*].

INTERPRETING AND EXTENDING
THE CHILDHOOD NARRATIVE

This narrative presents a set of rich characters in a plot that devolves from intimate tenderness to death, abandonment, and benign neglect. The strong-minded girl escaped, but in the process a door was closed that would not open again for nearly 40 years.

At the beginning of the story, several episodes of nurturance were described. The listener pictured a good mother whose relentless physical depletion increasingly constrained her caregiving, and a father who brought a shared delight in a storybook world to Ann's earliest childhood years. However, tenderness and nurturance are not the same as attachment, where security in the face of threat is tested.

The Attachment Episode and Ann's Attachment Status

In the attachment episode, Ann was brought in to be told about her mother's death. Despite her entreaties, her father, her attachment figure, rejected her efforts to seek proximity and would make no physical, verbal, or visual contact with her. In her narrative, this pivotal episode fixes her working model of attachment for the remainder of her childhood and most of her adult years. She suggested that her father's failure may have been even more traumatic than her mother's death. From an attachment theory perspective, this would be so. If the child understands that an attachment figure is unable to be present (as in death), proximity is not sought. By contrast, when the attachment figure is physically present but neither emotionally nor even physically accessible, the attachment system is both activated and thwarted. This kind of episode becomes the prototype for a working model of insecure attachment.

Because of their religious beliefs, family members deliberately did not respond to pain or distress—their own or their children's. However, it is exactly those times of pain and distress that activate the attachment system. Ann discovered that attachment-seeking actually caused caregivers to be less responsive, and that attachment needs, once activated, were most likely to be frustrated.

Ann's description of her life inside and outside the house conveys the feelings that underlie the internal working model of avoidant attachment. Inside the house, proximity did not bring comfort, prayer did not bring comfort, everyone was subdued, and death was "hideous . . . and available to me." In contrast, outside may not have brought comfort either, but there was action and distr-action, and few opportunities for the attachment system to activate. As Ann said, "Under the circumstances, I preferred neglect to attention. It was *fine*."

College, From the Longitudinal Archive

As she entered early adulthood, Ann maintained her preference for neglect over attention. As a research participant in college, her strategy was manifested in a vagueness, perhaps even a hint of indifference, about herself and her future plans. Only her personality inventory, which is designed to look beneath the surface, detected some of her actual complexity, conflict, and defense.

On questionnaires, Ann was careful. Her responses painted a pleasant picture and excluded a great deal. For example, asked to provide a thumbnail sketch of her mother and father, Ann made no mention of her actual mother or her mother's death. She wrote a sketch of her stepmother, not mentioning that it was not her mother. Here is the description she gave of her father:

> Very wise man who thinks clearly and deeply. Has a quick temper. Been through some trying experiences and shown real strength. Bogged down in the large aims of life (such) as his job and position, never financially terribly successful, but an excellent father, believing that children learn through understanding, not rigid discipline.

An English major, she was interested in dance and active in the campus Christian Science group. But her future plans were inchoate; she said that she expected to work after graduation, but was undecided about what kind of job to look for, and did not have expectations about how long she intended to work. On a checklist of choices regarding "marriage outlook," she checked "hope to marry at some indefinite time."

Her CPI profile reflected this pleasant surface but also revealed greater depth:

> The most conspicuous feature of this college profile is the high flexibility score; it suggests in this person a restless changeability, perhaps accompanied by feelings of conflict about competing ways of presenting herself in the world. On one hand, she is a responsible, optimistic, prudent person who is desirous of "making good" in rather conventional ways. At the same time, she appears individualistic, sophisticated, and motivated toward more original and innovative paths. Perhaps as a consequence, the profile reflects self-doubts, an introspective turn of mind, and a felt sense of uniqueness. She kept an open mind, a goal-directedness, and exercised a facility for adapting to a variety of social contexts.

Mobilizing some part of this constellation of traits, soon after graduation Ann adapted to the expectations for young middle-class women in the late 1950s, and "made good" on those conventional goals: She married her high school boyfriend, became a schoolteacher, worked as a secretary for her church, and soon was pregnant.

EARNING SECURE ATTACHMENT: ANN'S STORY OF CHANGE IN ADULTHOOD

Near its end, the Adult Attachment Interview asks, "How do you think your experiences in childhood affected your adult personality?" For most insecure respondents, the question yields a brief conceptual response. In contrast, Ann embarked on a new chapter of her narrative in which she told a story of transformation:

> [*Interviewer: In general, how do you think your experiences in childhood affected your adult personality?*] I think it lays the structure for your personality. Either you rebel against it, or you go with it—either way, it controls you. Or you do the very hard work of learning entirely new ways to turn some things around. I've done years of therapy, and I think all three of these things fit. Sometimes I'm doing just the opposite of what was done to me, and sometimes I'm doing exactly what went on, and sometimes I've learned a few new places.

"A Bone You Chew on All Your Life"

My fears of abandonment are just, have certainly, I guess that's the . . . Jung says there's a bone you chew on all your life, the same bone. I guess that's been my bone. It's certainly not an uncommon bone, but in many ways it's colored my friendships, and my expectations of people, and my fears and my anxieties, my insecurities: If you get too close to people, they may disappear. But I also think that I've healed myself of a lot of that.

I think that having my children has been the most healing thing that's ever happened to me [*touches eye with a tissue*]. Mmm. They're wonderful. I talked about the distance I have from people, and I used to wonder if I could ever really love anybody. People thought I was loving them, but I knew I wasn't, that something incredible was missing. But when my son was born, I just fell in love. He taught me how to love, and I taught him. I'm surprised at how emotional I am about this [*wipes her eyes*], but I don't know how I would be if I hadn't had children. He was an infant, under 2 years. We'd talk all the time, you know, babble babble babble. It wasn't that it didn't drive me crazy, and it wasn't that I didn't have a short temper. There were things I shouldn't have done at all. I'm not idealizing early motherhood; I don't think I'm actually very good with babies, but he opened my heart in the most profound way. That allowed me in some way to recover what I'd closed off when she died.

"It Became a Way to Understand What Love Is About"

And my daughter even more so—no, in addition to. And that became kind of the beam for "Okay, who do you really love? Who do you have a taint of that feeling for, that I have for my kids?" It became a way to understand what love is about. Even though it's different kinds of love, different kinds of people, you know, friends, lovers.

The whole parenting thing was greatly shaped by trying to re-do it, just not do it the same way. . . . I touched my kids a lot. I got that I wasn't touched, through therapy. So I reversed a whole lot of things. I think I married someone who was very much *not* like my father, in the sense that he was a very, very good father to young children and very loving. He's a very good father now, very gentle, and his touch is wonderful. He's good with animals. There are many reasons why he was intolerable for me, but my conscious reason for marrying him was that he would be a good father, and he has been.

"And That Opened the Whole Psychological World to Me"

When my daughter was 4, I began to have a lot of psychological difficulties and ended up in therapy. One of the things that came out of that, besides a difficult marriage, was that I was re-living my mother's death as my daughter approached the age that I was when she died. That parallel track was going on. So, for the first time at age 33, I really grieved her death . . . which was pretty late, and hard on my kids, but I just had to do that. And that opened up the whole world of psychological reality to me, once I broke through that denial in more than the top-level cognitive way. It shifted a whole lot of things. . . . There was a denial of her death in Christian Science, because life is immortal.

I did a whole lot of work, and then . . . I was done. I took a photograph of [my mother]—which I happened to have a duplicate of [*laughs*]—it was in a heavy metal frame, and I took it to the edge of the pier, and I dropped it in and watched her face just go down to the bottom of the ocean. And it was so wonderful, it was *so* wonderful. [I was saying to myself] "That's done, and I can now reclaim those parts of myself!" You know, I am talking about 3 or 4 years of work [*deep sigh*].

[*Interviewer: Is there anything else you'd like to add about your mother's death and its effect on you?*] Feeling responsible for her death, because I wasn't able to pray good enough, was certainly the biggest piece. That's been hard. It's tainted my spiritual life in a lot of ways.

I was determined, once I understood that I was going through this breakdown, when my daughter was 4, that I was going to be there for my kids. And it was a great triumph for me when she turned 7. . . . I healed something. I had beat the family odds, because [my mother's] mother had [also] died when *she* turned 6.

I know I've parented from my own need and my own neediness. I don't know who doesn't do some of that, and I think I've done a lot of that. But they're marvelous people. There's been a lot of healing. It's very moving to me. I'm just so grateful. I've been very fortunate to be able to do that.

INTERPRETING AND EXTENDING THE NARRATIVE
OF TRANSFORMATION IN ADULTHOOD

A person's working model of security rests on the confidence that "standing behind them, there are one or more trusted persons who will come to their aid should difficulties arise. The person trusted provides a secure base from which his [or her] companion can operate" (Bowlby, 1973, p. 359, cited in Bretherton & Munholland, 1999, p. 89). Lacking this assurance, the insecurely attached person adopts a pattern of thinking and acting that defends against this lack. Ann's style was avoidance, which led her to feel distant from others, dismissing of relationship. I believe this was what she meant when she said that she knew she was not able to love, that "something incredibly important was missing."

The Collision of Dismissing and Caregiving

Although Ann did many years of therapy, chose a caring husband, and built competence and confidence through her career, she attributed her transformation to the activation of the caregiving system: "I'm surprised at how emotional I am about this, but I don't know how I would be if I hadn't had children." This statement is consistent with the recognition by attachment theorists that the complementarity of the attachment and caregiver systems creates an avenue of reciprocal influence (George & Solomon, 1999).

Ann was also aware of the strong impact of her professional mentors, of her romantic partner, and of the feminist movement on her personal development and sense of fulfillment. Nonetheless, she recalled that it was through the experience of herself as committed wholeheartedly to be the secure base for her children that it became safe and rewarding to empathize with her children's attachment needs. Through her own behavior, she generated new expectations about what being in relationship can reliably provide, what the self can experience, and what the interpersonal world can be. As a result, her dismissive model of what people are like and how they can relate fell into question.

Although she wanted to give her children a very different childhood than her own, her narrative makes clear that the experiences that began her internal transformation did not take place through conscious planning. They took her by surprise, just as she was surprised to find herself weeping at the power of this redemptive turn (McAdams, 1993) in her story. Although her narrative is told in the past tense, she brings us into the present for a moment, as if the stage manager has walked on during the play, and draws us into the narrative, as listeners, in a new way. She tells us that she doesn't know how she would be if she didn't have children. She clearly believes that she would be as she had been—unable to fully feel connection with anyone, defended by that closed door through which no one else could enter, nor she depart.

Her caregiving experience was profound, and catalyzed change, but it did not complete the change. Ann said that one's experience in childhood "lays the structure of your personality. . . . Or you do the very hard work of learning entirely new ways to turn some things around." What was this "hard work," and when and where was it done? I have identified four areas—psychotherapy, parenting, marriage, and career—in which Ann found "entirely new ways to turn some things around."

Psychotherapy

The empathic connection with her children's attachment needs broke through Ann's defenses. Able to see the world through her daughter's eyes, she identified with her childhood self and became increasingly distressed as her daughter reached the age she had been when her mother fell terminally ill. During her years of psychotherapy, she experienced for the first time her anger and hurt at the loss of her caregiver and secure base, and her own vulnerability and longing for genuine connection and attunement. These recognitions moved her from the dismissive to the preoccupied attachment status.

In this new status, she could accept her attachment needs, and therefore, for the first time, generate the angry, painful protest that children make against separation and loss. Perhaps the reliable presence of an attentive therapist allowed her to know that her protest had been heard, held, and understood for the first time. Now aware of her needs and protest, she was in a position to rebuild her internal working model. I believe these are the parts of her psyche that emerged as she watched her mother's photograph drop from sight into the sea. As she said, "It was so wonderful. I can now reclaim those parts of myself!"

Parenting, From the Longitudinal Archive

From her narrative at age 61, it is clear that Ann began parenting afraid that she could not love, and one can infer what dread this must have brought. In 1963, however, when she was 27, her defenses were strongly mobilized. In response to a question that asked, "How did you feel and what were you like during the different periods of pregnancy? In personality were you pretty much the same as always or were you changed?" Ann wrote about physical changes. Noteworthy was the absence of feelings about becoming a mother. She said,

> First, I felt well, healthier than ever. There were no physical problems to mar life. If I got enough sleep, the emotional reactions of the early months, i.e. crying with little reason, etc., did not come up. . . . I felt more loving, radiantly beautiful than ever before. Physically, I *was* more beautiful. My complexion improved, my hair was shinier, superfluous hair stopped growing so I had no need to shave my legs.

Ann was not yet the person who could consciously acknowledge her fears about this life transition. However, she had entered that time when she unexpectedly fell in love with her first baby. When asked, "What have you found most gratifying about motherhood?" she revealed a glimpse of the experience that would break through her defenses. She said,

Don't feel I can adequately analyze this. I love watching an individual develop, trying to see life through a growing child's eyes. The natural good humor and joy of children makes them wonderful companions. I am far less lonely. The special kind of love you develop for a child, and their trust and faith in you is a priceless experience.

When Ann began by saying she couldn't "adequately analyze this" (an unusual way to respond), perhaps she was trying to say that there was something more that she could sense but not yet see and articulate. Nowhere else did she acknowledge any feelings of loneliness; these feelings are removed from conscious thought and self-description in someone with a dismissive attachment status. Perhaps the "priceless experience" of the reciprocal love between Ann and her children allowed her loneliness (her attachment needs) to move toward consciousness.

Writing at age 43, Ann tells us that the ensuing years were often difficult. Fearing the early death that befell her mother and maternal grandmother, Ann did the "very hard work" of psychotherapy necessary to turn that fear around by recognizing her separate self and its needs. Her husband was employed erratically; they were poor during these early years of parenthood. When Ann completed her psychotherapy, she reentered the workforce and was often the sole support for the family. As the marriage foundered, parenting was a pivotal concern. She recalled herself at age 34, when her children were 6 and 8:

> I tried to leave—walked out the door, and had terrific stomach pains. . . . The children were my main deterrent to leaving. I didn't feel I could work full-time as I was doing, and be a single parent. We needed each other for this task.

She was determined that, through the daily experience of parental availability, her children would know that they had "trusted people standing behind them." Although this was a gift to her children, it was also part of the "hard work" that she did to maintain her developing view of the potential for secure attachment. She and her husband continued to parent together. She was the steady source of financial support for the family for the next 5 years; her husband was often unemployed and the at-home parent. Her son had moved out and her daughter was 16 when Ann was asked (at age 43) about the impact that being a mother had on her. She responded, "[It has had the] single most important impact on me. Broadened my emotional/mental vision immeasurably."

The Couple Crucible, From the Longitudinal Archive

Ann was married for 23 years. Like all marriages, hers evolved in response to time and circumstances. In addition, as her internal working model of attachment began to change, Ann's experience of her marriage changed.

It had been important to choose a gentle, caring father for her children, and in those early days, the marriage brought her satisfaction. She wrote in 1963,

> It has oriented me to a broader . . . view of life, adding compassion and more scope. . . . I am less nervous, far more even tempered. I am more content to just live—exist and enjoy it—and do not always attempt to justify my actions in the light of some ideal. I am far more secure, loved and loving toward others.

Her personality profile allows a more complex view. It includes the greater evenness that Ann noted but adds the tension and conflict that might be expected as dismissive style and attachment needs collide. My interpretation of her profile read as follows:

> By 1964, she had married and devoted her energies to building a viable family structure. Like many young mothers, she had a new appreciation for stability and order. The unsettling feelings of uniqueness departed, and she was able to be more efficient. These seem to have been difficult years, necessitating some suppression of anger and impulse. While the wife and mother roles emphasize a communal outlook, the personality profile shows a growth in the need to achieve along independent lines, and increasing feelings of self-reliance.

From a 20-year perspective, Ann recalled that those early years encompassed the best aspects of her couple relationship: "Our times around parenting, kids, making a home, were *very, very* good." In other ways, the marriage was wanting. In therapy, after 9 years of marriage, she reports "the marriage was under terrific strain." At year 10, "I am nearly total support for family"; year 11, "totally exhausted . . . it's killing me." She returned to school and began a new career. Her husband too got a job. But in year 16 he was fired, and for the next 5 years, was intermittently employed, sometimes quitting jobs. At year 20 they began marriage counseling.

Ann wrote that marriage was "much harder" than she'd thought it would be. "I expected the man to be more security oriented, steady job, etc. I have had more responsibility than I dreamed of." Her husband was unable to establish himself as her adult attachment figure, to be "steady" and "security oriented" in an adult way, to be a "trusted other" on whom she could rely, to "come to her aid should difficulties arise." After psychotherapy, knowing she would (physically and psychologically) survive, and as her children got older and more independent, Ann became increasingly unhappy with her marriage partner.

This unhappiness, too, is part of the "very hard work." Ann was learning to want an age-appropriate secure attachment relationship (Crowell et al., 2002). At age 43, asked whether she felt changed as a result of difficult periods in the couple relationship, she responded,

Yes. More tough. More sure of my conflicts. Found myself through these conflicts. Slowly developed personal strength, but became poisonously bitter. It was the knowledge that I could not drop the bitterness and stay in the marriage that finally drove me out. . . . I tried to overcome this, but . . . it was only growing. I did not want to live the rest of my life with these feelings. I felt strong enough to make it on my own, so I left.

I believe that she was bitter because she finally understood that her husband did not have the qualities that could allow him to offer her the attachment security she now understood she longed for. By age 43, her internal working model had changed so drastically that she felt entitled to a trust-worthy, intimate, autonomous, and secure other. Her decision not to "live the rest of my life with these feelings" implies that she could now generate hope for a different life for herself; instead of feeling disappointed and pining for what she lacked, she could imagine having it. Asked in what ways the marriage was lacking, she wrote, "Intimacy. Deep personal connection." Asked whether, after divorce, she found herself reevaluating her ideas about relationships, she responded, "Only sure that I *wanted* an intimate relationship and was hungry for one."

The "Work" of Work, From the Longitudinal Archive

Change in the internal working model of attachment means a change in the self-concept as well. In her childhood narrative, Ann presented herself as a self-reliant young girl. In adulthood, however, as her defense started to unravel, Ann began to grapple with profound self-doubt. In 1963, asked to describe her strongest and weakest characteristics as a graduate student, she wrote, "My weakest was lack of confidence and ability to function under scrutiny as a student teacher. Strongest? It was a bad year. I was weak at everything."

The world of work offers opportunities to support the defensive self-concept of dismissive attachment, but also to challenge the self-concept of weakness and worried compliance associated with the preoccupied and disorganized/fearful attachment styles, as one acquires and manifests skills and is recognized as a sturdy, capable, and decisive person. Perhaps not coincidentally, 2 years after completing her therapy, once she could "reclaim those parts of myself," Ann went back to graduate school and began training for a new career.

At age 43, Ann noted the power of work-related experiences to shift her view of herself. When asked to describe four important people in her life, Ann included a professor "who strongly supported me . . . encouraged my training . . . found [a] job for me. But most of all, truly believed in my skills and abilities. Underlined those. Gave a necessary start to my sense of professional competence." Thus began the "hard work" in the area of work. Several years later, she accepted a challenging position (which she held until retirement). Looking back on this step at age 61, she recalled,

> When I first came . . . I intuitively and correctly felt that I wasn't strong enough, that it was going to be a *strong-minded* place. . . . I came in with some fear and trepidation and actually took myself back to therapy for a couple of months to get up my courage to take this job. Because I couldn't figure out why they hired me. . . . I was pretty intimidated about going there, so I came in humble and insecure. . . . Over the years, I came to feel and experience myself as very competent. I felt very good, and I got very confident.

Asked how she had changed most between her early 30s and 43, Ann said,

> Having a work life has been absolutely essential for change. As a result, I am sure of my competence and general effectiveness in the world, have a world "of my own," greater perspective, values shift—both more inner and more social–political.

At age 61, asked how her career goals had changed since age 40, she said, "Well, insofar as I finally got a few goals! I feel like I stumbled along in life and ended up doing things." As her new self-concept took hold in her internal working model, new possibilities opened up. Unhappy in her marriage for several years, it was only when her children were in their late teens and, as she said, "[when] I felt strong enough to make it on my own" that she left. Had work not afforded her that sense of effectiveness, would she have felt "strong enough"?

Asked to list her happiest years between ages 21 and 43, Ann includes two periods, each of 2 years duration, which she says were happy because of "recognition, encouragement professionally" and because "work is increasing my sense of competence." The second set of these "happy years" immediately preceded her divorce.

Her personality profile at age 43 detected several of these psychic gains as well as some ways that Ann's personality may have reflected her life transition and divorce experience:

> The present profile reflects the major reevaluation in which this woman is engaged. She appears to have withdrawn from many areas of interpersonal participation, and is holding her achievement needs in check at present. Her emphasis is on personal frankness and an insistence on being "her own person." Her level of insight has markedly developed, and less energy is being tapped by suppression of impulse. Even in the face of turmoil engendered by a radical life structure change, she is more genuinely accepting of self than at any previous testing.

LIVING IN A SECURE SELF:
ANN'S NARRATIVE ABOUT HER CURRENT LIFE

Ann concluded her story of transformation with appreciation for the opportunities to change (e.g., "It's very moving to me. I'm just so grateful. I've been very fortunate to be able to do that"). She then returned to the larger question—the impact of both the dismissive and the earned secure working models on her subjective experience of living. She said,

> I think [my childhood experience] put more emphasis than is intrinsic in my personality on emotional life. The last 10 years, I'm getting to exercise other parts of me. I think that my life has been unbalanced for who I innately am. . . . I'm beginning to feel like that balance is coming into play.
>
> I'm getting a cognitive strength that balances that incredible emotional life that is rich and vivid and there. And now, I am much more interested in [the hard sciences]. My mind is now more free! And it's yes! And I feel that's much more who I am. I have a lot more cognitive energy and curiosity than I have been able to get to for all these years. Fighting through that emotional stuff, I completed some things. I don't necessarily mean childhood things, because I don't know if we ever really complete that—but I mean raising kids, completing life tasks, has allowed me to be freer to use my mind. . . . Every once in a while, I think I've gone on a path that has been shaped way back, that may not have been my path if I hadn't had those particular experiences.

INTERPRETING AND EXTENDING ANN'S NARRATIVE
OF SECURE ATTACHMENT

Working within a new representational framework, Ann made many changes in the way she lived. She soon fell in love, and had been with her new partner, M., for 23 years. She continued working, but also returned to school and received her PhD at age 55.

The Multiple Meanings of Balance

A central theme in Ann's sense of secure attachment is that she had achieved a balance that had been disrupted. As she said, "I think that my life has been unbalanced for who I innately am. I'm beginning to feel like that balance is coming into play." Her subjective experience embodied what Holmes (1996) described:

> If intimacy and autonomy, like attachment and exploration, are reciprocally related, insecure attachment can be seen as an unbalancing of this reciprocity. The avoidant person . . . [is] detached but not autonomous. . . . The ambivalent individual is attached but cannot be intimate. . . .

Secure attachment provides a foundation for both intimacy and autonomy. (pp. 19–20)

Ann said that she was "getting a cognitive strength that balances that incredible emotional life." Several cognitive strengths are associated with secure attachment in adulthood: narrative coherence (Main & Goldwyn, 1984), metacognitive monitoring (Main, 1991), and the reflective self function (Fonagy, Steele, Steele, Moran, & Higgitt, 1991). These constructs partially overlap with aspects of ego strength such as object constancy, the observing ego, and the availability of a conflict-free sphere; they are negatively related to the use of defenses to edit unacceptable realities (Shapiro, 1965/1999) and to the use of dissociation to create a split between the ego and intolerable realities (Liotti, 1999).

From the Longitudinal Archive: Building a Life With a New Set of Blueprints

Ann's assessment of ways she was different, at 52, from her earlier self emphasized agency, self-acceptance, cognitive capacity, and joy. At 61, taking stock of her most valued accomplishments, Ann pointed to those domains—parenting, marriage, and career—where her hard work had brought about the changes described. Finally, data obtained at age 61 were used to describe Ann's current life.

Changes in the Self

At age 52, asked whether divorce had changed her, Ann said she felt "more confident, more in control, more *brave*, assertive, joyous!" Had her work changed its personal significance for her? "Yes. In 1985 I decided to finish a PhD and that meant a terrific overhaul of my professional identity and commitment. . . . I'm thinking better, more strongly, with great concentration and much pleasure and excitement."

In what ways had she changed since her early 40s?

[I am] less subservient, more direct and more risk-taking, able to appreciate friends, more politically aware, less religious. I am more sturdy and far less shamed. . . . It's all a process. The troubled times led to years of gradual shifts and integration. The troubles themselves just cracked open the tight systems. The actual perceptual changes took years.

Most Valued Accomplishments: The "Work"

When asked, at age 61, "What are your most valued accomplishments?" she said,

I've been an honorable and competent professional, and I value that a lot. My kids are the dearest accomplishment, but they're their own accomplishment. . . . I *really* value that I got out of a marriage and started

living with someone I really love. That was hard.[5] . . . It was a long process and it took a lot. So I'm pleased about that.

Pursuits and Key Relationships

At 61, Ann was phasing in retirement and was "much less stressed,
much more easy going." She was learning foreign languages, doing photography, involved in local politics, and often with her partner, family, and friends.

Asked how her relationships with her children had changed, she said,

> Oh! We like each other more. We do more together. I think it's deep-
> ened as they've grown. All three of us are very much out-door people, so
> we do more hikes together. . . . They've opened up my world amazingly.
> . . . And now they're both married and each of their partners like M. and
> me very much, and I like them. . . . They're enriching my life.

How would she describe her couple relationship? She chuckled lightly,
then said,

> At its best, playful. . . . Companionable, sensuous, deliciously comfort-
> ing, loyal, very individualistic. . . . M. opens up worlds for me. Having
> another perspective and viewpoint available and there, which is delight-
> ful to me. It's different from mine, and so it's like "Oh!" I like that part.
> . . . I think we really know how to trust each other, what areas to trust
> each other [in] and what areas we'll both goof up all the time, so the trust
> level has really deepened. And we've also been totally stalwart for each
> other at hard times . . . building a life with a new set of blueprints. . . . In
> the last 5 years I've felt infinitely happier and much more stable than I
> have in any other part of my life.

Ann's balance between emotion and cognition parallels the securely
attached child's ability to balance attachment and exploration, and the secure adult's balance of intimacy and autonomy. As Ann said, "My mind is
now free! And it's yes!"

CONTRIBUTIONS TO THE ATTACHMENT LITERATURE

This presentation of Ann's story contributes to the attachment literature in several ways. First, it brings the constructs and processes of attach-

---

[5]Ann's decision to live with someone she really loved was made additionally hard because her new
partner, M., was also a woman. As the relationship began, Ann was very concerned about
encountering homophobia, and especially worried whether her children could accept the relationship.
The revisions in Ann's self-concept and her worldview associated with a secure attachment status
seem to have enabled her to risk this change and carry it out successfully. Many factors influence a
life, and factors influencing Ann's life included the gain in authenticity she felt from coming out as a
lesbian and the ease and spaciousness that resulted from her transition from full-time employment at
age 61. Although this chapter focuses on processes central to attachment theory, I do not want to
imply that attachment theory is the only useful conceptual tool with which to comprehend this case,
or that attachment themes are the only important foci for the study of development.

ment theory to life; it reveals the cognitions, affects, and behaviors that make up insecure (dismissive) and secure attachment expressed in daily living. Because many research methods provide only statistics, the lived life is not visible there.

The clinical literature describes change in attachment patterns in the context of psychotherapy. However, Ann did not see therapy as the central change agent in her transformation. Instead, her story suggests that (although therapy surely helps) profound and positive psychological change can occur in the process of living.

Although there are many theoretical questions that the study of a single case cannot address, Ann's story provides attachment theorists with a map, showing where and how her attachment-related change was fostered. It depicts a change process in which, first, a viable context allows an emotional opening to be evoked by a new experience. Her defensive dismissing of attachment crumbles as she assumes the preoccupied attachment status—preoccupied with the pain, fear, vulnerability, and anger that have resulted from the chronic neglect of her attachment needs. She begins to be open to new thinking and experience, to rebuild her sense of self, and to revise her worldview to allow new possibilities. As possibilities become actualities, the texture of her life transforms, bringing the achievements associated with security of attachment.

Once begun, the change process entails a long period of strengthening the self. Ann's gradual and reciprocal increases in intimacy and autonomy were brought about through years of effort in the contexts of parenting, therapy, her marriage, and her career. Because of her participation in the longitudinal study, her work is visible; these are long-term processes that can be appreciated only through repeated sampling and multiple sources of data. Students of lives may want to recognize that changing the narrative takes time.

REFERENCES

Ainsworth, M., Blehar, M., Waters, E., & Wall, S. (1978). *Patterns of attachment: A psychological study of the strange situation.* Hillsdale, NJ: Erlbaum.

Block, J., with Haan, N. (1971). *Lives through time.* Berkeley, CA: Bancroft Books.

Bowlby, J. (1969). *Attachment.* London: Penguin.

Bowlby, J. (1973). *Loss.* London: Penguin.

Bowlby, J. (1988). *A secure base.* London: Routledge.

Bretherton, I., & Munholland, K. (1999). Internal working models in attachment relationships: A construct revisited. In J. Cassidy & P. Shaver (Eds.), *Handbook of attachment: Theory, research and clinical applications* (pp. 89–114). New York: Guilford Press.

Cassidy, J., & Shaver, P. (Eds.). (1999). *Handbook of attachment: Theory, research and clinical applications*. New York: Guilford Press.

Crowell, J., Treboux, D., Gao, Y., Fyffe, C., Pan, H., & Waters, E. (2002). Assessing secure base behavior in adulthood: Development of a measure, links to adult attachment representations, and relation to couples' communications and reports of relationships. *Developmental Psychology, 38*, 679–684.

Erikson, E. (1960). *Childhood and society*. New York: Norton.

Fonagy, P. (1999). Psychoanalytic theory from the viewpoint of attachment theory and research. In J. Cassidy & P. Shaver (Eds.), *Handbook of attachment: Theory, research and clinical applications* (pp. 595–624). New York: Guilford Press.

Fonagy, P., Steele, M., Steele, H., Moran, G., & Higgitt, A. (1991). The capacity for understanding mental states: The reflective self in parent and child and its significance for security of attachment. *Infant Mental Health Journal, 12*, 201–218.

George, C., Kaplan, N., & Main, M. (1985). *Adult attachment interview*. Unpublished manuscript, University of California, Berkeley.

George, C., & Solomon, J. (1999). Attachment and caregiving: The caregiving behavioral system. In J. Cassidy & P. Shaver (Eds.), *Handbook of attachment: Theory, research and clinical application* (pp. 649–670). New York: Guilford Press.

George, C., & West, M. (1999). Developmental vs. social personality models of adult attachment and mental ill health. *British Journal of Medical Psychology, 72*, 285–303.

Gergen, M. (1990). Finished at forty: Women's development within the patriarchy. *Psychology of Women Quarterly, 14*, 451–470.

Gough, H. G., & Bradley, P. (1996). *California psychological inventory manual*. Palo Alto, CA: Consulting Psychologists Press.

Helson, R., Mitchell, V., & Moane, G. (1984). Personality and patterns of adherence and non-adherence to the social clock. *Journal of Personality and Social Psychology, 46*, 1079–1096.

Helson, R., & Soto, C. J. (2005). Up and down in middle age: Monotonic and nonmonotonic changes in roles, status and personality. *Journal of Personality and Social Psychology, 89*, 194–204.

Holmes, J. (1996). *Attachment, intimacy, autonomy: Using attachment theory in adult psychotherapy*. Northvale, NJ: Jason Aronson.

Jordan, J. (1991). Empathy, mutuality and therapeutic change: Clinical implications of a relational model. In J. Jordan, A. Kaplan, J. B. Miller, I. Stiver, & J. Surrey, *Women's growth in connection* (pp. 283–290). New York: Guilford Press.

Klohnen, E., & John, O. (1998). Working models of attachment: A theory-based prototype approach. In J. Simpson & W. Rholes (Eds.), *Attachment theory and close relationships* (pp. 115–140). New York: Guilford Press.

Kraemer, G. (1992). A psychobiological theory of attachment. *Behavioral and Brain Sciences, 15*, 493–541.

Lieblich, A., Tuval-Mashiach, R., & Zilber, T. (1998). *Narrative research: Reading, analysis, and interpretation*. Thousand Oaks, CA: Sage.

Liotti, G. (1999). Disorganisation of attachment as a model for understanding disso-
ciative psychopathology. In J. Solomon & C. George (Eds.), *Attachment disorga-
nization* (pp. 291–317). New York: Guilford Press.

Loevinger, J. (1976). *Ego development.* San Francisco: Jossey-Bass.

Main, M. (1991). Metacognitive knowledge, metacognitive monitoring, and singular (coherent) vs. multiple (incoherent) models of attachment. In C. M. Parkes,
J. Stevenson-Hinde, & P. Marris (Eds.), *Attachment across the life cycle* (pp. 127–
159). London: Routledge.

Main, M., & Goldwyn, R. (1984). Adult attachment scoring and classification system. In M. Main (Ed.), *Systems for assessing attachment organization through discourse, behavior, and drawings.* New York: Cambridge University Press.

Main, M., & Hesse, E. (1990). Parents' unresolved traumatic experiences are related
to infant disorganized attachment status: Is frightened and/or frightening parental behavior the linking mechanism? In M. Greenberg, D. Cicchetti, &
E. Cummings (Eds.), *Attachment in the preschool years* (pp. 161–182). Chicago:
University of Chicago Press.

Main, M., Kaplan, N., & Cassidy, J. (1985). Security in infancy, childhood and adulthood: A move to the level of representation. *Monographs of the Society for Research in Child Development, 50*(1/2), 66–104.

Main, M., & Solomon, J. (1986). Discovery of a new, insecure-disorganized/disori-
ented attachment pattern. In T. B. Brazelton & M. W. Yogman (Eds.), *Affective
development in infancy* (pp. 95–124). Norwood, NJ: Ablex Publishing.

McAdams, D. P. (1993). *The stories we live by: Personal myths and the making of the self.*
New York: Morrow.

Rothbart, J., & Shaver, P. (1994). Continuity of attachment across the life span. In
M. Sperling & W. Berman (Eds.), *Attachment in adults: Clinical and developmental perspectives* (pp. 31–71). New York: Guilford Press.

Shapiro, D. (1999). *Neurotic styles.* New York: Basic Books. (Original work published 1965)

Sroufe, L. A., Egeland, B., Carlson, E., & Collins, W. A. (2005). *The development of
the person: The Minnesota study of risk and adaptation from birth to adulthood.* New
York: Guilford Press.

Sroufe, L. A., & Fleeson, J. (1986). Attachment and the construction of relationships. In W. Hartup & Z. Rubin (Eds.), *Relationships and development* (pp. 51–
71). Hillsdale, NJ: Erlbaum.

Wallin, D. (2002, March). *Attachment and intersubjectivity in the healing relationship.*
Paper presented at R. Cassidy Seminars, Oakland, CA.

Waters, E., Merrick, S., Treboux, D., Crowell, J., & Albersheim, L. (2000). Attachment security in infancy and early adulthood: A twenty year longitudinal study.
Child Development, 71, 684–689.

6

TRANSITIONS IN THE PROCESS OF IDENTITY FORMATION AMONG JAPANESE FEMALE ADOLESCENTS: A RELATIONAL VIEWPOINT

KAZUMI SUGIMURA

Accepting the fact that the human environment is social, the *outerworld of the ego* is made up of the *egos of others* significant to it. They are significant because on many levels of crude or subtle communication my whole being perceives in them a hospitality for the way in which my inner world is ordered and includes them, which makes me, in turn, hospitable to the way they order their world and include me—a mutual affirmation, then, which can be depended upon to activate my being as I can be depended upon to activate theirs. (Erikson, 1968, p. 219)

This study is based on data from Sugimura (2003). Portions of the study were presented at the meeting of the Annual Conference of the Society for Research on Identity Formation (Sugimura, 2001c). This study was partially supported by Grants-in-Aid for Scientific Research from the Japan Society for the Promotion of Science, 10710069, 1998–1999, and 17530474, 2005. I am thankful to Drs. Ruthellen Josselson, Jean S. Phinney, Toshio Kuze, Takeshi Sugimura, and Shinichiro Sugimura and Professor Hidenori Kageyama for their insightful suggestions during different phases of this work and Kazuyo Takamura, Shinji Nagamine, and Masako Ushida for their research assistance.

Some unique features of the study presented in this chapter have been altered, masked, or deleted to conceal the identity of the participants.

Relational aspects of identity formation form the core of Erikson's (1968) theories about identity formation. However, such aspects have been overlooked in research that stresses adolescents' separation and autonomy. Marcia's identity status model (Marcia, 1966; Marcia, Waterman, Matteson, Archer, & Orlofsky, 1993) includes, for example, exploration and commitment within specific identity domains but pays little attention to how adolescents understand the involvement of other people in the decision-making process for commitment. This issue is particularly critical when one attempts to elaborate identity formation processes in detail, that is, how adolescents transcend all previous identifications, construct a newly integrated whole that is greater than the simple sum of its parts, and integrate one's internal core and those of others. Identity researchers have recently begun to investigate such identity development mechanisms (e.g., Bosma & Kunnen, 2001; Kerpelman, Pittman, & Lamke, 1997; Kroger, 2003). In this chapter I describe a recent study in which I examined identity formation mechanisms from a relational viewpoint.

Erikson described identity as awareness of sameness and continuity in one's existence and the recognition of one's sameness and continuity by others. From this point of view, the commitments made by an adolescent need to be accepted by others in society. Therefore, identity formation can be described as the process of internalizing the expectations, needs, and opinions of significant others while recognizing and expressing one's own needs and interests. To accomplish this goal, adolescents must resolve disagreements between their own and others' perspectives through mutual regulation between self and others (Sugimura, 1998).

In this chapter, I focus on the way adolescents recognize and coordinate perspectives, that is, the way they construct a representation of the relationship between their own perspective and others' perspectives in the identity formation process. I specifically focus on identity exploration and examine how adolescents use and incorporate others' perspectives—that is, opinions, expectations, needs, and worldviews—into their own decision-making process about important life choices. Although the concept of *others* has various implications, in this chapter *others* refer to significant others, such as parents, friends, and dating partners, who play direct and important roles in identity formation in adolescence.

LEVELS OF RELATEDNESS IN IDENTITY EXPLORATION

In a series of my studies of female late adolescents (Sugimura, 1997, 2001b), I formulated six levels of relatedness in identity exploration. I built up the concepts of those relatedness levels by integrating theoretical formulations and the data collected in my studies. Theoretical accounts that focus on the development of relational understandings indicate that adolescents' recognition of the relationship between their own and others' perspectives in identity exploration changes over time (e.g., Fischer, 1980; Kroger, 2004; Selman, 1980). Selman (1980) described the relative sophistication of the ways children and adolescents assert themselves to other people while maintaining intimate relationships with them. In his model, a shift from undifferentiated perspective-taking to differentiated and mutual perspective-taking underlies these sophisticated relationship skills. Adolescents learn to understand how the perspectives of self and others can be coordinated. Fischer and his colleagues (Fischer, 1980; Fischer & Kennedy, 1997; Mascolo, Fischer, & Neimeyer, 1999) created a framework to examine microprocesses of cognitive development that is also applicable to the development of the self. His model provides the sequence of the different forms of relations among representations (i.e., single sets, mappings, systems, and systems of systems). These models suggest that adolescents recognize and differentiate between their own and others' perspectives and then gradually coordinate these perspectives.

In light of these theoretical accounts, I examined interview data of Japanese female late adolescents to elaborate the concepts of relatedness levels using the constant comparative qualitative procedure (Glaser & Strauss, 1967). As a result, six levels of relatedness were formulated (see Sugimura, 1998, for details of the analysis).

Exhibit 6.1 shows the definition and example of each of the six levels of relatedness in identity exploration. These levels are ordered according to the relative sophistication of adolescents' recognition of the relationship between their own and others' perspectives in identity exploration. Adolescents in the lower levels of relatedness (Levels 1, 2, and 3) do not construct representations of the relationship between their own and others' perspectives, whereas adolescents in the higher levels of relatedness (Levels 4, 5, and 6) construct representations of the relationship between these perspectives. In addition, adolescents in Levels 5 and 6 construct two different representations of the relationship between their own and others' perspectives and experience conflicts in dealing with these two different representations.

In a 2-year longitudinal study with Japanese female late adolescents from junior to senior years of university (Sugimura, 2001a), significant progression to the higher levels of relatedness (Levels 4, 5, and 6) was observed in three domains—occupation, friendships, and dating—but such progression was not observed in the sex role domain. It was also found that two factors were mainly associated with these changes. Those factors were job seeking or decisions on careers, and changes in relationships with friends or dates. However, that study did not examine how these factors affected each other and what steps were identified in the transition from the lower to the higher levels of relatedness. The question about how adolescents construct a representation of the relationship between their own and others' perspectives still remains. Therefore, in this chapter I focus on intraindividual changes

EXHIBIT 6.1
Definition and Example of Each of the Six Levels of
Relatedness in Identity Exploration

Level	Definition and example
Level 1	This level refers to the process of identity exploration without a representation of the relationship between one's own and others' perspectives. Adolescents do not recognize their own and others' perspectives. **Example:** [*What sort of role did your parents play when you made a decision about the roles of men and women?*] "Influence . . . I can't think of any exactly . . . perhaps none." (Sex roles)
Level 2	This level refers to the process of identity exploration with a vague representation of the relationship between one's own and others' perspectives. Adolescents vaguely recognize their own and others' perspectives. They understand which persons are involved in the process to some extent but understand little about how such persons relate to their decisions regarding their life choices. **Example:** [*What people or experiences exert major influence on your ideas?*] "I think my best friend is, I just think so, because I often talk with my best friend about this topic." (Friendships)
Level 3	This level refers to the process of identity exploration in which adolescents make important life choice decisions through the influence of others. Adolescents copy others' perspectives. **Example:** [*What sort of role did your parents play when you made a decision about the roles of men and women?*] "Quite significantly. . . . I think my parents both represent ideal roles. . . . When I ask my parents what they think about my opinion on sex roles and if they agree with me, I always feel relieved." (Sex roles)
Level 4	This level refers to the process of identity exploration with a representation of the relationship between one's own and others' perspectives. Adolescents recognize and coordinate their own and others' perspectives. They understand which persons are involved in the process and how such persons relate to their decisions regarding their life choices. **Example:** [*How did you come to decide your plan for the future?*] "My mother happened to mention a particular occupation . . . which I thought might be suitable for me, then I decided to pursue it. . . . I felt I was absorbing various ideas from older students, people whom I became acquainted with through club activities, and so on. . . . Biases develop if only one person or one thing is highly valued, so I think my ideas are formed by listening to as many opinions as possible." (Occupation)
Level 5	This level refers to the process of identity exploration with two different representations of the relationship between one's own and others' perspectives. Adolescents compare and contrast one representation with the other and experience a discrepancy between the two representations. **Example:** [*Have you ever had a time when you questioned men's or women's roles?*] "My mother often says to me I am a girl, and I should act in that way. Even though I disagree, I am still struggling with it. . . . (Is it solved?) In order to live all by myself, it is necessary to be capable of doing housework, and I know it is, but simply, when I'm told 'because you are a girl,' I feel dissatisfied with that. However, somewhere in my mind, I sometimes consider myself to be incapable of doing housework even though I'm a girl. So, I feel like as if I'm tied down . . . no solution in particular." (Sex roles)

Level 6   This level refers to the process of identity exploration in which
           adolescents resolve a discrepancy between two different
           representations of the relationship between their own and others'
           perspectives. Adolescents integrate the two representations through
           mutual regulation between self and others.
           Example (Negotiation): [*What are the important things about how a
           friend should be?*] "At first I thought that 'best friend' meant someone
           who I could tell my troubles to at anytime, but I had a quarrel with my
           best friend. . . . We hadn't talked to each other about what we really
           thought. The atmosphere between us soured. . . . Then I expressed
           what I was thinking in words for the first time. . . . And when I did that,
           I realized that my friend did understand how I was feeling. So, for me,
           a friend means someone with whom I can speak candidly. . . . We
           solved it while we were talking about various things. . . . We argued
           with each other, cried, but then the bad feeling dissipated."
           (Friendships)
           Example (Intrapsychic Negotiation): [*What made you think about the
           issue of the roles of men and women?*] "First . . . I heard the speech
           given by one of my female teachers. She successfully combined
           child rearing with a career. . . . I thought it was up to me to formulate
           my own thoughts about this issue. . . . Because my mother had been
           a housewife, I had the belief that a mother should stay home for her
           children, but I felt that the teacher gave me the opportunity to change
           my thinking. . . . I think it might be acceptable to become a little bit
           more advanced than my mother's model. . . . I thought I should
           consider various factors, so, I have weighed those factors to acquire
           balance." (Sex roles)

and investigate mechanisms of transitions to Levels 4, 5, and 6 of the relatedness levels in identity exploration.

CULTURAL CONTEXT OF IDENTITY FORMATION
FOR JAPANESE WOMEN

Women show the features of relatedness in identity development more
clearly than do men (Gilligan, 1982; Josselson, 1994; Skoe, 1998). For women,
identity emerges from relationships with others. According to Josselson
(1996), "the vitality and creativity" of women's identity "derive from and are
expressed in the flow of connection" (p. 237). In addition to this, Japanese
culture is characterized as being interdependent (Markus & Kitayama, 1991).
Japanese women in particular have been strongly expected to maintain harmonious relationships with others (Kashiwagi, 1997; Moriya, 1994). Young
girls are socialized so that they can consider others' feelings and attune themselves to others' wishes. These traditional expectations still remain in spite
of recent dramatic social and economic changes in Japan. However, for Japanese women, the options for life-courses and identity have been rapidly ex-
panding in the past 3 decades (Okamoto & Matsushita, 2002). This changing situation puts contemporary Japanese women in the crossroads between
traditional socialization forces that are exerted on relational issues and the

modern individualistic needs for achieving their own identity. Although female late adolescents in Japan, especially those university students who participated in this study, have been enjoying gender-free education, they may experience the potentially conflicting demands of maintaining a good relationship and of expressing their sense of self.

INTERVIEW DATA

Through narratives, an individual explores, finds, and ensures the purpose and consistency of his or her own life; thus, the narrated stories can be viewed as their own identity in which various elements of the self in different contexts and at different times are integrated in a meaningful way into a wholeness (McAdams, 1997). Carefully prepared questions about relational aspects of identity formation were asked with the intention of encouraging each female participant to create and tell her story about how she coordinates her own and others' perspectives.

Sample

The sample for this study consisted of 15 Japanese female late adolescents who were selected from 31 participants in a 2-year longitudinal study on identity formation (Sugimura, 2001a). The participants were 20 to 21 years old at the beginning of the study and were juniors from the Department of Education and Educational Psychology at a national 4-year university in Japan. They were unmarried and from two-parent families and had at least one sibling. The social status of participants' parents was upper middle class. I selected university students to represent late adolescence even though members of this age group are considered to be young adults in Western cultures. In Japan, they are categorized as late adolescents because of their lifestyles and psychological characteristics (Cabinet Office, 2005). They were interviewed three times up to age 22 or 23: the first semester as juniors before they began job seeking (Time 1), the first semester as seniors during job seeking (Time 2), and the last semester as seniors after job seeking (Time 3). Japanese college students usually come under strong pressure to find a job by the end of the 3rd year or the beginning of the 4th year of college. Therefore, the timing for interviews in the present study is particularly appropriate for the study of identity formation.

The following three criteria were used to select the sample from the 31 participants for the study: (a) those women who moved into Level 4 from the lower levels at Time 2 and remained in Level 4 at Time 3 ($n = 9$), (b) those women who moved into Level 5 from the lower levels at Times 2 or 3 ($n = 6$), and (c) those women who moved into Level 6 from the lower levels at Times 2 or 3 ($n = 5$), in at least one of the four identity domains. Five of these women came under two of the three criteria; thus, the total number of participants was 15.

Measurements

I expanded the Ego Identity Interview (Grotevant & Cooper, 1981) to include questions about relationships. The four domains of occupation, friendships, dating, and sex roles were chosen from the Ego Identity Interview because these were assumed to be important life areas among Japanese late adolescents. For each of those four domains, I added two sorts of questions aimed (a) to identify persons involved in the identity exploration process and their function in the process and (b) to probe the contents of the regulation between one's own and others' perspectives in the exploration process, if the regulation appeared in the participants' responses. Examples of those interview questions were presented in Sugimura (2001b). As the interviewer, and a female, I paid attention and tried to understand the whole picture of a participant's relational understandings in the exploration process for each identity domain. Whenever a participant made an articulate response that was not sufficient to determine a relatedness level, I asked her to give an example of the interaction between her and others in her own decision-making process so that she could explicitly elaborate her response, or further probed her recognition of others who were involved in the process, without asking any leading questions. I used the expanded Ego Identity Interview at all three interview points. At Times 2 and 3, the participants were also asked the reasons for the level change, if it seemed to have occurred. Each interview lasted between 1 and 3 hours, and each participant had three interviews in total.

The levels of relatedness in each domain were coded separately because, according to the focal model of adolescent development, the development of identity may or may not proceed at the same rate in different domains (Coleman, 1974; Grotevant & Cooper, 1981; Kroger, 1988). It is assumed that an individual functions at different relatedness levels in different identity domains although that person may have a basic capacity of social cognition that underlies different levels across domains. The relatedness levels are constructed by the interaction between a person and the environment. To assess the interrater reliability for the levels, a second rater (a male research assistant) independently coded 30 interviews (i.e., 10 interviews for each of the three interview points) selected at random. The rates of agreement were 80.0% for occupation, 90.0% for friendships, 73.3% for dating, and 70.0% for sex roles.

Procedure

To invite participants to the study, the author went to their class and extended a public invitation to the study at Time 1; those participants were informed of interview appointments by letter at Times 2 and 3. They were contacted by telephone a few weeks later to confirm participation and schedule an interview. They were interviewed individually at a laboratory in the department. At the beginning of the interview, the list of questions was provided to ensure their understanding of the items. For the questions about people involved in the identity exploration process, a list of people (i.e., mother, father, siblings, uncle and aunt, same-sex friends, opposite-sex friends, dates, school seniors, teachers, and others) was also shown to help them recall significant others. The interviews were tape-recorded and transcribed with the participants' names omitted.

Data Analysis

Each of those 15 women's interview transcripts was first analyzed individually, with a focus on the narratives that were offered at the interview point when a level changed but also with reference to the narratives that were created in other interview points. Each interview was read several times; triggers for level change, including specific events or internal changes, were marked, and how those women experienced the level change was highlighted. To abstract common features from the narratives, I then looked for similarities among the participants' own understandings and interpretations about the following points:

- For the transition to Level 4, the way those women recognized their own and others' perspectives and then the way they coordinated them into a representation of the relationship between their own and others' perspectives were examined.
- For the transition to Level 5, the way those women constructed a new representation of the relationship between their own and others' perspectives, which was incompatible with an existing representation of the relationship, was examined. The conflict between those two representations was also described.
- For the transition to Level 6, the way those women integrated an existing and a new representation of the relationship into a more complex representation was examined. Here, I tried to identify two types of integration, namely, "negotiation with others" and "intrapsychic negotiation between self and others," based on the findings in a pilot study (Sugimura, 1997).

MECHANISMS OF TRANSITIONS

The participants experienced their transitions to Levels 4, 5, and 6 through close encounters in daily life rather than through special events.

Although those transitions drastically changed their perspectives on important life choices, the transition process resulted from subtle swings between two different levels. In the following sections, I discuss similarities among the participants' narratives that implicate transitions to Levels 4, 5, and 6.

Constructing a Representation of the Relationship Between One's Own and Others' Perspectives: Transition to Level 4

Transition to Level 4 means that an individual recognizes and coordinates his or her own and others' perspectives. This transition was mainly triggered by the events that college youths experience in everyday life, such as the pressure of job seeking, changes in relationships with friends or dating partners, and course work in the university. When faced with these events, the women who moved into Level 4 first made meaning of their own or others' perspectives. Three slightly different stories for making meaning of perspectives were given by these women; I present one example from each story.

First, several of those women explained that they somewhat suddenly recognized their own or others' perspectives, which had probably existed but not been noticed until then. Typical descriptions were, for example, "I believe it was there before, but now I'm aware of it," "I feel it was . . . since the past," and "when I analyze rationally, I find. . . ."

Ayako, one of those women, exemplified this point well. At Time 1, she vaguely planned to be a counselor or something relevant to correctional institutions after graduation. Although she sometimes discussed these plans with her parents and friends, she stated that "They exert little influence over me." Thus, others' perspectives were unclear. At Time 2, she began serious consideration of occupational choices, and thus made the initial step to coordinate her own and her parents' perspectives. She first recognized her own perspective: that she was interested in a psychological position in the public service. This occupational option was based on her thought that she could make the best use of her major and aptitude in this occupational field. It is interesting that at the same time she was also beginning to recognize her parents' expectations about her occupation, which she had not noticed so far:

Interviewer: How did you decide to apply for a psychological position in the public service?

Ayako: I like psychology, and I want to make use of what I have learned. . . . When I wondered in which occupation my knowledge about psychology could come into play, I found a psychological position in the public service, and that's why it became one of the options. Then, the direction started to be obvious before my parents told me they wanted me to work for the government. . . .

> I felt they implied that, and I had to consider that. . . . Their feelings were that they wanted me to get a secure job.

Interviewer: What do you mean by "they implied that"? . . .

Ayako: Their auras waft and tell me they want me to get a well-secured job.

Her statements suggest that clarifying one's own perspective and clarifying others' perspectives are inseparably related to each other.

Ayako also elaborated on the process of constructing a representation of the relationship between her own and parents' perspectives. At Time 2, she emphasized that she fluctuated between the two perspectives:

Interviewer: What do you think about your parents' expectation?

Ayako: . . . It doesn't mean it is a heavy burden. But suppose if I select to be a government worker, it seems that I follow my parents' expectation, and that makes me feel frustrated. . . .

Interviewer: You have solved it somehow?

Ayako: I conclude that I should think about that when I pass, and that is out of my mind now. But I feel frustrated somehow. . . . I decide on my own, but when I think that my parents' wishes have been guiding me, then I wonder where my will is gone. I cannot tell the difference between what I do on my own, and what I do considering my parents' expectations; well, I cannot tell.

On the one hand, when she focused on her own perspective, she was sure that she decided her occupation on her own ("I decide on my own"). On the other hand, when she focused on her parents' perspectives, she felt as if she had deferred to parental wishes ("I wonder where my will is gone").

At Time 3, Ayako had passed the exam to become a psychology specialist in both the national and the local government and she had to decide between them. Her parents wished her to choose a local job and stay with them. However, she decided to become a national governmental official, which meant that she would live separately from her parents.

Ayako: I wanted to consider my parents' expectations if I could, but it's my life. Suppose if I had decided to follow my parents' expectation, and when something disagreeable occurs, that would provide me an excuse. So far, I made a choice that my parents would not feel ashamed of. From now on, it would be all right for me to do what I wanted. I decided to choose the opposite. . . .

Interviewer: How did you reach such solution?

Ayako: Suppose I remained here, meeting my parents' expectations, then it would be the same for marriage, whenever some big event arose, the same thing would occur. "We want you to do this, we want you to stay close." It would go on and on. But I cannot fulfill all of my parents' desires, so I thought I had to make my own decision at this point.

Interviewer: In the previous interview, you said, "It seems that I follow my parents' expectation and that makes me feel frustrated." But why do you think such feeling did not come up in this interview?

Ayako: My parents wanted me to work for a local government. But I decided to work for the national government, which gives me the feeling, "Can you beat it!" and I think my frustration is sublimated.

Ayako's narratives at Times 2 and 3 indicate that an individual fluctuates between one's own and others' perspectives immediately before those perspectives are coordinated. Through this process, she coordinated her own and her parents' perspectives and consolidated them into one decision while constructing a representation of the relationship—in her case, a more independent relationship with her parents.

Second, for other participants, actual separation or internal separation from significant others provoked them to begin to make meaning of perspectives. Eriko, for instance, reported that her exploration about future plans was facilitated by psychological separation from her father who had been influential in her consideration of occupational choices. At Time 1, she was interested in working in welfare facilities because her father was working in that area, and this interest was increased by his strong support: "My father gives me the opportunity . . . cheers me up . . . shares his knowledge with me . . . provides information, and helps me." She copied her father's perspective.

However, a change occurred by Time 2. Once Eriko was exposed to the pressure to start job seeking, she began to separate from her father's perspective and, at the same time, to recognize the perspectives of her friends at the university. The detachment from her father opened her to recognition of her friends' perspectives. Separation from familiar persons' perspectives may provide adolescents with internal space for obtaining new perspectives. She changed her future plan from something related to welfare to a position in private enterprises. In more specific terms, she first recognized her friends' perspectives and then elaborated her perspective through her friends' perspectives. Here, again, it was found that clarifying one's own perspective and clarifying others' perspectives are inseparably linked:

Before job hunting, everybody said, "Only one year remains" and then, those who are around me became frantic. . . . Now I think my friend exerts more influence. Because our life styles are similar, and our competence is almost at a similar level . . . while paying attention to my friend's actions, I thought I would be able to do something like that as well. . . . When I was talking about various things with my friend, and the friend suggested a job that I didn't know about, I thought it might be good to try.

It should be noted that Eriko had her own interpretation of why her father's influence decreased at this point:

Interviewer: Compared with the time when the previous interview was held, your father's role seems to have changed. What do you think exerted most influence upon such change?

Eriko: The time when I had to make a choice was approaching, my father . . . saw that I had started to apply for jobs. . . . I started to look in a direction that was different from that of my father, and my father might have thought [that] doing things while persisting in those in the past would not be good.

This excerpt implies that she had made meaning of her father's perspective, which had once been copied, as "other's" perspective. Taking both together, she constructed a representation of the relationship among her own, her friend's, and her father's perspectives.

Third, some participants illustrated how continuous interactions with significant others encouraged them to make meaning of their own and their significant others' perspectives and coordinate those perspectives. In close interactions with dating partners, those women faced new perspectives brought by their partners in the domain of dating. Although they were bewildered at the outset, they responded to the opinions of others. According to their descriptions, such as "gradually by deepening the relationship," "by interacting for a long time," and "by telling opinions to each other," their own and their partners' perspectives were clarified and coordinated step by step. Hitomi offers an example of this type of coordination.

At Time 1, Hitomi reported an ambiguous idea about dating based on what she had experienced in relationships with friends and others. However, at Time 2, she told a story about how her dating partner unexpectedly criticized her idea:

Interviewer: What do you expect from a dating partner? . . . .

Hitomi: I can be what I am—I can exactly express my feeling that I have at that time.

Interviewer: Has it changed since you started to go out with your dating partner?

Hitomi: Yes, I'm learning how to express myself, definitely, I think I have learned to do so.

Interviewer: How do you find yourself changing in that way?

Hitomi: At the beginning, I went out with him just like an ordinary friend, but he became upset. He told me, "You should express

yourself more." . . . My reply was "This is how I have been dealing with people."

Interviewer: What made you reply in that way?

Hitomi: I was shocked to be told such a thing, and I felt angry as well.

Interviewer: From that condition, how did you change yourself so that you could express your feeling exactly?

Hitomi: It took a tremendous amount of time to become what I am now, but . . . I started to be that way, as I went out more, and the opportunities for me to express myself gradually increased.

As illustrated in the narrative, her dating partner's perspective—that is, his criticism ("You should express yourself more")—brought her implicit perspective to light ("This is how I have been dealing with people"). Recognizing her own perspective, she gradually started to talk back to her partner and modify her dating attitude. As a result of these interactions with her partner and her own thinking about this issue, she formed a new idea: to "exactly express the feelings that I have at that time to a dating partner." This process of changing her ideas about dating can be viewed as the construction of a representation of the relationship between her own and her partner's perspectives.

In the transition to Level 4, each participant took actions to make meaning of her own or others' perspectives, and thus made the first step toward constructing a representation of the relationship between those two kinds of perspectives. Making meaning of her own (or others') perspective in turn illuminates others' (or her own) perspectives; and thus, the acts of clarifying her own and others' perspectives seem to conjoin with each other. This new recognition can be viewed as the progress from a vague worldview that lacks understanding of perspectives toward a clear worldview that is established by interpreting and making sense of perspectives about important choices for life—in some cases, as the process from meaning making based on identifications with significant others to meaning making of significant others' perspectives.

Kegan's (1982) model of the development of meaning-construction may provide theoretical accounts of these transformations. According to his model, change in the balance between self and other (or subject and object) facilitates the development of meaning construction, which allows an individual to interpret his or her life experiences in increasingly complex ways as he or she ages. In adolescence, individuals try to distance themselves from significant others' opinions in which they are embedded, make meaning of those opinions, and establish new relationships with those opinions. According to this notion, the women in the lower levels of relatedness (i.e., Levels 1, 2, and 3) were not capable of elaborating their own and others' perspectives because they were embedded in those perspectives. However, the women who moved to Level 4 could grasp them as they emerged from those perspectives in which they had been embedded, and understand such perspectives and objectively find the relations between them.

Also, some of the women who moved to Level 4 demonstrated a small but important step before coordinating perspectives; that is, after they clarified their own and others' perspectives, they fluctuated between the two perspectives. This fluctuation may be considered as a dialogue between the two perspectives within herself so that she can prepare to coordinate them.

Discrepancy Between Two Representations of the Relationship: Transition to Level 5

Once a representation of the relationship was constructed, the development of relatedness levels did not end for some participants. Changes toward more complex relational understandings were found, and these changes began with the recognition of the discrepancy between an existing and a new representation of the relationship between one's own and others' perspectives. Thus, these women constructed a new representation of the relationship that conflicted with an existing representation. The typical descriptions were expressed as "it was . . . in the past, but it started to . . ." and "I believed it was . . . , but I have found it is different." Those participants explained that significant others' acts that were incompatible with their own needs and interests mainly provoked them to construct new representations.

Kazuyo narrated the following story in the domain of occupation. At Time 1, she was interested in becoming a public official working with people with disabilities. She said that this plan was formed by integrating her own interest and her parents' expectation that their daughter should get a position in a well-established workplace, such as in public service or a major company. Thus, she had already constructed a representation of the relationship between her own and her parents' perspectives:

> Kazuyo: I'm interested in disabled people. I once thought of working at a facility which supports disabled people . . . but off days are not fixed, and I think it would be an extremely tough job. . . . [So] I think it would be good if I work for a government to serve disabled people, committing myself to policy making. . . . [Or] I think it would be better to work for a company or a government where I can properly take off on Saturdays and Sundays.

> Interviewer: What kind of expectation do your parents hold for you?

> Kazuyo: They say I should do whatever I want, but it seems that they want me to join a big company.

> Interviewer: How did you find it?

> Kazuyo: I might have accepted my parents' expectations exactly as they were. A big company has a hospital for its employees, for ex-

ample . . . provides various benefits. I want to keep on working after getting married and after giving birth, and I expect a big company provides satisfactory child-care leave.

At Time 2, Kazuyo changed her plan slightly, to getting a position in a general affairs department, where she would work with employees in a company rather than with people with disabilities. Yet, she was still exploring a compromise between her interest and parental wishes:

I haven't decided the type of business yet, but I'm thinking of some jobs at administration or human resources division; I want to support the employees who work there. Instead of finding something to do by myself, I think it might be more suitable for me to support others. . . . Long before, my mother told me, "For you, working at administration division would be suitable." Generally, companies seek for those who go ahead and do jobs, but I myself thought I wouldn't be able to do so. . . . So, when I had a personality test, . . . the result was as I had expected. Therefore, I thought, I was right. . . . I thought working at administration division would be suitable, and my mother's word made it sure and convinced me I was right.

Kazuyo's narrative, which represents the harmonious relationship between her own and parents' perspectives, was replaced with a different story at Time 3. Before this interview point, she actually got a job in a leading travel agency. Yet, her parents were disappointed with this decision and indicated that they did not view travel agencies as "well-established" companies. They wanted it to be Toyota Motor Corporation, which is one of the global companies in Japan. Here, all of a sudden, she faced the fact that the actual perspective of her parents differed from the perspective that she had assumed:

Kazuyo: So far, I was on a track that my parents said was "good, good," and I stayed on that track for a while. But then I changed my mind and took a different direction for the first time.

Interviewer: What do you mean?

Kazuyo: I decided to work for a travel agency, but it was not my parents' desire. . . . When an employment guarantee notice came from that travel agency, I immediately told that to my parents, expecting that they would be very pleased. But they were not at all pleased, which shocked me badly. I realized that they didn't think such a job was good. . . . I decided to work for the travel agency by myself, but at first, Saturdays and Sundays are not off days. . . . In addition, I feel anxious if I would not be able to spare time for myself because of busy schedules. . . . Whenever anxiety about my job arises, I think I should have joined Toyota as my parents advised me, and that makes me wonder whether I'm really doing the right thing. I wonder if I selected this job simply because I didn't give in to my parents' wish . . . but I know I feel excited about working for the travel agency in my mind . . . but I still vacillate.

The existing representation at Times 1 and 2 was characterized by the coordination of parental wishes and her interest. However, a new representation that emerges here is characterized by the coordination of her parents' disapproval and her deviation from parental wishes. Although she made a decision, she expressed insecure feelings about her future; thus, she seemed to waver between and was not capable of integrating those two representations into a whole, namely, a secure sense of occupational identity.

Miwa, another participant, reported an act by a significant other that was incompatible with her idea about friendships. At Times 1 and 2, she had already constructed a representation of the relationship between her own and her best friend's perspectives through continuous interactions with this friend. At Time 1, she explained how her best friend was important to her; for example, "the friend I met in my senior high school is slightly, rather significantly, different from other friends in the past" and "she plays an important role for me in my thinking about what I am." She also explained the process of forming her idea about friendships as follows:

Interviewer: What is the most important thing about how a friend should be?

Miwa: If she were my best friend . . . I could tell her what I think about her, and I would want her to tell me in the same way. . . .

Interviewer: What kind of role do you think your best friend plays in developing your idea about friendship?

Miwa: She told me whatever she wanted to tell me, even something I would . . . not tell if I were her, but she told me . . . [that] delighted me.

At Time 3, however, Miwa learned that her idea about friendship actually differed from that of her best friend. Then, she had to construct a new representation of the relationship, recognizing that her own perspective was completely different from that of her best friend:

The other day, I deliberated over what is important in a friendship. As the friend becomes closer, . . . I have a feeling I want to tell her negative things about her, even though the friend would be hurt. . . . So, I pointed out some negative things about my best friend, then that friend cried. . . . She said to me, "You usually don't talk that way to your best friend." That proved that her concept about friendship was totally different from mine. She said, "You are my best friend, but why do you put it badly in that way? A chum should never talk that way," that was her point. My point is different, and I think when we become closer, we can point out negative things more. That is what I experienced, and that is my concept. . . . I had believed that her thinking was the same as mine. [Because] she told me anything, and she advised me for everything when I conferred with her. She talked to me, and I talked to her. . . . But now . . . I learned it was not.

As shown in the preceding narrative, Miwa's familiar representation of the relationship was still rooted deeply in her mind. However, a new representation of the relationship was provoked at this point; this new representation consisted of her own perspective and her best friend's perspective, which was incompatible with her own. She attempted to resolve the conflict between the two representations through the mediation of another friend, but she failed to integrate them:

I expressed my opinions, and she told me her opinions. I was told by another friend that "your opinions are radically different, so you cannot resolve it, even if you discuss it." . . . I could not change her opinion any further. . . . I concluded in my mind that everybody has different opinions.

When constructing a new representation of the relationship in the transition to Level 5, the participants seemed to distance themselves from existing representations. If these women had remained embedded in the context of existing representations, they could have stayed in stable positions and had no need to construct new representations. However, their narratives show that the strong impact caused by significant others' acts forced them to step out of the context of their familiar representations. This process can be viewed as "decentration" (Kegan, 1982) from an existing representation; having different representations, the women clearly deliberated over their existing representations from the outside.

I inferred that those women fluctuated between the two representations, whether they explicitly demonstrated it or not. Although they understood both representations, they could not coordinate them. When they focused on their previous representations, they could not accept their new representations. Therefore, they did not tell stories about how they regulated those two different representations, but rather they told stories about what they experienced and how they endured this unstable and distressing situation. For these women, the relations between the two conflicting representations were yet to be rationalized or interpreted. In this transitional step these women were approaching integration of the two representations.

Integrating Two Representations of the Relationship: Transition to Level 6

For some of these women, once the discrepancy between two representations of the relationship was recognized, they began the process of reducing the discrepancy. The mutual regulation between self and others at Level 6 could be viewed as the act of coordinating two representations. As expected, two types of coordination were found: negotiating with significant others and intrapsychic negotiation between self and others. These women elaborated the process of regulation between the two representations.

Two of the five participants who moved up to Level 6 negotiated with their significant others. Nobuko, for example, negotiated with her dating partner about the idea of dating. At Time 1, she linked her own and her partner's perspectives superficially. In fact, she reported that her idea about dating—that is, being able to talk frankly with each other—was formulated because "my boyfriend urged me, 'please tell me everything,'" so she thought it was important that they openly tell each other everything.

At Time 2, Nobuko elaborated how her idea about dating was formed through continuous interaction with her partner. Thus, she constructed a representation of the relationship between her own and her partner's perspectives:

> I think he also restrained himself from telling me about the things he doesn't like. . . . After dating for a year, he started to tell me such things. . . . I also found myself telling him about the things I don't like. . . . He started to learn what I really felt when I told him about these things.

At Time 3, Nobuko experienced an event that caused her to construct a different representation. She had taken him into her confidence on the basis of "being able to talk frankly to each other." However, her partner disclosed confidential information to one of his friends. As a result, she constructed a representation different from the previous one:

> Step by step . . . we started to express exactly what we thought to each other. . . . [Then, I realized that] his character seems to be completely opposite from mine. . . . I found, in many cases, what I want him to keep absolutely secret from others was not particularly important for him.

Nobuko was upset by his unexpected behavior at first. However, this conflict was resolved after she protested to her partner and he discussed this issue honestly with her. From this experience, she learned an effective way of integration—that is, she negotiated with her partner without hesitation:

> When I told him politely, "Please do not tell that to others," he showed very deep remorse. . . . In this way . . . I learned how to change his attitude, [and since then] . . . I became less careful and started to speak "loud" and do whatever I wanted.

The remaining three women who moved to Level 6 integrated the two representations of the relationship intrapsychically rather than directly negotiating with others. Tomoko, one of these three women, had already reported two different representations in sex roles at Time 1. In one representation, she clarified her idea about sex roles by coordinating her parents' liberated way of dealing with housework and her own future plan, that is, to be a schoolteacher and continue working after marriage. However, she also constructed another representation by coordinating her own and her elder brother's perspectives. He worked in a private company and believed that it would be impossible for women to continue working in the male-dominant business society in Japan. Although she opposed his view, she understood the issue he raised. She fluctuated between these two contradicting representations:

> I have conflicts with my brother; he expresses his opinions as a man, and I express my opinions as a woman, and something like this happens. . . . Listening to my brother's opinion from a man's viewpoint, I think, "Ah, I see." I was offended at that time, but I thought, "Well, that may be true" . . . and some kind of compromise arose. I started to think, even though a woman joins a company for a career, but because of child care and marriage, many of these women reluctantly quit working or, in other words, quit working even though they want to keep on working. I might be like that. . . . [Listening to what my brother says, women having a disadvantage in the society] cannot be helped, but if we keep on saying so, the society itself doesn't change, so what shall I do? This is what I feel. . . . I can't find a solution.

In the narrative recorded at Time 2, the process by which Tomoko actively integrated those two representations was revealed. This process was part of her serious consideration of her future plans. She explored how she should deal with men's and women's roles in the family to continue working. She had discussed this issue with her elder brother and tried to integrate the two representations:

> Talking with my brother. . . . Even though I want to keep on working, but when I find my true love, and suppose if that person that I want to marry is a corporate employee just like my brother. . . . I wonder what I would do. If I became a teacher, which I have longed for since my childhood, and if I weighed the marriage and my career as a teacher in the scales, which side would I lean toward? . . . I asked myself.

In this narrative, Tomoko described that she was coordinating the two representations by "weigh[ing] . . . the scales" in her mind after the discussion with her brother. She achieved integration in the way that she chose liberated sex roles although she understood traditional sex roles: "I don't know which would be better for women in general [but] . . . when I think about myself . . . getting a job is more important than getting married."

The three stories of these women who integrated two representations by intrapsychic negotiation share a common characteristic in that they tried to discuss the issue directly with others before they coordinated the two representations intrapsychically. In fact, as can be seen in Tomoko's narrative, she talked with her elder brother before integrating the two representations in her mind. She also reported a similar method of integration regarding her occupation at Time 3. She planned to be a schoolteacher by coordinating her own and her mother's perspectives. Yet, because she failed the qualification examination, she planned to become a part-time teacher while studying for the examination the following year. However, her mother and elder brother opposed this plan and told her to focus on studying for the examination. Here, she constructed another representation by coordinating her mother's and brother's wishes and her rejection of their positions. Then, she began to resolve the conflict:

Interviewer: How did you solve the problem?

Tomoko: Quite carefully, I might have deliberated in my mind. When I talked with my brother, I told him what I had thought, and then I reviewed in my mind.

It should be noted that Tomoko stated, "I told him what I had thought, and then I reviewed in my mind." Although she could not resolve the conflict by discussion with her brother, this discussion might have led to her later consideration that enabled her to integrate the two representations. She decided to concentrate on studying, not working as a part-time teacher, because she understood that it would be a faster way to pass the qualification examination.

Yukiko, another study participant, also explained why she chose intrapsychic examination instead of negotiation; she refrained from negotiating with her father, whose traditional view on sex roles was incompatible with her liberated view. At Time 1, she reported only her emotional confusion and hatred for her father. At Time 2, however, she clearly recognized two distinct representations. On the one hand, she was exposed to a progressive view about sex roles through course work at the university. She constructed a representation of the relationship between her father's traditional view and her opposition to it. On the other hand, she came to understand her father's traditional view through her experience of job seeking, even though she often quarreled with him over this issue. Then, she began to integrate the views:

Interviewer: Was this discrepancy solved somehow?

Yukiko: During job hunting . . . I saw various companies, including small- and medium-sized companies. My father works in a company to earn and provide for his family. I realized how tough that is. . . . I believe that is what I may have learned. . . . Due to the recession, a mid-sized company may go out of business even now, [my father is working in such circumstances and] the work completely and fully occupies his head. . . . When that is considered, I could say nothing, because my father must be doing his very best. . . . I couldn't say anything to my father at that time.

This narrative suggests that Yukiko tried to negotiate with her father but hesitated to do so because she empathized with his feeling. Eventually she coordinated the two representations intrapsychically. The following statements at Time 2 indicate how she dealt with the two conflicting representations:

> What a job means, what working means . . . [through my job-hunting activity] I understand to some degree. I think I respect my father to some degree. . . . But I don't want to marry someone like him. . . . I love my father, I do respect my father, and from my father I inherit good stuff. However, if I would marry someone like my father, I wouldn't be happy.

These statements may indicate that Yukiko constructed a more complex representation of the relationship with her father in which she learned "to live with unresolvable conflict while still sustaining connection" (Josselson, 1994, p. 101). She understood the reason for her father's traditional view even though she opposed it; she refrained from protesting against her father, but she decided to choose a partner with liberated views on sex roles.

Transition to Level 6 involves the integration of two conflicting representations of the relationship between one's own and others' perspectives. The women who moved to Level 6 did not ignore these conflicting representations; rather they regarded them as an important part of their decision-making about life choices and dealt with them. Two methods of integration were found: namely, negotiation with others and intrapsychic negotiation between self and others. In these ways, the women gradually coordinated two conflicting representations.

Negotiation is a direct regulation between self and others. According to the research on interpersonal conflicts (Selman, Beardslee, Schultz, Krupa, & Podorefsky, 1986; Yeates, Schultz, & Selman, 1991), the negotiation strategy can be viewed as an effective tool for resolving conflicts in adolescent close relationships. In fact, the participants who indicated that they used negotiation as their approach found sufficient compromises between the two representations. However, not all the participants who moved to Level 6 achieved compromises through negotiation. Some participants explained that they once tried to negotiate with others but in the end they coordinated two representations intrapsychically for certain reasons. They clearly acknowledged that other people are involved in their own identity formation process, but they also understood that these people do not always attune themselves to their perspectives. Nevertheless, these women sought ways to construct a more complex representation of relationship that accommodates conflicting representations; they chose intrapsychic negotiation. Only the internal dialogue between two representations may work as a tool for coordination in such a situation.

Because some of those women, such as Yukiko, seem to live with contradictions without pushing themselves to resolve those contradictions, one may question whether this response may indicate one type of integration. However, according to Erikson (1968), the wholeness of identity allows various, even contradicting elements of the self to exist together. The ego's synthesizing function implies not only the integration of harmonious elements but also the dialectical integration of contradicting elements. Therefore, living with contradicting representations of relationship can also be viewed as a form of integration.

CONCLUSIONS

Concepts of different relatedness levels in identity exploration proved useful to understand how the participants recognized and coordinated their own and others' perspectives in the identity formation process. When the focus is on the transitions to the relatedness levels of 4, 5, and 6, identity formation can be described as a shift from meaning making based on significant others' perspectives or indistinct perspectives to meaning making of others' (or one's own) perspectives in making important life choices. Clarifying one's own and others' perspectives enabled the women to understand how those perspectives relate to each other and then construct a representation of the relationship between their own and others' perspectives. Likewise, further progression to construct a more complex representation of relationship can be explained by a similar mechanism; that is, the women emerged from the representations in which they had been embedded and made meaning of the representations. An individual's act of meaning making continuously promotes the processes of transitions to Levels 4, 5, and 6. This mechanism is consistent with Kegan's notion of gradual increase of self and other (or subject and object) differentiation.

These findings elaborate on Erikson's account of identity formation—that is, the process of transcending all previous identifications to construct a new whole that is greater than the simple sum of its parts. Thus, a series of transformations of meaning construction underlies this process; adolescents step out of a framework in which they are embedded and become aware of their own framework. Furthermore, they find ways of coordinating identity elements (i.e., perspectives or representations) beyond recognizing each of the elements. Experiencing wholeness by progressively synthesizing identity elements is also the core process of identity formation. In comparison with Marcia's model, the relatedness-level concept helps capture various dimensions of relatedness in identity formation more closely.

The other implication of this study is that the results contain some identity formation and relatedness characteristics that are specific to women in the Japanese cultural context. Although this topic was not a main purpose of this study, I want to point out two issues found in the female participants' narratives about transitions in the levels of relatedness. First, as shown in the case descriptions, several participants described the process of coordinating their own and others' perspectives as making a compromise between their own needs and parental wishes, especially in occupational domain. Despite the fact that their parents did not overtly express opinions, those women tried to consider the feelings and wishes of their parents. This process is different from identifications with their parents because they acknowledged and elaborated the process of coordination between both perspectives. For Japanese adolescents (both male and female), trusting their parents' expectations in their future plan is an indicator not of obedience but of a good relationship with their parents (Stevenson & Zusho, 2002). Hence, this feature of parent–adolescent relationship in Japan may be reflected in the content of perspectives and representations.

Second, in the transition to Level 6, the main way to regulate the representations of the relationship was intrapsychic negotiation rather than actual negotiation. This result may reflect relatedness characteristics that are specific to the Japanese culture. In Japanese culture, individuals are expected from childhood to recognize and attune themselves to the expectations of others (Rothbaum, Pott, Azuma, Miyake, & Weisz, 2000). Japanese women in particular are expected to maintain harmony with others (Kashiwagi, 1997; Moriya, 1994). Avoiding direct confrontation with others may be viewed as preferable behavior in conflict resolution. Therefore, Japanese women may tend to choose intrapsychic negotiation rather than actual negotiation with others in identity exploration. These women are embedded in the cultural context of identity formation whether they are aware of it or not.

In conclusion, the relatedness-level concept in identity exploration helps capture relational aspects of identity formation while allowing researchers to pay attention to identity formation for women and in cultural contexts. All these issues were not emphasized much in previous identity research. Therefore, although the concept and results of this study are exploratory and preliminary, this concept of relatedness-level classification in identity exploration adds to an understanding of how relationships between self and other are interwoven into the wholeness of identity.

REFERENCES

Bosma, H. A., & Kunnen, E. S. (2001). Determinants and mechanisms in ego identity development: A review and synthesis. *Developmental Review, 21*, 39–66.

Cabinet Office. (2005). *Seishounen hakusho* [White paper on youth 2005 in Japan]. Tokyo: National Printing Bureau.

Coleman, J. C. (1974). *Relationships in adolescence.* London: Routledge & Kegan Paul.

Erikson, E. H. (1968). *Identity: Youth and crisis.* New York: Norton.

Fischer, K. W. (1980). A theory of cognitive development: The control and construction of hierarchies of skills. *Psychological Review, 87*, 477–531.

Fischer, K. W., & Kennedy, B. P. (1997). Tools for analyzing the many shapes of development: The case of self-in-relationships in Korea. In E. Amsel & K. A. Renninger (Eds.), *Change and development: Issues of theory, method, and application* (pp. 117–152). Mahwah, NJ: Erlbaum.

Gilligan, C. (1982). *In a different voice: Psychological theory and women's development*. Cambridge, MA: Harvard University Press.

Glaser, B. G., & Strauss, A. L. (1967). *The discovery of grounded theory: Strategies for qualitative research*. Chicago: Aldine.

Grotevant, H. D., & Cooper, C. R. (1981). Assessing adolescent identity in the areas of occupation, religion, politics, friendships, dating, and sex roles: Manual for administration and coding of the interview (Manuscript No. 2295). *JSAS Catalog of Selected Documents in Psychology, 11*(52).

Josselson, R. (1994). Identity and relatedness in the life cycle. In H. A. Bosma, T. L. G. Graafsma, H. D. Grotevant, & D. J. de Levita (Eds.), *Identity and development: An interdisciplinary approach* (pp. 81–102). Thousand Oaks, CA: Sage.

Josselson, R. (1996). *Revising herself: The story of women's identity from college to midlife*. New York: Oxford University Press.

Kashiwagi, K. (1997). Koudou to kanjyou no jikoseigyokinou no hattatsu: Ikujibunka tono kanren de [Development of self-regulation in behavior and emotion: In relation to childrearing culture]. In K. Kashiwagi, S. Kitayama, & H. Azuma (Eds.), *Bunka shinrigaku: Riron to jisshou* (pp. 180–197). Tokyo: University of Tokyo Press.

Kegan, R. (1982). *The evolving self: Problem and process in human development*. Cambridge, MA: Harvard University Press.

Kerpelman, J. L., Pittman, J. F., & Lamke, L. K. (1997). Toward a microprocess perspective on adolescent identity development: An identity control theory approach. *Journal of Adolescent Research, 12*, 325–346.

Kroger, J. (1988). A longitudinal study of ego identity status interview domains. *Journal of Adolescence, 11*, 49–64.

Kroger, J. (2003). What transits in an identity status transition? *Identity: An International Journal of Theory and Research, 3*, 197–220.

Kroger, J. (2004). *Identity in adolescence: The balance between self and other* (3rd ed.). London: Routledge.

Marcia, J. E. (1966). Development and validation of ego-identity status. *Journal of Personality and Social Psychology, 3*, 551–558.

Marcia, J. E., Waterman, A. S., Matteson, D. R., Archer, S. L., & Orlofsky, J. L. (Eds.). (1993). *Ego identity: A handbook for psychosocial research*. New York: Springer-Verlag.

Markus, H. R., & Kitayama, S. (1991). Culture and the self: Implications for cognition, emotion, and motivation. *Psychological Review, 98*, 224–253.

Mascolo, M. F., Fischer, K. W., & Neimeyer, R. A. (1999). The dynamic codevelopment of intentionality, self, and social relations. In J. Brandstädter

& R. M. Lerner (Eds.), *Action and self-development: Theory and research through the life span* (pp. 133–166). Thousand Oaks, CA: Sage.

McAdams, D. P. (1997). The case for unity in the (post)modern self: A modest proposal. In R. Ashmore & L. Jussim (Eds.), *Self and identity: Fundamental issues* (pp. 46–78). New York: Oxford University Press.

Moriya, K. (1994). *Kodomo to fantasy: Ehon niyoru kodomo no jiko no hakken* [Children and fantasies: A picture book and a child's self-discovery]. Tokyo: Shinyosha.

Okamoto, Y., & Matsushita, M. (Eds.). (2002). *Shin jyosei no tame no life-cycle shinrigaku* [New life-cycle-based psychology for women]. Tokyo: Fukumura Shuppan.

Rothbaum, F., Pott, M., Azuma, H., Miyake, K., & Weisz, J. (2000). The development of close relationships in Japan and the United States: Paths of symbolic harmony and generative tension. *Child Development, 71*, 1121–1142.

Selman, R. L. (1980). *The growth of interpersonal understanding: Developmental and clinical analyses*. New York: Academic Press.

Selman, R. L., Beardslee, W., Schultz, L. H., Krupa, M., & Podorefsky, D. (1986). Assessing adolescent interpersonal negotiation strategies: Toward the integration of structural and functional models. *Developmental Psychology, 22*, 450–459.

Skoe, E. E. (1998). The ethic of care: Issues in moral development. In E. E. Skoe & A. L. von der Lippe (Eds.), *Personality development in adolescence: A cross national and life span perspective* (pp. 143–171). London: Routledge.

Stevenson, H. W., & Zusho, A. (2002). Adolescence in China and Japan: Adapting to a changing environment. In B. B. Brown, R. W. Larson, & T. S. Saraswathi (Eds.), *The world's youth: Adolescence in eight regions of the globe* (pp. 141–170). New York: Cambridge University Press.

Sugimura, K. (1997). A preliminary study on identity exploration among female adolescents from a viewpoint of relatedness. *The Bulletin of Aichi Gakusen University, 32*, 305–313.

Sugimura, K. (1998). Seinenki ni okeru identity no hattatsu: Kankeisei no kanten kara no toraenaoshi [Identity formation and relatedness in adolescence]. *Japanese Journal of Developmental Psychology, 9*, 45–55.

Sugimura, K. (2001a). Kankeisei no kanten kara mita jyoshiseinen no identity tankyu: 2-nenkan no henka to sono youin [A longitudinal study of relatedness in identity formation of female adolescents]. *Japanese Journal of Developmental Psychology, 12*, 87–98.

Sugimura, K. (2001b). A preliminary study of proposed levels of relatedness in identity exploration among female late adolescents in Japan. *Psychological Reports, 88*, 749–758.

Sugimura, K. (2001c, May). *Transition in the levels of relatedness in identity exploration.* Poster presented at the Eighth Annual Conference of the Society for Research on Identity Formation, London, Ontario, Canada.

Sugimura, K. (2003). *Identity exploration among female adolescents from a relational viewpoint: A two-year longitudinal study.* Unpublished doctoral dissertation, Nagoya University, Nagoya, Japan.

Yeates, K. O., Schultz, L. H., & Selman, R. L. (1991). The development of interpersonal negotiation strategies in thought and action: A social-cognitive link to behavioral adjustment and social status. *Merrill-Palmer Quarterly, 37,* 369–406.

7

THE RELATIONAL EMPLOTMENT
OF MIXED RACIAL IDENTITY

BRIAN SCHIFF AND TRACIE O'NEILL

In this chapter, we inquire into the part that relationships play in orienting persons to the cultural resources for identity formation. In our research, we consider how young adults with parents of different racial backgrounds come to rewrite their racial identity, becoming biracial, multiracial, or mixed race. We study the personal narratives of biracial youth to understand how they talk about arriving at these new self-identifications. The personal narrative is an attempt to make sense of the self through time (Cohler, 1998) by organizing experience into an understandable story of the past, present, and future (Ricoeur, 1984). Through the workings of plot, the personal narrative configures the *me* into a story that conveys a sense of identity (McAdams, 1996).

Although the personal narrative is the individual's story, it is constructed out of the building blocks, the cultural resources, of the social world. These cultural resources are manifest in a variety of forms, including works of art, styles of dress, and conventions of social interaction. However, as Wertsch

---

Some unique features of the study presented in this chapter have been altered, masked, or deleted to conceal the identity of the participants.

(2002) observed, "identity resources" often travel through the medium of language or discourse; they are "textual resources" that are encountered in interactions with others and their products. Each social world presents diverse opportunities for encountering and appropriating identity resources.

Although our research was concerned with social relationships, we did not directly observe relationships in action but used interviews that recorded the person's impressions of the social world. We researched how social relationships are written into the world of storied action and the function they perform in identity stories.

Our argument can be summarized as follows: These narrated relationships play a central role in connecting persons with cultural resources; they help to configure our account of arriving at particular conceptions of selfhood operating in the cultural world. Relationships are the point of contact for encountering cultural meanings and introducing people to various possible avenues for being a person. Although relationships are not the only means of encountering culture, they are a powerful instrument for sharing meanings and validating, or invalidating, various identity resources. On the one hand, narrated relationships determine who has access to particular identities, policing the boundaries of identity through the enforcement of power and privilege. On the other hand, relationships provide the necessary support over time, the scaffolding, for integrating meanings into how people perceive the world and tell their identity stories (Holland, Lachicotte, Skinner, & Cain, 1998). Finally, narrated relationships are part of the argument in establishing identity claims. Persons establish their identity by positioning themselves vis-à-vis other characters in the story world (Davies & Harré, 1990). The entry into a new identity requires the rebalancing of one's relational world in a way that is in harmony with this emerging sense of self. Lest one appear incoherent, balance must be achieved between one's identity choices and one's relationships.

MIXED-RACE AMERICA

Our interest in the identity stories of biracial youth stems from the ambiguity of their racial identity. In the face of ambiguity, many details must be clarified so that experience can be defined and communicated to others. Biracial identity is doubly ambiguous. On the one hand, multiracial identity is a cultural construct for which the language is evolving. This cohort of mixed-race youth has been witness to a historical shift in the meaning of race and mixed-race identity. Recent scholarship has argued that although race is socially meaningful, it has no biological significance (see Graves, 2001). On the other hand, the physical appearance of biracial individuals is often ambiguous and challenges identification with a single race, leaving open numerous options for self-identification.

Biracial, multiracial, and *mixed race* are emerging cultural resources for describing racial identity that are not yet fixed in American discourse. The terms connote a positive self-image; persons of mixed race have become fashionable in popular media (Williams-Leon & Nakashima, 2001). This cultural shift is a very recent development in the construction of a mixed-race collective identity (Daniel, 2002). In 1967, the Supreme Court declared that laws prohibiting the marriage of persons from different races—the so-called antimiscegenation or race defilement laws—to be unconstitutional, making mixed racial unions legally permissible. Public attitudes toward mixed-race marriage have only recently tipped in a positive direction; in a 1997 Gallup poll, 77% of Black participants and 61% of White participants stated that they approved of interracial marriage (Root, 2001b). Beginning in the late 1970s, organizations across the United States formed to promote awareness of multiracial issues and lobby for new methods of assessing racial identity (Daniel, 2002). These advocacy groups were successful in changing the way that *race* is publicly defined and counted. In the 2000 U.S. Census, respondents were permitted, for the first time, to choose more than one racial identity; in that census, almost 7 million Americans identified with more than one race (CensusScope, 2005). Groups of biracial students are now a noticeable presence on college campuses across the United States, with a growing number of organizations created to support multiracial identity.

Not only are the terms used to represent multiracial identity evolving but biracial persons are also often ambiguous in their physical appearance. Others are not sure what to make of mixed-race persons. At the same time that this ambiguity can be empowering, providing the space for creative play, it can also be distressing and alienating. The ever-present question "What are you?" can be a painful one for persons of mixed race. Race, like gender, religion, or sexual orientation, is a salient category in Western culture. Racial ambiguity elicits various social responses such as inquisitiveness, admiration, and discomfort.

Biracial persons maneuver through social systems of categorization that for others are matter of fact. At the same time that ambiguity presses the issue of race as a fact to consider, there is considerable difficulty in conveying the experience of being of mixed race because the terms for multiracial identity are still evolving. The ambiguity of biracial identity presents a unique opportunity to derive insight about the construction of racial identity in America.

RACE RELATIONSHIPS

In research on Black–White biracial individuals, Rockquemore and Brunsma (2002) argued that in combination with appearance, biracial identity is best understood through the lens of symbolic interactionism. Relationships provide push-and-pull factors, which help to explain patterns of identification with different identity options. Khanna (2004) has argued a similar point in examining the identity choices of multiracial Asians. Tatum (2004), in her study of Black adolescents who grew up in predominantly White neighborhoods, argued that there is a developmental need to associate with like-minded, and like-colored, individuals to form a secure and differentiated sense of racial identity. Specifically addressing parents and racial identity, Demo and Hughes (1990) argued that African American young adults who describe their relationships with parents as close have a more positive evaluation of their racial group.

Our interviews suggest that biracial identity is discovered and nurtured within a complex of social relationships, including lovers, teachers, friends, and siblings. In listening to our interviews and reading through the transcripts, we became interested in the place of parents in their children's identity claims. In the stories of biracial persons, the act of rebalancing parental relationships in young adulthood accrues new meanings. Because physical appearance is often ambiguous and race is associated with particular parents, parental relationships are intimately tied to racial identity. Feelings of affirmation and closeness or bitterness and distance become significant to the structure of one's identity story. At the center of their accounts, our interviewees talked about the significance of parents in their story of biracial identity.

IDENTITY STORIES

In this chapter, we analyze our conversations with two young women, Rachel and Jean, who were interviewed along with 6 other women enrolled in universities in the western United States in the spring and summer of 2004. This set of interviews was collected as the first round of a projected larger study on mixed-race identity. Interviewees were contacted through university diversity offices and student organizations for biracial and mixed-race students. We did not specify what counted as *mixed race* or *biracial* but, instead, interviewed all students who defined themselves in such a manner and were interested in talking about their life and identity. All interviewees had one White and one non-White parent. Non-White parents came from a variety of backgrounds, including Hispanic, Chinese, African American, Filipino, and Japanese. Our interview schedule included questions about family, peers, dating, religious belief, and identity. In designing interview questions, we followed the advice given by Chase (2003) to ask questions that "invite narratives." Interviews were, on average, 2 hours long.

Although Rachel's father was Hispanic and Jean's mother Chinese, the young women shared several important features in their life stories. Both women were in their early 20s, considered themselves White as children, and still find it easy to pass as White. The range of possible identities is more open for them than for someone with an African American parent, who could be positioned as Black because of the unspoken rule that people with one drop of Black blood are de facto Black (Root, 2001a). By virtue of their appearance, neither was forced into a non-White category; rather, they experienced some freedom to pick and choose among various possible identities. During their college years, Rachel and Jean rewrote their racial identity. For each, relationships played a key role in making this transformation. For both Rachel and Jean, this new self-understanding as biracial involved a reconfigured narrative of their non-White parent; a pattern that was evident in many of our interviews.

Repairing Father

> My identity, that's an interesting question because that's something that's come up a lot in my education classes that I've been taking and even with our discussions at the diversity center. . . . And I guess for me I would have to, first and foremost, I probably identify myself by race. And I probably say White simply because my parents got divorced when I was 2, and so I never grew up with my father. And so, my being White, or Caucasian, was who I was around or how I identified with most things. I mean, my school was pretty much a lot of Hispanic kids. I mean, I always fit in, even with my name and my darker complexion. When the sun comes out [*laughing*], it gives me color. But, um, and so it was never an issue. But I would probably have to say White. I mean, being here and being never really being exposed to Hispanic culture or anything like that.

This quote, which was told in response to a direct question about her identity, provides a good abstract of the plot of Rachel's story. At multiple moments in the interview, Rachel configured her parents' divorce, her relationship with her father, and her racial identity into an explanatory narrative. Her racial identity was connected to her experience growing up; she defined herself in relation to her absent father. In her childhood, she felt "White simply because [her] parents got divorced . . . so [she] never grew up with [her] father."

At the time of the interview, Rachel's identity was not settled. Her conversations in the diversity center and in education classes were ongoing. It was also unclear whether she still identified as White or whether she had abandoned this identification. As she said, "I would probably have to say [I am] White." Rachel did make it clear that her childhood identity was not determined by a sense of isolation—"my school was pretty much a lot of Hispanic kids"—or alienation—"I always fit in." Rachel's narrative of becoming mixed race was tied to her parents. For Rachel, being White meant identifying with her mother because she "was who I was around or how I identified with most things." The absence of a Hispanic identity was connected to her father's physical, emotional, and cultural distance.

Rachel's parents' divorce left a lasting impression on her life. Rachel's father, who was Mexican, left the family when she was 2 years old and, afterward, was no longer present in Rachel's daily life. Because of the early split in her family, Rachel was strongly aligned with her mother. What she knew about her father was filtered through her mother's eyes; the portrait is cast in negative hues. When she was asked how she resembles her parents psychologically, Rachel gave her mother's impressions of her similarities to her father: "She tells me about my dad." Rachel said that she is "impatient . . . [and has] little jealousy streaks and different things that [her mother] think[s] are like him." Even his physical appearance was described derisively: "My dad's the typical Mexican. I mean you know, thick black hair, really dark skin, dark, black-brown eyes. Well, I look more like my mom I think."

Rachel was emotionally and physically estranged from her father and his side of the family. On the day that her parents separated, when Rachel was 2 years old, her father brought Rachel and her older brother to his parents' house. Rachel's mother was annoyed because she did not like the children to visit their paternal grandparents. In evaluating this episode, Rachel described her mother's attitude toward her father's family and why she didn't want the children there. She said,

> It would be sort of stereotypical because . . . it's sort of a typical Mexican family, a lot of drinking, a lot of partying, a lot of, you know, 20 cousins around, um, was how his house was. My mom didn't want us over there a lot.

Rachel's attitude was stereotypical. But not all her impressions of Mexican families were negative. Rachel also related feelings of warmth and acceptance at the house of a Hispanic high school friend.

"I Was Denying Part of Myself I Suppose"

When asked about her comfort relating to Hispanic and White kids in school, Rachel responded that

> when you're being mixed, it's kind of interesting, because when you're around a lot of Hispanic people, you can kind of play off that side of you, but then if you're around a lot of White people, you can play off that side of you as well.

She then added, "so it's OK to kind of waver back and forth and then, but then, I guess, not even feel guilty about it." Her words "but then, I guess" seemed to contradict her declaration that she did "not even feel guilty about it." Did she mean that she didn't feel guilty about her identity shifts to match the majority racial group for the moment, or did she feel guilty about playing both sides of the fence? The interviewer asked, "You said that you didn't feel guilty about it and you didn't have to feel guilty about it before you. . . ." Rachel clarified her response, saying,

> At the time, when I don't think I knew I was doing it. But when, this was all before I was thinking of myself as a mixed-race person because my father was never around, and the more I confront that in college . . . or with different conversations, and I realized I did do that and . . . most of what I would do is pass off as White or something and not acknowledge the other side of me. I feel guilty for doing that. Like, I realize that by doing that I was denying part of myself I suppose, but um, I don't know. A lot of this stuff I'm still trying to, I don't know, figure out. Um, but I do know, when I think back, I used to do that a lot. Like I would say my name is. That's one reason I never correct people when they say, Rachel. I just don't want to. I don't want to seem, "Oh, you know, it's *Raquel*, you know, you're not saying it right, you know, it's Hispanic. . . ." So, I realize now that I used to do it a lot, and I don't feel good about it. At the time I thought it was fine, especially because I was, I think I had a lot of anger because of my dad and stuff and that side of me because I didn't want to have anything to do with it.

Rachel's facility in changing the pronunciation of her name to suit the needs of the situation raised guilt for "denying part" of herself. At the time of the interview, she could acknowledge that she did not "feel good about" her past actions. She indicated that her habit of hiding her Hispanic "side" was unexamined before she began to perceive herself as a "mixed-race person." Once she began thinking of herself as mixed race, Rachel felt guilt for avoiding the public acknowledgment of her Hispanic background. In college and "different conversations" Rachel began to "realize" that she did bury this side of her identity. However, Rachel's language in describing her entry into a mixed-race identity was far from decisive. She had not settled on how to think about these issues but she was "still trying to, I don't know, figure it out." In any case, only from the perspective of a changed, or changing, identity could Rachel feel guilt for avoiding the public acknowledgment of her Hispanic background. The contrast between these two periods from the vantage point of becoming mixed race appears to have driven her discomfort and guilt.

At the heart of Rachel's identity story is her parents' divorce and the absence of her father. Indeed, she didn't think of herself as mixed race "because [her] father was never around." In the past, she did not feel guilty about passing as White because she had "a lot of anger because of [her] dad." In fact, she "thought it was fine" to hide her Hispanic identity "especially because" she was angry at her father. One could speculate that this denial was a kind of emotional revenge directed at her father for leaving the family. Still, Rachel's narrative connects her negative attitude toward herself as part Hispanic to her anger toward her Hispanic father. This connection was clearly her interpretive strategy for distancing herself from a Hispanic identity in her youth and claiming a mixed-race identity in adulthood. Because of her anger, Rachel "didn't want to have anything to do with" the Hispanic part of herself. She let this side of herself fade away. Rachel's story weaves together her relationship to her father with her racial identity.

"Once I Realized That I Was Angry at My Father . . . "

One prominent figure in the plot of Rachel's narrative is her White boyfriend. In Rachel's account, the dialogue that set into motion a turn in her identity story was initiated by her boyfriend. The interviewer asked, "Is there a story about how you arrived at that conception of being more mixed race, being more Hispanic and White, is there a story of how you arrived at that?" Rachel's response is instructive:

> Yeah, I think it came to one of the many arguments that I would have with my boyfriend about, I don't know, it sort of came by serendipity, whatever, by accident . . . arguing about some random thing. . . . Early in our relationship I would always fight with him. If I was sad about something, I would immediately turn to anger, and so he would always be like, "Well, why are you doing this? Let's analyze this." I was like, "Oh my god. Here we go." And then, so I think one time we were, and I was talking about how growing up I hated people to feel sorry for me, and so I would try my hardest not to let that happen, and then I never wanted to admit any of the problems that I had because I felt like they would be too cliché and stupid. Like, you know, oh, girl never growing up, without her father, has all these relationship problems with men. I never wanted to say that, I never wanted to admit that could happen to me, but it did and I think, and once I realized that I was angry at my father for leaving and for never being there then I could accept the fact that I was a part of him and then start accepting the Hispanic part of me, I guess, and that all happened, like, my sophomore year, like, 2 years into our relationship.

At the beginning of their relationship, Rachel and her boyfriend had "many arguments" and "would always fight." By Rachel's account, the closeness made her emotionally unstable. Her feelings of "sad[ness]" would "turn to anger." However, her boyfriend's reaction was supportive, asking Rachel to explore the underlying reasons for her shifts in mood: "Well, why are you doing this?" and "Let's analyze this." His voice, as quoted in the context of Rachel's story, has a therapeutic or even clinical quality. Rather than letting these old feelings poison their relationship, they became an issue for discussion, clinical analysis, and, ultimately, a more profound closeness. In retrospect, Rachel thought that she tried her best not to "admit any of the problems" that she had because she "hated people to feel sorry" for her. In her eyes, her problems were not legitimate; they were "too cliché and stupid." As a result of these conversations, Rachel interpreted her past with new insight; she attributed "all these relationship problems with men" to the fact that she grew up without a father. Although not explicitly stated, Rachel appeared to be cognizant of the fact that she was repeating deep feelings of sadness, anger, and abandonment from her childhood in her present relationship.

An unforeseen consequence of these new insights was that Rachel began to revise her racial identity. In working on relationship problems with her boyfriend, Rachel allowed herself to acknowledge unresolved feelings of anger toward her father. She began to recognize that these negative feelings were affecting her in the present. The central line of the quote is

> and once I realized that I was angry at my father for leaving and for never being there, then I could accept the fact that I was a part of him and then start accepting the Hispanic part of me.

Rachel did not say that all her problems with her father were resolved but only that she was able to let herself be aware of these deep conflicts. Once Rachel acknowledged her anger, she could "accept the fact that [she] is a part of him," which allowed her to "start accepting the Hispanic part of me." The imagery of "parts" or "sides" is intriguing. Rachel was part her father and part Hispanic. In fact, it seems she was making an equation between the two. In Rachel's account, recognizing her anger for her father allowed her to acknowledge that she was part of him and this realization gave her the space and license to stake a claim that she was part Hispanic. It is interesting that Rachel appears to suggest the necessity for integrating these parts or sides to become biracial and feel a sense of wholeness.

"I Could Go There and Embrace My Hispanic Side"

Rachel's relationship with her boyfriend should not be viewed outside of the context of the wider set of relationships that were developing at the time. The experience of creating strong ties with other mixed-race students at the campus diversity center and hearing their stories is certainly a prominent theme in Rachel's identity story. As Tatum (2004) has argued, these kinds of supportive relationships assist in the affirmation of a positive racial identity and there is strong evidence for the influence of other biracial students in nurturing Rachel's emerging identity as a mixed-race person. To clarify the plotline of Rachel's story, the interviewer asked, "So you think it was one conversation with your boyfriend that started that off, at least consciously? Is that what you're saying?" Rachel responded affirmatively but added complexity and more social context to her narrative.

> I think so. Um, because that's when I started coming to terms with who I was, I believe. And then, I mean, going to the mixed-race students group [Fusion], which kind of happened simultaneously, and then talking out a lot of the stuff with them. And what it means to be mixed race. And what race means anyways . . . and feelings about certain things. All that helped, too, to bring that out, like self-identifying as a certain culture or group or wanting to be a part of a certain thing. All that became more clear and made more sense, I think, in terms of being something I

wanted and something that was a part of me. And I realized that. And so it was OK to be a part of that.

Rachel argued that both sources of social support—her boyfriend and Fusion—were critical in the development of her new self-understanding. Her boyfriend provided the initial emotional guidance and encouragement. The members of Fusion were instrumental in providing the scaffolding that confirmed this emerging identity, instructing Rachel in "what it means to be mixed race" and "what race means anyway." The members of Fusion also supported the idea that being mixed race is acceptable and even desirable; Rachel found out that being mixed race is "something [she] wanted" and that "it was OK to be a part of that."

Rachel chose to become involved in Fusion because, as she said,

> I wanted to do something, and I liked the idea of the diversity center. I liked the idea . . . that I could go there and embrace my Hispanic side, I suppose. And so I did. And Fusion was there, and I thought that was perfect.

On the basis of our interview, it is unclear what motivated Rachel to make the initial decision to become involved in Fusion. However, Rachel's involvement in Fusion made present and immediate the necessary resources for building a mixed-race identity. Rachel described Fusion as a warm group with other members facing similar challenges in defining their racial identity and encountering prejudice. As Rachel recounted, the group hung out and talked about "different things like . . . different experiences we had, who we were, who we thought we were, if we'd ever faced any racism." In the context of the group, these experiences were shared and affirmed. Fusion was a comfortable setting where Rachel gained access to the set of common stories and experiences of what it means to be a person with a mixed-race identity. Rachel used the imagery of sides or parts to describe the process of becoming biracial. Fusion supported the Mexican part of her; at Fusion, she could strengthen and "embrace [her] Hispanic side."

Rachel's mixed-race identity is still in process. However, her narrative bears the mark of significant relationships that assisted in the management of her racial identity. By helping Rachel to acknowledge unresolved feelings of anger with her father, Rachel's boyfriend motivated a new narrative beginning. In turn, this awareness opened the possibility of more closely aligning with what she cast as the Hispanic or other side of her. The support that Rachel received in conversation with other biracial youth in Fusion scaffolded her fledgling identity. Her friends in Fusion helped her to better understand the meaning and experience of being mixed race.

At the center of Rachel's narrative is her father, whom she connected time and again to her developing biracial identity. By Rachel's account, claiming a mixed-race identity had a lot to do with recognizing, and beginning to work through, her anger at her father. In response to "Do you feel like you're coming to terms with that anger [for your father]?" Rachel answered,

> I think so. I mean, the more, like I said, the conversations I have with people and in college, in the diversity center, and different situations, um, that it's easier to deal with my anger and just realize. I don't know. I shouldn't. Because different feelings I have towards my dad or towards anything. You know. This is who I am and just to be comfortable with that and realize that.

Rachel did not say that her problems with her father were resolved but that she was aware of these negative emotions from her past. This awareness allowed her to accept her father as part of her and to discover what being part Hispanic meant to her.

Reconfiguring Mother

Early in the conversation, the interviewer asked Jean, "So how would you describe your identity? Who are you?" Jean responded, "I would describe my identity at this point as being biracial, and I also identify with ethnic minority. But prior to maybe my sophomore year in working on my bachelor's, I identified myself as White." Jean's response foretold a rich and complex story.

> Okay. The reason why I identified as White is because, first of all, most people would identify me as White. . . . But I also have, like, very early memories of being 4 or 5 or whatever, and people would tell me I was White, and I would say, "Well, I bet you don't know that I'm Chinese," and they'd be like, "You can't be Chinese" or "No, you're not Chinese" or whatever. So it's like on one hand I have people telling me that I couldn't be Chinese or that I wasn't really Chinese, but then also from my Chinese mom.

Jean's words introduce a recurring theme in her identity story: Jean's identity is, in part, structured by the reactions of others to her appearance. As with Rachel, in Jean's identity story social relationships work in concert with physical appearance. Jean thought of herself as White because she looked White to other people. Even her objection "Well, I bet you don't know that I'm Chinese" was not met with affirmation and understanding but with skepticism and disbelief. These others encapsulate a host of interactions from the early part of her life.

Rockquemore and Brunsma (2002) argued that the interplay between socially perceived appearance and push-and-pull factors in social interactions influences the identity choices that people make. In Jean's narrative, anonymous others represent a significant push factor away from a Chinese self-identification. However, it is also critical to consider intimate social relationships that have names and a significant place in identity formation

(Josselson, 1994). Jean added at the end of the abstract of her early life, "but then also from my Chinese mom." Anonymous others challenged Jean's potential self-understanding as Chinese, but parental relationships had a powerful influence on Jean's identity story. "But then also from my Chinese mom" hints at the significance of Jean's family, in which being Chinese was downplayed.

> And I'm thinking that part of this is because of the time that she came to the United States, it was, like, late 60s or early 70s. She didn't really know anything about the Chinese Exclusion Act. So I'm thinking that chances are nobody really asked her to identify as Asian or Chinese necessarily. . . . I'm thinking, like, the categories back then were kind of different, like, maybe she didn't really stand out as Asian like she was asked to identify as Asian, so she would identify as White, too. So both of my parents would say that they were White, so I'm White. But I'm half-Chinese. Kind of like, "Oh, look, you're White, but you're half-Irish or half-German" sort of thing. So I identified as White until I started going to the university.

The method of historical thinking displayed in this quote is typical of Jean's cognitive style. She contextualizes her mother in the historical epoch in which she arrived in America and the culture that she encountered. Although Jean's mother looked Asian, her mother identified herself as White. Jean supposed that because her mother was never asked to declare herself Asian, she identified as White and just considered herself White. It might seem strange but for Jean's mother being Chinese was equivalent to being Irish or German; it was just another way of being White.

Although the equation is unusual, it is important to take note of the role of Jean's parents in how Jean understands this early part of her life. Jean's early account of her identity is structured through appearance and relationships with anonymous others. But it is also structured in her family's concealment of their Chinese identity. Later in the interview, when the conversation returned to the period that Jean thought of herself as White, the interviewer asked, "Did you think of yourself as being more White or more half-White or kind of ambiguous and you didn't know what it was?" Jean's response is poetic: "I didn't really know what it was. What I felt like I was, was a White girl with some Chinese secret or something. That's what I kind of felt like." In the early part of Jean's life, her Chinese identity was hidden beneath the surface.

"I Am Both These Things"

Jean's transformation from White to biracial, as she recounted, took place at the university in a psychology class that she happened to take. The moment was pivotal in her identity story. As Jean described,

What made me think more about identifying as biracial is actually a class where we used the Lonner and Malpass text. I took a psychology class called "Psychological Aspects of Racial Differences in the United States." One of the themes we ended up talking about in there—it was very brief, we spent, like, half a day on it—was biracial identity development. And that was like whoa, you know. So I learn stuff, like, about my mom and the tension in bicultural families. 'Cause my mom is an immigrant. She's first generation. So that was really interesting, learning about all of that. Then when I started learning about oh, wow, there's this whole other body of thought about people who are biracial, and then that was where I started identifying as biracial.

The text that Jean referred to, Lonner and Malpass's (1994) *Psychology and Culture*, was on the shelf of the interviewer's office. Before the voice recorder was turned on, Jean had already commented on the book. Although the influence of the book and the class on Jean's development is just the kind of impact that teachers crave hearing, we found no evidence that Jean might have contrived this story to please the interviewer. Her account was consistent throughout the interview.

As Jean told it, her educational experience was transformative. True, something about Jean, nascent at the time, might have compelled her to take the course. However, as she recounted, there was an element of serendipity in the discovery of her biracial identity. Jean was majoring in environmental studies, not psychology or sociology. The section on biracial identity in her course was only a half-day focus and not central to the theme of the class. But, there it was, and its presence had consequences for how Jean understood herself.

But what I did do that was different, too, was because I was starting to see myself as . . . what I started to my claim as being Chinese as legitimate. Like, I saw [my claim to being Chinese] as more legitimate now after having taken that class. It was like, well, yes, I'm biracial. I am both these things. I started identifying more as kind of looking into what's going on with the students of color on this campus and learning about them. And then also a whole other level of race relations awareness. It just totally stepped up a couple, more like 20, notches. A whole lot.

"What History Is She Coming From?"

It is significant that Jean's new understanding of culture and ethnicity led her to consider her mother differently. Before taking the class, Jean didn't understand many of her mother's actions and why certain situations bothered her so much. She often wondered, "What is she freaking out about?" But, as Jean recounted,

when I was in that class, and I was starting to learn all that stuff . . . I was, like, we don't get her because she's from a totally different world and we're from a totally different world. So she doesn't get us.

The course introduced her to a new way of thinking about her mother and her identity. She began to think about her mother not only as a person but as part of the culture in which she grew up.

Jean's identity story weaves together her evolving understanding of her mother with her emerging sense of self. As the character of her mother was placed within a new set of insights about culture and relationships, so too was Jean's identity reconfigured. This realignment in Jean's relationship with her mother was evident at several points in the interview; however, as Jean made clear, these revisions happened concurrently with her initial self-discovery. When she was asked, "Did [the class] change or motivate you to do anything differently with your life?" Jean answered,

> Well, I remember it motivating me to do different things with my life and also with how I interpreted my mom and interpreted things that were going on in my family. And that first, that same semester, there was a huge fight that my mom and I ended up having. . . . We went to Niagara Falls for the first time, and my mom has a sister . . . [who] was telling her "Oh yeah, when you go down to Niagara Falls, you have to cross the Canadian border. Just bring your driver's license; that should be fine." Well that of course wasn't fine. We didn't have our passports with us and the border people said that we needed to go to some other office first. . . . And my mom got really upset. She's like, "They're sending us there just because I'm Chinese, and if I wasn't Asian and we were all White they'd just let us pass through." And she was accusing them of being racist. And maybe they were, but I was saying to my mom that she couldn't automatically jump to that conclusion because, I said, "Canada is a foreign country, we are crossing a foreign border. Usually you should have your passport," like I was arguing with her about this point. And she got very upset with me, and she was like, "How could you side with them and not side with your own mother?" and blah blah blah blah blah blah. And then I started going into the stuff that I was learning about in my class, and I was trying to tell her that we were having some sort of cultural misunderstanding or whatever 'cause I'm not trying to side with them, and I was trying to be objective. Anyway, she just got really upset with me. I remember kind of going on for what seemed like hours; it probably was hours. . . . But at one point I remember her saying to me that she, basically in a nutshell, saying that I was full of it, culture has nothing to do with it, I'm just not being a good daughter because I'm not empathizing with her or siding with her. . . . But in our more recent interactions, just over the past 2 years or so maybe, she has acknowledged this culture stuff that I brought up 4 or 5 years ago. . . . When she starts doing things that I didn't understand before where I just would be like "What? What is she talking about? What is she getting all worked up about?" Now I really try to stop and think and be like "Where could she possibly be coming from?" You know, try to think of it in, like, as much Chinese understanding that I have. . . . I try to look at it from that angle, what history is she coming from?

As Jean described, the psychology class helped her to better understand her mother as part of her culture and history; it led to a new understanding of her mother and put their relationship on a new footing. She could contextualize the confusing style in which her mother divided up the world by asking, "What history is she coming from?" These insights reoriented Jean's relational world, helping her see her mother differently and securing a closer bond.

Although the complicating action of the "Niagara Falls" narrative is conflictual, the coda that brings the narrative actions to the present makes clear that her relationship with her mother has taken a significant turn: "But in our more recent interactions . . . she has acknowledged this culture stuff that I brought up." Rather than accusing Jean of "not being a good daughter," her mother validated Jean's understanding of cultural patterns of miscommunication in their household. Her mother's approval was not essential. However, the fact that Jean's mother appeared to have accepted her daughter's perceptions of the family's cultural conflict set the stage for closer interpersonal intimacy.

"That's Totally Me and My Mom"

A second change that resulted from the psychology class was Jean's decision to watch *The Joy Luck Club* (Wong, 1993). The film, based on the novel by Amy Tan, tells the stories of women and their struggles with self-definition in regard to their mothers and Chinese and American culture. Although her cousin had told her about the film several years before, Jean finally got around to watching it after taking the psychology class. Significantly, the first time that Jean watched the film was with her mom.

> I happened to watch it the first time with my mom. There were some things where, when mom would watch it, and she would have this, like, nostalgia of China and things like that. She'd be like, "Oh, yeah" . . . "Oh, [Jean], this happened and blah blah blah blah blah, and look at this, and see that necklace that she's wearing? You have one like that." . . . So, that was what my mom was doing when she was watching it, but what I was doing was tuning in on was, like, some scenes I was like, whoa, that's totally me and my mom.

Jean and her mom seemed to be watching two different films. For her mother, the film was a device for revisiting the culture that she left behind and sharing these profound remembrances with her daughter. For Jean, the film provided insight into her relationship with her mother and a deeper understanding of what it meant to be both Chinese and American.

During our conversation, Jean described several stories from the film that she "identified with." The film models the reconciliation of mothers and daughters who are strikingly similar to Jean and her mother, giving Jean insight into her mother's puzzling actions and Jean's participation in these interactions. Although these stories are universal in appeal, Jean found in them a sign of the intercultural misunderstanding in her household. Similar to the experience of Jean and her mother, the issues disrupting the relationships between the film mothers and daughters are also cultural. In a sense, the film had a similar effect as the psychology class did, allowing Jean to reposition herself toward her mother and clarify what it meant to be both Chinese and American.

"You Look Nothing Like Your Mom!"

The fact that Jean felt, quite firmly, "biracial" did not ease the pressure of her appearance. Jean is very sensitive to how she is perceived by others and continues to hunger for external recognition of her biracial status. She desperately desires the affirmation of her identity by outsiders. In this regard, Jean talked about her sister, whose Chinese facial appearance made social recognition easier and grounded her identity more firmly as half-Asian. In comparison to her sister, Jean felt that her own Asian identity was almost invisible. Jean acknowledged, "I would feel envious of people that would be recognized as being Chinese, like my sister." Jean was "disturbed" and "bothered" when she was not recognized as half-Chinese.

Appearance remains significant to Jean's biracial identity. Jean wants to look more like her mom. In such a way, she could position herself, like her sister, closer to her Chinese identity. But, given her appearance, she needs to be creative. When asked, "Can you tell me which of your parents do you resemble physically?" Jean first answered "Dad" and then changed her response to "Well, Dad and Mom." She said, "Where I resemble my dad, and I say that because of, at least in American society, people recognize people by their faces, and so facial structure is Dad. I definitely have my dad's eyes." Jean added,

> People often say to me and my mom, "You look nothing like your mom!" [*laughs*]. But what I totally have that is my mom though is her figure. . . . There was a picture of her and her dad, like, in an airport or something, and she was, like, just kind of posing with him. But I wasn't, like, actually looking at the picture at the time, it was something she had in her wallet, I didn't even notice or remember it. But I saw it out of the corner of my eye, and I was thinking in my head as I looked at it, what is this picture? I don't remember taking this picture. Except I thought it was me, and then I looked at it, and it was her, and I was like, "Whoa! That's cool!" because I want to look more like my mom.

However, physical appearance was not the only maternal quality that Jean saw in herself. She also had an internal sense of sometimes "acting like [her] mom because of the bicultural thing." Jean described several instances in which she found herself "thinking the same things I've heard my mom say." Jean explained that "because my mom comes from a kind of high-context background . . . I . . . just automatically do things and I've kind of been scolded by my mom when I have not automatically done things."

Jean recounted a memory from her early childhood that seemed to encapsulate many of her current feelings toward her mother. Jean remembered her mother's hands, holding her own to put her to sleep and comforting her when she was ill. She continued,

> I also remember saying to her when I was, like, 4 or 5 that if, whenever, she died that I would cut off her hands and keep them. . . . I was telling her that I always wanted to hold onto them.

Jean's mom took "it really well. . . . She's like, 'then they'll get really gross and so you'll have to keep them in a jar.'" For Jean, the memory was seen as affectionate and warm; she felt cared for and loved by her mother. It is interesting that she recounted this memory at a time when possessing aspects of her mother was central to her identity. Although the memory is open to various interpretations, it communicates the strong feelings that Jean had for her mother and the desire to take inside parts of her.

Making the case that she was half-Chinese was a difficult one for others to accept. Jean looked White to others but she identified emotionally with her mother and considered herself biracial. However, Jean claimed that they resembled each other in subtle ways, such as their "figure" and their emotional responses to others. These aspects of identity were not the ones that people notice but they helped Jean connect to her mother. Jean felt that she possessed important qualities of her mother and that she was close to her mother. This identification with her mother is especially critical because Jean's primary connection to being Chinese was through her mom; she didn't speak Mandarin or have an in-depth knowledge of Chinese culture. If Jean could recognize her mother in herself, then she could recognize the Chinese in herself and her biracial identity would be validated.

RELATIONAL IDENTITIES

In this chapter, we demonstrated how relationships help connect mixed-race youth with the cultural resources for creating a biracial identity. We showed that processes at the personal, social, and cultural levels of analysis are not separate but form a whole unit of analysis.

In the narratives of Rachel and Jean, a consonance was discovered between their interpretations of their personal history and the cultural resources for constructing a biracial identity. Because Rachel acknowledged her anger toward her father, she could distinguish between her feelings about her father and her thoughts about her Hispanic heritage. By virtue of this reinterpretation of her personal history, the cultural resources for a mixed-race identity became accessible, logical, and even desirable. At the time of the interview, there was a fit between how she saw her personal history and the cultural category of being mixed race. As Jean described, there was an immediate fit between her interpretation of her personal past and the cultural idea of what it means to be biracial. The fit was readily apparent and quickly embraced. For both women, an interpretive space was cleared to enter a biracial identity.

Although choosing a mixed-race identity indicates a personal willingness to imagine new possibilities, how Rachel and Jean made this choice and described their agency in the decision differs significantly. Rachel's progress toward a biracial identity was slow moving, gently nurtured by those around her, and still in process. Jean's progress was immediate and more complete; she appeared driven to figure out the implications of race in her life. Certainly, personal characteristics help to understand Rachel's timid and reserved story and Jean's exuberant, critical, and intellectual narrative. It is more in character for Jean than Rachel to take risks displaying biracial identity in an interpersonal context. This helps to explain Jean's enthusiastic acceptance, and display, of a mixed-race identity in contrast to Rachel's careful and reserved exploration.

Although personal characteristics are significant considerations in identity narratives (McAdams, 1996), a complete account must include a description of how relationships function in the management of identity formation. Social relationships are not separate from personal qualities or outside of culture but part of an interpretative whole that is necessary for a complex account of identity. Social relationships facilitate the process of entering into culturally derived modes of self-identification. They guide persons to identity options, confirm or deny their choices, teach them what these choices mean, and provide the evidence for their claims to new identities.

Without the support of critical relationships, Rachel and Jean's claim to a biracial identity would have been incomplete, fragmented, and dubious. Relationships played a central role in helping Rachel and Jean to make interpretations about their past and connected them with the larger cultural meanings of being biracial. Rachel's transformation from a young person passing as White to a person of mixed race was supported by significant relationships with her boyfriend and the members of Fusion. Jean's insight into her identity and the meaning of race were developed, tested, and confirmed in her family and other social relationships.

Although several important figures structured Rachel's and Jean's accounts of the past and played important roles in the plot of their identity stories, parents were among the most prominent characters in their narratives. Large portions of Rachel and Jean's identity stories concerned how perceptions of their non-White parent changed over time. Rachel recognized the influence of anger toward her father in her then-current relationship and its role in denying the "Hispanic side" of her. It is reasonable though speculative to surmise that Rachel hated her "Hispanic part" just like she hated her father. Once she recognized her anger, she could begin to disentangle feeling Hispanic from her disappointment in her father. In a similar way, Jean's perception of her mother had some negative aspects to it. Jean and her family thought of their mother's behavior as bizarre, unpredictable, and irrational. The insights that she gained about culture and identity allowed Jean to see her mother differently and to revise her misunderstandings. In this move, Jean could interpret her mother's behavior not as abnormal but as the product of her culture.

For Rachel and Jean, becoming biracial required the reinterpretation of their non-White parent. The internal sense of the non-White parent is especially salient to the racial identity of biracial youth because ideas of race are so intimately associated with the characteristics of their parents and their families. In each life story, there is a fit or consonance between this internal sense of the parent and the desire to take over the cultural terms for being biracial. It is interesting that Rachel and Jean both described the process of becoming biracial as discovering something on the inside. Rachel was finding her Hispanic part or side. Jean declared, "I am biracial. I am both of these things." One interpretation of these "parts," "sides," or "things" is that they represent an inheritance, genetic or cultural, of parents or their sides of the family. Claiming father or mother means to claim them as people, as good objects, but also to claim their inheritance as one's own.

Although various researchers have argued that relationships are significant in the identity stories of diverse groups of women and men (see Josselson, 1994; Mishler, 1999), it is possible that relationships have a heightened significance for our interviewees. First, by virtue of their ambiguous appearance, claiming a biracial identity was clearly a matter of choice. Neither Rachel nor Jean was forced by coercive social pressure to see herself as non-White. In making the decision to be biracial, they were asserting the importance and desirability of this identity resource. It is possible that parental relationships become more significant in identity stories in which social appearance is ambiguous or more closely resembles that of the privileged group. In the absence of clear social pressure or outright prejudice, feelings of affinity might have more salience in narrating racial identity. Second, researchers have argued that relationships are central to the development of American women (see Gilligan, 1982). Because these interviewees were female, this fact could account for the prominence of relationships in their identity stories. We don't know the shape of the stories of biracial men. These are questions that merit additional study.

REFERENCES

CensusScope. (2005). *Multiracial population statistics from 2000 United States Census*. Retrieved March 1, 2005, from http://www.censusscope.org/us/_chart_multi.html

Chase, S. (2003). Learning to listen: Narrative principles in a qualitative research methods course. In D. P. McAdams, R. Josselson, & A. Lieblich (Eds.), *Up close and personal: The teaching and learning of narrative research* (pp. 79–99). Washington, DC: American Psychological Association.

Cohler, B. J. (1998). Psychoanalysis, the life story, and aging: Creating new meanings within narratives of lived experiences. In J. Lomranz (Ed.), *Handbook of aging and mental health: An integrative approach* (pp. 255–280). New York: Plenum Press.

Daniel, G. R. (2002). *More than black? Multiracial identity and the new racial order.* Philadelphia: Temple University Press.

Davies, B., & Harré, R. (1990). Positioning: The discursive production of selves. *Journal for the Theory of Social Behaviour, 20,* 43–63.

Demo, D. H., & Hughes, M. (1990). Socialization and racial identity among black Americans. *Social Psychology Quarterly, 53,* 364–374.

Gilligan, C. (1982). *In a different voice: Psychological theory and women's development.* New York: Cambridge University Press.

Graves, J. (2001). *The emperor's new clothes: Biological theories of race at the millennium.* Piscataway, NJ: Rutgers University Press.

Holland, D., Lachicotte, W., Jr., Skinner, D., & Cain, C. (1998). *Identity and agency in cultural worlds.* Cambridge, MA: Harvard University Press.

Josselson, R. (1994). Identity and relatedness in the life cycle. In H. A. Bosma, T. L. G. Graafsma, H. D. Grotevant, & D. J. De Levita (Eds.), *Identity and development: An interdisciplinary approach* (pp. 81–102). Thousand Oaks, CA: Sage.

Khanna, N. (2004). The role of reflected appraisals in racial identity: The case of multiracial Asians. *Social Psychology Quarterly, 67,* 115–131.

Lonner, J., & Malpass, R. (Eds.). (1994). *Psychology and culture.* Boston: Allyn & Bacon.

McAdams, D. P. (1996). Personality, modernity, and the storied self: A contemporary framework for studying persons. *Psychological Inquiry, 7,* 295–321.

Mishler, E. G. (1999). *Storylines: Craftartists' narratives of identity.* Cambridge, MA: Harvard University Press.

Ricoeur, P. (1984). *Time and narrative* (Vol. 1, K. McLaughlin & D. Pellauer, Trans.). Chicago: The University of Chicago Press.

Rockquemore, K., & Brunsma, D. (2002). *Beyond black: Biracial identity in America.* Thousand Oaks, CA: Sage.

Root, M. P. P. (2001a). Factors influencing the variation in racial and ethnic identity of mixed-heritage persons of Asian ancestry. In T. Williams-Leon & C. Nakashima (Eds.), *The sum of our parts* (pp. 61–70). Philadelphia: Temple University Press.

Root, M. P. P. (2001b). *Love's revolution: Interracial marriage.* Philadelphia: Temple University Press.

Tatum, D. B. (2004). Family life and school experience: Factors in the racial identity development of Black youth in White communities. *Journal of Social Issues, 60,* 117–135.

Wertsch, J. V. (2002). *Voices of collective remembering.* New York: Cambridge University Press.

Williams-Leon, T., & Nakashima, C. (2001). Reconfiguring race, rearticulating ethnicity. In T. Williams-Leon & C. Nakashima (Eds.), *The sum of our parts* (pp. 3–10). Philadelphia: Temple University Press.

Wong, W. (Producer/Director). (1993). *The joy luck club* [Motion picture]. United States: Hollywood Pictures.

8

VICISSITUDES OF "HOLDING" IN THE IMMIGRATION EXPERIENCE: THE CASE OF ETHIOPIAN ISRAELI ADOLESCENTS

DANNA PESSACH-RAMATI AND RUTHELLEN JOSSELSON

Immigration, in encompassing many changes and much loss, demands a negotiation between old and new cultural norms and expectations, many of which are in the realm of relatedness and relationships. Because cultures differ in the way they perceive and construct relationships (Guisinger & Blatt, 1994; Josselson, 1992; Markus & Kitayama, 1991; Raeff, 1997), issues of relatedness often form the core of the immigrant's adaptation process. Adolescent immigrants, being developmentally in the midst of the process of shaping the self, are acutely attuned to these cultural differences in how relationships are to be conducted and experienced.

Accumulating research on immigration in adolescence thus far has focused on the intergenerational transmission of cultural values, the development of autonomy, and the maintenance of harmonious family relationships (for reviews see Kwak, 2003, and Mirsky, 1996). Both sociologists and psychologists have described the dilemmas of adolescents from nonindustrial

---

Identifying characteristics of the participants have been altered to conceal their identities.

cultures who have to transcend or struggle against collectivist family values to achieve the autonomy required by Western cultures. Kagitcibasi (1996, 2003) posits an "autonomous related self" that melds the need for autonomy with the need for embeddedness in the family, thus conceptualizing the way in which adolescents may successfully adapt to a more individualistic culture and also maintain their family ties.

Researchers have consistently found that familial support aids the process of adaptation (Darwish-Murad, Joung, Verhulst, & Crijnen, 2004; Mirsky, 1996; Zhou, 1997). However, the family may also be a delaying factor in the integration into the new society and may become an additional source of stress if the encounter with new cultural norms of behavior and relatedness undermines known patterns and creates conflicts and tensions (Gellis, 2003; Mirsky, 1996).

Migration can disrupt parent–child relationships in a number of ways following immigration: through a reduction in parental authority, different acculturation states, and so on (Zhou, 1997). Immigration and the acculturation process also affect the adolescent's ability to create social connection and gain support (Coatsworth, Maldonado-Malina, Pantin, & Szapocznik, 2005).

The challenge of making and maintaining supportive relationships with family and others is often central to the experience of immigration. Yet the phenomenological aspects of what constitutes "support" psychologically remain unexplored. What relational input do immigrants need to feel grounded in their bicultural experience? To whom do they turn for this relational connection? What relational dilemmas and pitfalls ensue from the changed relational context? What enables a family to provide adequate support for their teenage children and what enables the young person to experience his or her family as supportive?

In this chapter, we investigate these issues by focusing on the special case of adolescent Ethiopian immigrants in Israel. An understanding of their unique experience through listening to their relational narratives can enrich the body of knowledge on the dynamic between culture and relatedness and shed light on how relationships aid and impede the immigrants' adjustment.

BACKGROUND

The Ethiopian Jewish community in Israel has approximately 85,000 members, of whom 23,000 are Israeli born. Most of them arrived in Israel in two immigration waves during the early 1980s and early 1990s. In many cases the voyage to Israel was full of hardships and trauma, and the community suffered many losses of life. Ethiopian Israeli adolescents face some major difficulties. They are affected by the often low socioeconomic status of their families, and many of them feel alienated and withdraw from trying to integrate into Israeli society (Shabtay, 2001). Research has revealed the ways in which changes in parents' status and in connections between children and parents following immigration affected the processes of creating identity, forcing the Ethiopian teenager to maneuver between values he or she was brought up with and the often contradictory values that lead to success in Israel (Ben-Ezer, 1987; Bodovsky, David, Baroch, Eran, & Avni, 1994; Dotan, 1998; Shabtay, 1995; and more). The adolescent is often caught between the difficulties of trying to identify with parents whose values do not apply to the new reality and the dangers of rejecting this identification, which might lead to an unintegrated sense of self through disavowing some important parts of identity (Dotan, 1998).

These youths live in a unique relational context. In many cases, young immigrants, especially those who belong to the second generation, acquire the ethnic heritage through relationships with parents and family and no longer through the broader community (Kwak, 2003). In such cases, the relationships between children and parents carry a heavy cultural load. Thus, these youths must create relationships in a context that contains aspects and values from two cultures. Because the original culture and the new one may not endorse the same values, these teenagers may experience conflicts that are interwoven with the adolescent process of creating identity and building the self. It seems that relationships and relatedness play an essential and central role in this negotiation of values and are sometimes at the heart of the conflict.

RELATEDNESS

Psychologists are increasingly understanding that development takes place through social interactions (Raeff, 1997) and is tied both to preserving relations with others, both internally and externally, and to differentiating within them (Josselson, 1992). The sense of individuality and the sense of relatedness to others develop in an interrelated and dialectical manner (Flum & Lavi-Yudelevitch, 2002; Guisinger & Blatt, 1994).

Although relatedness is a universal phenomenon, the meaning and nature of connections are culturally dependent (Josselson, 1992). Modern Western society's stress on separation and individuality is not shared by all cultures (Guisinger & Blatt, 1994). Whereas in Western cultures the self is conceived as primarily independent, differentiated and separated from the other, in non-Western cultures, the self is construed from an interdependent position in the environmental context. In such a construal, the sense of belonging to a social connection becomes so powerful that it is more reasonable to think of the connection as the functional unit of conscious thinking and the self as being defined by relations with others (Markus & Kitayama, 1991).

The Ethiopian immigrants in Israel came from a society in which the social structure in the family unit and in the broader community was based on a hierarchy of authorities (Ben-Ezer, 1987). The extended family was the Ethiopian Jews' main communal and social unit (Barahani, 1990) and the family units were complex and large (Bodovsky et al., 1994). The family structure in Ethiopia was patriarchal and the husband or father had a major position. Adults constituted the center of the family and relationships with the children were based on authority, obedience, and respect toward the parents and adults in general, and toward the head of the family especially (Barahani, 1990; Bodovsky et al., 1994). According to the Ethiopian Jews' traditional perception, a person is an inseparable part of his or her familial and social unit, and self-image is derived through strong identification with the good name and honor of the family (Shabtay, 1999).

The social–behavioral norms governing relationships in Ethiopia included emotional restraint, indirect and ambiguous communication with sparing use of words, avoidance of direct confrontation, use of titles and honor designations, an emphasis on confidentiality and secret-keeping, and obligation for mutual help (Bodovsky, David, Eran, & Rozen, 1989; Shabtay, 1999). The respect concept was central in the Ethiopian culture and obligated the community members to behave honorably toward people higher in the social hierarchy (Ben-Ezer, 1987). Children's socialization process taught them the proper forms of obedience and respect for elders and authority figures, and the entire social order rested on the success of this process (Rosen, 1985). The adolescent period, called *the fire period* in this society, was regarded as a period in which the adolescent is expected to be hot tempered and impulsive, so the surrounding people were understanding and tolerant of the naughty behavior of adolescents (Bodovsky et al., 1994). Still, the nature and contents of the adolescence process in Ethiopia were very different from what is common in Western countries. Adolescence gave way to marriage and adult responsibility, all of which was governed by predetermined rules that were dictated by adult family members (Bodovsky et al., 1994; Shabtay, 1999).

With immigration and the transfer from a traditional rural society to an urban pluralistic industrial one, the social structure of the community was extensively changed. The extended family was frequently divided in the harsh immigration process (Barahani, 1990; Yilma, 1996). The parents' authority was undermined (Bodovsky et al., 1994; Shabtay, 1999), many children and teenagers were transferred to residential schools, and many parents felt that they lost control over their children. As a result, they "gave up" and passed on the responsibility of the children's education to the local authorities (Barahani, 1990; Bodovsky et al., 1994). In addition, the status of children in relation to their parents changed following the immigration. In the Ethiopian society the family as a unit was a top priority, whereas in Israel, the children receive much more attention than do adults in many areas. The Ethiopian community in Israel also has to deal with many other problems such as poverty, unemployment, and negative attitudes toward their skin color, which is experienced as a main category of difference, and sometimes marginality (Ben-David & Ben-Ari Tirosh, 1997; Rosen, 1995).

As these young Ethiopian immigrants make efforts to adapt, their interpersonal relationships play a crucial role. Connection to the family, attention and care from authority figures (Shabtay, 1995, 1999), and identification with important others (Flum, 1998) were found to be associated with good adaptation of Ethiopian youth in Israel. Still, cross-cultural literature points to the notion that interpersonal relationships and concepts such as "connection to the family" or "care" may convey very different meanings for people who live in the context of different cultures. This situation may be seen in research that compared Ethiopian and Israeli students' adjustment in college (Ben-David & Leichtentritt, 1999) and found that Ethiopian and Israeli students perceived their family's functioning differently. Although family was important as a support system and affected adjustment in both groups, family cohesion was an important resource for Ethiopian students in contrast with the Israeli students who stressed other family factors. In this chapter we attempt to understand some aspects of how the bicultural context is expressed by and constructive of Ethiopian students' relational frame of reference, especially in the context of their relationship with their parents and what it means to them to feel supported.

RELATIONAL SPACE MODEL

Josselson's (1992) relational space model allows for the investigation of complex relatedness. This model parses relational experience into its components and distinguishes among different relational experiences, thus offering a language by which it is possible to describe extensively and deeply the ways people connect to others. This multidimensional model of relatedness details eight dimensions of connection, which represent eight primary ways by which people make connections. In the beginning of life, these relational connections are concrete and basic; they later become more symbolized and differentiated. The eight dimensions can be described briefly as follows: holding—the experience of being held, contained, supported, and anchored by others; attachment—the experience of being close to a reliably responsive, unique, and irreplaceable other; passion—whereby the other is a source of exciting pleasure and drive gratification; eye-to-eye validation—in which the other reflects the self and provides the feeling of existing and being seen, known, and valued (or not valued) by others; identification and idealization—a connection based on the attempt to emulate others to acquire qualities the others are perceived to possess; mutuality—the experience of companionship and friendship, of harmonic movement together as *we*, and the creation of a connection that is a product of two; embeddedness—a sense of belonging to a group, of fitting in, having a place and role in society; and care—connecting to others through tending and responding to their needs.

These eight dimensions are sometimes interwoven but remain distinguishable emotional experiences. This model, however, was created on the basis of experiences of people from Western cultures, and does not include experiences of people from non-Western cultures. Thus we had to be very sensitive to cultural variations and be ready to "hear" previously unnamed relational dimensions.

THE RESEARCH PLAN

In-depth interviews were conducted by the first author. Participants were 11 Israeli adolescents, 5 girls and 6 boys, of Ethiopian origin, ages 16 to 18. Four of them were born in Israel, one arrived at age 12, and the rest arrived at ages 5 to 8. Participation in the study was voluntary and the researcher approached the participants through contact persons in the community. All of the participants spoke Hebrew well enough to be interviewed in this language. All of the participants were in high school; four studied in residential schools. Ten of the interviewees described a low familial socioeconomic status. Three of the participants lived in Israel without their parents, who had either died or stayed in Ethiopia. Two of these lived with their older siblings and one lived by himself with guardian supervision. Another three participants lived with their mothers and were not in touch with their fathers. The remaining five lived with both their father and mother.

THE INQUIRY

The researcher, in a preliminary conversation, presented the study to the participants as "a research about the social connections of teenagers from Ethiopian origin, which is aimed to better understand the world of these youth." A payment of $18 was offered to each participant as a reward for the time and energy invested in the interview. At the beginning of the interview meeting, the interviewer presented the topic and purposes of the interview again. She emphasized that the participant could stop the interview at any point, and said that participants were free to avoid dealing with any subject that was uncomfortable for them. The issue of confidentiality was stressed.

The participants were asked to draw relational space maps (Josselson, 1992), graphic descriptions of their inner sense of meaningful connections to others at three points in their lives: age 5, age 10, and today. The maps served as a basis for an in-depth interview in which the participants were asked to describe how—in which ways—the people represented in the maps are or were important and meaningful to them. (For a fuller description of the relational space map and the exact instructions, see Josselson, 1992.) This procedure helps focus the interview on the participants' relational systems and their meanings and the participants' development through the years. Most of the participants did not show any difficulty in understanding the explanation and drawing the maps, although some flexibility was necessary. Some of the participants, for instance, did not draw all three maps (e.g., they drew two maps that represented "childhood" and "today"), and some of them started with one of the maps and drew the other maps during the interview. Nevertheless, in all cases, this procedure led to a rich representation of the participant's relational networks and served as a useful framework for interviewing.

During the interview that followed, the interviewer asked questions that clarified how people were important to the participant and asked for examples and specific events that illustrated the nature of the connection under discussion. At the end of the interview, the participants were invited to ask questions or to talk about topics that had not come up during the interview. Most of the participants mentioned that they enjoyed the interview and experienced it as meaningful.

The interviews were conducted in Hebrew and lasted 1.5 to 3 hours. The interviewer was aware of the language difficulties that arose with some of the participants whose Hebrew was still somewhat awkward and tried to overcome these difficulties by an invitation to elaborate and give examples. The interview was recorded and transcribed, and all identifying material has been changed to protect confidentiality.

ANALYSIS

The data were coded according to the eight relational dimensions in Josselson's (1992) model, and attention was given to other themes and dimensions that appeared in the interview but not in the model. An attempt was made to create a relational profile for each participant. In a second stage, we tried to trace major themes and to find repeated issues in each interview. We attended to metalanguage and the emotional tone that accompanied the content and its meanings, as well as the strategies the participants chose for presenting their narrative. Finally, we tried to synthesize an understanding of the relational themes that characterize this group of participants. A special emphasis was given to clarifying concepts with cultural meanings and to examining them in the bicultural context.

FINDINGS AND DISCUSSION

Each narrative demonstrated a different relational constellation and presented different dominant dimensions and themes. In this chapter, we focus on holding as a central dimension in the construction of the participants' relational world because this dimension most closely maps onto the concept of support and seemed especially sensitive to the participants' cultural context.

Among the eight dimensions in the relational space model, holding is the primary and most basic relational dimension in development (Josselson, 1992). We human beings fundamentally and physically experience holding as the feeling of having arms around us, surrounding, supporting, and keeping us from falling through limitless space. These arms serve as a barrier between us and anything that might be harmful or overwhelming in the surrounding environment.

Winnicott (1975, 1979) saw a holding environment as the first and most important factor that allows the baby to maintain "continuity of being," enabling the emergence and expression of the infant's inner potential. Extending this idea, Bion (1962) spoke of *container* and *contained* whereby the mother helps the infant manage emotional experiences, providing security for what is inside.

The physical holding of infancy develops into a more symbolic type of holding with maturation and operates as support (Josselson, 1992). It evolves into a sense that others are there and will support us, keeping us from feeling powerless and helpless. Holding can be experienced as a sense of emotional containment by which people in our lives manage stimulation for us. A sense of support also includes an experience of certain figures acting to protect us and provide for our needs. Holding gives the sense that there is someone to depend on. Such experiences throughout development advance the expression of self and autonomy. A sense of sufficient holding allows the individual to gain hope and to dedicate resources toward directing him- or herself to the future (for more on the holding dimension, see Josselson, 1992).

Although many people grow attached to those who hold them, holding is not the same as attachment in Bowlby's sense. It is possible to be held by people to whom we are not attached or to be attached to those who do not hold us. Attachment implies continuing powerful bonds to particular others from whom one can expect responsiveness, but the nature of the response can vary widely. Holding, on the other hand, can be offered by many others, with or without the promise of ongoing relationship; holding can also be experienced from internalized others.

The need for and availability of holding was repeated as a dominant concern in all of the interviews. Each interviewee of course contributed his or her unique shades and colors to the dimension. Many focused on their difficulties in obtaining holding from important figures in their current life, especially in their relationships with their parents. Many of the interviewees described experiences of lack of sufficient support. Feelings of having no anchor and a fear of falling and decline arose often in the interviews.

We begin by describing the expressions of the holding dimension in the participants' narratives, particularly in connection with relationships with their parents. We also describe and discuss the meanings they give to terms related to holding, and the way they deal with the lack of holding in their lives. (Because the relational space model and the definitions of the holding dimension were derived from the experiences of Western people, it is reasonable to assume that non-Westerners may define related concepts in different ways.) Our attention is on what exactly the interviewees meant when they talked about support and what exactly they seemed to need from a holding relationship.

Haila

"This is what happens to all the kids here, they give up [become desperate]."

Haila is an 18-year-old boy who moved to Israel with his family at age 8 and now studies and lives in a residential school. Haila presents a difficult life situation and repeatedly raises relational elements that are connected with holding—and its absence.

Haila chose to begin the interview with a description of his relational world in the present time. When Haila describes how his parents, whom he regards as the most important people in his life, matter to him, he first mentions the fact that his parents care about him, and that they know and take an interest in whatever happens to him. He says, "It makes me feel that there's someone who knows what's going on . . . that there's someone who will be with me my entire life." This is a clear statement of his sense of attachment to his parents, and the feeling that they are a constant part of his life is very important to him. Yet, Haila describes his brothers and sisters as the figures who help him and take care of him. He depicts his older sisters as those who raised him and cared for him along with his parents, and his brother as someone who helps him out in need. "Whenever there's a problem I go to him. Money problems and all, all sorts of problems." One of his sisters is also described as one who helps and fills in for his parents when he does not want them involved. "If I have a problem at school, she takes care of it, this sister. . . . If there are problems I don't want my parents to know about, she takes care of it right away."

When Haila draws his current relational map, he includes his residential school in it as well, and relates to it as an important "image" in his world. He describes hard feelings following "bad treatment" by the staff, which includes experiences of discrimination and injustice. Haila feels that he does not get the treatment and care he deserves, feels unloved and rejected, and says, "They don't like me here, so what am I doing here?" Haila tries to emphasize that in addition to these feelings, he lacks something even more basic than the wish for love and acceptance. Haila wishes for a strong figure who will help him and make things better. He says that he considered reporting the situation in the school to an inspector from the ministry of education, who will come and fix what is unjust. He describes a sense of helplessness and lack of power to act because he has to cope on his own with his difficult situation.

Haila describes how his sense of helplessness increases because he feels that his parents do not back him up when he wants to complain and oppose the system. Haila feels that his parents, who are important to him as major attachment figures, have difficulty supporting him in his confrontation with the system. He wishes for active support (i.e., backing, holding) from his parents. He wants them to act on his behalf, fight his battles, and be the agents of his needs and rights in the world, but his parents urge him to restraint and silence according to what he perceives as the Ethiopian behavioral code. He says,

> My mama and papa saw this too, you see. It's not that they didn't see, I tell them this. . . . What did they say? "Until you finish the year, even if a counselor beats you, you shut up . . . don't respond, shut up. Shut up. You get more but finish the year quietly. . . . Don't complain. If you complain you won't get anything, you'll have more, you see." That's my mama, it really annoys me.

Haila perceives the parents' push for restraint not just as a message for choosing not to act but also as a message for his helplessness against the system. He quotes his parents as saying, "You can't do anything." He feels that he lacks the power to act on his own and that there is no one by his side to help him in doing so. He says, "There are no people here, the people who can really fight it. Me, what can I do, you see, nothing."

Although he perceives his parents as caring, because of financial difficulties and lack of education they cannot provide him with the support and guidance that will help him to press forward in the world.[1] "I don't study at home, maybe . . . there's no one to help me at home, help me to read this and give me money for extra lessons and all. The situation doesn't allow it." Haila says that these circumstances led him to living in a residential school. Feeling that he has to cope on his own, Haila describes a strong feeling of helplessness and uses the phrase "no choice" frequently. This leads to despair and hopelessness. He says, "This is what happens to all the kids here, they give up [become desperate]."

When Haila speaks of his relational world at age 5 or 6, when he still lived in Ethiopia, he nostalgically describes the memory of a safe and happy childhood. He begins with describing his school, contrasting it with his cur-

---

[1]In a way, we felt that Haila highlighted his parents' importance and the fact that they cared for him because he wanted to stress that they still had an important role in his life even though they were not holding figures. It may be that he wanted to present to the interviewer and to himself their strengths as parents.

rent school. Haila describes the school as a place with very defined rules and strict behavioral norms, a place with clear lines of authority. "It's a school of many kids . . . about 60 to 70 people in each class. . . . I don't remember the teachers. The headmaster, I never saw him." There were hard punishments, including corporal punishment, for improper behavior. Nevertheless, he speaks of the school with much appreciation and describes it very positively.[2] He says, "There I felt good, good. What can I tell you, it's a school. Great school." When the interviewer tried to find out what element of school created the good experience, Haila said, "Everything was organized there. . . . That way, if you do everything on time and all, you're guaranteed to succeed. There's no such thing, no. There are no failures. And even if there are failures, you get over them."

The clear rules and limits of the school in Ethiopia protected him and served as a source of support and holding, thus allowing him to develop and act assuredly within them. Haila adds,

> It's also education, you see, but a different kind of education, not like here. Here education is "stop this," and all, and if you don't feel like it don't and all. There's no such thing there as "I can't." There is no one that can't. . . . I like that form of learning better.

The fact that the school rules posed difficult but concrete demands apparently enabled Haila to trust in his ability to succeed. Clear limits form an important component of support. Haila's choice to begin the narration of his childhood relational world with this subject and the comparisons he makes with his current situation indicate how he misses such restrictions from the people in his relational world today.

Later, Haila describes the neighborhood in which he grew up, where, according to him, "everybody knew everybody." Having many people involved in his life gave him a feeling of being held, but in a different sort of way. He says,

> When you have a little problem, suddenly a gazillion people appear and take care of the problem. There's no such thing as bystanders and . . . solve your own problem or anything. There's a problem, 300 people take care of it. And with 300 people taking care of the problem, the problem goes away in seconds.

It seems that those two bodies—the school that provided clear and defined boundaries that one can lean on, and the people of the neighborhood that provided multiple figures who can help—provided holding and support. This situation created a bounded, predictable, and therefore stable childhood environment within which he could develop. The nostalgia and idealization in

---

[2]The interviewer felt that this appreciation was unexpected, and it surprised her during the interview. Later on she had to check herself and try not to let her value system, which does not favor corporal punishment and a strict educational attitude, interfere with accepting and understanding what Haila had to say.

Haila's tone and words suggested that he used these memories to cope with his current loneliness and helplessness.

The holding dimension is at the center of Haila's relational world partly as a result of the pain he feels at its absence. Similar issues appeared in different form with almost all interviewees. For these young people, support in the holding context refers to structure and the sense of a predictable world with people who can take their part and advocate for their needs. In the conceptual model, the negative pole of the holding dimension is *falling*—this sense, the sense of being ungrounded, is what these young people described.

Presence and Concern as Manifestations of Holding

Almost all of the interviewees (except those whose parents are dead or completely out of touch with them) mentioned the relationship with their parents or other adult caretaker as representing holding in some way. Haila described the experience of his parents as accompanying figures who are interested in what he is going through as a primary experience in the relationship. Although he does not describe them as holding figures in the sense of protecting him or being able to intervene at his school on his behalf, their presence is perceived as encouraging and somewhat strengthening. Malka, by contrast, describes her parents as "supportive the whole way" and focuses on how her parents' presence in different situations is experienced as holding. She says, "They accompany you through this. . . . They stand behind you." The very presence of the parents was described by almost all the interviewees as a primary factor in that relationship. Josselson (1992) described *thereness* as a basic experience of holding (and, often, attachment as well), an experience of another person that provides anchoring. For our participants, their sense that their parents are present in their lives offers a strong support that they can lean on in time of need. (The interviewees whose parents were not part of their lives supported this impression when describing experiences of absence or loss of support and backing in the context of the parents' absence.)

In addition to their presence, most interviewees mentioned the parents' interest or caring as an experience that provides, among other things, a sense of holding. The caring and interest were described in many of the interviews by means of the term *concern*.[3] The interviewees gave the term *concern* several meanings. First, the term refers to a sort of tending, in the sense of taking care of needs. In addition, the term appeared in the sense of worrying. Zaudo, for example, described his mother's concern as the primary aspect of their relationship: "She worries about me, whenever I go outside, she worries about me." Barahanu also mentioned his mother's worry for him as an important factor in their relationship. He describes her concern as a need

---

[3] *Concern* in Hebrew is *de'aga.*

to know where he is and what he is doing. He interprets this concern as a certain kind of holding and protection. He says, "I don't take care of myself. She looks after me." It seems that the parents' worry somewhat relieves these young people from the need to be worried. When the parents hold these worries as their own, they contain certain kinds of anxieties, and by doing so, allow their teenagers some respite from anxiety.

Although most of the interviewees described their parents as having some holding functions, many spoke with pain of the absence of or reduction in their parents' holding role. The need for holding is often most clearly visible when the provision of what is needed in the holding environment falters or is absent.

The Socioeconomic Situation and Its Impact on Holding

During the interviews, the participants often mentioned their socio-economic situation and its impact on their relational world. Although low socioeconomic status is not a purely relational issue, it is a part of the overall context in which the participants live and as such it influences subjective feelings and experiences and the nature of the relationship systems. The issue of economic distress and its influence on relationships arose in 10 of the 11 interviews we conducted.[4]

The participants in the study seemed to experience financial distress as a factor that makes it difficult for their families to be supportive at the basic level of life. Many of the interviewees were very occupied by this subject and spoke with pain of the need to survive on their own and provide for themselves without financial support from their families. Tadila, for instance, says the following:

> The familial situation, the financial state, that's something that really influences the . . . attitude you have towards yourself, towards society, in comparison to society and . . . it's not easy. . . . I have to finance myself, I have to provide. . . . You get along on your own and have to take care of everything, take responsibility for what you are. Very hard.

The loss of economic support by the family is entwined with the adolescents' evaluation of their parents' capabilities and competency. The participants seem to experience their parents as incompetent in many areas, not just the financial one. One can safely lean only on someone strong and stable, and the parents seem to them to be unable to provide holding and support

---

[4]Although this sample is not statistically representative, there is no doubt that the Ethiopian community in Israel was suffering from economic hardship. According to the Central Bureau of Statistics, only 53% of the 25- to 54-year-olds of Ethiopian descent participated in the workforce in 1999, as opposed to 76% of the entire Israeli population in this age group (Central Bureau of Statistics, 2001a). As a result, many Ethiopian families depended on social security support and suffered poverty and harsh conditions.

where most needed. These young people experience their parents, in many cases, as people who want to provide support but are unable to do so efficiently because they lack the appropriate resources.

Most participants mention that their parents lack language abilities, education, and other skills that are needed for adapting to everyday life in Israel. Haila described his parents' incapacity to help him in his schoolwork as the reason for his move to a residential school and the ensuing loss of the everyday emotional holding he needs. Similar descriptions appeared in many of the interviews. In response to their parents' difficulties, the teenagers sometimes assumed part of the role that traditionally belonged to the parents. As Uri put it,

> I think that today parents use their kids more because they [the parents] don't do anything. They need their kid to come with them to social security . . . and all that to explain to them, the electricity bills, to pay and everything. He plays many roles.

Malakamo said, "They want to help me, but they don't, they can't." The parents' lack of skills is seen as the inability to act usefully in the world, despite their good intentions. Our participants' focus on their parents' competency and with their need for holding in their current relationship with the parents seems to be connected with their developmental stage. During adolescence, many individuals first develop the cognitive ability to experience the lack of holding and discover their parents' inability to fully protect them (Josselson, 1992). This realization raises many questions as to the competency of the parents, who were previously experienced as protective and omnipotent during childhood. In view of the cultural transition their families experienced and the upheaval in their adaptive abilities, the adolescents' questions concerning the parents' competency are intensified, and their ability to experience them as strong, capable, and therefore adequate holders is damaged.

Holding and Cultural Norms

The lack of skills and abilities is a result of the parents' status as immigrants who have not acculturated and have yet to familiarize themselves with the new environment. Parents also lack knowledge of Israeli culture and have difficulty embracing new behavioral codes. The interviewees therefore view their parents' conduct as incompetent according to Ethiopian social and behavioral norms.

Some of the interviewees described situations in which the parents' clinging to the Ethiopian codes of obedience and respect for authority figures prevents them from standing behind their children and supporting them when they feel thwarted in the new culture. We have shown how Haila experiences his parents' insistence on the Ethiopian code of obedience and restraint in the interaction with authorities as their inability to support him in his struggles against the system. The difficulty, incapacity, or unwillingness of their parents to argue, be assertive, and stand up for their children's' rights was described in many of the interviews. Malakamo, for example, says, "Father, if they [teachers] tell him I'm no good, your son is no good, then he takes it more . . . negatively. He can't argue with the teacher, maybe you're no good and all, stuff like that." The interviewees explicitly connect these situations to the traditional Ethiopian behavioral codes, and many times compare their parents' behavior with the Israeli parents' behavior, as they perceive it. Malakamo, for instance, later on says, "The Israelis, the parents argue, the parents are always on their children's side. The Ethiopians, well, it's different."[5]

Holding As Emotional Support

Many of the participants expressed the wish for more logistical support from their parents. Beyond experiencing their parents' concern for them, some of the interviewees expressed a wish for support also in the form of serving as a source of advice and guidance. Many of the interviewees described their parents as unable to guide them because of their different cultural background and the lack of similar experiences in the parents' past.

David says the following about his mother: "I can't come, come and ask her about the army. Or, like, discuss whether I should join the army or not. Because no, she doesn't have a clue." Malka, who spoke a lot about the support she receives from her parents, qualified that by saying that in certain areas she does not go to her parents for support: "They weren't born in Israel, they came from Ethiopia. They didn't go to school. They, like, didn't have this whole thing. They didn't go through what I'm going through."

These feelings, of course, are not unique to Ethiopian youths. The experience of the generation gap and the perception of parents as not understanding are not unknown to children of native-born Israelis as well. Often, however, the experience of adolescents who complain that their parents don't understand them is intertwined with elements of the eye-to-eye validation dimension, which includes wishing the other would see them as they are (Josselson, 1992). Here, this experience is described in the context of the holding dimension, a reflection of the parents' ability to contain, advise, and guide. The teenagers experience not being understood as a problem that pre-

---

[5]A similar phenomenon was also reported in regard to Hispanic adolescents. Coatsworth et al. (2000) suggested that Hispanic parents' cultural tendency to behave with respect and conformity toward institutions may cause them to be inhibited with regard to approaching school representatives to advocate on behalf of their children, and thus they become less involved in school. Coatsworth and colleagues (2000) also found that more family involvement in school was related to lower levels of behavior problems among young Hispanic girls, especially for recently immigrated (and probably less acculturated) families.

vents them from receiving aid from their parents, and eventually mars the relationship with them.

In addition, some of the participants described their parents' views, which they experience as different from the views of most Israeli parents, as another cause of emotional distance. Uri, for instance, compares the sort of relationships he sees in Israeli families to the situation in his family and in Ethiopian families in general. He says,

> And this we can't do, come to father and tell him, listen father, I don't get along here because of this and that. Either he doesn't have any clue about it. . . . There is no such thing as friends and going out and all, he has no idea. Or that you're ashamed because, because he's more, educates [disciplines] you, not helping and laughing with you and everything, but more educating . . . fathers are mainly for educating you, not being with you, son, and coming to Superland [an amusement park] with you and all that stuff.

Uri wishes for this kind of mutuality with his father, but his father's unfamiliarity with such a father–son relationship leads Uri to experience his father's unavailability as a failure in holding.

Uri's quotation also offers a view of the parents' perception of the sort of holding they should provide.[6] The parents grasp their tending function as educating and disciplining, teaching behavioral codes, and passing on the tools needed for survival (tools that may no longer be suitable to Israeli life). Uri describes a wish for support in the sense of containing and processing his problems, but feels that the nature of his relationship with his parents does not allow turning to them for that. Similar feelings came up in many of the interviews and were experienced as impaired parental holding and support.

These descriptions are compatible with research findings that suggest that parenting styles that are adaptive in collectivist societies may be less adaptive in a new society because adolescents adopt the new culture's construction of the self. Examining the connection between parenting style and self-esteem, Herz and Gullone (1999) showed that a parental pattern that involves high levels of control and restriction and the communication of minimal amount of affection and care, a style that is prevalent in traditional collectivistic societies, was connected to lower self-esteem for Vietnamese Australian immigrant adolescents just as it was for nonimmigrants. There is no evidence that such a style is connected to low self-esteem in collectivistic societies. Thus, the researchers suggested that when the cultural context that serves as a buffer for self-esteem (e.g., the communication of the importance of obedience to the family and society or implicit communication of affection) is removed, the pattern is no longer adaptive. In the present study, a similar parental behavior that might have been adaptive in Ethiopia is experienced in the relational realm as a lack of holding.

---

[6]As it is perceived by the adolescents.

Coping With the Experience of Impaired Parental Holding

Most interviewees express mixed feelings concerning the holding dimension in their relationship with their parents. As we have shown, interviewees mention holding functions as important and central to the relationship. Most regard their parents as concerned about them yet unable to protect or guide them in the new cultural setting. The teenagers view these difficulties in holding with empathy and understanding and often accept them forgivingly. Still, the participants also express anger and disappointment in their parents. Malakamo, for instance, says, "I'm fed up of it, of them trying to help you, but can't." He adds, "I say it doesn't matter and all, it's not that bad, even though it does matter, and in my heart I know it matters."

The experience of lack of holding is accompanied by great pain. Earlier, we noted the feelings of despair that Haila described following the lack of holding he was experiencing at the time of the interview. Similar feelings were described by most of the interviewees. Descriptions often included words such as *despair, break up,* and *deterioration* as interviewees dealt with emotions associated with lack of holding. Uri, for instance, speaks generally and in third person when he deals with the difficulty accompanying lack of holding[7] and says,

> He [the Ethiopian] plays many roles and somewhere in the way he becomes despaired, he says, "What do I need all this nonsense for?" . . . There isn't the help for the community, someone has to pick up this community, to pick it up. And many youngsters fall out in the end.

(We note that the imagery of "picking up" and "falling" is that of the holding experience.)

There are, in fact, occurrences that may be seen as deterioration and decline among the youngsters in the Ethiopian community. According to data published by The Israeli Association for the Ethiopian Jews, in 1998, 6.2% of Ethiopian Israeli students ages 14 to 17 dropped out of the education system, as opposed to 3.5% in the general Jewish population. The rate of delinquency is also steadily rising among them. According to the Central Bureau of Statistics (2001b), the percentage of dropouts is even higher (around 16.5%) among students who came in the more recent immigration wave (immigrating to Israel between the years 1996 and 1999). Indeed, some of the interviewees described taking up crime, as well as drug and alcohol abuse, as common occurrences among Ethiopian youths. Three of the participants in the study (all male) described periods of leaving the school system, use of addictive substances, and even periods of loitering and homelessness. Both those who experienced it themselves and those who watched it happen in

---

[7]This use of general speech about "the problems of the community" or of third-person speech was common among the interviewees when they dealt with painful subjects.

their surroundings associated these occurrences with factors involved in lack of holding and support.

Most interviewees describe their efforts to cope with the lack of parental holding. One prevalent way is searching for a holding relationship with other figures. All interviewees mentioned important relationships with adults that provide holding and support. In most cases, including Haila's, these people are older siblings, but sometimes they are educational figures, or even friends from the same age group.

The interviewees described the holding these figures provide as replacing and filling the place of the parental holding. Malakamo, for example, describes the relationship with his older siblings and mentions that he approaches his siblings as holding figures because his parents, for different reasons, cannot play this role. Of his parents he says, "It's not that they can help me or anything. . . . The siblings, yes, the siblings can. . . . That's why the siblings are more. . . . I love my brothers and sisters because they do things for me."

The presentation of the siblings' (or other figures') holding as a substitution for parental holding shows that the participants had expected holding to come from their parents as it had in early life. Receiving holding from other figures is only a replacement. Therefore when the parents do not fulfill the holding role, the relationship with them is impaired, and pain, anger, and disappointment appear. One may assume that it is a deepening process. Impairment of holding leads to distancing from the parents, which then weakens the tendency to approach them when in need, thus blocking the possibility of holding and support, which in turn causes more distancing. Malakamo, feeling that his parents would not understand and accept his actions, does not approach them for help.

On the other hand, some of the interviewees experience the need "to get along on their own" as a factor that helped them acquire important skills. Uri, for instance, describes a painful experience of "breaking down" and leaving the system but later on says, "I managed to get along. And that's it, ever since, I say, I can get along, I don't have to depend on others." Interviewees such as Uri do not ignore the need for holding and the pain connected with the lack of it, but cast their need to do without as a strengthening factor that helps them develop independence and adaptability. Several of the teenagers told stories in which lack of support from their surroundings fostered their will to prove themselves and succeed against the odds. Tadila describes her family's difficult situation and the necessity "to get along" on her own, but she also says, "I feel that I have to fight in order to prove. To prove that my success depends only on me, only on me, and not on anybody else. Motivation to succeed, to go on." The ambition to succeed and prove that they can cope with the difficult circumstances serves as a kind of holding factor in itself, by providing a meaning system that gives order and direction.

Authority, Idealization, and Holding

The changes that the Ethiopian community went through as a result of the immigration to Israel undermined the parents' authority in relation to their children. Causative factors included adaptation difficulties, intervention of external figures in family matters, and the children's transfer to residential schools (Bodovsky et al., 1994; Shabtay, 1999). In light of the emphasis the Ethiopian culture and traditional social structure give to authority and rules of behavior toward authority figures (Barahani, 1990; Ben-Ezer, 1987; Bodovsky et al., 1994; Rosen, 1985), this loss had a big effect on family life and on the relationships between parents and children.

Some of the participants described loss of parental authority, and often linked it to descriptions of decline and failure. Zaudo, for instance, explains why he thinks many Ethiopian youths drop out of school: "In Israel the parents don't have the right to tell them. . . . The parents lost their right. The parents tell them something, ah, 'leave me alone, I have a right here, I can do whatever I want to do, whatever I want'." When he was asked to explain the term *right*, he said, "Here the parents don't have a right. To speak here, to tell him, or beat him. It's for his own sake . . . because here, the children have power, the parents don't have power."

Literature on immigration and adaptation often divides parental factors into parental support and parental control (e.g., Buriel, 1993). From our interviews, it appears that these aspects of the parent–child relationship are interwoven. Parental authority and control are often experienced as support. Perhaps a certain degree of authority is necessary to be an adequate holder— at least for an adolescent.

Unhelpful parental guidance can be experienced as a failure of holding, which further undermines the sense of parental authority. Thus, a destructive circle results: The impairment of parental authority damages the experience of being held, which weakens the adolescents' ability to view their parents as valued authorities.

Ben-Ezer (1987) described the Ethiopian respect code as bidirectional, a code compelling respect for the authority figure one addresses but also compelling the authority figure to act helpfully. According to Ben-Ezer, the authority figure is viewed as powerful, knowledgeable, and having the ability to help (or harm), which indicates that this figure has the ability to hold and care. In fact, for the figure to be viewed as authoritative, the figure must have the ability to hold and care.

When the dynamics between authority and support are viewed from a relational perspective, it seems that the idealization or identification dimension plays an important role in this equation. As seen in the participants' statements and Ben-Ezer's description, authority belongs to strong and valued people; one must be at least somewhat idealizable to effectively hold others.

In light of this, it is possible to say that adequate holding is essential for idealization to take place, and that this idealization is necessary for obeying adult figures and accepting (and being held by) their authority. To the extent that the participants view their parents as incompetent, they cannot experience them as idealizable self-objects (Kohut, 1977), and it is no wonder that their authoritative position is undermined. The difficulties in holding impair the idealization and authority, and the impairment of these others' ability to be idealized also damages their capacity to provide holding in the sense of setting limits and giving guidance.

Holding and Grief

As we have shown, many of the participants view their parents as limited in their ability to act usefully in the current cultural environment. Most interviewees associated this lack as a loss: The parents had many skills and abilities when they lived in Ethiopia, but these abilities were lost, or became irrelevant, with the immigration to Israel. When the participants speak of their relationship with their parents during childhood, many of them describe their parents' respectable position and their talents at the time. It is interesting to observe that this perception of their parents' earlier competence and authority also appeared in narratives of the Israeli-born participants, who did not experience their parents' lives before the immigration (although they probably heard stories about it).

Conceptual models of the immigration experience relate to loss of functions, position, identity, values, skills, and so on as a result of leaving the home country (for a review, see Mirsky, 1996). Many models depict the immigrants' adaptation process as parallel to a grief process following the loss of a loved one (Leherer, 1993; Mirsky, 1996). In the context of the present study, the participants did describe an experience of loss and sometimes even grief. However, it seems that this is a complex experience of loss. The adolescents were grieving for the skills and status their parents lost rather than for their personal losses. Immigration hurt their parents' ability to fit in, and that had profound impact on the relationship with them. They grieved for the loss of holding that might have been. In this sense, even the youths who were born in Israel and did not experience the immigration themselves, as well as those who did immigrate but feel they adjusted well, experienced themselves as having been influenced by the effects of the immigration process on their parents. The experience of loss and the grief that accompanied it was implanted in the experience of the relationships with the parents.

SUMMARY AND CONCLUSIONS

Our purpose in this work was to investigate the relational experience of Ethiopian Israeli youths, particularly in terms of their experience of support and holding as they make their way in the bicultural context they live in. We were specifically trying to examine how holding operates phenomenologically in the experience of adaptation following immigration.

We found that the holding relational dimension was strongly apparent in the descriptions of the participants' relationships with their parents. Parents were experienced as providing some holding functions, described by the participants in concepts of "thereness" and "worry" or "care." When this holding felt adequate, participants perceived their parents as supplying an anchor in the world, tending to and fulfilling their needs and sometimes containing their anxieties. At the same time, the participants experience a lack of holding in their relationships with their parents, who do not seem strong or capable enough to protect them and provide a buffer in the new culture. Sometimes the children feel called on to exercise a holding function for the parents.

The participants described a lack of financial holding and of emotional support in the sense of guiding, containing, and sharing emotions. This lack was attributed to a number of elements, including the parents' difficulty in integrating and adjusting in Israel, their lack of modern skills, and, more important, their adherence to traditional Ethiopian norms that were described as no longer adaptive. These elements prevent the parents from fulfilling what their children expect from a holding other in the new culture.

The experience of lack of holding is accompanied by feelings of anger and despair which may underlie the unfortunately common phenomena of destructive and self-destructive behaviors among this adolescent group. Those who are adapting better are those who cope with the lack of parental holding by finding some substitute figures that meet this relational need. Still, these connections are described as substitutions, and holding is defined as a parental role and duty by its essence. Thus, parental failure in fulfilling this role damages the connections with the parents and the distance created may prevent further possibilities of receiving support from parents in the future. Some of the participants also used the perception of "making it on my own" as a meaning-making system that has a holding value and provides motivation and a will to succeed.

The holding concept illuminates, from a relational point of view, the dynamics of the decline of parental authority that has been described before in the professional literature. Obeying parental authority is a central concept in the Ethiopian culture, as it is in many nonindustrial cultures. The traditional authority structure, however, presupposes an authority figure who can be idealized or at least regarded as competent enough to protect, guide, and support. Impairment of the parents' perceived ability to hold also impairs their capacity to express their authority or to be experienced as such by their adolescents. We have discussed the sad circularity in which the difficulties in holding hurt the possibility to idealize the parents and therefore accept their authority, which in turn hurts their ability to hold in the sense of guiding and setting limits.

We found evidence of a mourning process for the holding functions that once existed and were lost. This experience seems to be one of second-hand loss: The adolescents grieve over qualities that their parents lost which in turn affect them. It is therefore possible to say that the loss experience is carried by the Ethiopian Israeli culture and passed to the next generations.

These findings help put the immigration losses described in the literature in a relational perspective. Concepts such as decrease in authority or conflicted values are imbued with relational significance.

REFERENCES

Barahani, Z. (1990). The family and community life of Jews in Ethiopia and at the transition to Israel. *Sugiot be'Nosey Mishpacha shel Yehudey Ethiopia* (Publication 4) [Booklet]. Jerusalem: Beitachin.

Ben-David, A., & Ben-Ari Tirosh, A. (1997). The experience of being different: Black Jews in Israel. *Journal of Black Studies, 27*, 510–527.

Ben-David, A., & Leichtentritt, R. (1999). Ethiopian and Israeli students' adjustment to college: The effect of family, social support and individual coping styles. *Journal of Comparative Family Studies, 30*, 297–313.

Ben-Ezer, G. (1985). Cross-cultural misunderstandings: The case of Ethiopian immigrant Jews in Israeli society. *Israel Social Science Research, 3*(1–2), 63–73.

Bion, W. R. (1962). *Learning from experience.* London: Heinemann.

Bodovsky, D., David, Y., Baroch, E., Eran, Y., & Avni, B. (1994). Ethiopian Jews in the cultural transition: The family and the life circle. *Sugiot be'Nosey Mishpacha shel Yehudey Ethiopia* (Publication 5) [Booklet]. Jerusalem: Beitachin.

Bodovsky, D., David, Y., Eran, Y., & Rozen, Y. (1989). Customs and culture: Implications for developing professional relationships. *Sugiot be'Nosey Mishpacha shel Yehudey Ethiopia* (Publication 2) [Booklet]. Jerusalem: Beitachin.

Buriel, R. (1993). Childrearing orientations in Mexican American families: Influences of generations and sociocultural factors. *Journal of Marriage and the Family, 55*, 987–1000.

Central Bureau of Statistics. (2001a). *Sikrey koach adam* [Man-power survey]. Jerusalem: The State of Israel.

Central Bureau of Statistics. (2001b). *Hatmada balimudim ve'neshira shel yalmidey batey ha'sefer ha'al yesudim* [School persistence and dropping out rates of high-school students]. Jerusalem: The State of Israel.

Coatsworth, D. J., Maldonado-Malina, M., Pantin, H., & Szapocznik, J. (2005). A person-centered and ecological investigation of acculturation strategies in Hispanic immigrant youth. *Journal of Community Psychology, 33*, 157–174.

Coatsworth, D. J., Pantin, H., Mcbride, C., Briones, E., Kurtines, W., & Szapocznik, J. (2000). Ecodevelopmental correlates of behavior problems in young Hispanic females. *Applied Developmental Science, 6*, 126–143.

Darwish-Murad, S., Joung, I. M. A., Verhulst, F. C., & Crijnen, A. A. M. (2004). Determinants of self-reported emotional and behavioral problems in Turkish immigrant adolescents aged 11–18. *Social Psychiatry and Psychiatric Epidemiology, 39,* 196–207.

Dotan, T. (1998). Adolescence in transition: Ethiopian adolescents in Israel. In M. Golan, R. Duck, B. Vezunsky, M. Yakuv, & A. Nudelman (Eds.), *Hagesher el ha'kesher: Sugiut be'Inyaney mishpacha kehila be'pnimia* [The bridge to connecting: Family, community and residential school issues] (pp. 33–48). Jerusalem: Ministry of Education and Culture.

Flum, H. (1998). Embedded identity: The case of young high-achieving Ethiopian Jewish immigrants in Israel. *Journal of Youth Studies, 1,* 143–161.

Flum, H., & Lavi-Yudelevitch, M. (2002). Adolescents' relatedness and identity formation: A narrative study. *Journal of Social and Personal Relationships, 19,* 527–548.

Gellis, Z. D. (2003). Kin and nonkin social supports in a community sample of Vietnamese immigrants. *Social Work, 48,* 248–258.

Guisinger, S., & Blatt, S. J. (1994). Individuality and relatedness: Evolution of a fundamental dialectic. *American Psychologist, 49,* 104–111.

Herz, L., & Gullone, E. (1999). The relationship between self-esteem and parenting style: A cross-cultural comparison of Australian and Vietnamese-Australian adolescents. *Journal of Cross-Cultural Psychology, 30,* 742–761.

Josselson, R. (1992). *The space between us: Exploring the dimension of human relationships.* San Francisco: Jossey-Bass.

Kagitcibasi, C. (1996). The autonomous-relational self: A new synthesis. *European Psychologist, 1,* 180–186.

Kagitcibasi, C. (2003). Autonomy, embeddedness and adaptability in immigration contexts. *Human Development, 46,* 145–149.

Kohut, H. (1977). *The restoration of the self.* New York: International Universities Press.

Kwak, K. (2003). Adolescents and their parents: A review of intergenerational family relations for immigrant and non-immigrant families. *Human Development, 46,* 115–130.

Leherer, Z. (1993). *Psychology shel hagira: Skirat safroot* [The psychology of immigration: Literature review]. Jerusalem: I.D.F/Joint-Brookdale Institute.

Markus, H. R., & Kitayama, S. (1991). Culture and the self: Implications for cognition, emotion, and motivation. *Psychological Review, 98,* 224–253.

Mirsky, Y. (1996). Hebetim psychologim bewhagira: Skirat safroot [Psychological aspects of immigration: Literature review]. *Psychology, H*(2), 199–214.

Raeff, C. (1997). Individuals in relationships: Cultural values, children's social interactions, and the development of an American individualistic self. *Developmental Review, 17,* 205–238.

Rosen, H. (1985). Core symbols of Ethiopian identity and their role in understanding the Beta Israel today. *Israel Social Science Research, 3*(1–2), 55–61.

Rosen, H. (1995). A government anthropologist among the Ethiopian Jews in Israel. *Israel Social Science Research, 10*(2), 55–68.

Shabtay, M. (1995). The experience of Ethiopian Jewish soldiers in the Israeli army: The process of identity formulation within the military context. *Israel Social Science Research, 10*(2), 69–80.

Shabtay, M. (1999). *"Hachi achi": Masa hazehut she hayalim olim me'Ethiopia* ["Best brother": The identity journey of Ethiopian immigrant soldiers].Tel-Aviv: Chirikover.

Shabtay, M. (2001). *Bein reggae le'rap: Etgar ha'hishtaychut shel noar yutse Ethiopia be'Israel* [Between reggae and rap: The integration challenge of Ethiopian youth in Israel]. Tel-Aviv: Chirikover.

Winnicott, D. W. (1975). *Through pediatrics to psycho-analysis.* New York: Basic Books.

Winnicott, D. W. (1979). *The maturational processes and the facilitating environment.* London: Hogarth Press.

Yilma, S. (1996). *From Falasha to freedom: An Ethiopian Jew's journey to Jerusalem.* Jerusalem: Gefen.

Zhou, M. (1997). Growing up American: The challenge confronting immigrant children and children of immigrants. *Annual Review of Sociology, 23*, 63–95.

9

CONNECTIONS OF CARE: RELATIONSHIPS AND FAMILY CAREGIVER NARRATIVES

JENNIFER F. DOBBINS

There are only four kinds of people in the world:
those who have been caregivers,
those who are currently caregivers,
those who will be caregivers, and
those who will need caregivers.

—*Rosalyn Carter* (1996)

According to current census projections, over 50 million people in the United States provide care for a family member, significant other, or friend who is aged, ill, or disabled (National Family Caregivers Association, 2005). Caring for a loved one was once considered a family matter—invisible work nested within the private sphere of home. Over the past couple of decades, however, advances in medical technology, altered illness patterns, extended life spans, and changes in traditional family structure and dynamics have rendered informal or family caregiving and caregivers visible. There is an increased awareness of what such caregivers do, and a growing acknowledgment that they need to be supported and sustained in the caregiver role over time.

I would like to acknowledge Dr. Suzanne Ouellette for her invaluable assistance in the preparation of this chapter and the editors of this special issue for their thoughtful and provocative commentary on earlier drafts. Special thanks are due to those whose willingness to share their caregiving experiences have made this chapter possible and, most especially, to Jean and Arnold Dobbins, my first and best models for family care.

What do family caregivers do? They provide critical assistance with day-to-day living, monitor symptoms and illness progression, research treatment options, and offer comfort and support (Levine, 2002; Pearlin, Mullan, Semple, & Skaff, 1990). They negotiate with the medical care providers and insurance companies and are often expected to master complicated medical technologies and procedures (Ayres, 2000; Levine, 2002; Wrubel & Folkman, 1997). Caregiving, however, is more than the tasks caregivers perform on behalf of those they care for; it encompasses a series of relationships that are constantly being reconfigured and renegotiated. Yes, caregivers are caregivers—but they are also spouses, parents, children, siblings, friends, and relations. Family caregiving never takes place in a vacuum but is rather woven into the rich matrix of activities, events, roles, and relationships that make up lives.

Psychological and medical literature on family caregivers has traditionally focused on caregiver stress, strain, and burden; from this perspective, caregiving tends to be treated as a variable to be isolated. As researchers, we need to find tools and perspectives that reflect the embeddedness of caregiving in social life, so that we can better understand what caregivers do and how they do it. The close examination of caregiver narratives is one approach.

CAREGIVING AS RELATIONSHIP; RELATIONSHIP AS CAREGIVING

If you look up the term *relationship* in any dictionary, you will find the word *connection* somewhere in the definition. Human relationships reflect the multiple ways in which we are bound to each other: by blood, by law, by choice, and by chance. Caregiving can be considered one expression of that bond. Sociologists Leonard Pearlin and his colleagues (Pearlin et al., 1990) made the connection clear: "Whereas caring is the affective component of one's commitment to the welfare of another, caregiving is the behavioral expression of this commitment. Giving care to someone is an extension of caring about that person" (p. 583). Disability activist Richard Gottlieb (2002) put it even more simply: Caregiving is "embodied love" (p. 226).

For some, caring for a loved one is simply part and parcel of a given relationship; they resist the title of caregiver, because it seems to negate the other relationships they hold: "I don't look at myself as a caregiver; I am a husband in love with his wife" (Senor, 2001, p. 77). Others find that their relationships with those they care for—and indeed with all those they care about—flounder under the weight of caregiving:

> Caregiving, which previously might have been but one fleeting component of an encompassing relationship, can come to be the dominant, overriding component. Under conditions of chronic and progressive impairment, therefore, caregiving may imperialistically expand to the

point where it occupies virtually the entirety of the relationship. (Pearlin et al., 1990, p. 583)

It comes as no surprise that caregivers find their day-to-day relationships disrupted by the inexorable duties of caregiving. However, recent research indicates that much of the stress family caregivers report doesn't come from what they do, but rather from the meanings they ascribe to what they do (Ayres, 2000; Wrubel & Folkman, 1997). These meanings arise through people's ongoing interactions with others. As Virginia O'Leary (1998) observed, "Meaning derived through mutual relationships is a critical source of personal validation, because the concepts of meaning and validation are linked to culture and socially defined." She further noted that people's dealings with those close to them provide more than the exchange of emotional and practical support; they also serve as "reality checks—a way to validate one's personal sense of meaning and social identity" (p. 436). The ways in which caregivers experience their important relationships then become important to their understanding of themselves as caregivers and as people in the world.

In this chapter, I explore the ways in which evolving relationships shape the experience of caregiving, and how caregiving in turn shapes critical relationships. To do this, I examine an exchange between five members of an online support group created by and for family caregivers. I use positioning theory (Davies & Harré, 1999) to explore the different relationships that emerge from this caregiver narrative: connections between caregiver and care recipient, between caregiver and other caregivers, and between caregiver and other people (friends, other family members, medical professionals, etc.). The process of creating and negotiating the caregiver role is revealed as the caregiver conversation unfolds; an understanding of this process and of caregiving itself as a series of interrelationships becomes contextualized.

THE CAREGIVERS' SUPPORT GROUP

The narrative selected for review, "Crisis—Not a Vent," was generated by five members of an Internet-based message board called Caregivers' Support. The board had been in existence for almost 6 years and within that time, the format and structure of the group had been repeatedly revamped by the Internet service provider network on which it was residing. There was also a considerable turnover in membership; people came and went as the need for support ebbed and flowed over the course of the caregiving experience. However, the basic function of the board remained constant: to provide ongoing support to family members caring for family and friends who are chronically ill or disabled.

Like many popular virtual forums, the Caregivers' Support group was peer-led—that is, run by caregivers for caregivers without any kind of professional intervention or moderation. Such groups are based on the premise that people facing similar challenges are best equipped to help each other find productive ways of dealing with them (Davison, Pennebaker, & Dickerson, 2002; McKenna & Green, 2002). Members swap stories; exchange emotional support, practical tips, and information; and together explore different models of caregiving. "The power of this approach lies in the belief that a collective wisdom is born through the shared experience of participants rather than through the professional training or style of the leader" (Davison et al., 2002, p. 206).

At this point, it may be helpful to consider what *relationship* means in an Internet-based context. Virtual interactions have certain key features that clearly mark the boundaries between online and offline worlds. Online relationships are unique in that participants can remain anonymous, physical distance no longer matters, time is immaterial, physical appearance and visual cues no longer act as gatekeepers, and conversational turn-taking is equally shared by all participants (McKenna & Bargh, 2000). These features are particularly relevant to the study of Internet-based support groups such as Caregivers' Support. Participants in such groups may speak more openly online than they would in a face-to-face setting; they forge intimacies more quickly and feel freer to ask for what they need. Without physical or visual cues to act as gatekeepers, there may be a greater openness to feedback. Unlike actual self-help groups that meet at specified intervals, caregivers can access a virtual group 24 hours a day, and a person always gets a turn to speak (McKenna & Bargh, 1998, 2000).

Another finding comes directly from my own observation of virtual support groups: A person doesn't have to be in direct contact with others to feel connected to them. Research on the Internet mentions *lurkers*, those who read message-board posts but don't respond. Within these support groups, it's not uncommon for people to lurk for some time before making their presence known. People can therefore come to know each other before they ever share an interaction—and if and when the interaction does take place, it is informed by this prior knowledge. The careful observer can often pinpoint the moment at which people first *express* their online relationships as the point at which they first respond directly to another's posted message. It's not as clear, however, when that sense of relationship truly begins.

The Internet allows people to come and go at will, to express themselves without the usual boundaries of face-to-face interactions, to transcend the limits of time and space. Although this freedom is potentially liberating, it can also be very frightening. People who seek online support need to create safe spaces in which they can reach out to others. The creation of relationships in this context is a critical part of creating safe space—quite literally an act of good faith. At the most basic level, virtual relationships arise from the same impetus as those in real life: the desire to connect with others.

The Caregivers' Support group uses a message-board format[1] for member communication. Message boards function in a straightforward way: Someone posts a topic of interest—a question, a problem, a story to share; others respond, and a conversational thread[2] ensues. Multiple threads take place simultaneously at any given time; some begin and end in a couple of exchanges, and some roll on for months. Interactions can take the form of a lively debate between many different participants or an intimate chat between just a few. Message-board communications are unique in that they combine the call and answer of conversation with the introspection of a journal. As the following analysis shows, the "Crisis—Not a Vent" thread forms a narrative that simultaneously reflects the interior monologue of each participant and the joint efforts of all participants to address the topic at hand. This narrative reveals the process of creating the caregiver role, as members individually and collectively work out what it means to be a family caregiver.

"CRISIS—NOT A VENT": AN OVERVIEW

The thread I've chosen for analysis is an exchange between five caregivers entitled "Crisis—Not a Vent." The "Crisis" thread is composed of an original message posted to the Caregivers' Support message board, the four responses elicited by that post, and the original poster's response to all who responded. I selected this particular thread because it reflects a particularly focused interaction; the participants stayed firmly on the topic at hand, and the whole conversation took place within a relatively short time frame (approximately 24 hours total). The "Crisis" thread works well as a series of individual contributions, as a shared moment in time, and also as part of an ongoing conversation that might be extended into the future. The five women who engaged in the exchange had strong and highly individualized voices; both the range of individual orientations and narrative styles as well as the collective voice that started to emerge through their interaction can be heard. Finally, I chose this thread because it provides a particularly fine exemplar of the kind of work caregivers did together as they interacted in this virtual forum.

---

[1] Message-board forums, such as the one discussed in this chapter, are held within the public domain; anyone with access to the Internet can read the messages posted there. All narrative content quoted in this chapter, however, is used with permission of the authors. Some unique features have been altered, masked, or deleted to conceal the identity of the authors.

[2] The definition of *thread* used here is derived from standard message-board (not electronic mailing list) format and follows the usage indicated by the Internet service provider network that hosted this particular group. A thread is composed of an initial post and all the responses and interactions that arise in response to that post, pertaining to a given topic or subject. It does not refer to individual posts or conversational turns.

The details of the "Crisis" thread are thoroughly explored in the analysis sections of the chapter; what follows here is an overview of the thread to orient the discussion to come.

Connie, a relatively new poster,[3] opened the conversation with a heartfelt plea:

> Help.
>   This time I am flat-out asking for help, and not just venting and opening up for the benefit of others who post. I am being selfish (do we caregivers even KNOW the meaning of that word?), and I want anybody's help.

Connie's dad, who was suffering from dementia, had been transferred from the hospital to a skilled nursing facility while necessary repairs were done to his home. Connie said that Dad was well aware of the damaged roof and the need for repairs; she had repeatedly explained to him that, for his own safety, he couldn't come home until these repairs were made. The repairs were almost done, and hospice was standing by to facilitate the move. But Dad wanted to come home right away, and Connie described the barrage of phone calls "begging, threatening, or bribing me in order to come home." The latest phone call—the one that pushed her over the edge—came at 3:00 in the morning: "He was in the ER after falling out of his bed being treated for a laceration and a large lump on his head."

As Connie's narrative unfolded, other relationships came into play. Connie was not only Dad's daughter and caregiver; she was also a wife, a mother, and the caregiver for two brothers who are severely disabled. She summed up her situation simply ("My strength is gone") and asked the group for guidance: "How do I cope with someone in his condition? And do it in the weakened state that I have reached since my Mom died?" She closed her post with a rueful reflection on how things were going:

> I have held it together pretty good for 10 months but with things seeming to be at their worst, that "full plate" everyone talks about me having is seeming more and more to be made of paper.

In a relatively short time (a little over 24 hours) Connie received four responses to her note. Nancy, Beverly, Karen, and Lucy[4] offered advice, practical tips, and emotional support; they interpreted Connie's significant relationships, and reflected on their own. Connie responded in turn to the group, and the conversation—for the time being—was closed.

The analysis and interpretation of the "Crisis" thread is based on a combination of positioning theory and the multiple reading method. In the section that follows, I describe my method of analysis.

---

[3]At the point of this post, Connie had been active on the board for only about 6 months; however, she may have been lurking for much longer (see earlier discussion on lurking).

[4]Names used are pseudonyms, as is the name used for the support group. Again, all content is used with permission of the authors.

POSITIONING THEORY

Davies and Harré (1999) defined *positionality* as "a discursive practice whereby selves are located in conversations as observably and intersubjectively coherent participants in jointly produced storylines" (p. 37). Positioning reflects where people stand within a given discourse, a given social context, a given relationship. It can be interactive, as one person positions another; it can be reflexive, as one positions oneself within the discourse. Michael Bamberg and others described three different levels of positioning (Bamberg, 1997; Talbot, Bibace, Bokhour, & Bamberg, 1996). The level of then-and-there represents the actual story that is being told. The here-and-now level reflects the relative positioning between the narrator and the audience. At the self-to-self level, the narrator positions him- or herself vis-à-vis him- or herself.

THE MULTIPLE-READ METHOD

Using a variant of Brown, Debold, Tappan, and Gilligan's (1991) multiple-read method, I applied these three levels of positioning to the "Crisis—Not a Vent" text to explore caregiving as a series of interrelationships that evolve over time. The multiple-read method is based on two fundamental premises: (a) each speaker, author, or narrator speaks from multiple voices, stances, and positions and (b) the act of reading is in and of itself relational in character (Brown et al., 1991, pp. 25–27). By reading the same text multiple times for different voices or positions, one can identify how these different positions shape, color, and work through the tale being told. This process in turn leads to richer, deeper understanding of the text, at the same time illuminating the relationship between narrator and audience. The exploration of emergent relationships between narrator and multiple audiences is particularly salient in light of the present data. Not only are there multiple authors, but there are multiple readers as well: the caregivers who read each other's posts, I myself as researcher and interpreter, and those who read this chapter.

For the analysis presented in this chapter, I read the entire "Crisis—Not a Vent" thread for each of the three levels of positioning: the then-and-there, the here-and-now, and the self-to-self:

- At the then-and-there level, I identified the key relationships referenced by each caregiver and the ebb and flow of those relationships over the course of the narrative.
- At the here-and-now level, I explored the relationships that developed between the members of the group over the course of their exchange.

- At the self-to-self level, I sought out the interior monologue the narrator held with herself as she worked out the emerging relationship with herself as caregiver.

Level 1: Then and There

How are the characters positioned in relation to one another within the reported events? At this level, we attempt to analyze how characters within the story world are constructed in terms of, for example, protagonists and antagonists or as perpetrators and victims. More concretely, this type of analysis aims at the linguistic means that do the job of marking one person as, for example: (a) the agent who is in control while the action is inflicted upon the other; or (b) as the central character who is helplessly at the mercy of outside (quasi "natural") forces or who is rewarded by luck, fate, or personal qualities (such as bravery, nobility, or simply character). (Bamberg, 1997, p. 337)

This is the level of "What happened?": the level that permits one to identify the key players and events in the narrative, to map out the narrator's position relative to significant others in the story, and to trace shifts in those positions over time. The then-and-there reading of the "Crisis" thread reveals how these caregivers collectively and individually sought to restore balance to their relationships, relationships that had been thrown out of kilter by the disruption of illness. From this perspective, the events described are more than what happened; they are important markers for relationships in flux.

Connie's initial post presents the chain of events that had led her to her present state of crisis. First, a bit of history:

We have had to do roof repair and mold removal in order to make it safe and healthy for Dad to come home from the "skilled nursing facility" where he has been for 8 days since released from a hospital stay of a little over a week.

Then there's the recurring event of Dad's phone calls: "I have just had yet another phone call from him begging, threatening, or bribing me in order to come home." Finally there's the precipitating event that brought Connie to the group for help: "I got a phone call at 3 a.m. this morning because he was in the ER after falling out of his bed being treated for a laceration and a large lump on his head." Connie offers these events in precise order, as a kind of map for Dad's downward spiral. In doing so, she creates a background that evokes the sense of agency she once had regarding her caregiver role—and it is against this background that the foreground of an uncertain future has begun to emerge.

However, two events that are not presented as part of this chain of events are equally important to understanding Connie's experience. The first is the death of Connie's mother, an event that is mentioned only in passing at the end of her post ("the weakened state that I have reached since my Mom died"). The second event—the main event—is the one that has not happened yet: Dad coming home. From the stance of the then-and-there, this preevent is as significant a marker of Connie's position relative to those around her as those events that have already taken place, especially in what it says about Connie's relationship with her father.

Connie's presentation of this escalating chain of events not only maps Dad's decline but also charts the decline in their relationship, as she is less and less able to deal with him. Dad has become simultaneously the agent of power ("begging, threatening, or bribing") and the object of pity and concern ("He is a sun downer and the dementia has worsened").[5] Connie does her best to keep their relationship on an even keel ("We can safely bring him home Tuesday, which has been explained to him several times"), but is thwarted by Dad's inability to understand ("Rational explaination [sic] does not help"). Her frustration mounts as she first takes on Dad's point of view ("It's my entire fault. My fault he can't come home") and then counters with her own ("Like I enjoy driving 40 minutes one way to see him, often in restraints").

But Connie's relationship with her Dad is not the only one at risk. Significant others in her life are affected by this situation as well:

> This I do between caring for the quadrapalegic [sic] brother and doing his wound care, seeing to the needs of my oldest brother (45yo with the mind of a teen due to brain damage), *trying to be a Mom* to my girls, and *attempting to be a wife* [italics added].

Caring for her siblings, trying to be a mother, attempting to be a wife—Connie seemed to feel that all her relationships are on shaky ground. Her inability to meet the needs of the rest of her family weighs on her heavily; her struggles to make Dad understand why he can't come home now mirror her attempts to keep up with the rest of her life. And this tension between love and frustration gets her down: "And when he starts one of his tyrades [sic] that I know he can't help, it simply does me in."

Nancy is the first person to respond to Connie's post; her reply was brief but to the point:

> My suggestion is to contact Medicare. If they are insisting that the repairs are needed before he can come home let them pay for them. I bet they would rather pay for the repairs then [sic] continue to pay the hospital bills.

---

[5] A *sun downer* is a person with Alzheimer's who experiences episodes of disorientation, anxiety, and/or agitation toward the end of the day, into the evening hours, and sometimes, throughout the night. This pattern of behavioral disruption is called Sundown or Sunset Syndrome.

Nancy does not merely respond to a very specific event in Connie's story; she restages the event by proposing a redistribution of responsibility: Let those who dictated this major renovation bear some responsibility for it. In doing so, Nancy attempts to shift the weight off Connie's relationship with her dad; Connie does not have to be the villain or the victim.

Beverly, the next to respond, acknowledges the power of Connie's story, and offers some key events and relationships of her own. She begins by restating the power dynamic that Connie has implied: "Your father is still attempting to control you, even though he is suffering from dementia." Beverly draws on her own experience of caring for her mother to illustrate how the balance of power can be shifted back to Connie in a loving, caring way:

> It might be helpful to write a note, in large print, and post it on the wall where he can see it—that would reassure him that you will be bringing him home as soon as the house is ready. (I did that with my Mom because she would forget as soon as I left her.)

Beverly's latest event, her husband's hospitalization, is offered as an experience that parallels Connie's:

> Even now, when my husband has been hospitalized, I am not there every single day because it just wears me out. Once he is out of danger, and recovering, I give myself permission to let the professionals take care of him.

Like Nancy, Beverly attempts to shift Connie's then-and-there narrative—and by extension Connie's position in relation to her dad—by shifting the boundaries of agency and responsibility: "You must tell yourself that you are the one in charge now, not your Dad."

Karen jumps right in with an anecdote about her mother-in-law:

> When MIL [mother-in-law] was in a nursing home after a broken hip, she would call us at all hours of the day and night. I finally instructed the staff not to bring the telephone to her. That helped.

Like Connie's dad, Karen's mother-in-law "also has tirades, and gets very snide and nasty"—so much so that Karen guiltily described another event: "It's almost a relief when she has a TIA [transient ischemic attack] as she becomes so docile during those periods." And like Connie herself, Karen is preoccupied with the big event that hadn't happened yet: the placement of her mother-in-law in a specialized facility. Karen uses the then-and-there events (her mother-in-law's outbursts) as a way to rehearse for this preevent, which necessitates a shift in her own position: "I have been thinking very seriously about placing her after the holidays, if I can get through the holidays with her in our home. If her behavior keeps getting worse, she may go sooner."

Lucy claims solidarity with Connie as the one who is ultimately responsible: "I am an only child and the mother of an 8 yr. old . . . bottom line, it all falls on me." She describes the illness trajectory of her own father as a series of escalating health crises: "He had been battling health issues on and off for years with several stays in intensive care, 2 months in intensive care and then hospice care." The hospice care experience is presented as the defining event in Lucy's then-and-there narrative: "I think that after years of health issues, I was finally able to realize that for my Dad being there was the BEST place for him." The hospice people knew exactly what to do for Dad and were particularly supportive of Lucy: "They were also wonderful in helping me prepare my then 4 yr. old son for the inevitable passing of his beloved Pop-Pop." Lucy described a kind of hermeneutic circle of relationships between herself and her father, her father and her son, her son and the hospice workers, and so on. She finds comfort in these multiple relationships, using them to strengthen her own connection to her father. Her list of practical tips is all about fostering the care recipient's sense of connection to others; keeping Dad connected to the rest of the family keeps Lucy connected to Dad. These multiple relationships sometimes intersect in chaotic ways:

> Like the day my son ran into the corner of the wall in the hospice and needed stitches, my Dad tore his iv off and trach tube to try to get to his grandson and the staff was trying to help me and my Dad. The hospice staff drove my son and I to the hospital and was greeted by a dr. who asked me if I wanted a drink, a prayer or a bed to collapse in! I told him I think I needed all three!

How does Connie respond to all this? When it is read specifically for the then-and-there, there's not much to be found in her concluding post. Connie's repeated expressions of thanks and her reflections on what this exchange meant to her more properly belong to the here-and-now level of analysis. An important shift happening, however, as Connie signifies her willingness to try reframing her story in light of what she has now heard: "I wholeheartedly accept every bit of advice that your experienced posts give."

Across this caregiver conversation, the then-and there reading becomes a narrative about restoring a sense of balance to important relationships. Connie's "problem" is not just her relationship with her Dad but the toll that it has taken on the other important relationships in her life. She struggles to balance the background story (all the events that had led up to that moment) with the as-yet-unknown foreground story of her dad coming home. The others offer their own experiences and reflections as an exploration of how a new balance can be achieved: by shifting priorities, by redefining responsibilities, by identifying turning points, and by taking and sometimes relinquishing control.

Level 2: Here and Now

> *How does the speaker position him- or herself to the audience?* At this level, we seek to analyze the linguistic means that are characteristic for the

particular discourse mode that is being employed. Does, for instance, the narrator attempt to instruct the listener in terms of what to do in face of adversary [sic] conditions or does the narrator engage in making excuses for his actions and in attributing blame to others? (Bamberg, 1997, p. 337)

I use the level of the here-and-now to explore the emerging relationship between caregivers as it unfolded within this conversation. As an individual, each narrator explicitly presented herself to the others to forge a mutually supportive relationship. They simultaneously work together to construct a collective caregiver narrative for themselves and also for an audience that extends beyond themselves—an audience that does not yet fully understand what it was to be a caregiver.

As indicated in my earlier discussion of virtual relationships, it's difficult to determine how well these five women knew each other prior to the "Crisis" thread. Connie and Beverly had interacted before on another caregiver message board. Beverly was a long-time member of the Caregivers' Support group, whereas Karen was a relative newcomer; however, both were prolific posters and so were "knowable" to others who read. Lucy posted regularly prior to her father's death; this thread marked her first appearance in some time. Connie and Nancy usually posted in response to others, but as yet had not offered much of their own history. From this perspective, Connie's post can be seen as a statement of her intention to create a new kind of relationship with others:

> This time I am flat-out asking for help, and not just venting and opening up for the benefit of *others who post*. I am being selfish (do *we caregivers* even KNOW the meaning of that word?), and *I want anybody's help*. [italics added]

Of course, Connie does not want just anybody's help; she wants the help of people who know from their own experience just what she is going through. In describing the events of the past 10 months, she oscillates between the recitation of what happened next ("We have had to do roof repair and mold removal . . ."; "I got a phone call at 3 a.m. this morning because . . .") and the toll this situation had taken on her life overall ("It's all my fault. My fault he can't come home"; "My strength is gone"). She was doing fairly well ("I have held it together pretty good for 10 months . . .") but feels that she cannot keep it up ("That 'full plate' everyone talks about me having is seeming more and more to be made of paper"). This pendulum swing between what happened and the implications of what happened ends with an overt call for help: "How do I cope with someone in his condition? And do it in the weakened state that I have reached since my Mom died?"

But what kind of help is Connie seeking? At the simplest and most obvious level, she is asking for a response from the other caregivers: advice, guidance, feedback, reaction. However, Connie is seeking a very specific kind of response, and in presenting her story to the others, she stacks the deck to ensure that she gets it.[6] In this introductory post, Connie deliberately presents herself to the others in a negative light. She refers to herself as selfish ("I am being selfish") and then immediately qualifies the statement ("Do we caregivers even KNOW the meaning of that word?"). She uses the strongest terms to describe her responsibility ("As the only non-disabled child, all responsibility lies in my hands") and her guilt ("It's my entire fault. My fault he can't come home"). The chain of events that create a kind of temporal order at the then-and-there level of analysis become a chain of evidence, a way for Connie to present her case to the others: Am I *really* that responsible (or guilty or selfish)? Connie thereby opens the door for others to respond in kind: "It's not your fault. The responsibility isn't yours alone. You're not selfish." Connie's request for help, then, is twofold: (a) What should I do? How do I do this? and (b) What kind of caregiver (or person) am I?

The task at hand for the other caregivers is multilayered as well: They must find a way to offer practical support and emotional comfort without compromising Connie's already fragile sense of agency. In presenting her case, Connie clearly differentiates between just venting and requesting help. This differentiation marks a critical shift for Connie; in caregiver circles, the ability to frame the right questions, to appropriately ask for help, is a sign of mastery. Venting is not interpreted as an agentic act but rather as a necessary evil, something a person does because there's nothing else to be done. Connie is asking the others to help her create a caregiver role that encompasses a greater sense of agency than the one she now experiences.

Nancy takes a practical approach to Connie's questions: "My suggestion is to contact Medicare." At first glance, Nancy's response seems terse; she doesn't overtly acknowledge or address Connie's need for emotional support. But Nancy helps where she can, in being the first to respond to Connie's note and in taking a triage approach to Connie's stated emergency. Nancy not only answers Connie's implicit question about responsibility but also provides the direct hyperlink to Medicare in her post so that Connie didn't have to scramble to find it.

Beverly responds with a heady mix of emotional support and advice. She immediately addresses Connie's implicit questions ("Connie, you are NOT being selfish, not even for a moment") and fully acknowledges Connie's painful situation ("Your situation is almost impossible . . ."; "My heart goes out to you"). Beverly pulls no punches in offering advice, peppering her response with phrases such as "you must" and "you should," as in the following excerpt: "You *must* consider your own health and your own family (your husband and girls). They *should* [italics added] be your first responsibility, at least in my opinion". Speaking as an experienced caregiver, Beverly provides Connie and the others with a model for caregiving:

---

[6]This interpretation was originally offered by a reviewer of an earlier draft of this chapter.

Even now, when my husband has been hospitalized, I am not there every
single day because it just wears me out. Once he is out of danger, and
recovering, I give myself permission to let the professionals take care of
him. When he returns home, my real caretaking begins, so I try to take
care of myself before then.

Like Beverly, Karen's first words to Connie are to offer emotional support: "Connie, I think you have done extremely well. You have taken on a
tremendous load, and I don't know how you have held up so well up until
now." Karen takes on a kind of expert status as she echoes Beverly's advice
on prioritizing relationships: "You need to put yourself and your husband and
children first, and everyone else should come later. I know that is easy for me
to say, but I know it is true." Karen is also the first to directly answer Connie's
call for affiliation with other caregivers. She marks the parallel between
Connie's dad and her own mother-in-law:

> Is it possible for you to have your father placed in a secure facility for
> people with Alzheimer's and dementia? We are fortunate to have three
> in our area, and I can see the time coming soon with [sic] MIL will have
> to go there.

That sense of connection and affiliation is then extended to the group as a
whole: "I wish I could be of more help to you, but it is really good for you to
unload about this to us. It helps to know that others are in the same boat."
For Karen, the whole was greater than the sum of its parts; the collective
wisdom of the group transcended the limitations of what each individual
caregiver has to offer.

By the time Lucy responds, a clear pattern of communication has been
set. She too begins with a strong statement of emotional support and acknowledgment: "My heart goes out to you . . . your situation is nearly impossible." Lucy, like Karen, strives to show Connie that she is not alone ("I
totally understand your position; I know that it is certainly not easy"). She
restates what has now become a recurrent caregiver theme—the need to prioritize relationships ("your daughters and husband come first")—and clearly
affiliates herself with the other "experts" ("I agree with Beverly and others
. . ."). However, the advice Lucy gives is tempered by a kind of humility:

> There are times when I look back now or others remind me of that time
> and how it was unbelievable that I did it all. I wish I could tell you how,
> I think you just do the best you can do and some days are better or worse
> than others.

From the here-and-now perspective, Lucy offers her list of practical tips in
the same spirit as Beverly's story of her husband's hospitalization: as a potential model for caregiving that Connie and the others might find useful. Lucy
says, "All of this seemed to help him stay more connected even though he
didn't remember much and at times was incoherent." She closes with a
semihumorous telling of a very bad day and ends her note with a chuckle: "I

was greeted by a dr. who asked me if I wanted a drink, a prayer or a bed to collapse in! I told him I think I needed all three!"

In the concluding post, Connie is clearly overwhelmed by the responses she has received—responses that addressed both her questions. She singles out Beverly ("Beverly, I have called you our 'Angel' on this board before, and as always, your words are not just of great comfort but of wisdom, as well") and extends her thanks to the others ("You were joined by some other Angels as well, and I thank all of you"). She gratefully endorses the expert status claimed by each of her correspondents, and by the group as a whole ("I whole heartedly accept every bit of advice that your experienced posts give"). Connie responds strongly to the collective embrace she received from the group ("I don't know what I would do without this board") and draws a connection between the relationship that she is building with these people to another cherished tie: "Reading each of your posts, I heard my Mom's voice echoing things you all said."

The here-and-now reading illuminates the various ways in which members of the group position themselves in relation to each other. Connie takes the role of novice, presenting her story in a way that requires the other caregivers to fill in the gaps with their own experiences. Nancy responds as the practical, pragmatic one, Beverly is the "Angel," and Lucy and Karen respectively are the voices of caregiving past and future. Connie seems to have gotten what she came for in terms of practical and emotional support. However, this interaction transcends simple call-and-answer; it serves as the foundation for ongoing conversations and for emerging partnerships. Connie, Nancy, Beverly, Karen, and Lucy are more than an audience for each other. They are collaborators in a joint product (e.g., the redefinition of agency) and their collaboration creates a discourse of caregiving that can be shared with each other and with others outside their immediate circle.

Level 3: Self-to-Self

> *How do narrators position themselves to themselves?* How is language employed to make claims that the narrator holds to be true and relevant above and beyond the local conversational situation? In other words, we hold that the linguistic devices employed in narrating point to more than the content (or what the narrative is "about") and the interlocutor. In constructing the content and one's audience in terms of role participants, the narrator transcends the question of: "How do I want to be understood by you the audience?" and constructs a (local)[7] answer to the question: "Who am I?" (Bamberg, 1997, p. 337)

---

[7]Bamberg warned that the answers to the self-to-self question "Who am I?" are by necessity local: "Any attempted answer to this question is not one that necessarily holds across contexts, but rather is a project of limited range" (Bamberg, 1997). I'm not entirely convinced of this; the discussions that emerged in this exchange suggest a life that extends outside the confines of this particular conversational thread.

At first glance, one may wonder how the self-to-self level of analysis could be useful to the narrative study of relationships. The self-to-self reading is used here to reveal a special kind of relationship between the narrator and herself as audience. In telling her story to others, each caregiver is also telling it to herself. The interaction between the narrator and herself as audience invests the narrative with meaning, as she seeks to connect her "caregiver self" to her sense of herself as a person.

Connie begins by recognizing that she is speaking from a different place than usual: "This time I am flat-out asking for help and not just venting and opening up for the benefit of others who post." Who is Connie to Connie in this moment? She is guilty ("I am being selfish"; "It's all my fault. My fault he can't come home."). She tries to be understanding about her father's condition ("When he starts one of his tyrades [sic] that I know he can't help . . .), but cannot quite pull it off ("He was well aware of the roof damage . . ."; "Like I enjoy driving 40 minutes one way to see him, often in restraints"). She strives to be everything to everyone:

> This I do between caring for the quadrapalegic [sic] brother and doing his wound care, seeing to the needs of my oldest brother . . . trying to be a Mom to my girls, and attempting to be a wife.

However, she is failing ("My strength is gone"; "it simply does me in"; "the weakened state that I have reached"). Connie's final estimation of herself paints a bleak self-portrait:

> I have held it together pretty good for 10 months but with things seeming to be at their worst, that "full plate" everyone talks about me having is seeming more and more to be made of paper.

As previously remarked, Nancy's post is brief and practically oriented; she suggests that if Medicare requested the roof repairs, Medicare should help to make it all happen: "If they are insisting that the repairs are needed before he can come home let them pay for them." Nancy positions herself to herself as the practical one, the one who knows how the world really works: "I bet they would rather pay for the repairs then [sic] continue to pay the hospital bills."

Beverly used her response to set forth some very personal statements about caregiving and about relationships in general. The advice she offers reflects Beverly's hard-won sense of herself as caregiver: "You must consider your own health and your own family (your husband and girls). They should be your first responsibility. . . ." Beverly's meditation on her own caregiving experiences reflects a kind of self-project that helps her to learn who she is:

> Once he is out of danger, and recovering, I give myself permission to let the professionals take care of him. When he returns home, my real caretaking begins, so I try to take care of myself before then.

Karen's self-to-self narrative is about expectations ("I can see the time coming soon with [*sic*] MIL will have to go there") and boundaries ("If her behavior keeps getting worse, she may go sooner"). She uses her response to think herself into the kind of caregiver—the kind of person—who will ultimately place her mother-in-law into a secure facility: "I have been thinking very seriously about placing her after the holidays, if I can get through the holidays with her in our home." Karen's sense of herself as a caregiver seems to be about turning points: At what point did she tell the nursing home staff not to bring her mother-in-law the phone? At what point will the decision to place her mother-in-law become inevitable? And who will Karen be in that moment?

Lucy, like the others, takes this opportunity to identify those beliefs that are crucial to her understanding of herself as a caregiver. She positions herself to herself as someone who had been on a long journey; her post is filled with references to her own evolution ("I was finally able to realize"; "there are times when I look back now"; "I only knew that after my Dad had passed away," etc.). Her caregiving is regarded as an act of good faith: "All you can do is do the best that you can do and at some point you will know that you did your best." Lucy's musings reflect a strong temporal sense that extends beyond the experience of caregiving: What can we know about our most profound experiences at any given time?

> I only knew that after my Dad had passed away—I knew I had tried so very hard and I know that my Dad knew it too. That has been what has given me peace—but it was much later and it wasn't [*sic*] there when I was caregiving.

This is what makes this narrative unique: Lucy's father has died, her time of caregiving is technically over, and yet she still identifies herself as a caregiver and is actively engaged in a self-to-self conversation about what that really means.

Finally, I return to Connie. In her opening post, Connie makes it clear that she is forced to go outside her own comfort zone to ask for help: "This time I am flat-out asking for help, and not just venting and opening up for the benefit of others who post." By the last post, things are starting to change: "I am not good at accepting help, but for some reason, I whole heartedly accept every bit of advice that your experienced posts give." Connie strives to connect the help she receives from the group to the help she might have received from her mother: "Reading each of your posts, I heard my Mom's voice echoing things you all said." In doing so, she shifts her position in relation to herself, rejecting the one she does not want to recognize ("I am being selfish . . . and I want anybody's help") to envision a self that suits her better: her mother's daughter. This shift is very much a work in progress for Connie; she is struggling to absorb all that she's heard, and is unsure what to do with it all at the moment of response: "I cannot explain how much that means to me. I don't know what I would do without this board." It's difficult to analyze a self-to-self narrative that has not quite happened yet, but that may be what makes this level of analysis so powerful in the long run. Perhaps, like the preevents that inform the then-and-there reading, the most powerful self-to-self narrative is the one that has yet to take place.

I previously described the message-board format as a blend of conversation and personal journal. The self-to-self reading taps into this narrative as a journal, or as an open letter to oneself. By positioning themselves simultaneously as narrator and as audience, participants shift the critical issues under discussion. The question is no longer "Who is a caregiver, and when, and how?" but rather "Who am I as a caregiver, and how does that fit into the rest of my life?" The self-to-self reading is the level at which meaning is made—meaning with implications that extend beyond the caregiving experience itself.

LOOKING ACROSS THE LEVELS

Now that I have considered each level separately, it's time to put the pieces back together. In doing so, one can see all three levels of positioning simultaneously at work in what Gadamer called a "fusion of horizons . . . in which the perspective of text and reader are combined into a new and more encompassing horizon" (Gadamer, as cited by Widdershoven, 1993, p. 13). In the section that follows I consider three of the key findings that emerged from this analysis and reflect on what they may add to the study of caregiving.

Caregiving Is Inherently Relational

Biomedical and psychological research has traditionally focused on the caregiver in isolation or, at most, the caregiver–patient dyad. Lyoness Ayres (2000) suggested that "this deconceptualized approach to caregiving may have led researchers to attribute depression, strain or burden to caregiving rather than to the complex life experiences of which caregiving was a component" (p. 425).

In the present analysis, three separate but related sets of relationships are revealed through each positioning level: between the caregiver and the important people in her "real" life, between the five caregivers as they interact with each other online, and between each caregiver and herself, as she struggles to create her own unique and personal variant of the caregiver role. These relationships are not mutually exclusive; rather, they overlap, color, and shape each other to create new perspectives.

As Connie interacts with the other caregivers, and then internalizes those interactions, she brings a new sense of herself as caregiver to her real-life relationships, thereby changing those relationships. If and when Connie returns to the group, she will have new stories to share—stories that will in turn change her interactions with the group and the work they do together.[8] In following Connie as she moves through the different interactions and relationships that make up her world, one comes to a deeper understanding of where the stress and strains of caregiving really live and what resources and support are most needed to alleviate them.

Caregiving Is More Than a Series of Events—It's a Process

Much of the research on informal caregivers focuses on a particular caregiver event: a health crisis, the decision to institutionalize the patient, the moment of caregiver collapse, and so on (Navaie-Waliser et al., 2002). Assessment tools similarly tend to focus on specific tasks performed at specific moments (Reinhard, 2004). The problem with this event-specific approach is that it cannot capture the temporal trajectory of the caregiving experience, that is, the ways in which situations and relationships change over time and the implications of those changes for those who live through them (Ayres, 2000; Neufeld & Harrison, 2003; Reinhard, 2004; Wrubel & Folkman, 1997).

This analysis opens up the concept of caregiver time by framing it in terms of relationships. Although Connie came to the board with a specific anticipated event (Dad coming home), the discussion that unfolded traveled both backward and forward through time. The trajectory of caregiving, like the span of a relationship, covers both the known and the unknown; as Shakespeare put it, "We know what we are, but know not what we may be." Taken together, these three levels of positioning allow the reader to go beyond the moment in time, to capture the temporal aspects of the caregiver narrative: the then-and-there of the past, the here-and-now of the present, and the potential of the self-to-self. Connie spoke as a caregiver on the day of her first message, but may come to speak as an "Angel" tomorrow.[9]

Caregiving—and the Discourses of Caregiving—
Are Constantly Being Renegotiated

The most intriguing finding—and the one most potentially useful to the study of caregiving—is the realization that those who research caregiving must learn how to truly listen to what caregivers say. The words that appear and reappear in the caregiver research literature (*stress, empowerment,* and *support,* to name a few) may have very different meanings within the literatures generated by caregivers themselves. In an earlier section, I described how the concept of agency was turned upside down by these caregivers; venting is not empowering after all, but asking for help is a sign of caregiver

---

[8]This discussion encapsulates my own caregiver identity model (Dobbins, 2002).
[9]As I write this, I have just learned that Connie's father died within 2 weeks of her initial post.

mastery. This kind of redefinition is an important addition to the existing literatures on help-seeking behaviors and coping or support systems.

In a similar way, the group called into question the very definition of family, as they worked out the question of who should come first. Connie was strongly urged to put her family first; *family* was specifically defined as her husband, her daughters, and herself. Did this mean that Dad was no longer "family"? Would Connie really be able to enact this redefinition of family? And what would it cost her to do so? Richard Gottlieb (2002) described this quandary as a practical, psychological, and moral one: "Who receives in this emergency room of family life, the benefits of triage?" (p. 230). Connie, Nancy, Beverly, Karen, and Lucy are actively engaged in creating a vocabulary that reflects their collective and individual understandings of caregiving. The work undertaken by caregivers through their caregiver talk—specifically, the creation, development, and negotiation of caregiver vocabulary, identity, and role definitions—serves as both welcome addition and much-needed reality check to existing biomedical and psychological research literatures.

FINAL THOUGHTS

I began this chapter with a call for tools and perspectives that allow the exploration of caregiving in the context of a fully realized life. By bringing together narratives created by and for caregivers, positioning theory, and the multiple-read method, I've discovered a fruitful venue for exploration, a productive and generous framework for interpretation, and a viable methodology. I extended Bamberg's three levels of analysis to capture the unique qualities of the phenomenon in question:

- The then-and-there level has been expanded to include the discussion of anticipated events.
- The here-and-now level reflects a more generous construction of audience.
- The self-to-self level is now explicated as a true relationship.

These augmentations allow researchers and interested others to take full advantage of the rich narratives provided by these caregivers. As relationships unfold within and across all levels, we can appreciate both the contexts in which they emerge and the meanings that they hold for those engaged in them.

Before closing, and as a way to move the discussion forward, I'd like to clarify a couple of key issues in reference to the work presented here. The theoretical underpinning of my research is based on a favorite quote by Widdershoven (1993):

> By telling a story about our life, we change our life. In doing so, the story itself becomes *richer* [italics added] as it is filled with life experience. Thus

experience and story can be said to communicate with each other. (p. 13)

In the course of my ongoing research on virtual caregiver support groups (Dobbins, 2002, 2004), I've certainly found this statement to be true: Caregivers bring their life experiences online, take their revised life stories offline, and then return with new stories based on their latest real-life experiences. However, not every story is a happy story; not every narrative contains a healing plot. Nor do I mean to suggest that richer stories are necessarily better, healthier, more positive, or productive. They are simply richer; they have more going on, more layers to interpret, and more to take into account and to think about. Finally, I do not suggest that the sharing of such stories is a healing activity in and of itself—only that stories are being told and that we as researchers can learn much from them.

It should also be noted that the "Crisis" thread was generated by caregivers who overtly identified themselves as such. By participating in a forum specifically labeled by and for caregivers, Connie and the others lay claim to a caregiver identity that was related to but also separate from their other relational roles. However, many people who care for loved ones who are chronically ill or disabled do not call themselves caregivers.[10] Such caregivers speak with a different voice; the stories they tell are different as well (Dobbins, 2004). The caregiver story that emerges from the "Crisis" thread is not the only caregiver story to be told. However, the story generated by these self-identified caregivers may be used to suggest ways in which the stories of those who don't think of themselves as caregivers can be heard.

As researchers and health care professionals work to understand the phenomenon of family caregiving, as we strive to create interventions that alleviate the stress, strain, and burden of family care, we must also seek to understand the meanings caregivers ascribe to what they do and who they are. I see the present study as part of an evolving partnership of research—a new kind of relationship—between caregivers and those who study them. Caregiving is more than a collection of variables, a given set of tasks to perform, or a political platform for instituting social change, although it encompasses all of these things and more. Caregiving is first, foremost, and always about relationships between people—relationships that are continually in motion.

REFERENCES

Ayres, L. (2000). Narratives of caregiving: The process of making meaning. *Research in Nursing & Health*, *23*, 424–434.

---

[10]The Senor quote noted earlier in this chapter bears repeating: "I don't look at myself as a caregiver; I am a husband in love with his wife" (Senor, 2001, p. 77).

Bamberg, M. W. (1997). Positioning between structure and performance. *Journal of Narrative and Life History, 7*(1–4), 335–342.

Brown, L., Debold, E., Tappan, M., & Gilligan, C. (1991). Reading narratives of conflict and choice for self and moral voice: A relational method. In W. Kurtines & J. Gewirtz (Eds.), *Handbook of moral behavior and development: Theory, research, and application* (Vol. 2, pp. 25–61). Hillsdale, NJ: Erlbaum.

Davies, B., & Harré, R. (1999). Positioning and personhood. In R. Harré & L. van Langenhove (Eds.), *Positioning theory* (pp. 32–52). Malden, MA: Blackwell Publishers.

Davison, K. P., Pennebaker, J. W., & Dickerson, S. S. (2002). Who talks? The social psychology of illness support groups. *American Psychologist, 55*, 205–217.

Dobbins, J. (2002). *Supporting the supporters: Informal caregivers and the use of virtual support groups.* Unpublished manuscript, The Graduate School and University Center, City University of New York.

Dobbins, J. (2004). *"Voices": Family caregivers and the discourses of care.* Unpublished manuscript, The Graduate School and University Center, City University of New York.

Gottlieb, R. (2002). The tasks of embodied love: Moral problems in caring for children with disabilities. *Hypatia, 17*, 225–237.

Levine, C. (2002). Hospital-based family caregiver programs: Building institutional resources and community ties. *Journal of Palliative Medicine, 5*, 175–180.

McKenna, K. Y. A., & Bargh, J. A. (1998). Coming out in the age of the Internet: Identity "demarginalization" through virtual group participation. *Journal of Personality and Social Psychology, 75*, 681–694.

McKenna, K. Y. A., & Bargh, J. A. (2000). Plan 9 from cyberspace: The implications of the Internet for personality and social psychology. *Personality and Social Psychology Review, 41*, 57–75.

McKenna, K. Y. A., & Green, A. S. (2002). Virtual group dynamics. *Group Dynamics: Theory, Research, and Practice, 6*, 116–127.

National Family Caregivers Association. (2005). *Who are family caregivers?* Retrieved August 11, 2005, from http://www.thefamilycaregiver.org/who/stats.cfm

Navaie-Waliser, M., Feldman, P. H., Gould, D. A., Levine, C., Kuerbis, A. N., & Donelan, K. (2002). When the caregiver needs care: The plight of vulnerable caregivers. *American Journal of Public Health, 92*, 409–414.

Neufeld, A., & Harrison, M. J. (2003). Unfulfilled expectations and negative interactions: Nonsupport in the relationships of women caregivers. *Journal of Advanced Nursing, 41*, 323–332.

O'Leary, V. (1998). Strength in the face of adversity: Individual and social thriving. *Journal of Social Issues, 54*, 425–446.

Pearlin, L., Mullan, J., Semple, S., & Skaff, M. (1990). Caregiving and the stress process. *The Gerontologist, 30*, 583–594.

Reinhard, S. C. (2004, April). *Family caregivers on the job: What do ADLs and IADLs tell us?* Paper presented at the meeting of the United Hospital Fund, New York.

Senor, S. (2001). Tips from a caregiver husband. In G. Barg (Ed.), *The fearless caregiver: How to get the best care for your loved one and still have a life of your own* (pp. 73–77). Herndon, VA: Capital Books.

Talbot, J., Bibace, R., Bokhour, B., & Bamberg, M. (1996). Affirmation and resistance of dominant discourses: The rhetorical construction of pregnancy. *Journal of Narrative and Life History*, 6, 222–251.

Widdershoven, G. A. M. (1993). The story of life: Hermeneutic perspectives on the relationship between narrative and life history. In R. Josselson & A. Lieblich (Eds.), *The narrative study of lives* (Vol. 1, pp. 1–20). Newbury Park, CA: Sage.

Wrubel, J., & Folkman, S. (1997). What informal caregivers actually do: The caregiving skills of partners of men with AIDS. *AIDS Care*, 9, 691–706.

10

TELLING STORIES ABOUT THERAPY: EGO DEVELOPMENT, WELL-BEING, AND THE THERAPEUTIC RELATIONSHIP

JONATHAN M. ADLER AND DAN P. McADAMS

My therapy helped me understand what I have to do to live a more successful life. I believe without it, I would have been lost and probably
back to my rock bottom, which I believe I hit. It was the hardest thing I
have ever done, but I'm glad I done it. A lot of ups and down, but I
needed them. I needed to face them and therapy helped me do that. . . .
I'm glad to tell you about it.

—*Study Participant*

From the perspective of narrative theory, psychotherapy represents a
unique experience in the life—one in which the individual seeks assistance
in the telling (or retelling) of his or her story so that events or occurrences
that do not fit with the ongoing personal narrative, or that call into question
the established story, may be incorporated (Josselson, 2004; Singer, 2005;
Spence, 1982; White & Epston, 1990). Significant negative experiences such
as the onset of a major depressive episode, a battle with an eating disorder, or
severe relationship distress are precisely the type of troubles that present the
most difficult narrative challenges for people, for they are often especially

This research was supported by a grant to the second author from the Foley Family Foundation to
establish the Foley Center for the Study of Lives at Northwestern University. We would like to thank
Katie Weisz-White, Raelle Wilson, and Katie Magrino-Failla for their participation in coding, and the
rest of the Foley Center for the Study of Lives for their support.

Some identifying features of the study participants described in this chapter have been altered,
masked, or deleted to conceal their identity. All names have been changed.

hard to reconcile with one's ongoing self-story. They directly resist easy resolution in the search for happiness and they often require difficult work for meaning to be made out of them. Thus, psychotherapy can be understood as an unusual personal project in which the individual seeks help working on his or her story in an effort to move closer to a personal narrative that supports desired outcomes. White and Epston (1990) concluded, "When persons seek therapy, an acceptable outcome would be the identification or generation of *alternative stories* that enable them to perform new meanings, bringing with them *desired possibilities* [italics added]" (p. 15). Thus, there is good reason to investigate the "alternative stories" that are generated through psychotherapy to understand those narrative qualities that support these "desired possibilities."

From a clinical perspective, well-being (WB) is likely one of the *most* desired possibilities that bring people into psychotherapy. Indeed, positive affect and life satisfaction are privileged outcomes in the psychotherapy outcome literature (Seligman & Csikszentmihalyi, 2000) and figure prominently in lay conceptions of "the good life" (King, 2001; King, Eells, & Burton, 2004; King & Napa, 1998). In the narrative realm as well, several studies have sought to determine the relationships between particular narrative patterns and WB (i.e., Adler, Kissel, & McAdams, 2006; McAdams, Reynolds, Lewis, Patten, & Bowman, 2001). But the sole emphasis on WB as a desired outcome has several drawbacks, as outlined by King (2001). These include the tendency to portray negative emotions as inherently problematic, to foster a conception of the happy person as immune to the inherent vicissitudes of life, to ignore other facets of experience as outcomes in and of themselves, and to neglect the "rich truth of lived experience" (p. 54). Grounded in her work on folk concepts of "the good life" (King, 2001; King & Napa, 1998; King et al., 2004), King identified having a sense of one's life as meaningful as an important additional outcome. In assessing this quality, King has used the concept of ego development (ED).

ED was introduced into the psychological literature by personality psychologist Jane Loevinger. For Loevinger, the ego is the individual's subjective sense of self, akin to James's *I* (Loevinger, 1976). It is the structure through which one interprets and makes sense of the content of his or her experiences, the master synthesizing *I*. So, ED involves the shifting structures through which meaning is made. Loevinger conceptualized ED as a life-span developmental construct—one characterized by several stages through which people progress. What changes from one stage to the following one is the degree of complexity with which the person is able to conceive of himself or herself and his or her world. Thus, for the purposes of this chapter, ED will be defined as *the degree of complexity an individual uses in making meaning of his or her lived experiences*. With this unique emphasis, ED has become one of the most widely used constructs for assessing the sophistication of individual meaning-making processes (Westenberg & Block, 1993). Furthermore, it is important to note that a large body of empirical work suggests that ED and WB are not correlated (Bauer & McAdams, 2004, 2005; Helson & Roberts, 1994; King, 2001; King, Scollon, Ramsey, & Williams, 2000; Vaillant & McCullough, 1987; Westenberg & Block, 1993).

Thus, the desired possibilities that serve as optimal outcomes of psychotherapy referred to by White and Epston (1990) may be understood as comprising stories that support two distinct qualities: high levels of WB and complex meaning-making processes, or high ED. In an investigation of the alternative stories that individuals generate in psychotherapy, those stories that support these two qualities can therefore be regarded as especially successful.

It is from this perspective that the present investigation originates. Although an emerging body of work is concerned with the narrative basis of psychotherapy (i.e., Angus & McLeod, 2004; Lieblich, McAdams, & Josselson, 2004; Singer, 2005), there is currently a dearth of work in the narrative tradition that is specifically focused on the qualities of the successful alternative self-stories that are proposed to follow from psychotherapy (though see Lieblich, 2004). In this relative vacuum, we have chosen to take a small, preliminary step toward addressing this larger matter. Indeed, with the work reported in this chapter, we did not directly address the larger topic of how people change their life stories through psychotherapy. Instead, we sought to narrow our focus to look deeply at the narratives that individuals who differ in their levels of ED and WB construct about their experiences in psychotherapy. As such, the present study does not attempt to speak to the larger issue of the alternative self-stories that result from psychotherapy. This is not an investigation into stories constructed *from* therapy, or of stories told *in* therapy; instead, we are interested in retrospective stories *about* therapy. In his classic book on psychotherapy, *Persuasion and Healing*, Frank (1961) suggested that the storying of psychotherapy—weaving the "myth" of the therapeutic experience—is vital to the individual's continued optimal functioning. Although focusing on the personal myth about therapy does not allow us to make any direct causal inferences regarding the role of the therapeutic process in generating these stories, or about the actual lived experience of the psychotherapy that is the main topic of these stories, the personal accounts we provide do offer a window into an important matter. These stories are about an experience in people's lives that was presumably concerned with the creation of more viable alternative self-stories. Understanding the different ways in which individuals who vary in ED and WB reconstruct these experiences is an important first step in the endeavor of explicating the most successful alternative self-stories that emerge from the therapeutic process. In addition, rich narratives of psychotherapy enable an initial attempt at understanding different types of reconstructions of the therapeutic relationship and how those reconstructions relate to ED and WB. Furthermore, the present investigation also provides insight into those themes that support

TABLE 10.1
Demographic Characteristics

Demographic characteristic	Number (%)	M (SD)
Sex		
Male	26 (34%)	—
Female	50 (66%)	—
Race		
African American	22 (29%)	—
Asian American	3 (4%)	—
Caucasian	47 (62%)	—
Hispanic	4 (5%)	—
Age (years)	—	35.28 (10.37)
Education level[a]	—	3.50 (1.03)
Income[b]	—	2.12 (1.53)

[a]Education level was coded on a 5-point scale, where 1 = *less than high school*, 2 = *high school*, 3 = *some college*, 4 = *college (BA or BS)*, 5 = *graduate work*. [b]Annual income was coded on a 7-point scale, where 1 = *<$20,000*, 2 = *$20,000–40,000*, 3 = *$40,000–60,000*, 4 = *$60,000–80,000*, 5 = *$80,000–100,000*, 6 = *$100,000–120,000*, 7 = *>$120,000*.

ED and WB. Finally, it has been proposed that the sharing of stories about emotionally disruptive events relates to personal growth (Alea & Bluck, 2003; McLean, 2005; Pasupathi, 2001; Thorne, 2000). Thus, this work also has some implications for the ongoing process of narrative identity construction, growing out of the particular narrative choices made by individuals in this study with different constellations of functioning.

METHOD

We collected therapy stories from 76 adults recruited from the greater Chicago area. These individuals had all been in therapy (individual or couples, for at least eight sessions) in the past 5 years, but were not in any form of treatment at the time they wrote their story. Demographic descriptions of the sample are included in Table 10.1. Each participant wrote extensive narrative accounts of five key scenes in his or her therapy story: The Problem (a specific scene in which the presenting problem was especially clear or vivid), The Decision (a specific scene in which it was decided that the participant would go to therapy to address the problem), Most Important Session (a specific session that the participant deemed the most significant), Another Important Session (a specific session, different from the previous one, that the participant deemed significant; obtained to gather more data on the process of psychotherapy), and Ending (a specific scene that describes a time at or after termination in which the impact of the therapy was especially clear or vivid). An optional sixth scene was also available so participants could write any other important information they felt was not captured in the rest of the narrative. Based loosely on the procedure used by Bauer and McAdams (2004) in their narrative study of occupational and religious transitions, our method provides an explicit format for organizing a therapy narrative. We realize that if asked simply, "Tell us about your therapy experience," many people might not follow a script like ours, wherein they begin with the problem and then move to decision, main scenes from therapy, and an ending. Nonetheless, we believe that our format, like that used in Bauer and McAdams (2004), holds the advantage of presenting a sensible, chronological script that most individuals can readily follow. Furthermore, because the script is standardized across participants, we are better able to compare and contrast the stories told.

The participants also completed a series of questionnaires designed to assess self-reported current-state WB—Satisfaction With Life Scale (Diener, Emmons, Larson, & Griffin, 1985), Positive and Negative Affect Schedule (Watson, Clark, & Tellegen, 1988), Psychological Well-Being Scales (Ryff & Keyes, 1995), and Hopkins Symptom Check List (Derogatis, Lipman, Rickels, Uhlenhuth, & Covi, 1974)—as well as Loevinger's Sentence Completion Test as a measure of ED (Hy & Loevinger, 1996; Loevinger & Wessler, 1970). Given the relatively normal distribution of both ED and WB, we divided the range of ED and the range of WB in two on the basis of median splits and labeled each participant as either high or low in each of these variables. Several other characteristics of the therapeutic experience, including duration of therapy, were also assessed. Neither demographic characteristics nor any of these variables were significantly correlated with ED or with the composite of WB, and thus assignment to 1 of the 4 groups was not affected by any of these factors.

In analyzing the narratives, we used qualitative methods based in grounded theory, a system designed for approaching the analysis of data to facilitate the emergence of theory (Glaser & Strauss, 1967; Strauss & Corbin, 1994). It is typically used in the absence of a preexisting explanatory system for assessing a phenomenon of interest. Although the "alternative stories" framework for psychotherapy was developed by White and Epston (1990) and others, to date there have been no suggestions as to what specific narrative patterns might characterize such stories. The purpose of this research, then, is to identify narrative patterns that characterize the four groups with their different constellations of current functioning.

Following the grounded theory approach, we began qualitative work with a careful initial reading of the data accompanied by an uncensored recording of all phenomena of interest (Glaser & Strauss, 1967; Strauss & Corbin, 1994). Anything distinguishing or remarkable was noted with no attempt to provide order to the material. After the initial reading, an effort was made to categorize, code, and sum the notes in various ways that facilitated comparison and contrast. Emergent working hypotheses or propositions, derived from the data, were developed, and a second reading was undertaken with these organizational points in mind. The process was iterative, requiring the repeated reexamination and revision of these propositions and their accuracy of fit to the data. This process continued until the point of saturation—when no further categories were found and all data were accounted for by the propositions (Strauss & Corbin, 1994).

In the present study, these qualitative methods were undertaken by a group of coders to minimize the inherent biases introduced by relying on only one perspective toward the data. This group was composed of five individuals: one senior PhD-level personality psychologist (the second author of this chapter), one doctoral-level student in clinical and personality psychology serving as a practicing therapist (the first author of this chapter), one doctoral-level student in human development, and two masters-level students in counseling psychology serving as practicing therapists. The readers were diverse with respect to age, gender, and race, as well as in their formal training in psychotherapy and familiarity with grounded theory methodology. Over the course of several months, this group of readers used these methods to elucidate the narrative patterns that distinguish the four different groups of participants.

The narrative reconstructions of the therapeutic experience differ across the four groups in numerous ways, which are discussed elsewhere (Adler & McAdams, 2007). Given this volume's emphasis on relationships, we focus on the particular ways in which participants described the role of interpersonal relationships, especially with the therapist, in their stories. As stated earlier, the themes we identified in these stories may not convey what these relationships actually felt like at the time of therapy, but rather the ways the participants recalled and reconstructed them when they wrote their stories. Thus, although we are not able to comment directly on the relative importance of the therapeutic alliance for people differing in ED and WB, we hope to elucidate the different ways in which individuals who varied on these dimensions *reconstructed* that special relationship. To do so, we chose to focus on the relational aspect of stories told about psychotherapy in an effort to suggest some narrative patterns that support current levels of ED and WB.

Given the space constraints, we chose to focus on 2 of the 4 groups in our sample: the high-ED–high-WB group and the high-ED–low-WB group. Restricting our discussion in this way allows us to provide a lengthy case example of each group, followed by supporting illustrative examples from other individuals in the same group. In addition, these two particular groups provide an interesting contrast in their portrayals of the therapeutic relationship.

THERAPY NARRATIVES OF INDIVIDUALS HIGH IN EGO DEVELOPMENT AND HIGH IN WELL-BEING

Nora opened her story at a time when she was 23 years old and her boyfriend insisted that she get treatment for the eating disorder that was becoming more and more destructive in her life and in their relationship. "It started as a way to help me feel better about a specific incident or the ways things were going in my fated relationship," she described, "but soon turned into an overall habit, and then my day wasn't complete without several binge–purge sessions." In Nora's words, the bulimia "overtook" her, as if it was an external force with its own distinct power. She even gave it a name: "I called it the 'Walk Of Shame' in my head," she said.

As she told it, Nora was resistant to the idea of therapy at first, as it felt like an enormous challenge. She explained that by the time her boyfriend confronted her, "I had intensely struggled for a few months. I was ready to admit my daily struggles, but not ready to change—it became, by that time, a part of my identity." Nora wrote that her boyfriend agreed to accompany her to the first session and she soon began seeing a therapist privately.

Treatment was rocky from the start, Nora explained. She said she felt that her therapist was too passive, noting that "I didn't click with the coun-selor . . . (he used the 'how did that make you feel' approach)." After a short period, she dropped out of treatment. This lapse strained her relationship with her boyfriend and they eventually separated. But, Nora continued, "After a humiliating sexual assault incident, I decided to go back into counseling and discovered I didn't recover as fully as I thought I had." She described this second round of therapy as having gotten off to a better start. Two sessions into this second attempt, she felt like things finally clicked. Nora explained,

> My counselor started pinpointing things that we had never thought of before. It was so interesting to see how the past qualities may have been linked to childhood events and possibly ADD, a concern we never thought of. All of a sudden, it became more clear, we had broken through the eating disorder symptoms, to find another cause of my behavior. . . . I felt so relieved that my counselor and I had found agreement on a topic and both were enthusiastic about finding a solution. I knew things were, or had, changed, as I was willing to look at all alternatives as my solution.

This revelation turned things around for Nora. She felt her treatment was more effective, she began a new romantic relationship, and she started work-ing on mending the tensions she felt with her parents. Indeed, in contrast to her first experience in therapy, Nora said that she "grew to respect" her thera-pist this time around. But Nora explained that she soon came to feel that her second therapist was pushing too hard. If her first attempt at therapy had felt too passive, as she told it, this time Nora came to feel overly controlled. When her therapist suggested they invite Nora's parents to come to a ses-sion, Nora said she "felt totally betrayed." She also believed that her thera-pist "was trying too hard to push medication on me." She says she ultimately "decided I could recover on my own" and left therapy again.

At this point in the story, Nora jumped ahead in time, to a moment months after leaving therapy that she felt captured her progress. She talked about the night before the day of a half-marathon race she was participating in. She went to a restaurant with some friends and discovered that

> The various veggie dishes were cooked with oils which made me feel uncomfortable. I remember feeling it in my stomach and thinking how nauseous I was. . . . I knew I would be ruining my body's chance for a good time for the run—but it was a struggle. The next morning I woke up and was so thankful for the dinner—it gave me so much energy for the run! Oh, and the run itself was, for the first time, not obsessively trained for—I actually limited my mileage and didn't feel compelled to do anything extraordinary.

Nora's story has several qualities that make it a model example of those told by participants in the high-ED–high-WB group in our sample ($N = 21$): the theme of personal agency; a powerful, personified problem; a turning point of revelation in her treatment; and, perhaps most important, a relationship with her therapist marked by conflicting attitudes.

The Theme of Personal Agency

Nora's story, like that of many participants in this group, is all about agency. She began by describing her powerlessness and "intense struggles" at the hands of her bulimia. The impulse to get treatment came from an external source—her first boyfriend—and she acquiesced even though she did not feel "ready to change." As she told it, her first encounter with her therapist soured because Nora experienced the therapist as too passive, and Nora left treatment. It was as though her therapist didn't assert enough agency to convince Nora that they could overpower her problem. Nora added emphasis when she stressed that returning to therapy was her own decision ("I decided to go back . . ."), a reassertion of her personal sense of capability. This second time, Nora spoke of working with her therapist as a team—she shifted to using the pronoun *we* instead of *I* ("we had broken through . . ."). Yet when Nora described her therapist as having become overly forceful, Nora's personal sense of agency was reinvigorated and she decided "I could recover on my own." Nora's story ended with an image of her continued struggles, but one that portrayed her as empowered and in charge: She was "no longer compelled" by external forces.

This theme of agency runs throughout the stories told by participants in the high-ED–high-WB group. Often they opened with a description of a once-strong hero descending into passivity. Indeed, the stories of many other participants in this group showed evidence of this theme. Here are a few emblematic quotations:

- A woman, age 56: "After an adult life of frequent large moves, some of them Trans-Pacific, this seemed like nothing. So, I felt myself woefully unprepared for the inevitable transitional difficulties that did accompany this move. . . . I felt like I was at the bottom of a well, unable to think or move."

- A woman, age 45: "I had hit a plateau—unable to grow and too far gone to turn back."
- A man, age 57: "Soon I realized that I had not cried since I was a small child, despite other important losses. This was the biggest low point in my life. . . . After several attempts and opportunities afterwards, I still could not shed even a tear!"
- A woman, age 25: "I had become a mere shell of the strong person I used to be and I wanted to find her again, to start over."

But when these beaten-down heroes entered therapy, like Nora they often experienced the caretaking of their therapists as disempowering. One participant explained, "Some of my problems were because of decisions I had made. My counselor never told me that. She treated me like a victim. It made me feel more stuck." Feeling so ineffectual was such an aversive experience for these individuals that they sometimes interpreted their therapists' efforts as simply reinforcing their powerlessness. Just as Nora felt her therapist had "betrayed" her and "was trying too hard," other participants in this group could not tolerate their therapist's active efforts. Indeed, as was the case for Nora, these experiences often led these individuals to rebuff their therapy, asserting that they needed to do the work of healing on their own. One participant echoed this sentiment, stating,

> I believed I had made progress but that I was beginning to feel that the work I needed to do was more inside myself rather than inside a session. . . . I had learned a lot from my sessions but was feeling as though I had some work to do by myself. Work that could not be done by or with someone else.

She ultimately viewed her work as internal and solitary, suggesting that she hit a point at which the relational realm was not the right context in which to heal. Another participant made a similar statement, writing,

> The therapy became more of a safety net after a while. I didn't need it. I was ready to make something of my life. I'm an artist. I made art instead of therapy after it ended. . . . I was ready to become healthy.

The Powerful, Personified Problem

Though Nora and the other participants high in both ED and WB described their therapists as sometimes overly assertive, they certainly had respect for the power of another character in their narratives—that of their problem. Nora personified her problem; she said that it "overtook" her and infiltrated her sense of self, becoming "a part of my identity." She even gave it a name, explaining, "I called it the 'Walk Of Shame' in my head."

This pattern is very common across participants in this group, many of whom wrote about their problems as fully realized characters in their stories, villains of sorts. They often ascribed physical characteristics to their problems. One man explained, "I had been carrying all of it." Another added, "My problems piled on me." A third wrote, "The words [haunted] me." They also tended to locate their problem in physical space. Like the woman quoted earlier, several participants described their problems as a "well." For example, another woman described her situation as having been "led to this deep well of low self-esteem." The image of the well is powerful. It connotes a dark place, one below the surface of the ground, full of dank, stagnant air. The well is where babies fall and get stuck, requiring heroic efforts to be saved. Thus, by invoking the well, these individuals tapped a culturally loaded symbol of dire circumstances and the urgent need of rescue. Most notable, however, the high-ED–high-WB participants ascribed a great deal of power to their problems—more power than they possessed. "What a *paralyzing* fog it was I was in!" noted one participant. "There was [a] problem somewhere, something tying me up in knots," described another, female participant. Notice that this woman discussed her problem as being suffered at the hands of a powerful external agent. A third participant echoed this sentiment, asserting that her anxiety "did not let me live in peace with myself and my family. . . . My disorder did not allow me to even think right." In this story, her anxiety had the power to control her thoughts, disrupting her life and her relationships. Another participant wrote, "I was struggling to get out of [its] grasp." Thus, the high-ED–high-WB participants tended to personify their problems, elevating them to the status of a major character in the narratives. Indeed, for the normally agentic protagonist, the problem presented a worthy foe, a powerful and destructive force in opposition to which the thrust of the narrative is structured.

Revelation

Nora used the language of revelation in talking about a turning point in her therapy. "All of a sudden, it became more clear," she said. "We had broken through the eating disorder symptoms, to find another cause of my behavior." This abrupt and essential insight allowed Nora to feel as though she and her therapist were on the same team, taking on her challenging problem. It energized her and may have proven to be the crucial spark that reignited Nora's personal sense of agency, which ultimately led to her leaving treatment to "recover on my own."

The description of therapy as being punctuated with dramatic revelations, insights that changed the course of treatment, is frequent in the stories told by these individuals, and unique to this group. One participant, an actress, wrote,

And it was there and then where I heard the answer for my life that came like lightening. I said what a pity that nobody told me that 6 years ago so I could save at least 5 years of my life. . . . I felt such a relief after this discovery! . . . I could sleep, and eat, and think, and act again.

All of a sudden, this woman unlocked the powerful "answer for [her] life," and everything fell into place. The language of such sudden and powerful changes is common among the individuals in this group; their progress is marked with new perspectives and deeper understandings. Another participant explained,

Never could I remember a time before when I could conjure up a positive, detailed memory from my past. . . . This positive insight into my past—the discovery that it was not all lost—made me feel very happy and hopeful.

A third wrote, "I was able to give my fears a source, an 'etiology,' and as soon as they were 'explained,' they dissolved." Yet another noted, "I felt instantly a little better because I was taking some action to solve my problem." Indeed, insight and new understanding were the most common mechanisms through which high-ED–high-WB participants described their treatments working, and they invoked words such as "discovery" to convey these changes. Although these insights arose in the interpersonal context of therapy, they were often framed as shifts in the narrator's own perspective and ultimately were not shared with the therapist. Nora said she knew she had changed because "I was willing to look at all alternatives." Another participant, the actress quoted earlier, cast her revelation in terms of what it enabled her to do—to sleep, eat, think, and act again. And a third individual also talked about how she felt: "very happy and hopeful." In each of these examples, the revelation is framed more in terms of the protagonist's own success than in terms of a healing relationship with the therapist.

Conflicting Attitudes Toward Therapist

What is evident across the three themes we have discussed is that participants in this group told stories that expressed a good deal of ambivalence toward their therapists. Therapists were described as both overly passive and too pushy; unlike the individuals' problems, they were not portrayed as richly realized characters, and the truly curative powers of therapy were often ascribed to a mysterious and sudden revelation that was ultimately internal, not to the therapeutic relationship or the hard work of the therapist in facilitating that insight. In the rosiest parts of Nora's story, she said she "grew to respect" her therapist and felt as if they were on the same team, "both enthusiastic about finding a solution." But Nora was also deeply dissatisfied with her therapist at times, noting that they "didn't click" at first and later feeling "totally betrayed."

The presence of such conflicting attitudes toward the therapist is common in the stories of the participants in this group. Unlike Nora, many of these individuals tried working through their problems with other people, before turning to therapy. "I talked about this with a friend," wrote one woman, "but her help was insufficient." A man explained, "I talked to a friend because I was pretty distraught, [but] my friend referred me to a counselor." Throughout the narratives told by people high in ED and WB was the implication that therapy offered the participants something that could not be obtained elsewhere in their lives. Indeed, they expressed these sentiments even in comparison with alternative treatments. One woman noted, "I should have started getting counseling, but I didn't until months later. Instead, I just took medication. It made me feel really numb—emotionless." At the same time, this special regard for therapy was seen as scary by some of these participants. "I was afraid, like many people are, of psychologists—that they might go too deep into you," shared one woman. Another overcame her fears and felt it was the right choice. She wrote,

> I used to think 'I'm not crazy, I don't need a psychiatrist, that's a crazy person's doctor. I don't even want to be seen going into his office.' But after you've lived through the symptoms . . . not even your family doctor, or a Tylenol pill will help you address your problem. . . . A therapist . . . can really help you.

Yet even though these individuals clearly respected the power of therapy, when telling their stories they looked back at their experiences with therapists with a great deal of negativity as well. Nora felt her therapist "was trying too hard to push medication" on her. Another man talked of a similar disappointment with his therapist. He wrote, "I'm pouring out my heart and she seems like she's spouting out the most generic psycho-babble. . . . I am emptying myself and she's just saying 'it's not your fault.'" As he narrated it, this man felt as though the language of therapy was too clichéd and not strong enough to contend with his story of anguish. Another participant, a woman, explained, "[My therapist] actually viewed me as much less capable than I am and this pissed me off and motivated me to prove her wrong." Indeed, she noted how her resentment of the therapist motivated her to get better.

The other three themes we have discussed certainly relate to these conflicting attitudes. As explained earlier, participants in this group saw themselves, at the time they wrote their story, as strong, capable people and described their past experiences in therapy as coming about in response to an especially powerful and challenging problem that weakened them significantly. So, within the logic of the story it makes sense that they might have some ambivalence about being helped to overcome their hardships. Therapists were described as professionals, but ones who had the power to push too hard and see too deep, which was experienced as intrusion. Indeed, many of the participants in this group, including Nora, described refinding their own sense of personal agency in reacting to their therapist's efforts. Although they suggested that doing so gave them the boost they need to heal, the therapeutic relationship was often cast in a negative light.

Thus, individuals in the high-ED–high-WB group tended not to reconstruct their relationships with their therapists as being central to the healing process. The therapists tended not to attain the stature of fully realized characters in the stories of this group, although in contrast, the problems these people faced often were personified and described as if they themselves were individuals. The therapeutic relationship often was portrayed ambivalently, as both a necessary step toward healing and, for some, an unwanted intrusion into the personal agency of the protagonist. The therapy story that these individuals tended to tell was therefore largely characterized by the redemptive journey of a near-self-sufficient protagonist (i.e., McAdams, 2006). The narrator opened the story presenting a weakened hero, brought down by the powerful foe of his or her problem. Seeking therapy was a way to heal, and specifically a place to find new insights about the secrets that sustain the problem, but it was also a place where the therapist, only a supporting character, could assert him- or herself too much (or too little), infringing on the protagonist's agency. In the end, the protagonist reclaimed his or her own capability, threw off the no-longer-wanted help of the therapist, and worked toward health with his or her own will.

A CONTRAST: THERAPY NARRATIVES OF INDIVIDUALS HIGH IN EGO DEVELOPMENT AND LOW IN WELL-BEING

If the stories of the high-ED–high-WB group go along with a highly desirable constellation of functioning, one that supports both complex ways of making meaning out of their experiences and high levels of WB and life satisfaction, the stories of the high-ED–low-WB group accompany similarly complex systems of meaning making but generally less satisfaction with life. These people were deeply in touch with the nuances of their experiences but tended to see life in darker hues than did the high-ED–high-WB individuals.

Willy was 44 when he opened his therapy story. He explained that 7 years prior, his wife had left him and moved with their young daughter across the country. Willy had been struggling with depression and alcoholism for many years, though he had managed to keep up in a high-pressure advertising job throughout his marriage, eventually running the agency. "I have always taken great pride in my career and qualifications," Willy explained. But he said that he had never really been happy. "I felt that alcoholism was just a symptom of other root problems/issues I [had always] faced," he wrote. Following his divorce, Willy noted that his drinking got worse, and he ultimately lost his job. Eventually, he sought out Alcoholics Anonymous and was able to maintain his sobriety successfully, an accomplishment he was proud of; nevertheless Willy felt down. "After four years in A.A., I was still ashamed of my past and terrified of the future," he wrote. "I *still* felt rotten about myself. I was broke—financially and spiritually."

Willy described undergoing what he called "a year of wandering." He "tried lots of things: more A.A. meetings, ongoing education, self-help tapes, more exercise, dating, job interviews, etc. Nothing helped." Eventually, at the prompting of a friend, Willy decided to give therapy a try. "I didn't believe counseling would work," he wrote. "(I mean, what could they tell me about me?) But, I figured it couldn't hurt. So, I did the research, found [a] free counseling [center] and made the appointment."

Very early on in his treatment, as Willy described it in his narrative, he felt cared for by his therapist, whose name he gave in his narrative (we'll call her Ava). He explained,

> A crucial turning point in therapy was when I communicated this story [about my past] to my therapist. Obviously, the loss of my family was devastating. What was awesome about this early session was the fact that Ava showed genuine empathy and cared about my feelings.

He continued, "The fact that Ava showed real care about me, but also helped me also see my ex-wife's position, bolstered my affinity and trust in her and the counseling I was receiving."

Several months into therapy, as Willy described it, Ava began to push him to get a new job. He felt that there weren't any available jobs worthy of his qualifications and "scoffed at the notion that I [would] take a 'lesser' position." Willy explained, "Ava flipped the coin on me and demanded (strongly suggested) that I fill out an application and at least interview for a position at [a book store]. I didn't want to do it, but I did." Willy was offered the job, and although he turned it down, he felt the experience "was a lesson in humility."

Willy explained how, after 5 months, he received a call from Ava who told him that she had accepted a position at a university that was out of state and would be going away soon. "I was disappointed she was leaving," Willy said. "I liked her and felt I had made progress. It was good to have somebody on my side." He decided to terminate treatment instead of transferring to another therapist. Willy summarized, "In general I was very satisfied with my time with Ava. She allowed me to tell my story, was empathetic, and helped me devise action solutions." He didn't say much about what had happened in his life since the end of this episode, except to mention that he had had one relapse in his drinking, which he felt he handled very well, and was sober again at the time he wrote his story.

Willy's story is obviously quite different from Nora's and those told by the high-ED–high-WB participants. In contrast to their therapy stories, Willy's story includes several typical themes common in the narratives told by individuals in the high-ED–low-WB group ($N = 17$), including the following:

a long-standing, internally located problem; a fully realized character of the strong therapist; and an attribution that the therapeutic relationship was the source of healing.

The Long-Standing, Internal Problem

Willy's drinking played a large role in his marital problems and his eventually losing his job. But he reconstructed the drinking as only the surface incarnation of other "root problems/issues." Indeed, even after he regained sobriety, Willy explained, "I *still* felt rotten about myself." Unlike the high-ED–high-WB participants, Willy never labeled his root problem or gave it a name the way Nora had. Instead, he suggested that it had always been with him, an integral part of who he was.

This regard for the problem as innately tied up with one's sense of self is common in the stories written by participants high in ED but low in WB. For instance, one woman explained, "I have always been a private, quiet, sad person." Another man added, "I've always felt disconnected from myself." A third noted, "I always felt like I couldn't change and that I was gonna forever be a hopeless, helpless case." From these individuals' perspective, their problem was not some powerful other with which they must do battle, but a flaw in their very nature. This long-standing, internal description of the problem is unique to the high-ED–low-WB group. And certainly, it is a striking contrast to the way participants in the high-ED–high-WB group wrote about their problems.

Therapist As a Strong Character

Willy described having tried a huge variety of interventions for addressing his problems: "more A.A. meetings, ongoing education, self-help tapes, more exercise, dating, job interviews, etc." But he suggested that none of these treatments really helped him get to the core of the issues. When his friend suggested he try therapy, Willy was willing, but pessimistic. But after just a few sessions, Willy says he felt cared for by his therapist and was on the road to healing. This idea that the therapist offered something above and beyond what other treatment options could deliver is a theme that was also evident in the stories told by the high-ED–high-WB participants, but it created a very different impact when framed by the participants in the high-ED–low-WB group.

Many of the individuals in the high-ED–low-WB group wrote about the unique advantages of professional help, benefits that exceeded those they could find elsewhere in their lives. One woman explained that "talking to my girlfriends helped somewhat, however they were involved in their own relationship struggles." Her implication was that because her therapist would leave her personal problems at the door and focus solely on the client's own troubles, she would be a more effective healer than her girlfriends would be. Indeed, later in his own narrative, Willy also observed the same result for him: "Of real importance was the idea that I was dealing with a trained professional, rather than the 'ad hoc' advice given by friends, family, A.A., and self-help books." Willy, like the other individuals in this group, described therapists as possessing specialized qualities that were linked to their ability to help. The very status of therapists as professionals seemed vital to these participants. One woman noted, "My Dr. was the Chief of Staff—Dr. Levi. I remember being so optimistic at the thought of 'little old me' having 'the head guy' on my case." In each of these examples, the personal qualities of the therapist were seen as special and described as the seat of their healing powers. Like the individuals in the high-ED–high-WB group, the high-ED–low-WB participants valued the perceived professional status of their therapists. However, the high-ED–low-WB individuals' attitudes toward this advanced position were uncomplicated and positive, whereas the high-ED–high-WB participants described seeing in this standing the potential for unwanted intrusion.

The Healing Connection

Much of Willy's narrative is concerned with the connection he felt with Ava, his therapist. He talked about the "genuine empathy" he felt coming from her and how that connection allowed him to overcome his initial pessimism regarding the power of therapy. Indeed, even when he felt unduly pushed by Ava to apply for a job that he believed was beneath him, he embraced her suggestion, applied for the job, and described the experience as "a lesson in humility." Willy plainly narrated the therapeutic relationship as the central locus of healing.

This tendency to cite the therapeutic relationship as the curative ingredient is common throughout the high-ED–low-WB group. A woman in this group noted, "What made it work for me was because I finally found a person whom I could trust and wasn't afraid to be open and honest with." She also clearly described how telling her story was curative. Another individual explained, "I felt it worked because I liked my therapist and trusted her." These high-ED–low-WB participants felt that something in the relationship with their therapist provided them with the crucial ingredients to get better. "I don't know why I couldn't do it myself. My therapist had to help me," said a man in this group. "I know now that I would have never been able to look that deep inside or be that honest without my doctor's help," added another.

It is interesting that even when high-ED–low-WB individuals felt very negative about their treatment, their therapists remained key players in the story, and a lapse in the therapeutic relationship was seen as the problem. One woman described a disagreement with her therapist:

She told me that I could heal my heart and that my emotional healing would soon follow. I disagreed because I don't think that I can ever overcome these feelings. She continued to say that I could but that I was just holding back. It made me very defensive and a little aggressive in my words, causing me to withdraw.

This woman did not believe her therapist's hopeful assertion that she had the power to heal, and this divergence of opinion had a strong impact on her behavior in future sessions, causing her to retreat from the relationship. Indeed, conflict between the protagonist and the therapist was the source of another woman's breakdown in progress as well. She felt that her therapist made an erroneous interpretation of her behavior. She continued,

I considered this, and then her words hit me in a way that sounded so phony I couldn't stand it. After that I just started to make things up to get through the sessions without feeling as though I had been raped.

Her language is surprisingly strong and vivid; she ascribed to her therapist the power of a rapist in her analysis. Once again in this example, while the valence of the impact of the therapist was negative, it was quite intense and the rupture in the alliance was seen as violent and detrimental. Thus, for the high-ED–low-WB individuals, whether they regarded their therapists as positive or negative, they wrote about them as very important characters and their relationship as quite powerful. Indeed, for these participants, therapy was fundamentally about an interpersonal relationship.

A NOTE ABOUT OTHER PARTICIPANTS

As explained earlier, we chose to restrict our discussion of the accounts collected for this study to 2 of the 4 groups of participants. Descriptions of the other groups (low-ED–high-WB, $N = 16$, and low-ED–low-WB, $N = 22$) are available elsewhere (Adler & McAdams, 2007). In addition, in light of this volume's focus on relationships, the narrative patterns observed in the two groups we have described encapsulate the richest contrast we uncovered that is specifically concerned with narratives of interpersonal dynamics. Although the other participants did write about the therapeutic relationship, this discussion was not one of the prevailing themes that emerged in these two groups. Instead, the most salient patterns observed in these groups concerned other matters, such as the coherence of the overall narrative and the tone of their conclusions.

INTERPRETING THESE STORIES

Our emphasis in this chapter has been on describing stories told by individuals who had been in therapy and, at the time they wrote their story, expressed optimal functioning, defined as the combination of high levels of ED and high levels of WB. What we found in comparing the stories of those participants who espoused both of these characteristics with those of participants high in ED but low in WB is that the former tended to deemphasize the role of the therapist and the therapeutic alliance as instrumental to their healing. This conclusion seems puzzling at first glance, but we hope to offer an interpretation that is grounded in what we know of these participants.

First of all, in addressing this question it is important to distinguish between therapy-as-experienced and therapy-as-narrated. An enormous body of literature suggests that the therapeutic alliance is important to successful therapy (i.e., Beutler et al., 2004; Martin, Garske, & Davis, 2000; Miller & Stiver, 1997; Orlinsky, Rønnestad, & Willutzki, 2004; Safran & Wallner, 1991), so therefore it should also be important in the construction of viable alternative self-stories that White and Epston (1990) suggested are the outcomes of successful therapy. The present study cannot speak to the components of the actual lived experiences in therapy that these participants had. Instead, our data provide a window into the ways in which individuals who, at the time they write their story have differing levels of two valued outcomes, vary in their *reconstructions* of the experience. On the basis of the body of both theory and research on the therapeutic alliance, it seems curious that individuals who have high levels of ED and WB would not have experienced this bond as important. The narrative accounts we collected, however, do not directly address that matter. The question that the accounts do allow us to address is this: Why did these individuals choose to *narrate* the therapeutic experience in a way that deemphasized the role of the therapist?

In tackling this question, we must first ask why people choose to narrate their lives in certain ways, from a general narrative perspective. McAdams (1993, 2001) has suggested that one of the primary functions of the life story is to provide the individual with a sense that his or her identity has both unity and purpose. Therefore the process of storying the self involves weaving together events into a largely coherent story. In doing so, the individual must reconcile events that do not easily fit into the established and ongoing personal narrative. As explained in the beginning of this chapter, difficult life events of the type that lead people to seek psychotherapy are precisely the types of events that provide challenges to the ongoing construction of a coherent and unified narrative of the self, marking low points and turning points in the life story (McAdams & Bowman, 2001; Schultz, 2003). This is why the work of therapy has been conceived of as striving in the service of better story generation. Successful alternative stories either assimilate the pretherapy problems into the ongoing personal narrative or adapt so that the existing self-story can be revised to accommodate them. From a narrative perspective, for the present study we collected stories from individuals that describe a point in their life when a problem challenged their ability to construct a self-story that supported optimal functioning. These problems brought the individual into therapy in a search for a more successful alternative self-story. In other words, the stories we collected are reconstructions of this process of alternative story generation. Thus, although our data do not directly speak to the matter of life-story construction, the manner in which individuals reconstruct these episodes must fit into their larger self-story to support good functioning.

This perspective provides a route for resolving the apparent conflict between the literature that asserts that the therapeutic alliance is central to successful therapy and the deemphasis of the alliance in the stories of those participants who evidence the best functioning at the time they write their story. Recall that the narratives of the individuals in our sample who were high in both ED and WB were centrally about the ebb and flow of personal agency that this episode entailed. They wrote about themselves as typically empowered individuals who were suffering at the hands of a powerful and personified problem. For this group, the story of therapy was fundamentally about their struggle to regain agency. Once reempowered, they largely described having solved their own problems, sometimes repudiating the therapist's role in their narratives of progress.

Against this backdrop it becomes clearer why this group of participants might have chosen to deemphasize the therapeutic alliance in their descriptions of their experiences. These participants narrated their pretherapy selves as largely competent, agentic individuals. In fact, many of them suggested that precisely what made the episode recounted in their story stand out for them was how unusual it was for them to feel so ineffective in fixing their problems. Although many of them suggested that the work of therapy was an ongoing project in their lives, their stories concluded with the protagonist returned to his or her previously empowered state. And in light of their levels of high ED and high WB at the time they wrote their story, it seems reasonable to assume that their ongoing personal narratives continued to successfully support these positive components of functioning. So, the individuals in this group narrated this episode in their lives as an anomaly with respect to their personal agency: In their stories they were effectual prior to this episode, and they were effectual following it, but the episode itself represented an unusually disempowered period in their lives. As such, it seems likely these high-functioning individuals found a way of narrating this unusual episode in a way that did not once again make them feel disempowered. It is as though recounting this episode was akin to returning to "the scene of the crime" and it was likely important to the narrators to avoid again experiencing the powerlessness of the protagonist they were describing. If so, then we can understand why these high-ED–high-WB individuals might reconstruct their therapy experiences in ways that emphasized their own agency in healing themselves, while relatively minimizing the therapeutic alliance. Although we did not collect full life stories from these participants, it seems possible that recounting this important episode and sharing it with us, the researchers, provided the high-ED–high-WB individuals with an opportunity to reinforce the personal narrative they had about themselves as effective agents at the time they wrote their story, given that the therapy story is so concerned with personal agency. Indeed, this type of personal memory telling has been viewed as a key component of personality development (i.e., Alea & Bluck, 2003; McLean, 2005; Pasupathi, 2001; Thorne, 2000).

How then should we interpret the stories of the high-ED–low-WB participants, who did emphasize the therapeutic alliance in their reconstructions of the therapy experience? This task proves to be far less challenging, for the highlighting of the role of the therapist in the stories of these individuals is more in line with the expectations of the literature on therapy process and outcome. The participants in this group described their problem as long-standing and internal; many said they could not remember a time when it wasn't part of who they are. It seems likely therefore that therapy represented a special time when these individuals were in a relationship that they experienced as warm and supportive. Although at the time of writing their story, they saw themselves and the world in relatively complex terms (high-ED), they also reported low levels of current WB. Thus, against this picture, it doesn't seem surprising that therapy would be remembered warmly, especially in the interpersonal context of the therapeutic alliance.

In the stories of individuals high in ED but relatively low in psychological WB, the healing therapeutic relationship itself, rather than the problem that brought them into therapy in the first place, represents the key departure from life as it usually is. As they described it, these insightful but relatively unhappy people saw the world as a complex and dangerous place, and they saw themselves as vulnerable. Unlike the usually agentic protagonists in the stories told by individuals high in ED and high in WB, they were more familiar, we suspect, with long-term dissatisfaction in life. As they told it, they entered therapy in response to what they perceived to be long-term, even chronic, problems, rather than in response to the kind of anomalous breakdown of agency described by individuals with high ED and high WB. They described having found in therapy a kind of effective and supportive relationship with another. According to their descriptions, they lived much of their lives in need of help and therapy provided them with the healing relationship, even if it did not, in the long run, enable them to live happily afterward. In contrast, their happier counterparts who were also high in ED suggested that the therapeutic relationship was more contentious and problematic. For them, the therapeutic experience challenged their agentic narrative of self. They were not as comfortable receiving this kind of help, for it threatened their agentic narrative of self. Their preferred narrative was one in which the strong protagonist, once humbled, regained his or her strength.

CONCLUSION

White and Epston (1990) and others (e.g., Angus & McLeod, 2004) have suggested that psychotherapy is fundamentally concerned with the generation of alternative self-stories that support "desired possibilities" of functioning. The body of literature on lay conceptions of "the good life" indicates that two of the most valued of these desired possibilities are high WB and complex ways of making meaning, as captured by the concept of ED. However, there is a dearth of research on the qualities of those self-stories that support this combination of high WB and high ED. With the study described in this chapter, we have begun to address this matter. Although the nature of our data did not allow us to speak to the actual lived experiences of the participants or to the causal nature of therapy in generating these alternative self-stories, they did provide us with a rich source of information about how individuals with different constellations of current functioning choose to reconstruct and narrate their experiences in therapy. The story of therapy is therefore one component of their current life story and is specifically focused on an experience that likely impacted their WB and self-understanding. In focusing on the narrative patterns of relational dynamics, specifically with regard to the therapeutic relationship, we have highlighted one key source of variation in these stories: Individuals considered to have had the best functioning at the time they wrote their story—those high in ED and high in WB—deemphasized the role of the therapist in their narratives, whereas those high in ED but low in WB featured the therapeutic relationship prominently in their stories. This finding suggests that the sharing of these tales was shaped differently for individuals in these two groups, to serve different psychological needs. For the high-ED–high-WB individuals, the episode was regarded as anomalous in their lives; it was a time when they described themselves as being uniquely disempowered. As such, the telling of this story at a time when they were functioning quite well may have called on them to distance themselves from the central relationship from that troubled time and allowed them to reinforce their current understanding of themselves as empowered. In contrast, for the high-ED–low-WB individuals, the relational component was largely narrated as a warm and supportive bond, set against a lifetime that was perceived as having been plagued by internal problems.

The research presented here thus marks an initial step toward understanding the larger matter of therapy's role in generating specific types of alternative stories that support the desired possibilities of increased WB and enhanced ED. In addition, the findings suggest specific roles that constructing and sharing the memories of psychotherapy may serve for individuals with different constellations of current functioning.

REFERENCES

Adler, J. M., Kissel, E. C., & McAdams, D. P. (2006). Emerging from the CAVE: Attributional style and the narrative study of identity in midlife adults. *Cognitive Therapy and Research, 30*(1), 39–51.

Adler, J. M., & McAdams, D. P. (2007). *Therapeutic narratives of the good life.* Manuscript under review.

Alea, N., & Bluck, S. (2003). Why are you telling me that? A conceptual model of the social function of autobiographical memory. *Memory, 11,* 165–178.

Angus, L. E., & McLeod, J. (2004). Toward an integrative framework for understanding the role of narrative in the psychotherapy process. In L. E. Angus & J. McLeod (Eds.), *The handbook of narrative and psychotherapy: Practice, theory, and research* (pp. 367–374). Thousand Oaks, CA: Sage.

Bauer, J. J., & McAdams, D. P. (2004). Personal growth in adults' stories of life transitions. *Journal of Personality, 72,* 573–602.

Bauer, J. J., & McAdams, D. P. (2005). Interpreting the good life: How mature, happy people frame their autobiographical memories. *Journal of Personality and Social Psychology, 88,* 203–217.

Beutler, L. E., Malik, M., Alimohamed, S., Harwood, T. M., Talebi, H., Noble, S., & Wong, E. (2004). Therapist variables. In M. J. Lambert (Ed.), *Bergin and Garfield's handbook of psychotherapy change* (5th ed., pp. 227–306). New York: Wiley.

Derogatis, L. R., Lipman, R. S., Rickels, K., Uhlenhuth, E. H., & Covi, L. (1974). The Hopkins Symptom Checklist (HSCL): A self-report symptom inventory. *Behavioral Sciences, 19,* 1–15.

Diener, E., Emmons, R. A., Larson, R. J., & Griffin, S. (1985). The satisfaction with life scale. *Journal of Personality Assessment, 49,* 71–76.

Frank, J. D. (1961). *Persuasion and healing: A comprehensive study of psychotherapy.* Baltimore: Johns Hopkins University Press.

Glaser, B. G., & Strauss, A. L. (1967). *The discovery of grounded theory: Strategies for qualitative research.* New York: Aldine.

Helson, R., & Roberts, B. W. (1994). Ego development and personality change in adulthood. *Journal of Personality and Social Psychology, 66,* 911–920.

Hy, L. X., & Loevinger, J. (1996). *Measuring ego development* (2nd ed.). Mahwah, NJ: Erlbaum.

Josselson, R. (2004). On becoming the narrator of one's own life. In A. Lieblich, D. P. McAdams, & R. Josselson (Eds.), *Healing plots: The narrative basis of psychotherapy* (pp. 111–127). Washington, DC: American Psychological Association.

King, L. A. (2001). The hard road to the good life: The happy, mature person. *Journal of Humanistic Psychology, 41,* 51–72.

King, L. A., Eells, J. E., & Burton, C. M. (2004). The good life, broadly defined. In A. Linley & S. Joseph (Eds.), *Positive psychology in practice* (pp. 35–52). Hoboken, NJ: Wiley.

King, L. A., & Napa, C. K. (1998). What makes a life good? *Journal of Personality and Social Psychology, 75,* 156–165.

King, L. A., Scollon, C. K., Ramsey, C., & Williams, T. (2000). Stories of life transition: Subjective well-being and ego development in parents of children with Down syndrome. *Journal of Research in Personality, 34,* 509–536.

Lieblich, A. (2004). The place of psychotherapy in the life stories of women in households without men. In A. Lieblich, D. P. McAdams, & R. Josselson (Eds.), *Healing plots: The narrative basis of psychotherapy* (pp. 171–188). Washington, DC: American Psychological Association.

Lieblich, A., McAdams, D. P., & Josselson, R. (Eds.). (2004). *Healing plots: The narrative basis of psychotherapy.* Washington, DC: American Psychological Association.

Loevinger, J. (1976). *Ego development: Conceptions and theories.* San Francisco, CA: Jossey-Bass.

Loevinger, J., & Wessler, R. (1970). *Measuring ego development: Vol. 1. Construction and use of a sentence completion test.* San Francisco, CA: Jossey-Bass.

Martin, D. J., Garske, J. P., & Davis, M. K. (2000). Relation of the therapeutic alliance with outcome and other variables: A meta-analytic review. *Journal of Consulting and Clinical Psychology, 68,* 438–450.

McAdams, D. P. (1993). *The stories we live by: Personal myths and the making of the self.* New York: Guilford Press.

McAdams, D. P. (2001). The psychology of life stories. *Review of General Psychology, 5,* 100–122.

McAdams, D. P. (2006). *The redemptive self: Stories Americans live by.* New York: Oxford University Press.

McAdams, D. P., & Bowman, P. (2001). Narrating life's turning points: Redemption and contamination. In D. P. McAdams, R. Josselson, & A. Lieblich (Eds.), *Turns in the road: Narrative studies of lives in transition* (pp. 3–34). Washington, DC: American Psychological Association.

McAdams, D. P., Reynolds, J., Lewis, M., Patten, A. H., & Bowman, P. J. (2001). When bad things turn good and good things turn bad: Sequences of redemption and contamination in life narrative and their relation to psychosocial adaptation in midlife adults and in students. *Personality and Social Psychology Bulletin, 27,* 474–485.

McLean, K. C. (2005). Late adolescent identity development: Narrative meaning making and memory telling. *Developmental Psychology, 41,* 683–691.

Miller, J. B., & Stiver, I. P. (1997). *The healing connection.* Boston: Beacon Press.

Orlinsky, D. E., Rønnestad, M. H., & Willutzki, U. (2004). Fifty years of psychotherapy process-outcome research: Continuity and change. In M. J. Lambert (Ed.), *Bergin and Garfield's handbook of psychotherapy change* (5th ed., pp. 307–390). New York: Wiley.

Pasupathi, M. (2001). The social construction of the personal past and its implications for adult development. *Psychological Bulletin, 127,* 651–672.

Ryff, C. D., & Keyes, C. L. M. (1995). The structure of psychological well-being revisited. *Journal of Personality and Social Psychology, 69,* 719–727.

Safran, J. D., & Wallner, L. K. (1991). The relative predictive validity of two thera-peutic alliance measures in cognitive therapy. *Psychological Assessment, 3,* 188–195.

Schultz, W. T. (2003). The prototypical scene: A method for generating psychobiographical hypotheses. In R. Josselson, A. Lieblich, & D. P. McAdams (Eds.), *Up close and personal: The teaching and learning of narrative research* (pp. 151–175). Washington, DC: American Psychological Association.

Seligman, M. E. P., & Csikszentmihalyi, M. (2000). Positive psychology: An intro-duction. *American Psychologist, 55,* 5–14.

Singer, J. A. (2005). *Personality and psychotherapy: Treating the whole person.* New York: Guilford Press.

Spence, D. P. (1982). *Narrative truth and historical truth.* New York: Norton.

Strauss, A., & Corbin, J. (1994). Grounded theory methodology: An overview. In N. K. Denzin & Y. S. Lincoln (Eds.), *Handbook of qualitative research.* Thousand Oaks, CA: Sage.

Thorne, A. (2000). Personal memory telling and personality development. *Personal-ity and Social Psychology Review, 4,* 45–56.

Vaillant, G. E., & McCullough, L. (1987). The Washington University Sentence Completion Test compared with other measures of adult ego development. *American Journal of Psychiatry, 144,* 1189–1194.

Watson, D., Clark, L. A, & Tellegen, A. (1988). Development and validation of brief measures of positive and negative affect: The PANAS Scales. *Journal of Personality and Social Psychology, 54,* 1063–1070.

Westenberg, P. M., & Block, J. (1993). Ego development and individual differences in personality. *Journal of Personality and Social Psychology, 65,* 792–800.

White, M., & Epston, D. (1990). *Narrative means to therapeutic ends.* New York: Norton.

11

GIVE LOVE A CHANCE: DIFFICULTIES OF YOUNG ADULTS IN ESTABLISHING LONG-TERM ROMANTIC RELATIONSHIPS

ALON RAZ, HADAS WISEMAN, AND RUTH SHARABANY

Establishing long-lasting romantic relationships is one of the most important issues for young adults. In developmental and cultural terms, this task is age-appropriate, and failure to establish such relationships is one of the main reasons young adults seek psychotherapy. The stress experienced by these emerging adults (Schwartzberg, Berliner, & Jacob, 1995) is attributed partly to social pressure from parents and others, partly to the risk of becoming less attractive to partners with increasing age, partly to direct social pressure from parents and others.

Many of the young adults who participated in our study regarded their lack of lasting romantic relationships as a "black hole" in their life story. They had difficulty fitting it into the story they told themselves of who they are. As one of our interviewees put it,

> I am frustrated over the fact that my romantic relationships have never lasted more than a few months. I consider myself as being above average

The identities of the participants in this chapter were masked.

in my ability to reflect upon my experiences and get down to the root of things, but *I just cannot resolve the riddle of romantic relationships.*[1] People say I look fine, I know I am fun to be with . . . so what the hell is the problem? Sometimes I feel I can't make any real progress in my life without solving this issue somehow.

DIFFICULTIES IN ESTABLISHING LONG-TERM ROMANTIC RELATIONSHIPS AS A PERSONAL NARRATIVE

This study explored personal narratives about romantic experiences told by young adults who had difficulty in establishing long-lasting relationships. Could any specific aspects of their narratives about experiences in romantic relationships—whether the main themes or the way they told the narratives—shed some light on these difficulties? This was the main question of our study. We focused on the individual's narrative as largely independent of potential partners. We chose this focus on the basis of the observation that, over time, the difficulties recurred with a variety of potential partners.

We chose to use the term *difficulty* because it reflected the agonizing unfulfilled wish that was expressed by our participants to form and to maintain such relationships. We thereby excluded from the investigation those who were not interested in establishing such relationships and therefore did not experience stress over the matter.

When we approached the topic at hand we were surprised by the paucity of studies in this area (Raz, 2003). What may be a little confusing is the fact that a related area of research, that of relationship maintenance, has been investigated quite extensively. Its focus is current relationships that are relatively long-term (e.g., Campbell, Simpson, Boldry, & Kashy, 2005). In contrast, difficulty in establishing stable premarital romantic relationships has received very little attention. The few studies that have addressed this topic directly focused on relatively older participants (over 40) who had passed the normative developmental window (e.g., Kelly, 1977; Waehler, 1995).

In light of these findings, we used a specific working definition for "difficulty in establishing long-term relationships" based on a preliminary study (see Raz, 2003). This working definition included (a) an objective parameter that referred to the individual indicating that in the past 3 years he or she had not been involved in romantic relationships that lasted longer than 1 year and (b) a subjective aspect that consisted of a self-report indicating that the individual perceived him- or herself as experiencing such difficulty.

Given the aforementioned paucity of previous research, we resorted to studies of relationship maintenance, specifically to those that suggested some understanding of why established, ongoing relationships, usually marital ones,

---

[1]Italics here and elsewhere denote the original emphasis of the speaker.

become unsatisfactory or break up. A thorough search of the research literature about relationship maintenance revealed that it is largely based on attachment theory. Empirical evidence for the relationship between attachment styles and level of satisfaction and stability of romantic relationships has been well documented (e.g., Bartholomew, 1997; Campbell et al., 2005; Feeney & Noller, 1990). This being the case, we were interested in how the attachment framework may apply specifically to difficulties in young adults in establishing long-lasting romantic relationships. To address this question we turned to relational schemas, or the story-like structures, that form the basis of attachment dynamics, namely the internal working model (Bretherton & Munholland, 1999).

Working models are internalized representations of self and others following continuous experiences with attachment figures related to issues of adjustment and satisfaction of attachment needs (Main, Kaplan, & Cassidy, 1985). These representations reflect past relational experiences and constitute a framework of expectations regarding future experiences, thus affecting social interactions as a whole. Reactivation of the working models of self and other can occur in any significant human encounter. In the case of romantic relationships, these encounters, perhaps especially at the stage of establishing new romantic attachment relationships, may be characterized by very high emotional intensities. We can therefore hypothesize that at this stage, rigid, inappropriate, or conflictual working models are one of the sources of difficulties in establishing the relationship.

Most findings involving attachment styles and strained romantic relationships are based on a categorical attachment styles approach, connecting a certain attachment style with a particular difficulty (e.g., Monteoliva & Garcia-Martinez, 2005; Shaver, Collins, & Clark, 1996). We argue that we need to go beyond these findings to an examination of the kind of inner scripts or narratives involved in the unfortunate results of experiencing difficulties in establishing long-lasting romantic relationships. Many studies focus on the general style of attachment, but do not probe either the internal dialogue or monologue that is the unique experience of each person or each person's specific difficulties in the area of romantic relationships. A more specific uncovering of the contents and the process that is activated in attachment-related representations of self and other is needed to obtain deeper insights into the experiences of young adults who have these difficulties. Such an understanding is likely to contribute to both theory and clinical practice.

PARTICIPANTS

Our participants were young adults in their 20s and 30s, equal numbers of men and women, who responded to an advertisement at the University of

Haifa in Israel to take part in a study on "close relationships." Thirty-two of our 80 interviewees heard about our study from other participants. The participants were paid and selected from screening questionnaires so that they were equally divided between those who experienced and those who did not experience difficulties in establishing long-lasting romantic relationships. In this chapter, we focus exclusively on those who experienced such difficulties ($n = 40$).

RELATIONAL NARRATIVES AND THE RELATIONSHIP ANECDOTES PARADIGM INTERVIEW

Participants were interviewed using the Relationship Anecdotes Paradigm (RAP; Luborsky, 1978), which requests interviewees to relate a significant interaction with another person. In the RAP, participants are encouraged to describe the interaction freely and are asked questions about it only if the interviewer feels that clarification is needed. In the present study the participants were asked to narrate two relational episodes describing significant interactions with a past or present romantic partner. Interactions told during RAP interviews have been shown to represent common themes in close relationships (see, e.g., Wiseman & Barber, 2004) and to be a reliable source for exploring transference relationships in therapy (Luborsky & Crits-Christoph, 1998). The idea of transference being a manifestation of inner relational schemas or working models transferred from one relationship to another (Waldinger et al., 2003) suggests that RAP interviews may be a suitable tool for exploring deeply the concept of the internal working model in romantic relationships.

THE NARRATIVES ON ROMANTIC RELATIONSHIPS

In this chapter we present and discuss our analysis of two narratives collected by the RAP method. The relationship episodes presented here reflect themes that we found characteristic of the participants in our study who fit the criteria for those with difficulties in establishing long-term romantic relationships (Raz, 2003).

In our analysis of these episodes, we focus on two dimensions: the central themes (content) of the narrated interaction and the characteristics of the individual as a story narrator (process). The underlying assumption was that given that difficulties in establishing long-lasting romantic relationships recurred with different partners, the individual characteristics that contributed to the narrator's difficulties would be expressed in the narrative. Furthermore, the narrative represents above all the narrator's perception of the relationship episode that he or she had described, and not that of the partner in the interaction. Thus, our focus is exclusively on the narrator and on trying to understand the way the relationship episode was perceived through his or her working models of other and self.

The first relational narrative describes a meeting between a young woman and her romantic partner and the disappointment she felt over one specific answer of his that led to an immediate breakup. The second relational narrative describes a rapid escalation of bad feelings and conflict between a young man and his romantic partner, which left the narrator with substantial doubts about the romantic relationship.

Story 1—Tamar: "Wrong Answer, and That Was It"

Tamar, a 27-year-old woman experiencing intense frustration over her continued failure to be involved in a long-lasting romantic relationship, described a meaningful moment when she met with a man who could have been a potential romantic partner:

Tamar: So this guy I was dating on and off at the time. One time when we were in touch again he came over to my place, after I hadn't seen him for a very long time, and I asked, I wanted to know what he felt for me after such a long time. And he responded, "I *like* you very much." In retrospect, I realize now that the fact that he said it doesn't necessarily mean that's how he felt, I mean it could also have been deeper, but these were the words he blurted out, and I remember that in that situation, although we were physically close, it was . . . it was *simply like the wrong answer, wrong answer, and that was it, that was it.* I remember being very angry, very offended, very hurt, and I just wanted him to go, like, so he got up. It was I who caused this, I don't know whether to call it a break-up, but the fact was that at that moment, he got up and went home.

Interviewer: How did you make him go home, what did you say?

Tamar: It was clear to me that I didn't like the sound of it, I don't remember my exact words, but I made it clear that this was not what I expected to hear and that it was unacceptable to me. Looking back, I now see things differently, but at the time, it was extremely sensitive.

Interviewer: There's anger in your words; was it reflected also in your tone of voice?

Tamar: I guess so, *but like always I did not share with him what it did to me, but more like attacking as a way of defense. To be aggressive, to be strong, to be snappy, goodbye.*

Interviewer: In this situation you are relating, did you already know what your feelings for him were?

> *Tamar:* This was already at a later stage, I knew what I was feeling, but it was not like I was crazy about the guy, in love and wanting him. . . . But I knew we had a lot of emotion . . . intensity. . . . But then again, it was more important for me to know *how the other party felt. To gain security through what he felt.* This is actually, like a condition that is necessary for me to be able to loosen up.

Let us look first at the story of the interaction between Tamar and the young man in this episode. Tamar had a certain need: to be told she was loved. She did not share this need with her partner and it seems that this need could be fulfilled only with a very specific response. In other words, this was a testing situation for the partner. The partner reacted in a way that disappointed her, so he failed the test. She, in return, felt hurt and angry and counterattacked ("as a way of defense"), making him leave. The content of the narrative reflects a working model that can be articulated as a need to be loved (wish) that is followed by an interpretation of the response from the other as dangerous for the self—the other being rejecting or posing a potential threat of a future rejection (responses from other). This, in turn, activates painful feelings of the self (response of self) and a defensive action—breakup (outcome). In terms of internal representations, what is striking here is the fact that the internal working model, which is shaped by previous experiences, acts in a way that is aimed at defending the participant's emotional world, while in fact contributing to her future unfavorable pained view of men in general and her perception of self in romantic relationships. In that sense, working models of other and self may act as double-edged swords: Aimed at protecting the self, they end up becoming part of a vicious circle of emotional pain.

In terms of conflict management, it seems that the conflict in the episode described earlier escalated drastically and quickly to a point of no return. Although several explanations may be offered, such rapid escalation of conflicts was a common theme among our interviewees. The following verbatim transcript from another female participant demonstrates further such rapid escalation of conflict—here too as a result of a wish that was not verbalized:

> *Iris:* And the situation was that I came to his house to stay over the weekend, and he had friends with him, but I wanted us to be alone together, *so I just got up and left.* He realized I was angry, and he stayed with his friends until they left . . . and he didn't understand what had gone wrong.

Going back to Tamar's account of the process of escalation, two kinds of dynamics appeared to be involved: The first was that the conflict was initiated by an inner alarm bell, set off by an internal working model shaped by experiences and calling for a clear-cut reaction. The second was Tamar's very specific, unspoken expectation—leaving no room for a variation—of acceptable, negotiable responses from the other. It is as if the whole conflictual dialogue had already taken place in Tamar's head, and the "wrong answer" she received was the closing argument of that inner dialogue.

Many of the episodes told by our participants reflect very specific, narrowly defined expectations with regard to physical appearance, personality, and behavior. When these expectations were not met fully, a feeling of deep crisis arose in the relationship. Frequently, this dynamic was reflected in the many variations of the testing situation theme illustrated earlier. The following verbatim report by Karen gives a good idea of how such a dynamic may sound:

> We went to a hotel, actually more a seaside resort, and I very much wanted us to swim together, to play ping-pong and to do things together, and all he wanted was to sit alone and read the newspaper. I remember being very upset, here we came to spend a vacation together, let's enjoy the hotel, what's the point of just sitting down like that. . . . You can do that at home. He told me that this was something he needed, "to be with myself." We started fighting. I just left the pool and went up to the room for all to see *and thought to myself, let's see how long it takes before he notices I'm not there.* And I got into the room crying a lot, thinking he doesn't want me at all, all he wants is to be by himself, *and this relationship has no future.* I wept and then I washed my face, went down, and pretended nothing had ever happened and spoke to him pretty normally. Then we played ping-pong and went swimming together. And then somehow we left it behind us, but it wasn't really forgotten.

The expectation that the other meet a very specific set of behavioral demands seems to be a crucial obstacle in establishing romantic relationships. When these demands are not met, the relationship shifts into the "wrong answer" mode. In that sense, *wrong answer* may be considered a central metaphor for understanding the phenomenon at hand. The themes (content) identified in Tamar's episode appeared to represent some common dynamics among many of our interviewees. This episode represented also another common characteristic of our participants: that of the individual as a story narrator (process). We would like to suggest a distinction between a positivistic and a narrative-playful manner of thinking about one's love life and romantic partners.

Tamar's response—"wrong answer"—may represent a positivistic attitude indicating that the story of the relationship must follow some prewritten external script. This is in contrast to allowing the story of the relationship to unfold and be a creation of the moment. Winnicott's ideas (1965, 1971) are highly relevant here. It seems that when Tamar was expecting a very narrowly defined specific answer, an answer dictated in advance, she lost the potential space needed to create a story. She no longer could stand in the transitional space that allows one to play with many possibilities, with the many possible developmental lines the story may have.

In this regard, it is useful to draw on Sternberg, Hojjat, and Barnes's (2001) taxonomy of love stories. One type of love story they described, termed *theater,* is characterized as follows: "Love is scripted with predictable acts, scenes and lines" (p. 203). In that sense many of our participants shared this type of love story. However, in our view it may be somewhat confusing to call it a "type of a story" because in a way this is exactly what is missing here—the story, that is, the playful quality from which genuine stories are born.

Winnicott (1965, 1971) saw the ability to play as developing through a number of steps. When play becomes social, children move through two distinct steps: at first, they need the other only as a witness. With time, they actually begin to play *with* the other but expect the other to follow their own rules. It is only when their ability to play matures that they allow the other to become an active partner in the play and to initiate his or her own moves. At that stage, an important part of the joy that accompanies playing stems from the innovation and surprise of the other's moves in the mutual play, which the child has minimal or no control of. It may be that romantic relationships in general, but certainly at their beginning, call for the same quality: really allowing the other to be involved in the writing of the mutual story, and really being able to assess—with minimal judgment and with acceptance— the other's contribution to the "love story" that the two are writing together. From this viewpoint, Tamar's clear-cut answer—"wrong answer"—represents a fundamental characteristic of the difficulty in establishing long-lasting romantic relationships. It involves the general ability or disability to approach one's own love stories more as flexible collaborating co-writer, and in a playful manner, rather than as a writer who holds a prewritten fixed script for the developing relationships.

Story 2—Itai: "I Started Thinking, What Was It That She Saw in Me"

Itai, a 28-year-old man, had never experienced a long-term (in his case, no longer than 6 months) romantic relationship. In fact, the relationship he narrated in the following episode was the longest of his romantic experiences. An important perspective to keep in mind while considering this episode is that Itai believed that this first ever romantic experience had shaped, in his eyes, his romantic experiences ever since. He had been in love with a girl he dated for 5 months, and it seemed to him at the time that it was mutual. Then, without any preliminary indication or warning signs, she ended the relationship, with no explanation, and he didn't ask for one. According to him, ever since then, whenever a relationship "threatened" to become a serious relationship he broke it up on his initiative.

The following interaction occurred in one of the relationships that he ended.

Itai: We went on a trek with some nice guys, and after several days of trekking I felt she was talking to these guys more and more, and ignoring me, and *I carried that feeling inside me all day without telling her anything,* because we were riding horses, and she's also a professional rider, and she just skipped from one guy to the other without hardly ever talking to me during the day.

Interviewer: How did you feel about it?

Itai: That what is happening here? . . . we are together all the time and suddenly on the trek. . . . *I felt insecure about how she felt about me, and why. . . .*

Interviewer: What did you feel?

Itai: A kind of dejection, uncertainty, insecurity. . . . This was also because on that very day, whatever I said or did she said, "Why did you start making a fool of yourself? . . . This isn't like you," and all that. But I felt it was like me. It added to the insecurity regarding what she felt about me. There were dogs there guarding the alpacas. Usually you don't get near them, and there was one nice dog that approached me, and I petted it, I like animals very much, and this also made her mad at me. . . . Rabies and stuff. . . . And I told myself, this is how I define myself, it's part of my nature—loving animals—and now she can't accept that either so maybe. . . . Gradually, I started thinking, *what was it that you saw in me to begin with. . . .* I felt too much criticism on her part. The way I see myself, I really don't have any problem taking criticism, but nevertheless this seemed like the kind of nonconstructive criticism of who I really was. In the evening we stopped for dinner and a rest, and *I gave her this sour face,* to make her understand. She asked, what's up, and I told her, "OK, you want to know what's going on then let's talk." So I told her more or less everything I told you now, how I felt about today, about what went on here. . . . "You start criticizing me about everything, ignoring me during the day. I start thinking, *what do you find in me, what are you looking for.* All the time you tell me you feel a certain way, and today I didn't feel you behaved that way."

Interviewer: How did she react?

Itai: As far as I can recall it was that I shouldn't be looking for reasons for the way she felt about me. This was her basic message. I don't exactly remember the conversation. That you don't need reasons for that, if she feels that way, and that she said it to me plenty of times and that when she has something to say she says it and that this is the way she is, a little critical, and that I shouldn't take it the wrong way. . . .

Interviewer: And how did you feel about her response?

> *Itai:* Not 100%. . . . I wouldn't have behaved that way; I still thought
> that something in my interpretation may have been right.

Certain points stand out in this episode. The first is that Itai kept his hard feelings for a while to himself, at least verbally, communicating them at first in only a nonverbal way ("I gave her this sour face") and expecting, perhaps testing, his girlfriend to read the nonverbal signs and approach him. The second is the vicious circle that arose by his not confronting his girlfriend with his bad feelings: He got even deeper into an inner, self-enhancing negative dialogue, ending with a profound feeling of insecurity. Every event during the day was interpreted and given a meaning that enhanced seeing things through those gloomy dark glasses. The fact that Itai's feelings were kept inside verbally and were communicated only nonverbally (sour face) created a testing situation for the partner similar to the dynamics that we identified in Tamar's story.

Campbell et al. (2005) suggested that individuals who hold an anxious attachment model tend to be oversensitive to indications of threat in the relationship—that is, they tend to "flunk" their partners in "the test," often without reason. In terms of internal working models, Itai's story, like Tamar's story before, reflects an anxious internal working model, one that requires only weak external cues to form an unfavorable picture of the self in relation to the other. What seems to be crucial here is the fact that these cues become significant, hurting, and irrefutable facts, in a process that does not involve the other. Because feelings and thoughts are not dealt with directly and immediately, they become, with time, much more significant and threatening, and much less resolvable.

Not communicating one's own anger or hurt, and expecting the other to "read" them without words, may have many origins and many conscious and unconscious motives, but is most likely to be destructive for the relationship. It results in conflicts whose starting point leaves very little room for maneuver, other than breaking up. This tendency to hold hard feelings unspoken was termed by Thompson, Whiffen, and Aube (2001) "silencing of the self" and was one of the most common themes in the interactions told by our interviewees. *Self-silencing* refers to any inauthentic behavior in a relationship, and one important aspect of it is the lack of expression of negative feelings. We present some variations on this very common theme, especially among female participants in our study.

The first verbatim text is taken from the same episode that was partially presented earlier by Iris, the young woman who got angry because her boyfriend didn't realize that she wanted to be alone with him. Later she was asked whether there was something in that situation that was familiar or typical of her, and she replied,

> *Iris:* Yes. The inability to discuss what I'm going through in relation-
> ships. I think that in general I'm waiting to be asked and that

I'm sort of reluctant to speak up. *Especially if it's something I'm mad about. It's more like I let it eat me up and feel there's nothing to talk about.*

Another example of self-silencing can be found in the following episode. A female participant, we shall name her "Dalia," told us about a situation in which she was having trouble parking her car; she called out to her boyfriend, who didn't hear her at first but then came to help her park her car. When he parked the car he noticed that he almost ran over his dog. He told her that she was very fortunate, because "the dog is the most precious thing to me besides you." She was very offended by his remark but said nothing, and her description of the situation reveals the dynamics of self-silencing entrapment.

Dalia: It was very unpleasant for me, but I told him nothing.

Interviewer: What was unpleasant?

Dalia: The general feeling.

Interviewer: What made that general feeling?

Dalia: All sorts of things, in general. I thought the dog was indeed more important to him than I was. I also expected him to hear me and wait for me, because he knew I was coming.

Interviewer: How was all this significant for you?

Dalia: At the beginning of our relationship, he used to kind of wait, sometimes even with a flower . . . and now he barely heard me calling.

Interviewer: Did you tell him anything about the way you felt?

Dalia: No, I didn't, because first, he said I was more important, so what's the point of quarreling with him? And second, I couldn't say anything because I felt very guilty over the fact that the dog almost got run over because of me.

The ability to express both positive and negative feelings is one of the backbones of close intimate relationships (Sharabany, 1994). Murray and Holmes (1999) suggested that avoiding the expression of difficult feelings in relationships, as in the previous example, eventually creates the impression that the difficulties experienced in the relationship are insoluble. In turn, when parties can no longer hide the things that bother them, this notion leads to breakups because partners are convinced they are unable to overcome their strong feelings and differences. Such avoidance of expressing difficult feelings has been found to correlate negatively with satisfaction with relationships and positively with depression and with the degree of criticism by the partner (Thompson et al., 2001) and with oversensitivity to signs of rejection (Knoblach & Carpenter, 2004).

Going back to Itai's story, one is struck by his description of the situation in which daily cues were magnified, resulting in profound insecurity. On the basis of our clinical experience, we suggest another possible explanation for this mechanism, which may be particularly relevant to the history of Itai's romantic relationships. Because Itai ended all his relationships whenever he felt they were threatening to become serious, it may be that seeing the other as rejecting is a sophisticated mechanism to avoid guilt feelings. This way, the other becomes bad and rejecting, and not the self. Many of those in our study who were experiencing difficulties in establishing long-lasting romantic relationships reported such a theme. They claimed that a central reason for their hesitation to give new relationships a chance was their wish to avoid contending with hurt feelings following breakups that they initiate. For example, consider the passage taken from one of the male participants who described an episode in which he initiated a breakup. The interviewer asked him further what was significant for him in the interaction he had described. He responded,

> I hate the feeling it arouses. I feel so bad about it that I take a long timeout from romantic relationships altogether. Then I try again, but I am so cautious, trying to make sure that the new relationship is different, that I will not have to face the same ugly situation again, that I prefer at most times to say "bye bye" right at the beginning and not after we have got to know each other a little, because then it is always the most difficult.

Itai's insecurity was made up, perhaps, of two complementary feelings: the feeling that his girlfriend was ignoring him, and his being perceived incorrectly by her. In fact, he felt that his girlfriend saw him in a way that completely missed one of the most central aspects of his self-definition. Regarding the latter of the two feelings, Itai seemed unable to attribute to his girlfriend any real, genuine love or concern for him, such as when she suggested that he should avoid petting a dog that might carry rabies. Instead, even in retrospect, he viewed her remark as sheer criticism directed at no less than "who I am."

On the basis of many of the interactions told by participants in our study we suggest that over and above any specific dynamics or content of the specific interaction, our participants were unlikely to tell a good (favorable) story about their partners. As we argued in Tamar's case, this unlikelihood may reflect the inability to consider different possible meanings of the partner's responses as well as the tendency to confuse hypotheses with presumably truthful "facts." Not only did Itai lose the intermediate space from which different meanings could be explored hermeneutically, but specifically he made no effort to take his partner's point of view or see her favorably. Recent studies in fact have suggested that couples who have successful and enduring relationships tend to idealize their partners, or perceive their behavior in a particularly positive or tolerant way (Murray, Holmes, & Griffin, 2004). This does not mean that one altogether ignores bad moments or is involved in prolonged denial. It means an active and prolonged effort to see the other and interpret his or her action in a favorable manner. It is a continuous process of choosing what kind of a story one would like to tell oneself about one's partner and about the partner in relation to oneself. This active and prolonged effort ends with a good story about a romantic partner that too often was absent from the interactions told by those experiencing difficulties in establishing long-lasting romantic relationships. Being able to see a situation from multiple or at least not solely egocentric points of view might be considered one important factor in the process of telling a positive story. This ability seemed to be missing from many of the interactions we studied, as the following demonstrates:

> We were snorkeling and she was afraid to put her head under the water. I told her how beautiful it was and that she must try, but she refused. She said she was afraid. I got very mad, *why couldn't she even try?* It was the beginning of a big fight that continued all through that vacation, and at the end of it, we broke up. We just were not speaking the same language.

In contrasting those individuals who did not experience difficulties in establishing long-lasting romantic relationships with those who did have such difficulties, we found that their narratives reflected an almost equal number of conflicts. However, there were two main differences: The escalation of conflict was generally more moderate, and conflicts, in most cases, did not reach the point of no return. Furthermore, the tendency to tell a favorable story about the other, and especially being able to describe the situation from the other's point of view and acknowledge his or her pain, was very common in this other group. As a result, conflicts were commonly viewed in that group as strengthening the relationships rather than weakening them. The participants under consideration here, however, tended to narrate conflict as fatal to a positive view of the other.

Some Methodological Considerations

In the RAP, the participant is asked to describe an interaction, in this case with romantic partners, but is not asked to reflect on it. We added to the standard RAP interview a single question at the end of the participant's account of each episode: "Do you feel the interaction you have just described, or some aspect of it, is *typical* of your interactions with romantic partners in general?" However, understanding these narratives could benefit from a more comprehensive reflection of the participants' own perspective in regard to experiencing (or not experiencing) difficulties in establishing long-lasting romantic relationships. Future studies that append the subjective reflection and a subjective evaluation of the state of difficulties could illuminate an additional important aspect of the difficulties in establishing long-lasting romantic relationships.

CONCLUSIONS

The narratives told by those experiencing difficulties in establishing long-lasting romantic relationships suggest that aspects of the internal working models play an important role in the difficulties that we examined. In general, these models, based on previous experiences, portray a negative image of both self (not worthy to be loved) and other (rejecting, unreliable). The following are the most prominent themes that emerged from our narrative data.

Lack of Open Dialogue

Overall, distinct patterns of lack of communication of negative feelings arose in the interaction with the partner, and the most common, prominent, and destructive of these patterns was not expressing them at all. This tendency to self-silence seems to involve a repeatedly failing magical wish that the other will know and feel without words what the person needs and wants from him or her. Two other patterns of communicating hard feelings were destructive: expressing them nonverbally and expressing them but not leaving room for the partners' perspective. The latter pattern was most noticeable in Tamar's "wrong answer" story, in which the whole conflictual dialogue had seemingly already taken place in her head and the wrong answer was the closing argument of that inner dialogue, leaving no room for any real dialogue with her partner.

Testing Situations

Our participants were most likely to hold very specific expectations of their partner and reacted with disappointment when these were not met. These specific expectations involve examining closely the investment of the other before the narrator extends him- or herself and risks getting hurt. This position introduces skepticism into the relationship and places the partner in a situation in which he or she has to prove something before the narrator allows him- or herself to invest more in the relationship. This testing situation is especially destructive because it is often not communicated, leaving the partner with a very high probability of failing the test. Any such failing of the test serves as proof of the validity of the working model that created the test in the first place, thus supporting further avoidant or ambivalent behavior.

Acute Sensitivity to Rejection and Wide Safety Margins

Those experiencing difficulties in establishing long-lasting romantic relationships are often characterized by a heightened sensitivity to signs of rejection—seeking these signs and interpreting relationships from this perspective. Downey, Freitas, Michalis, and Khouri (1998) suggested that such high sensitivity to signs of rejection often leads to behavior arousing the other's anger and impatience, and eventually to rejection on their part. This acute sensitivity can therefore act as a self-fulfilling prophecy. It also appears to evolve as a means to prevent further hurtful experiences at any cost. For this, very wide margins of safety are created, such as expecting the other to pledge his or her love first or else not allowing oneself to really get involved in the relationship.

Together, these two tendencies—acute sensitivity to rejection and wide safety margins—often pull those experiencing difficulties in establishing long-lasting romantic relationships away from the relationship because the other does not provide the degree of security needed to risk getting close again.

Beyond Specific Themes: The Difficulty of Telling a Positive, Favorable Story

Over and above the content of specific themes that were shared by many of our interviewees, we identified a certain distinct quality in the way they told their stories about these interpersonal interactions. Very often, the stories of our interviewees, men and women alike, reflected what we termed a positivistic view of both their partners and romantic relationships in general. They frequently expected situations and partners to follow some prewritten scripts or made their partners play certain predesignated roles. Interactions were frequently devoid of a playful atmosphere and left the impression of what one may call a thin story.

It appears that seeing the partner as a coauthor rather than an actor in one's own script, and seeing relationships more as a developing story rather than having to fit an existing but nonworking old narrative, may give love a better chance. A real love story may potentially be an enriching dialogue of multiple stories, but when such dialogue is restricted, one is left, in the end, alone.

REFERENCES

Bartholomew, K. (1997). Adult attachment processes: Individual and couple perspectives. *British Journal of Medical Psychology, 70,* 249–263.

Bretherton, I., & Munholland, K. A. (1999). Internal working models in attachment relationships. A construct revisited. In J. Cassidy & P. R. Shaver (Eds.), *Hand-*

book of attachment: Theory, research, and clinical application (pp. 89–111). New York: Guilford Press.

Campbell, L., Simpson, J. A., Boldry, J., & Kashy, D. A. (2005). Perceptions of conflict and support in romantic relationships: The role of attachment anxiety. *Journal of Personality and Social Psychology, 88,* 510–531.

Downey, G., Freitas, A. L., Michalis, B., & Khouri, H. (1998). The self-fulfilling prophecy in close relationships: Rejection sensitivity and rejection by romantic partners. *Journal of Personality and Social Psychology, 75,* 545–560.

Feeney, J. A., & Noller, P. (1990). Attachment style as a predictor of adult romantic relationships. *Journal of Personality and Social Psychology, 58,* 281–291.

Kelly, K. (1977). Lifestyle of never-married adults (Doctoral dissertation, University of Nebraska, Lincoln, 1977). *Dissertation Abstracts International, 39,* 5026-B.

Knoblach, L. K., & Carpenter, T. K. E. (2004). Topic avoidance in developing romantic relationships: Associations with intimacy and relational uncertainty. *Communication Research, 31,* 173–205.

Luborsky, L. (1978). *The relationship anecdotes paradigm (RAP) interview: A TAT like method using actual narratives.* Unpublished manuscript.

Luborsky, L., & Crits-Christoph, P. (1998). *Understanding transference: The CCRT method.* Washington, DC: American Psychological Association.

Main, M., Kaplan, N., & Casssidy, J. (1985). Security in infancy, childhood, and adulthood: A move to the level of representation. *Monographs of the Society for Research in Child Development, 50*(1–2), 66–104.

Monteoliva, A., & Garcia-Martinez, J. (2005). Adult attachment style and its effect on the quality of romantic relationships in Spanish students. *Journal of Social Psychology, 145,* 745–747.

Murray, S. L., & Holmes, J. G. (1999). The (mental) ties that bind: Cognitive structures that predict relationship resilience. *Journal of Personality and Social Psychology, 77,* 1228–1244.

Murray, S. L., Holmes, J. G., & Griffin, W. (2004). The benefits of positive illusions: Idealization and construction of satisfaction in close relationships. In H. T. Reis & C. E. Rusbult (Eds.), *Close relationships: Key readings* (pp. 317–338). Philadelphia: Taylor & Francis.

Raz, A. (2003). *Meafeinim ishiutiim, temot merkaziot shel yahasim, veyecholot bein ishiot bekerev hamitkashim beyetzirat kesher zugi mitmashech* [Personality, central relationship themes, and interpersonal competence among young adults experiencing difficulties in establishing long-term romantic relationships]. Unpublished doctoral dissertation, University of Haifa, Haifa, Israel.

Schwartzberg, N., Berliner, K., & Jacob, D. (1995). *Single in a married world.* New York: Norton.

Sharabany, R. (1994). Intimate friendship scale: Conceptual underpinnings, psychometric properties and construct validity. *Journal of Social and Personal Relationships, 11,* 449–469.

Shaver, P. R., Collins, N., & Clark, C. L. (1996). Attachment styles and internal working models of self and relationship partners. In G. J. Fletcher, J. O. Garth,

& J. Fitness (Eds.), *Knowledge structures in close relationships: A social psychological approach* (pp. 25–61). Mahwah, NJ: Erlbaum.

Sternberg, R. J., Hojjat, M., & Barnes, M. L. (2001). Empirical tests of aspects of a theory of love as a story. *European Journal of Personality, 15*, 199–218.

Thompson, J. M., Whiffen, V. E., & Aube, J. (2001). Does self-silencing link perceptions of care from parents and partners with depressive symptoms? *Journal of Social and Personal Psychology, 18*, 502–516.

Waehler, C. (1995). Relationship patterns of never-married men and their implications for psychotherapy. *Psychotherapy, 32*, 248–257.

Waldinger, R. J., Seidman, E. L., Gerber, A. J., Liem, J. H., Allen, J. P., & Hauser, S. T. (2003). Attachment and core relationship themes: Wishes for autonomy and closeness in the narratives of securely and insecurely attached adults. *Psychotherapy Research, 13*, 77–98.

Winnicott, D. W. (1965). *The maturational processes and the facilitating environment.* New York: International Universities Press.

Winnicott, D. W. (1971). *Playing and reality.* Middlesex, England: Penguin.

Wiseman, H., & Barber, J. P. (2004). The Core Conflictual Relationship Theme approach to relational narratives: Interpersonal themes in the context of intergenerational communication of trauma. In A. Lieblich, D. P. McAdams, & R. Josselson (Eds.), *Healing plots: The narrative basis of psychotherapy* (pp. 151–170). Washington, DC: American Psychological Association.

12

ONGOING RELATIONSHIPS: RECOUNTING A LOST PARENT'S LIFE AS A MEANS TO RE-MEMBER

RON NASIM

Only those who took up the lyre
even among shadows
can render unending praise
out of a sense of foreboding.

Only those who partook of the poppy
sharing their meal with the dead
will never lose
the softest sound.

However much the mirror reflection in the lake
may blur and dissolve us,
thou knowest the image [italics added].

Only in the twilight zone
do the voices become
eternal and mild.[1]

The publication of Klass, Silverman, and Nickman's *Continuing Bonds: New Understandings of Grief* (1996) marked a decisive shift in 20th-century grief literature. Whereas Freud (1917/1993) and other psychoanalytically oriented theorists had emphasized the importance of relinquishing the strong affective bond with the deceased person, it has recently been proposed that the very continuation of the bond facilitates adjustment (Klass & Walter, 2001). *Continuing bonds* is generally understood in the scientific community as denoting the presence of an ongoing inner relationship with the deceased person by the bereaved individual (see Field, Gal-Oz, & Bonanno, 2003; Shuchter & Zisook, 1993). In recent years, grief researchers have shown that

---

[1]From *Sonnets to Orpheus* (IX; S. Kitron, Trans.), by R. M. Rilke. Reprinted with permission of the translator.

Some unique features of the study presented in this chapter have been altered, masked, or deleted to conceal the identity of the participants.

there are indeed different kinds of continuing bonds within various groups of bereaved, but whether these bonds are necessarily healthier for the individual is still a moot point (Stroebe & Schut, 2005). Whether or not such bonds are beneficial for the grieving process, they may still be central in the lives of certain grieving individuals and may have great importance for their self-understanding and identity formation.

In this chapter I present four narratives of individuals who lost a parent at an early age (9–15 years old) and whom I interviewed about 10 years after their loss. My main aim is to examine the various ways in which these individuals narrate the story of their parents as well as the impact of these narrations on their own self-defining life stories. I argue that within this process, one can observe and learn about the continuation of the bond with the deceased. I describe how reinterpretations of the parents' stories enabled the children to widen the inner representation of the parent and, at the same time, describe how they struggled to define the way it fit or did not fit their own self-narrative. Through this description I use and expand the concept of re-membering (Meyrhoff, 1982). From this discussion I hope to draw the conclusion that the way people re-member their lost loved ones may change over time according to their changing psychological needs and that grieving individuals in general may strive for a right balance between continuing the bond and letting it go.

CONTINUING BONDS WITH A LOST PARENT

The basic thesis in Klass et al.'s (1996) book was that "the resolution of grief involves continuing bonds that survivors maintain with the deceased. . . .These continuing bonds can be a healthy part of the survivor's ongoing life" (Klass et al., 1996, p. 22). Evidence for this claim was drawn from a variety of sources, including studies on the retaining of ties in other cultures (Klass, 1996; Stroebe, Gergen, Gergen, & Stroebe, 1992). Klass (1996), for example, described ancestor worship in Japan, whereby an elaborate set of rituals enables the living to maintain emotional bonds with their deceased loved ones. Ancestor worship, seen within the context of Buddhist beliefs and practices, was understood to be "an expression of the human community that cannot be separated by death. . . . The rituals provide a vehicle by which resolution of grief is accomplished" (Klass, 1996, p. 59).

Continuing bonds have also been observed within Western culture (Stroebe et al., 1992). For example, the Harvard Child Bereavement Study, analyzed by Silverman and Worden (1992), involved a nonclinical sample of children between the ages of 6 and 17 who lost a parent. These children devoted considerable energy to maintaining a connection to the deceased parent. They did this through dreams, by talking to the deceased, by feeling that the dead parent was watching them, by keeping things that belonged to the dead parent, by visiting the grave, and by frequently thinking about the dead parent. The authors stressed that in previous clinical studies such behaviors had been labeled "preoccupation with the deceased," which implied a symptomatic behavior that should end. However, most of those studies were based on clinical observations (Dietrich & Shabad, 1989; Volkan, 1981) and did not deal with a nonclinical population. Therefore, the authors concluded, "The parent may be dead, but the relationship did not die" (Silverman & Worden, 1992, p. 315). In the long run, Silverman and Worden claimed, accepting the reality of death may mean finding a way for the dead parent to live in some way within the child's life (Rubin, 1985; Silverman & Worden, 1992; Worden, 1991). Silverman and Nickman (1996) interviewed children at similar ages as well as their surviving parent, and found that children retained ties to their deceased parent by experiencing the deceased as a disciplinarian, keeping a belonging of the deceased parent, or reminiscing about the joint past.

An early psychoanalytic contribution to the understanding of the continuing-bonds phenomena in children is Schafer's (1968) thesis that in psychic reality the object (parental inner image) is immortal. Therefore, he argued, it makes more sense to speak of the various fates of the immortal object than to speak of object loss pure and simple. From the subject's standpoint, there can be no thoroughgoing object loss. Only the higher levels of function, those more or less dominated by the secondary process, recognize "no," death, and loss. What is more, he claimed that there are fundamental, indissoluble links between the child's self and parental object representation, and between the child's attachments to both; the child can consequently no more give up or lose an object entirely than he can entirely give up or lose his subjective self. Thus, the parental object is ever-present, ever-available, and indestructible. According to Schafer, the way in which the object is "ever-present, ever-available" is through the process of identification, in which the object is moved from the external world into the child's inner world (Schafer, 1968).

Stroebe and Schut (2005) recently published a review of research on the continuing–breaking bonds controversy. They concluded that it is not possible to determine with any certainty whether either the continuation or the relinquishment of the bond is generally helpful and that researchers need to work toward understanding how and for whom continuing or relinquishing bonds furthers adjustment (Stroebe & Schut, 2005).

It is important for me to note my own personal journey through this work. Having been a grieving child myself after losing my father to cancer when I was 13, I started this study with an absolutely dichotomous and unbalanced view: On one side—the side I favored—stood continuing-bonds theorists and practitioners who encourage the continuation of the relationship and emphasize its positive contributions. On the other side were "letting go or saying goodbye" theorists who emphasize the importance of relinquishing the tie and moving on to form new relationships. What I discovered was that letting-go as well as continuing-bonds narratives were presented as a dialectic in the interviewees' subjective experience. From what I could gather from my interviewees as well as from reflections on my own experiences, both narratives seemed crucial to the preferred development of the self-narrative. Therefore the end point for my journey was a more balanced view in which acknowledging the reality of the death and the parent's absence exists side by side with the experience of an ongoing relationship. Through the conceptualizations and the analysis of the narratives in this chapter, I hope to show how mourners may strive to find the right balance between the two.

RE-MEMBERING AND THE TWO MODES OF EXPERIENCE

A continuing relationship with a lost loved one, especially with a lost parent, may be formed internally, through the process of identification (Schafer, 1968), or externally, through the felt presence of the deceased (Silverman & Worden, 1992). Yet questions remain. How is the tie with the lost parent, which may partly be unconscious, experienced consciously? How do various subject–object relationship patterns, which may form part of an inner reality, become manifest in the outer reality of life? If various parts of the parental object were internalized through the process of identification, what parts manifest themselves in the mourner's life and when? Finally, how and when does a grieving child actively bring the parent's image or their relationship pattern into a self-narrative?

Re-membering

Barbara Myerhoff (1982), who studied elderly Jews in a secular senior citizen center, observed a specific type of recollection in the members' struggle to retain the past. To signify this specific type of recollection, she suggested the term *re-membering*,[2] which stresses the active nature of how the members brought images and stories about the deceased closer to their current lives. According to her, re-membering calls attention to the reaggregation of members—the figures who belong to one's life story—one's own prior selves, and significant others who are part of the story. It was termed "a purposive, significant unification, quite different from the passive, continuous fragmentary flickering of images and feelings that accompany other activities in the normal flow of consciousness" (p. 110).

---

[2]This concept has been readdressed in the work of narrative therapist Michael White (1997) and recently elaborated on in the book *Re-membering Lives: Conversations With the Dying and the Bereaved* by Lorraine Hedtke and John Winslade (2004).

Myerhoff's emphasis in the phenomenon she observed was on the "incorporation into the present" and on the active restoration of lost members into the mourners' lives. She also claimed that the process of re-membering is part of the "full recovery" from mourning. However, her conceptualization can be used in general to define any process of bringing a relationship pattern, or image of the deceased, from a subconscious to a conscious level of experience. These special moments of recollection may pertain to joint experiences or to stories that stress the unique knowledge the parent had of certain aspects of the child's self (White, 1997). In the context of the lives of the people who participated in my study, at the time of the interview, a remembered sense of their lost parent may have connected with certain aspects of the children's self-presentation, character traits, and current relationship patterns.

White (1997) suggested the metaphor of a club—a club of life—to describe significant relationships and affiliations in a person's life. According to him, this club of life is composed of members who have played a significant part in a person's life story; in this club, each member has "membership status," which may change over time. Following Myerhoff's (1982) conceptualization, he invited his clients to engage in "re-membering practices," a process in which they revised the memberships of their club of life. White (1997) claimed that this invitation allowed his clients to have a greater say about the status of particular memberships—to suspend or elevate, revoke or privilege, and downgrade or upgrade specific memberships of their lives (White, 1997). Hedtke and Winslade (2004) described "re-membering conversations" they conducted within families, in which the therapist invited each person to tell stories that constituted the living legacy of a loved one who, though physically absent, remained very much a "member" of his or her life (Hedtke & Winslade, 2004).

Such revisions of membership status may occur naturally throughout life, without any therapeutic intervention. In light of Schafer's (1968) definition of identification, the club-of-life metaphor can be viewed as different object representations that have been incorporated into various aspects of the self-representation. It is important to note, though, that Myerhoff and Schafer regarded the term *incorporation* differently. According to Schafer (1968), when an object is incorporated or fully identified with, it gets absorbed into the self and loses its object-ness. Thus, as I demonstrate later, if one "becomes" one's mother, the mother as a distinct being disappears. In contrast, the club-of-life metaphor (White, 1997) and the incorporation of lost members into the present (Myerhoff, 1982) can keep the image of the person separate and alive. Throughout the four narratives I present later I quite broadly use the concept of re-membering to point to any active process of bringing (or choosing not to bring) the deceased parent's image or story closer to the interviewee's consciousness.

Two Modes of Experience: Separateness and Oneness

The conceptualization of re-membering and the notion of the club-of-life members have a common denominator: The ongoing relationship with the parent, even if it reflects and influences the subjective self, still stems from a differentiation between self and other. The subject may try to be like the object (Schafer, 1968) but clearly recognizes his or her separateness from the other. Yet, a subjective feeling of a total identification or *merger* between child and parent might be reported as well. In this process the parental object is incorporated or identified with fully. Absorbed into the self, it loses its object-ness.

Erlich (2003) offered an understanding of experience as stemming from the operation of two contiguous, ongoing modalities of processing internal and external input, and reflecting two polarities of the subject–object experience: one of separateness, and another of oneness. In the first modality, subject and object are experienced as separate from each other, as two distinct, interactive entities. The experience is then one of having or not having the object, which may give rise to a range of feelings: a feeling that one needs the object and is motivated or moved toward it; feelings of loss, longing, missing, wishful desire, or a need to test the object's durability and realness; and so on. In the second experiential mode, subject and object are not experienced as separate and distinct from each other. On the contrary, Erlich claimed that the fundamental experiential qualities in this mode are their merger, identity, and fusion. Boundaries cannot and do not play the crucial role they occupy in the first one. In this mode, experience has little or nothing to do with manipulating, affecting, or being affected by the other. Likewise, it is not based on or generative of desire, as the object is not experienced as an other to be had for some purpose (Erlich, 2003).

Although Erlich offered his understanding of the general modes of experiencing and did not consider the experience of a lost object in particular, his conceptualization may contribute to the analysis of the material in this study. His claim that the experiential modes operate constantly and are always parallel with each other may illuminate the subjective experience that the parental object exists in two dimensions and that in both modes it is felt differently. In two of the analyses presented in this chapter, I try to reconstruct how both modes of experience are narrated. I also explore whether a dominant mode of experience of the lost object can be shown within the participants' narratives and how this connects to the conceptualization of re-membering.

RECOUNTING THE PARENT'S LIFE STORY AND THE SELF-NARRATIVE

The way I intended to investigate the continuation of the bond with a lost parent was through the narration of the parent's life story by the child.

Attig (1996) has said that "As we come to know and love others, we come to know and cherish the stories of the lives they live. . . . Our knowledge and love of the stories remain after the loss of the presence of the deceased" (pp. 179–180). Attig further noted that reinterpretation of stories is always possible and can yield new insights into the lives of deceased loved ones. Such new insights are especially likely to occur as one ages and encounters changing life circumstances—circumstances that enable one to consider the deceased from a different vantage point (Attig, 1996; Rando, 1993).

Rosenblatt and Elde (1990) and Walter (1996, 1999) have similarly hypothesized that one significant way in which the dead may become a valued part of the survivor's biography is through talking to others who knew the deceased and asking them about his or her life story. This activity may be particularly important in certain relationships in which large parts of the dead person's life are unknown to the mourner (Klass & Walter, 2001).

One cause for gaps in the mourner's knowledge is the fragmentation of modern life, particularly the split between home and work: In many cases of bereavement, significant parts of the deceased's life are typically unknown to the mourner (Klass & Walter, 2001). Another explanation may be the veil of silence drawn over the period between the onset of a parent's fatal illness and its final outcome, especially when children are involved. Davidman (2000), for example, has claimed that her respondents' ability to reconstruct narratives about their lost mothers was hampered by the silence surrounding this event. Yet a third explanation is that some parts of the parent's life story may be chosen to be left unknown because they contradict or in some way threaten the self-development of the child.

Within this dynamic of knowing or not knowing the parent's story, it is important to stress that even known facts may be reinterpreted and reunderstood during different stages of the survivor's life. Thus, the recounting of the parent's life story, without the actual presence of the parent to negotiate these understandings, can serve as a lens through which to view the ongoing relationship with the parent's image. The parent's life story can also be examined in relation to the mourner's self-narrative (Neimeyer, 2004).

Neimeyer (2005) claimed that in narrative terms, significant losses challenge the self-narratives of survivors, in terms of both their personal sense of autobiographical continuity and the social construction of their postloss identity. He further argued that the central role of meaning reconstruction by the survivor in response to the loss (Neimeyer, 2001) shows increases in narrative complexity. For example, he demonstrated that after their loss, widowed persons were left with a self-narrative that was more complex and more sophisticated but not necessarily more unambivalently positive than the self-narrative that preceded the loss (Neimeyer, 2005).

I think that some of the postloss challenges to the self-narrative that Neimeyer mentioned are related to the way survivors may understand and recount the life of the person who died. The comparison to their own self-narrative may inevitably reveal similarities as well as differences and thus, in time, contribute to its complexity. Therefore, I would like to find out to what extent the parent's story evolves or is regarded as static over time. How will participants engage in a revision of the story as they grow older and encounter changing life circumstances? To what extent does the child's story merge with or diverge from that of the parent? Finally, in what ways does this reconstruction of the story shed light on the modalities (separateness or oneness) in which the lost object is experienced?

PARTICIPANTS, METHOD, AND CHAPTER OVERVIEW

Eight individuals, from a nonclinical population, in their early to late 20s, who lost a parent when they were children (ages 9–15), were interviewed in the narrative-research tradition.[3] An ad posted in different areas of the university campus invited people to volunteer to participate in the study. The people who answered the ad were asked to answer a few general questions over the phone, concerning relevant facts regarding their gender, current age, the age when the parent died, cause of death, and number of siblings. On the basis of their answers to these questions, I put together a group that reflected some of the variance that exists in the larger society of bereaved children. I interviewed the participants either at the university or at their home for, on average, an hour and a half.

In all interviews, the general question of how relationships with a lost parent evolve over the years was introduced, followed by a set of more specific questions. Then I introduced the topic:

> I'm interested in learning more about how and when you envision your father/mother. When do you think about him/her today or over the years? How do you imagine him/her? I'm also interested in finding out how you think about who he/she was, what you understand about his/her life story, and how these images or memories may have influenced you. So I'd really like you to begin with any of these questions and tell me how you think about your father/mother as part of your own life story.

During the interviews I tried to be very flexible and allow the conversation to flow. In addition, I introduced more specific questions during the course of the interview only when they seemed they would elaborate the story that was told.

All interviews were conducted in Hebrew, recorded, and then transcribed by a professional transcriber. The materials were then analyzed in a concept-directed content analysis in light of the concepts mentioned earlier. I conducted multiple readings, during which I assessed how the relationships were described, what the nature of the parent–child bond was, and whether

---

[3]These persons were interviewed for an MA thesis submitted to the Hebrew University in Jerusalem, Israel. Names of study participants were changed to protect confidentiality.

it had changed over the years. Another focus in my readings was the nature of the parent's representation as it was depicted in his or her life story and how it reflected on the child's self-narrative. While doing the analyses I also tried to find clues for the way these individuals re-membered their parents and in what modes of experience the parental object was experienced over the years.

My approach to the readings was mainly a holistic-content one (Lieblich, Tuval-Mashiach, & Zilber, 1998), in which each story was taken as a whole, and sections of the text were integrated in the context of other parts of the narrative. This analysis approach seemed appropriate as I sought the special meaning each bereaved young adult gave to the connection with the late parent (Neimeyer, 2001). However, I also used a categorical-content approach (Lieblich et al., 1998) in which the original story was dissected and sections belonging to a defined category were collected from the several texts belonging to a number of narrators. This approach helped me bring out the general themes underlying the phenomenon of continuing bonds with a lost parent and give a fuller description of the concept of re-membering and the two modes of experience as it appeared across narratives.

To ensure trustworthiness (Merrick, 1999) and further enhance the analyses, I organized a discussion of findings and processes with a narrative research study group who also read and commented on the interviews.

As mentioned earlier, in this chapter I focus on the narratives of four interviewees. First I describe Danny's narrative, in which a persistent feeling of "missing out" in his relationship with his late father set forth a dynamic of knowing and not knowing his father's life story. Through Danny's story I aim to show how, in the process of recounting a parent's life story, parallels can be drawn with the self-narrative, which may become a central part in the ongoing relationship. Sharon's story further exemplifies this idea. Her ongoing relationship with her late mother revolves around three ways in which she re-membered her. I argue that these three different forms of re-membering are connected with the gradual formation of Sharon's identity. Both Danny and Sharon's narrations led me to the conclusion that a mourner may use his or her parent's story to satisfy a current psychological need. Through the comparison to Maya's story, I strengthen this point. Although she displayed a completely different and static form of an ongoing relationship with her late mother, what Maya re-membered still reflected what she needed from her mother even years after her death. Sharon's and Maya's stories also form the base for a discussion about the concept of re-membering in light of the two modes of experience. Finally, I present the analysis of Niebal's interview, which shows that a certain form of re-membering does not always fit one's current stage in life. Thus, a mourner may choose not to re-member. This analysis takes me back to discuss the general idea of ongoing relationships and the continuing versus relinquishing bonds debate and some of the questions it may raise.

DANNY: THE DECEASED FATHER'S LIFE STORY
AND THE THEME OF MISSING OUT

Danny was a 25-year-old student who lived with his mother and younger brother. He lost his father when he was 14, after long months in which his father struggled with cancer. Danny said that following his father's death he was "lost for a long period of high school." His relationship with his brother deteriorated and he felt depressed. During the end of high school and the beginning of his army service a turning point came in his life, in which "this issue [of the father's death] didn't occupy me any more." From then on he started to make "a sort of new acquaintance" with his father and gradually realized the complexity of his father's life and character.

The theme that accompanies Danny's story is the theme of missed opportunities. "Missing" runs like a fine thread through the story beginning with his father's premature death, which left Danny with a memory of an old father "from another generation . . . more like a grandfather than a father," a father with whom he found it hard to communicate when he was alive. He "missed out" on the opportunity to enjoy things his father could have shared with him in adulthood, such as literature, history, and politics, which Danny started to appreciate only when he grew older. The missing out is also revealed in the life story of the father himself and exists as a threat to Danny's life story: At the time of the interview he was dissatisfied with what he was studying and with the direction he had sought out in his life.

Danny recounted his father's life story in a way that showed how the life story of a deceased parent can, on the one hand, be intriguing and draw the child to investigate and burrow into it, but on the other hand, present a kind of threat: "Because at first I wanted to know as much as possible, but then I arrived at the conclusion that it could also only harm the way I remember him." This statement, which recurred throughout the interview, made me wonder why knowledge of Danny's father had turned into a threat that could have dire consequences. Further analysis revealed that the threat was not only against the positive memory of the father but also at the same time against Danny's self-development. From his story it is apparent that the parent's story may have adverse effects when it is treated, consciously or unconsciously, as a prophecy, not necessarily positive, regarding the offspring's fate.

Danny described how he went about investigating his father's history: "And because I am by nature a curious person, I went straight ahead to investigate his entire life, its unfolding, and I discovered all sorts of amazing things." He interviewed family members, posed questions to his aunt, and read the letters his father had left behind. He recounted that his father was born in Italy and raised in Tunis; he immigrated to Israel to fight as a volunteer in the 1948 War of Independence and then returned to Europe to pursue higher studies. Living and studying around the world probably created a very educated person, "an erudite . . . who knew seven or eight languages," who translated and edited books for several publishing houses for a living. Yet, in spite of his father's erudition, Danny described a person who could not use his many talents and could not support his family honorably. This is the theme of missing out, interwoven in the father's life story.

In contrast to his desire to learn about his father's studies and education and listen to heroic stories from the war, Danny often refrained from probing further into the father's past, because knowledge might become harmful. Thus, when he got to a description of something that was missed out on or had not been completed in his father's life, he stopped: "and he did not complete his doctorate, and all kinds of things, that is to say, there is a hole as far as I am concerned, I don't know everything, I also don't know how much more I would like to know, in addition to what I know." Again and again, throughout the interview, Danny resumed the story, and then stopped when an issue such as this came up. To the story Danny constructed through the years about his father, unflattering, frustrating details were added, and Danny faced them as if facing an eternal truth. Thus, a tension could be felt between his quest to deepen and reinterpret the story and between his acknowledgment that certain unpalatable facts will never change.

The Father's Story and the Self-Narrative

Danny's ambivalent attitude toward knowledge of his father's life was paralleled by his ambivalent attitude to what he would like to take, reconstruct, or see as part of his own life: "And I also felt like being a little like him, study languages, experience his life in some way, consciously or unconsciously, because he was a humanist by nature so I learned these fields." This statement presents the part of him that wants to be similar to the father and follow in his footsteps. But when continuing that sentence he said, "But I am not particularly satisfied." When the story was directly connected with his own life story, Danny feared that he would relive the narrative of missing out. If he repeated the "same follies" that his father committed, he would also be leading his own narrative to a similar ending: "I feel, I don't really think that I can be really like him. I also try to avoid the follies, the mistakes and the stupidities he was guilty of in life, unsuccessfully so far."

The interesting thing here is the mechanism, which is half-consciously selective. Danny knew that from a certain point onward he did not want to obtain further knowledge of his father's life, because he might have found the story to bear unfavorable similarities to his own story. Therefore, at these points in time, he activated the selection mechanism and chose not to ask further questions, chose not to know. In other words, he actively re-membered only certain aspects from his father's story into his own self-narrative.

For example, he chose to connect his academic choices and ambitions with his father's humanistic inclinations. Yet he was constantly afraid of any sign of uncertainty or hesitancy in himself: "Now that I am at an age of a grown up person, (I hope . . .), I see similar patterns [to my father's], and it sometimes scares me, sort of complicated, hesitant, indecisive [patterns]." These similarities apparently scared Danny and thus he added, "Of course, on the whole, we are two different characters, and we were also brought up in different times and in a different atmosphere and different history." I think that with this differentiation, Danny was making an astute sociological and historical observation, but nevertheless this observation might have been conveying part of his will to shape his life independently of his father.

He later added, "His entire life story is something that is truly fascinating, and it could have been a great pride to be with a person that no longer exists today, and I assume that on many occasions I would see things the same way he would have seen them, if I only had that chance." Danny emphasized that part of what made his story different from his father's was the different times in which they grew up. This may point again to being a child of an older father, but also to the missed opportunity of bringing their stories closer, as he grew older.

In summary, the theme of missing out that underlay Danny's father's life story might have given rise to a dynamic between knowing and not knowing his father's story. Knowing his father's life story might have served Danny's curiosity about his father's character and his need to re-member or re-connect with him. Not knowing or not wanting to know might have appeared when parts of the father's story posed a threat to the development of his self. Danny might have consciously as well as unconsciously used a selective mechanism to discriminate between parts of his father's story that he would have or wouldn't have liked to be exposed to. The very similarities between their stories both inspired and frightened him. They served as a role model but also as a warning not to repeat the mistakes his father had made in his life.

The main point here is that recounting the parent's life story may be a central part of the way an ongoing relationship with a lost parent can be conducted. The possibility of gaining new information and the ability to reinterpret and to be in a dialogue with that story are ways to be in a dialogue with the lost parent. As I showed, this dialogue may sometimes be complicated as the stories show similarities as well as differences compared with the mourner's self-narrative. Nevertheless, the possibility of reconstructing the parent's narrative as one ages may enable one to feel the relationship as dynamic, which some of the interviewees said they were very much striving for. If one believes that one's self-narrative is reauthored as one ages and that through this reauthoring one can experience self-growth and change (White, 1997), one may need to be attuned to the life stories that shaped that self-narrative.

The next two stories, Sharon's and Maya's, further exemplify this idea. The interpretations of the life stories of their deceased mothers had an important impact on the way these women experienced an ongoing relationship with them as well as on their self-narrative. I would also like to stress how the different relationship patterns that emerged from the analyses show that the nature of the continuing bond with a lost parent might be a function of a developmental need. Both girls kept alive a complex representation of their mothers but drew on only those aspects that they needed at their current psychological stage.

SHARON'S STORY: THREE FORMS OF RE-MEMBERING

Sharon is the second of four siblings. Her mother, an elementary school teacher, died in a car accident when Sharon was 13. Sharon, who was in the car along with her two older sisters and younger brother, said, "A strange fact about the way she died is that there was no visible harm to her body. There were no scratches, bruises or blood." She further said, "She died in her wholeness. . . . Her body, as part of her whole soul, went up to heaven in its wholeness, in a beautiful way, without suffering." The mother apparently died from internal injuries but all her children survived the crash. Sharon believed that God wants and takes "the best" and that the mother was "too good to be in this life."

The last two remarks, which are of a strongly religious nature, apparently reflect the religious atmosphere in the Jewish house she was brought up in. The birth of Sharon's brother, the mother's "first male child," for whom she "had been waiting for many years," had a very strong religious effect on Sharon's mother. As part of that transformation, Sharon's mother started to cover her hair and decided, for the first time, to spend the holidays at home observing all the religious customs. However, during the years that have passed since their mother's death, all the children have turned away from religion, and only the father has remained an observant Jew. At the age of 25, Sharon was studying communication and sociology at the university and living with her boyfriend, her father, and her younger brother.

From reading Sharon's interview it was very much apparent that there was a lively ongoing relationship or dialogue with her lost mother, even though 12 years had passed. When I tried to capture the underlying dynamics of this ongoing relationship, two main categories were formed: being like the mother and turning against the mother. Each of these categories is represented by a "plot" in Sharon's narrative: "being like" is expressed by the story of the upbringing of Sharon's younger brother; "turning against" is manifest through the story of turning away from religion. These contradictory features of the relationship seemed to coincide with contradictory characteristics of the mother's inner representation and life story.

> She was a very very unique combination. All in all, she was a simple moshav[4] girl, but no, she really broke through all the normative bound-

---

[4]An Israeli cooperative settlement consisting of small separate farms.

aries of a family of Yemenite origin; a daughter should be at home and raise children; as for education?—high school at most. She very much broke this, went to the university, started on a teaching career, traveled the world . . . and on the other hand she was very classy, very refined . . . although [what she had done] was very rebellious. . . . My grandfather, this is how my grandmother tells it, did not get angry with her because she did it in such a diplomatic way.

So, in Sharon's mind, the mother was an individualist and did things her own way, but still conformed to her family, displaying a softer, diplomatic side. She managed to break away from what her family might have destined for her but still stay part of the broader family and feel connected to it. The mother thus resembled "a very very unique combination" of a conformist and an individualist. Sharon explained,

So this is something that we [the sisters] tried to internalize. That is, to incorporate that thing of pushing forward, to move on for your own right . . . because she really pushed us toward education and academic achievements and all that, but, like, to do all you want, and stand up for yourself but still keep that diplomacy.

In this quote, I think Sharon was saying that she was constantly moving between two poles: At one pole, which coincides with the mother's characteristic of being a conformist, she wanted to be "like" her and follow in her footsteps to make an academic career. Even if in the context of Sharon's mother's family this development might have been considered rebellious, Sharon actually conformed to the norm her mother laid down. But at the other pole, to be like the mother is also to rebel, to be an individualist and to act differently. For Sharon, rebelling meant turning against the norms and against the mother herself. I suspect that turning away from religion might reflect this side in her. In contrast, the story of the upbringing of her younger brother might fit the first, conformist side.

Sharon said,

And we three girls—we simply took the motherly role in the house and brought up my little brother . . . and my brother is the crowning glory [*laughs*]; he is the jewel in the crown of this family and part of the reason for this is that my mother really loved him.

The girls "strictly kept the house exactly as [their] mother liked it, in the way we cleaned and in the way we behaved." The brother was the reason to keep things static, routine: "he wouldn't allow anything different. . . . He would not do without the traditional Yemenite food for even one Saturday." Sharon repeatedly used the word *protect* when she referred to her brother and said the girls "wrapped cotton wool around him." Presumably, through the upbringing of the brother, the daughters kept alive that part of their mother that was protective and caring, thus actively re-membering the soft and motherly role. By re-membering her mother's motherly role, Sharon conformed to the conformist side of her mother.

In contrast, the story of turning away from religion stands out in its individualistic and rebellious nature. The "religious revolution" that happened in the family after the mother's death was very much connected with her death. It is hard to tell whether the way the mother died eventually made her children stop believing, or whether the mother's absence took the vitality out of religious observance. However, by turning away from religion, even if considered as a form of re-membering the mother's individualistic side, Sharon may have felt inwardly torn.

Therefore, there seems to be an inner conflict between the two sides of her mother's inner representation, as displayed in Sharon's self-narrative. It was thus interesting to discover a third way in which Sharon re-membered her mother, specifically when struggling with identity issues and loneliness. This third way was her mother's encouragement of her artistic side when she was a child and the way Sharon developed it at certain times in life after her mother had passed on.

Sharon's favorite childhood memories of her mother were presented as follows:

> She [the mother] was a teacher of fifth and sixth graders. And when I was about that age, she used to take me to all sorts of evenings in which an organ player was needed . . . or when she started to decorate the class before the beginning of the school year, so I have an artistic touch, so she always promoted this and loved this.

Along with the music and decorations, another memory Sharon presented was that of joint visits to the market and of cooking together. She remembered all the colors and the smells from these special days.

Part of the reason these memories of shared creativity had become cherished is because they represented something different and unique. First, in them Sharon is differentiated from her sisters for having a certain quality that her mother had recognized and encouraged. Second, all these memories are very sensory by nature. However, what is most interesting is the way Sharon turned to these memories and re-membered this special, "good" part of the mother–daughter bond at certain times in her life.

She said that at the time that her family was torn apart after her father remarried, she actively developed her creative talents. At other hard moments of loneliness and longing she experienced during high school, she developed her musical skills. It seems that during these times, the membership status of the mother, or more specifically, the part of their creative bond, was upgraded. It was given a special privileged place, in contrast with what was happening with Sharon's other club-of-life members (White, 1997). After his second marriage, her father drifted away to form a new relationship, physically and emotionally. In contrast to what seemed as a decrease in her father's membership status, Sharon re-membered her unique and cherished bond with her mother. In a similar way, during her high school years Sharon felt lonely and jealous of the other girls. Again, she actively re-membered her mother's encouragement of her creative side and developed it: "[These creative] things that were at the beginning [at the time she was alive], I really really fostered them."

In summary, Sharon stressed the contradicting features of her relationship with her mother before as well as after her death. The three aspects of their ongoing relationship—of being like (conforming), turning against (individualizing), and creativity—all point to her own identity formation process. It is quite apparent in her story how much she needed her mother's help in her quest for her preferred identity, her prime psychological need at the time the interview took place. The mother's image and story were being revisited so she could better understand who she was and what she wanted in life.

The tension between two contradicting sides in the parent's story was also depicted by Danny. However, although Danny chose not to know one side of his father's life story, Sharon tried to develop a third side that she remembered from the mother–daughter bond. This third, "preferred" or "good" part of the mother–daughter bond exemplifies how "re-membering practices" may lessen the sense of isolation and give strength and courage to mourners at difficult times (White, 1997). It may also exemplify what Hedtke and Winslade (2004) tried to foster when engaging in "re-membering conversations" with bereaved families.

In contrast to Sharon, Maya retold her relationship with her mother in a way that solely centered on her self-image of a cherished and loving daughter. In the way she actively re-membered the protection and care of her mother at different moments in her life, she actually kept their relationship pattern completely static.

MAYA'S STORY: "A CHILD OF DIAMONDS"

Whereas Sharon lost her mother at the age of 13, Maya lost her mother at the younger age of 9. Her mother died of cancer after 3 years of illness. In contrast to the lively and dynamic nature of the life story of Sharon's mother, as recounted by her daughter, Maya offered a minimalist story of a brief biography that stated major facts and life events. Maya's mother's life story revolved around her wish to bring children into the world. Maya told her story as if the mother's life preceding that pregnancy had been empty, and giving birth to Maya was what improved it. The most detailed part of Maya's narration centered on the theme "a child of diamonds," a term that Maya's mother coined. When interviewed for a radio talk show during her pregnancy she said she would call the child to be born "a child of diamonds" (Maya was one of the first test-tube babies in Israel). And so, accordingly, they changed the name of the radio program to this name. I found this "child of diamonds" theme to be the most significant one in Maya's story.

At the time of the interview, Maya had recently gotten married and was working in a day-care center with children who were taken out of their homes. She said,

> Every person that takes a meaningful place in my life, I immediately tell him about what happened to me with my mother and about my mother, because it's like, I feel it is *a part of me* [italics added]. And as long as he doesn't know it, he, in a sense does not know me.

I think that in this statement Maya emphasized the ongoing presence of the mother as a crucial part of her feeling complete, secure, and whole. Her conception story captured Maya's feeling of being her mother's diamond. The feeling was that the mother waited so long for her arrival that when she was born, it was an amazing thing. In this story, Maya narrated her feeling of being loved and cherished but also of "her side" of the relationship, in which she enabled the mother to bestow these feelings on her.

In a similar way, Maya described her relationship with her mother, before and after her death, as an exclusive one. By *exclusive* I mean that besides being unique and special to her mother, she was also the first and foremost guardian of her mother's memory. The exclusiveness of the mother's memories appeared very clearly when she talked about her younger brother, who turned to her for the memories of their mother. Referring to her father she said, "I always *am* his memory [of her]," which means that she was the main representative of her dead mother in his life, too. She mentioned that many people said that they look alike; she also resembled her mother in her laugh, her smile, and her joy of life. In those shared characteristics, the distinction between the mother and herself had been eliminated.

Maya gave an example of this resemblance in a story about a job interview she had, in which she competed with other candidates: "When I asked the interviewer why she had picked me and not the other women, she said that I had been smiling all the time; during the entire interview I was smiling and laughing . . . and so I always connect it with my mother." In her understanding, the joyful qualities she shared with her mother enabled her to win the job and generally succeed in life.

Maya's story also offers an extraordinary example of a reinterpretation of a parent's life story. When she was 16, Maya had a big fight with her stepmother, "S," after which she consulted a rabbi. The rabbi told her that every man has a partner who is fated to be his mate. He told her that her father's fated partner was in fact S. The problem was that S was infertile, and because of that, Maya's mother's purpose in life had been to give children to her father and leave at some point, because she was not his match. Maya adopted this story, which gave a new meaning to her mother's life purpose, again emphasizing her own uniqueness to her mother. This story also gave her the legitimization to find new ways of relating to S, and maybe even to forgive her father for marrying again.

I think that the most extreme expression of the mother–daughter fusion is the reversal of the basic feature of the mother–child relationship, the first giving birth to the second. In Maya's experience, the mother stayed alive for another 3 years because she wanted to be with her: "It seemed like a bear hug that will not leave us and will not let us be alone." Apparently the "bear hug" involved a mutual nurturing between mother and daughter and created an illusion of one unit, in which the mother and children give life to each other reciprocally. Therefore, their relationship was characterized mainly by mutuality: Maya gave her mother a reason to live whereas her mother's mission in life had been to give life to Maya. According to Maya's stories, this pattern was continuing in their relationship: Maya referred to her mother as a live person, kept alive through her own existence and through the similarities between them.

SHARON AND MAYA: A COMPARISON

A comparison of these two very different stories demonstrates that an ongoing relationship can be experienced as dynamic and ever changing (as in the case of Sharon) or as static, frozen in time (as in the case of Maya). However, a dynamic relationship pattern does not mean that the felt presence or significance of the parent is necessarily greater in the mourner's life. Rather, the pattern of the relationship represents the dynamic or static quality of the inner representation of the parent and may indicate what the child needs from the parent at the current stage in life. For Maya, the most basic need for love and protection from her mother persisted throughout life, and thus their relationship pattern did not change from the way it was experienced in childhood. In contrast, for Sharon, it seems that her goal in their ongoing relationship was to first understand the mother separately from herself and then reincorporate this knowledge into her understanding of her self. This goal entailed a dynamic and changing quality for their ongoing relationship. Nevertheless, for these two women as well as for other grieving children, this relationship remained central in their lives.

Another way to understand the differences between these relationship patterns is through the conceptualization of separateness and oneness of subject and object (Erlich, 2003). As I showed, Maya's most basic mode of experience of her ongoing relationship with her mother was that of oneness. In contrast, it can be claimed that Sharon's most basic mode of experience of her ongoing relationship with her mother was that of separateness. Whereas for Maya a fusion existed between herself and her mother's image and story, Sharon portrayed her mother as a separate and distinct being.

Re-membering: Separateness or Oneness?

Taken together, both concepts—separateness and oneness—illuminate the narratives of Sharon and Maya. It seems to me that for the whole process of re-membrance to occur, both modes of experience are needed. As an example, for Sharon, re-membering the creative aspects that her mother acknowledged and encouraged in her called for experiencing her mother as a separate "member" in her life. An object (the mother) identified and encouraged these aspects in the subject (herself). However, to feel these aspects as part of her life as an adult, she needed to experience oneness. These talents were no longer only external knowledge that came from the outside, but part of her own being. Sharon's evocation of childhood memories, and their incorporation into her present life, may thus have called for experiencing the mother–daughter relationship in both realms of separateness (retrieving the memory) and oneness (the sense that these parts of her mother are parts of her self). In the way Maya re-membered her mother's protection and care, even in her present life, she may have felt a fusion, an experience of oneness with the mother. However, the feeling of fusion still rested on childhood memories in which the mother was experienced as distinct from her and thus a constant unconscious shift to the separateness modality must have been happening as well.

In my analysis of the three stories presented thus far, I have shown various ways in which individuals narrate the story of their parents as well as the impact of these narrations on their own self-defining life stories. In all of these stories the children actively re-membered parts of the parent's image or of the child–parent bond and I suggested how this process functioned as part of their self development. For Niebal's story, I would like to show that a certain form of re-membering does not always fit one's current stage in life. This example may hint that sometimes, for the sake of the preferred development of the self, one may actually choose to not re-member or to distance oneself from the image of the deceased and thus relinquish part of the bond.

NIEBAL'S STORY

Niebal's story may serve as a negative instance for the thesis that the very continuation of the bond facilitates adjustment (Klass & Walter, 2001). She chose to relinquish the tie with her late father and move on in her life. In terms of her self-narrative, not keeping her father's image or memory close to her may have made it easier for her to seek her own way to growth and independence. In other words, a certain way in which she may have re-membered her father did not fit in with her development at that stage of her life.

Niebal came from a relatively large Islamic family residing in one of the mixed Arab-Jewish cities in the north of Israel. She was 21, the youngest of seven, with four older sisters and two older brothers. Her father died of a heart attack when she was 9. During our interview, she repeatedly said that she "does not remember too much." I got the feeling that somehow she was afraid she fell short of my expectations by failing to give a full account of who her father was and how she kept his memory alive. "I've never felt that there is something that is really, really missing. . . . In almost everything I have chosen to disengage and move on" were her words when describing the years after his death. She attributed this feeling to the fact either that she "was too young [when he died]" or that she had gotten "used to it."

Niebal's story seems to exemplify the pattern of successful grieving as it is presented in traditional grief literature. That is, her father had been metabolized in some way in her and did not resemble a living presence for her. Similar to Maya's experience, her memories of him were of being a prized child who was the youngest, in need of care, protection, and pampering. However, this self-image of being protected and cared for, given her developmental stage at the time of the interview, was one that she might have been trying to transcend. Furthermore, her father may still have been a strong presence in her family, and to some extent, some of his parental style—being conservative and strict—jeopardized her wishes for leaving the traditional way of life.

One of the most striking facts about Niebal's story was that throughout the interview she constructed her father's image as well as her relationship with him through the stories and reminiscences of others in her family. She repeatedly questioned her own knowledge about her father, and in various ways she said that she did not know or remember: "Mother always tells me how he was helping me with homework and things, but I don't remember anything—really anything."

This failure to remember gave rise to a feeling of guilt. She apologized to me, the interviewer, for not being able to present a fuller account of her memories, and of who her father was. Likewise, she had mislaid two significant mementos, symbolic presences of her father. One was a videotape from her sister's wedding (the last time he was captured on video) and the second, a key chain with a small photo of her father: "All of us have a key chain with a photo of my father and I can't find where it is; I need to look for it." I think that these last two examples exemplify the underlying theme in Niebal's story about her father: "distancing the memory."

When I reflected on the range of feeling that I had experienced when listening to and reading Niebal's interview, I found that I, too, had been feeling a tension between bringing my father's memory closer to my current life and distancing it. I lost my father when I was 13 and throughout the years that have passed I tried to re-member him into my life in various ways, but at other times, I found that I was better off when distancing his memory. So I tried to understand why at the current stage in her life it was better for Niebal not to experience her father as a dominant member in her club of life. I answered this question by examining her own self-narrative in comparison with the father's image in her family and his relationship with her when she was a child.

Niebal was the youngest daughter in her family, born when her father was relatively old. Her most cherished and memorable events of her father were accompanying him on house calls he made to people's homes, fixing washing machines and other devices at their houses. In contrast to portraying the father's memory as constructed by others, discussed earlier, the "house visits" memories were told in a very personal and emotional way: "The guests there always loved me and gave me all kinds of chocolates . . . [and] he always bragged 'I have a small daughter' and I really enjoyed every minute. . . . This is my clearest memory." Niebal's clearest memory, so different from other blurred memories of her father, was of being together with him, loved and admired for being his youngest.

However, she said that she was still treated as the youngest and the fragile one at home: "and even today, when I am 21 and a half, they still treat me as 'the youngest,' the one to be looked after, and to be sent food to and all sorts of things like that." This situation may conflict with the way she wishes to see herself today. Niebal had chosen to move away from her hometown and family and make the courageous effort to study in Jerusalem: "I deliberately chose to come and study in Jerusalem only for this reason, like, not to be dependent upon my family."

Niebal's father's presence in her life, not only in the physical sense, but also in a re-membered sense, may have made it more difficult for her to develop in the direction she chose: "and I don't think that if my father were with us, I don't think he would allow me to come to Jerusalem." Thus, this certain way of re-membering her father and her childhood interactions with him may have put her back in the position of being her father's youngest, with its implication of her self-image being small and fragile.

Apart from the pattern of the relationship with her father as his youngest, the father's parental style, as being strict and conservative on family matters or women's place in society, may also have been in conflict with Niebal's developing self:

> I don't really remember this, but I know from my sisters that my father was strict. Not too strict. He was conservative, so yes, I don't think he would have allowed me to come [to Jerusalem]. And my sister always reminds me and says that if my father were still with us he wouldn't approve.

It seems that knowing or remembering her father as a conservative and strict person may have again endangered her striving for growth and independence. Leaving his character to an outsider's knowledge, that of her mother or her sister, may have eased the sensed conflict between her father's wishes and her chosen way of life.

A good example of this conflict between what her father would have wanted for her and what she herself wanted is her story about wanting to get a tattoo:

I first consulted my mother, and she, of course, categorically refused. . . . According to our tradition this is really not done; so she [the mother] used the argument of "customs" and said that according to our [Islamic] religion it is forbidden, and in the Koraa'n it is written that it's forbidden. . . . [*sigh*] Then the issue of my father was brought up, and she [the mother] also told me, that my father wouldn't even have considered . . . saying "yes," and also my sister said [the same], but I think I intentionally chose not to listen because in this way it is easier.

Eventually, Niebal did choose not to listen, and got the tattoo.

Thus, this certain way of re-membering her father may have called on parts of Niebal's self that were connected with being small, fragile, and his youngest. Second, her image of her father as a strict or conservative person included his disapproval of her moves away from home or of her modern lifestyle in Jerusalem. Thus, for Niebal, keeping a lively ongoing relationship with her father in this particular way may have led to a felt conflict between the preferred independent development of her self and the feeling of an "over-sensitive" and fragile little daughter. By distancing herself from her memory of the father or even by choosing to ignore what her father might have wanted to tell her, she apparently succeeded in fulfilling her dream of studying in the university and seeking her own preferred identity.

NIEBAL, MAYA, SHARON, DANNY, AND OTHERS

Niebal's choice not to re-member may call to mind Danny, who chose not to know certain aspects of his father's story. I'd like to suggest that they both described this happening because of a sensed conflict that had arisen with the development of their self. Sharon was similarly trying to foster a conflict-free part of her relationship with her mother to cope with contradicting features in her mother's image. Maya reinterpreted her mother's life story in a way that would fit the dominant way she wanted to go on re-membering her. I think all these stories show that the way people re-member their lost loved ones may change over time according to their changing psychological needs. Sometimes their need is actually not to re-member or to partly relinquish the bond. Therefore I think that the continuing-bonds phenomenon, at least in children, may be a function of a developmental need. Through recounting the deceased's life story, survivors may keep alive complex representations of the deceased. From these representations they may choose what to draw on or not draw on at different stages in their lives. This is how I also understand the dialectic between "letting go" and "continuing bonds" in the interviewees' subjective experience.

Therefore, I would like to suggest that when listening to stories of bereaved individuals, one may need to be attuned not only to what a mourner may wish to re-member but also to what aspects he or she chooses not to remember, and why. I think that the four stories in this chapter show that this process may be understood only within the context of the ongoing relationship and in light of the current psychological need of the survivor.

Recent decades have witnessed a revolution in bereavement theory, calling into question time-honored formulations of grief predicated on presumably universal symptoms or stages (Neimeyer, 2005). Joining leading grief theorists who are now emphasizing that there is no one universal way to grieve, I'd like to add that there is no one way to re-member. Indeed, there may be a certain dominant way in which a deceased might be re-membered, and this dominant way may or may not fit a certain stage in the mourner's life. However, I believe that these four narratives demonstrate that life is indeed multistoried (White, 1997) and that there always exists a new way to re-member.

CONCLUDING REMARKS

"Ongoing relationships," as a framework of listening and thinking about mourners, even years after their actual loss, is quite different from the still dominant Western view of "saying goodbye" as it is portrayed in popular psychology textbooks and social conventions (Stroebe et al., 1992). Taking the perspective of ongoing relationships helped me describe how these individuals felt their parents' presence at different periods or events in their life and their manifold reactions to what they imagined their parents' attitude might have been.

Stroebe and Schut (2005), reviewing the continuing–breaking bonds controversy, concluded that it was not possible to determine whether the continuation or the relinquishment of the bond was generally helpful. I did not try to determine which furthered adjustment more, but I do argue that grieving individuals in general always strive for a right balance between the two. I also hold the view that even if a continued sense of the deceased implies some sort of inner denial of his or her absence, this grief reaction need not be regarded as pathological. The club-of-life metaphor and the notion that lost others can be re-membered into the life of the mourner can enrich the mourner's self-narrative and enhance his or her self-perception. When listening to survivors, therapists have to be very sensitive to the various ways in which a lost other is re-membered and ask ourselves whether these ways fit the survivor's development at the current stage of his or her life.

If one chooses to regard relationships with deceased members as possessing the qualities of a real relationship, one has to be aware of the manifold forms that this relationship may take. A relationship with the deceased can be invigorating and meaningful, but at the same time frustrating and confusing. Both possibilities were shown within the analyses of the ongoing relationships in this chapter. Because the lost member was a parent, it was not always simple to define where the inner representation of the parent ended and the self-perception of the child began. Thus, within this certain subgroup, the implication of continued relationships as presenting an inner dialogue between different aspects of the child's self was highly important. I referred to this duality as experiences of separateness from and oneness with the parental object.

The ongoing relationship was intimately linked to the mourner's self-narrative (Neimeyer, 2004) and the current stage of the development of his or her self. It also seemed that these postloss self-narratives showed high complexity and displayed multiple representations of self and other. It would have been interesting to investigate whether the task of meaning reconstruction in response to the loss actually contributed to this narrative complexity (Neimeyer, 2005). In addition, the different relationship patterns that my analysis identified clearly had links to the attachment histories of these individuals (Bowlby, 1980). A great deal of work has been done in recent years linking attachment theory and continuing bonds following bereavement (e.g., Stroebe & Schut, 2005). It would be interesting to find out whether these individuals' attachment histories shed light on the way they recounted their parents' life stories and on what they chose to re-member from their stories.

As I came closer to these people's losses, I also gained a better understanding of my own personal grief. Through a process of finding new reference points and identification, I came to acknowledge my own ongoing relationship with my late father and to deconstruct previous assumptions about my own story. I found this experience to be both educational and healing. Looking at the harsh reality of daily life, which unfortunately is fraught with death and loss, I hope that learning about the different ways in which people conduct an ongoing relationship with a lost loved one can serve others. My work may help broaden the academic discussion about ongoing relationships and also serve as a guideline, especially for therapists, in their journey to help their clients find new ways to re-member their lost loved ones and strike the right balance between continuing the bond and letting it go.

REFERENCES

Attig, T. (1996). *How we grieve*. New York: Oxford University Press.

Bowlby, J. (1980). *Attachment and loss: Loss, sadness, and depression* (Vol. 3). New York: Basic Books.

Davidman, L. (2000). *Motherloss*. Berkeley, CA: University of Berkeley Press.

Dietrich, D. R., & Shabad, P. C. (1989). *The problem of loss and mourning*. Madison, CT: International Universities Press.

Erlich, S. (2003). Experience—What is it? *International Journal of Psychoanalysis, 84,* 1125–1147.

Field, N. P., Gal-Oz, E., & Bonanno, G. (2003). Continuing bonds and adjustment at 5 years after the death of a spouse. *Journal of Consulting and Clinical Psychology, 71*, 110–117.

Freud, S. (1993). Mourning and melancholia. In G. H. Pollock (Ed.), *Pivotal papers on identification* (pp. 21–39). Madison, CT: International Universities Press. (Original work published 1917)

Hedtke, L., & Winslade, J. (2004). *Re-membering lives: Conversations with the dying and the bereaved.* Amityville, NY: Baywood Publishing.

Klass, D. (1996). Grief in Eastern cultures: Japanese ancestor worship. In D. Klass, P. Silverman, & S. Nickman (Eds.), *Continuing bonds: New understandings of grief* (pp. 59–70). Washington, DC: Taylor & Francis.

Klass, D., Silverman, P. R., & Nickman, S. L. (1996). *Continuing bonds: New understandings of grief.* Washington, DC: Taylor & Francis.

Klass, D., & Walter, T. (2001). Process of grieving: How bonds are continued. In M. Stroebe, R. O. Hansson, W. Stroebe, & H. Schut (Eds.), *Handbook of bereavement research: Consequences, coping, and care* (pp. 431–448). Washington, DC: American Psychological Association.

Lieblich, A. R., Tuval-Mashiach, R., & Zilber, T. (1998). *Narrative research: Reading, analysis and interpretation.* Thousand Oaks, CA: Sage.

Merrick, E. (1999). An exploration of quality in qualitative research: Are "reliability" and "validity" relevant? In M. Kopala & L. A. Suzuki (Eds.), *Using qualitative methods in psychology.* Thousand Oaks, CA: Sage.

Myerhoff, B. (1982). Life history among the elderly: Performance, visibility and re-membering. In J. Ruby (Ed.), *A crack in the mirror: Reflexive perspectives in anthropology* (pp. 99–117). Philadelphia: University of Pennsylvania Press.

Neimeyer, R. A. (2001). Reauthoring live narratives: Grief therapy as meaning reconstruction. *Israeli Journal of Psychiatry, 38*(3), 171–183.

Neimeyer, R. A. (2004). Fostering posttraumatic growth: A narrative contribution. *Psychological Inquiry, 15*, 53–59.

Neimeyer, R. A. (2005). Widowhood, grief and the quest for meaning: A narrative perspective on resilience. In D. Carr, R. M. Nesse, & C. B. Wortman (Eds.), *Late life widowhood in the United States* (pp. 228–254). New York: Springer Publishing Company.

Rando, T. A. (1993). *Treatment of complicated mourning.* Champaign, IL: Research Press.

Rosenblatt, P. C., & Elde, C. (1990). Shared reminiscence about a deceased parent: Implications for grief education and grief counseling. *Family Relations, 39*, 206–210.

Rubin, S. (1985). The resolution of bereavement: A clinical focus of the relationship of the deceased. *Psychotherapy, 22*, 231–235.

Schafer, R. (1968). *Aspects of internalization.* New York: International Universities Press.

Shuchter, S., & Zisook, S. (1993). The course of normal grief. In M. Stroebe, W. Stroebe, & R. O. Hansson (Eds.), *Handbook of bereavement: Theory, research, and intervention* (pp. 23–43). New York: Cambridge University Press.

Silverman, P., & Nickman, S. (1996). Children's construction of their dead parent. In D. Klass, P. Silverman, & S. Nickman (Eds.), *Continuing bonds: New understandings of grief* (pp. 73–86). Washington, DC: American Psychological Association.

Silverman, P., & Worden, W. (1993). Children's reaction to the death of a parent. In M. S. Stroebe, W. Stroebe, & R. O. Hansson (Eds.), *Handbook of bereavement: Theory, research, and intervention* (pp. 300–316). New York: Cambridge University Press.

Stroebe, M., Gergen, M. M., Gergen, K. J., & Stroebe, W. (1992). Broken hearts or broken bonds: Love and death in historical perspective. *American Psychologist, 47,* 1205–1212.

Stroebe, M., & Schut, H. A. W. (2005). To continue or relinquish bonds: A review of consequences for the bereaved. *Death Studies, 29,* 477–494.

Volkan, V. (1981). *Linking objects and linking phenomena.* Madison, CT: International Universities Press.

Walter, T. (1996). A new model of grief: Bereavement and biography. *Mortality, 1,* 7–25.

Walter, T. (1999). *On bereavement: The culture of grief.* Buckingham, England: Open University Press.

White, M. (1997). *Narratives of therapists' lives.* Adelaide, South Australia: Dulwich Centre Publications.

Worden, W. J. (1991). *Grief counseling and grief therapy: A handbook for the mental health practitioner.* New York: Springer Publishing Company.

AUTHOR INDEX

Numbers in italics refer to listings in the references.

Noble, S., *234*
Noller, P., 239, *252*
Nudelman, A., *187*
Nussbaum, M., 39, 47, *49*

O'Leary, V., 191, *210*
Olsen, C. S., 78n, *90*
Orlinsky, D. E., 230, *235*
Orlofsky, J. L., 118, *140*

Pan, H., *115*
Pantin, H., 166, *186*
Parkes, C. M., *116*
Pasupathi, M., 216, 232, *235*
Patten, A. H., 214, *235*
Pearlin, L., 190, 191, *210*
Pellauer, D., *162*
Pennebaker, J. W., 192, *210*
Peperzak, A. T., *19*
Person, E. S., 39, 41, 42, 43, 46, *49*
Pittman, J. F., 118, *140*
Podorefsky, D., 137, *141*
Pollock, G. H., *279*
Pott, M., 139, *141*
Pratt, M. W., 77, *90*

Quintana, S. M., 77n, *90*

Rabin, A. I., *48*
Raeff, C., 165, 167, *187*
Ragland-Sullivan, E., 54, 73, *74*
Ramsey, C., 215, *235*
Rando, T. A., 261, *279*
Raz, A., 238, 240, *252*
Reed, J. A., *89*
Reinhard, S. C., 207, *210*
Reis, H. T., *252*
Renninger, K. A., *140*
Reynolds, J., 214, *235*
Rholes, W., *115*
Richardson, L., 53, *74*
Rickels, K., 217, *234*
Ricoeur, P., 143, *162*
Roberts, B. W., 215, *234*
Robinson, F., 22, 22n, 23, 24, 25, 26, 27, 28, 29, 30, 31, 32, 33, 35, 36, 37, 39, 41, 43, 44n14, 45, 48, *49*
Rockquemore, K., 145, 153, *162*
Rogers, A., 53, 54, *74*
Rønnestad, M. H., 230, *235*
Root, M. P. P., 145, 147, *162*
Rosen, H., 168, 169, 183, *188*

Rosenblatt, P. D., 261, *279*
Rosenzweig, F., 12, *19*
Rothbart, J., 95, *116*
Rothbaum, F. 139, *141*
Rozen, Y., 168, *186*
Rubin, S., 257, *279*
Rubin, Z., *116*
Ruby, J., *279*
Runyan, W. M., 42, *49*
Rusbult, C. E., *252*
Ryan, R. M., 76, *91*
Ryff, C. D., 217, *236*

Safran, J. D., 230, *236*
Saraswathi, T. S., *141*
Schafer, R., 257, 258, 259, 260, *279*
Schepeler, E., 34, *49*
Schneider, B., 87, 88
Schneidman, E. S., 42, *49*
Schultz, D., 84, *91*, *142*
Schultz, L. H., 137, *141*
Schultz, S. E., 84, *91*
Schultz, W. T., 39, *49*, 230, *236*
Schut, H., 256, 257, 277, 278, 279, *280*
Schwartzenberg, N., 237, *252*
Scollon, C. K., 215, *235*
Sedikides, C., 88, *91*
Segura-Herrera, T. A., 77, *90*
Seidman, E. L., *253*
Seligman, M. E. P., 214, *236*
Selman, R. L., 119, 137, *141*, *142*
Semple, S., 190, *210*
Senor, S., 190, 209n, *211*
Shabad, P. C., 257, *278*
Shabtay, M., 167, 168, 169, 183, *188*
Shapiro, D., 112, *116*
Shapiro, E. R., 21n, 40, *49*
Sharabany, R., 247, *252*
Shaver, P., 95, *114*, *115*, *116*, 239, 251, *252*
Sheinberg, N., *74*
Sheridan, A., *74*
Shuchter, S., 255, *280*
Silverman, P., 255, 256, 257, 258, 279, *280*
Simpson, J., *115*, 238, *252*
Singelis, T. M., 76, *91*
Singer, J. A., 213, 215, *236*
Skaff, M., 190, *210*
Skinner, D., 144, *162*
Skoe, E. E., 89, 121, *141*
Smollar, J., 83, *91*
Solomon, J., 96, 97, 105, *115*, *116*
Soto, C. J., 94, *115*

SUBJECT INDEX

287

dismissing, 97, 108, 109, 111, 114
disorganized/fearful, 97
insecure, 96–97, 101, 105, 111
preoccupied, 97, 114
secure, 96, 97, 108–109, 111–113
working model as, 95, 96, 109 (*see also* Working models)
Attachment theory and literature, 95
and Ann's story, 101, 113–114
and bereavement bonds, 278
on complementarity of attachment and caregiver systems, 105
and relationship maintenance, 239
Authority, in holding study on Ethiopian Israeli adolescents, 183–184, 185
Autoethnography, 53
Autonomy
and adolescent immigrants, 165–166
vs. connection, 76
and relationships, 76
Autoscopy, 60
Avoidant attachment style, 97
in Ann's story, 101
Ayres, Lyoness, 206

Balance
in Ann' life, 111, 111–112, 113
in caregiver responsibilities (mutual support group participant), 199
between continuation and relinquishment of bond with lost loved one, 256, 277, 278
between identity choices and relationships, 144
Barahanu (Ethiopian Israeli study participant), 176
Behavior modeling, 84
Bereavement theory, 10
revolution in, 255, 277
See also Continuing bonds with lost parent
Beuret, Rose, 55–56, 56, 57, 63, 64, 70
Beverly (virtual support group participant), 194, 198, 200, 201–202, 203, 204, 208
Biracial identity, narratives of, 144, 159–161
of Jean, 146–147, 153–161
of Rachel, 146–153, 159–161
Biracial youth
and internal sense of non-White parent, 161
and racial identity, 144–145 (*see also* Racial identity)

Bohemianism, and Douglas's biography of Morgan, 24
Boucher, Alfred, 55
Brady, Ivan, 53, 73
Buber, Martin, 11–12
on "devotional objects," 16–17
on living as meeting, 47
on means as obstacles, 15
on narrative integrity, 16, 17
on three spheres of relation, 12–15
Bulimia, in therapy narrative, 219, 220

California Psychological Inventory (CPI), 94, 102
Camille With Short Hair (Rodin sculpture), 56
Caregivers' Support Group, 191–193
Caregiving, 189–190
conflicting responsibilities in (virtual support group participant), 197
and need to prioritize, 202
and "Crisis—Not a Vent" thread, 193–194
and multiple-read method, 195
and positioning theory, 195–206
and virtual caregiver support, 209
and message board group (Caregivers Support), 191–193
parents' system of, 96
as process, 207
as relational, 190–191, 206–207, 209
renegotiation of, 207–208
vocabulary of, 208
Carter, Rosalyn, quoted, 189
Claudel, Camille, 51–52, 54–55, 57
relationship of with Rodin, 56–57, 57–58, 63–64
and Liscomb, 64
in Rogers' poems, 64, 65–66, 71, 73
Claudel, Paul (brother), 57
Club-of-life metaphor, 259, 260, 269, 277
Cognitive strength, and secure attachment, 112
Coherence, in life story, 96
Communion, vs. agency, 3–4
Community, and American identity, 76
Concern, in Ethiopian Israeli adolescents study, 176
Conflict
and difficulties with romantic relationships, 249

escalation of, 242
Connection
    vs. autonomy, 76
    as functional unit (non-Western cultures), 167
    healing connection, 228–229
Connie (virtual support group participant), 194, 196–197, 199, 200–201, 203, 204, 205–207, 208, 209
Consciousness, shared, 45
Constant comparative qualitative procedure, in study of Japanese female adolescents, 119
Continuing bonds (with deceased), 10, 255–256
Continuing bonds with lost parent, 256–258
    and choice not to re-member, 276–277
    as dynamic vs. static, 272
    narratives of, 260–263
        Danny, 263, 264–267, 276
        Maya, 263, 270–273, 274, 276
        Niebal, 263, 273–276
        Sharon, 263, 267–270, 272–273, 276
    through re-membering, 258–259, 260, 270, 273 (see also Re-membering)
    through separateness vs. oneness, 260
        in narratives of Sharon and Maya, 272–273
Continuing Bonds: New Understandings of Grief (Klass, Silverman, and Nickman), 255
"Continuity of being," holding as factor in, 172
CPI (California Psychological Inventory), 94, 102
"Crisis—Not a Vent" (virtual support group thread), 191, 193–194
    and caregiver identity, 209
    and Caregivers' Support Group, 191–93
    and caregiving as process, 207
    and caregiving as relational, 206–207
    and multiple-read method, 195
    and positioning theory, 195–196
        then-and-there level (level 1), 195, 196–199, 208
        here-and-now level (level 2), 195, 199–203, 208
        self-to-self level (level 3), 196, 203–206, 208
    and renegotiation of caregiving, 207–208

Cross-cultural literature, on variation in relational concepts, 169
Cultural context
    and adaptiveness of behavior patterns, 180
    and Ethiopian Israeli adolescents
        and holding, 172
        and relational frame of reference, 169
    of identity formation for Japanese women, 121–122, 138–139
        interview data on, 122–124
        mechanisms of transitions in, 124–138
Cultural meanings, and relationships, 144
Cultural norms, and holding (Ethiopian Israeli adolescents), 178–179
Cultural resources, in personal narrative, 143–144
Culture
    Japanese, 121, 139
    and relationships, 9, 46, 165
        cultural meanings, 144
        of Christiana Morgan and Henry Murray, 41

Dalia (participant in study on romantic relationships), 247
Danny (participant in study on continuing bonds), 263, 264–267, 276
Dating, in study on Japanese women's identity formation, 128–129, 134
David (Ethiopian Israeli study participant), 179
Death of Ivan Ilych, The (Tolstoy), 13–15, 16
Decentration, 133
Desire, Lacan on, 61
Despair, as break in narrative integrity, 16
Development
    and longitudinal data, 93
    and relationships, 76–77
    See also Identity development
Devotional objects, 16–17
"Diptych: Father and Child" (Rogers), 67–68
Dismissing attachment style, 97
    vs. attachment needs, 108
    in story of Ann, 105, 109, 111, 114
Disorganized/fearful attachment style, 97
Distancing the memory, of lost parent, 274
"Double" (Rogers), 65–66
Douglas, Claire, 22

Hispanic adolescents, 179n
Holding, 77, 169, 172
  vs. attachment, 172
  and Lorenzo, 79, 83–84
  in study of Ethiopian Israeli adolescents,
    171–173, 184–86
    authority and idealization in, 183–
      184
    and cultural norms, 178–179
    and delinquency, 181–182
    and emotional support, 179–180
    and getting along on own, 182
    Haila (participant), 173–176, 178,
      181, 182
    and loss or grief, 184
    and parenting, 174, 176–181, 182,
      183, 184, 185
    and presence or concern as manifes-
      tation of holding, 176–177
    and socioeconomic situation, 177–
      178
    and substitute parenting figures, 182,
      185
Holistic-content approach to readings, 263
Homberger, Erik (later Erik Erikson), 32n
Hopkins Symptom Check List, 217
Hotteé du Diable ("devil's basket"), 54
Hypotheses, and romantic relationships, 248

Idealization and identification, 77, 169
  of Lorenzo, 79, 85
Identification, and continuing-bonds phenomenon, 257, 258
Identity(ies), 76
  for African American men (friendships
    in), 82
  caregiver, 209
  masculine, 81
  and narrated relationships, 144
  racial, 9, 144–146 (see also Racial iden-
    tity)
  and relationship, 8, 77, 159–161
    context in development of, 77
    cultural resources for, 143
    in story of Lorenzo, 78–88
  and self, 76
  of youth at Boys & Girls Club, 80
Identity construction, narrative, 216
Identity development
  and adolescents, 76, 77
    in story of Lorenzo, 78–88
  biracial

of Jean (interviewee), 155, 158, 159,
  160, 161
  in psychology class, 155
Erikson on, 76
Identity formation or exploration, 118, 138
  and continuing bonds, 256
  Erikson on, 118, 138
  levels of relatedness in, 118–121, 138,
    139
    mechanisms of transition for, 124–
      138
  and meaning making, 138
  in narrative of bond with mother
    (Sharon), 270
  relational aspects of, 118, 122
    cultural resources for, 143
Identity formation for Japanese women, cultural context of, 121–122, 138–139
  interview data in, 122–124
  mechanisms of transitions in, 124–138
Identity resources, 143–144
Identity stories, 146, 159–161
  of Jean, 146–147, 153–161
  of Rachel, 146–153, 159–161
Illusion, Morgan–Murray relationship as, 39
Imaginary, in Lacanian theory, 63
  and Rogers' poem, 65, 66
Immigration, 165–166
  of Ethiopian Jews to Israel, 168–169 (see
    also at Ethiopian Israeli community)
Independence, Lorenzo's description of, 82
Individualism
  language of, 43
  Western emphasis on, 76
  See also Autonomy
Individuality, Western society's stress on, 11,
  167
Individual responsibility, as American model,
  88
Insecure attachment, 96–97, 105
  in Ann's story, 101
  as unbalancing, 111
Integration of viewpoints (Japanese female
  adolescents), 133–138
Integrity, sense of, 16
Interanimation, in Morgan–Murray relation-
  ship, 43–44, 45
Interdependence
  in Black and Hispanic communities, 81
  and Lorenzo, 83
Internet, and relationship, 192
Interracial marriage, approval of, 145

Intersubjectivity, as narrative context, 42–45

Intimate exchange, 46

Intimate social relationships, and self-identification, 153

"Invisibility syndrome," 86

Iris (participant in study on romantic relationships), 242, 246–247

Israel, Ethiopian immigrants in. *See at* Ethiopian Israeli community

Itai (participant in study on romantic relationships), 244–249

Japanese culture, 139
  as interdependent, 121

Japanese women. *See* Identity formation for Japanese women, cultural context of

Jean (biracial interviewee), 146–147, 153–161

Josselson, Ruthellen
  relatedness dimensions proposed by, 77
  relational space model of, 169

Jouissance, 58, 61–62, 63
  in poems on Claudel and Rodin, 64, 66, 67, 69

Joy Luck Club, The (film), 157

Jung, Carl
  Ann on, 103
  and Murray–Morgan relationship, 24, 25, 26, 26–27, 27, 31, 37, 41
    in discovery of archetypes, 42
    and individuation, 43
    Morgan mistreated by, 34
    Morgan's contributions, to (Douglas), 35
    and the Tower, 30
    and unconscious, 23
    in understanding of relationship, 36

Karen (participant in study of romantic relationships), 243

Karen (virtual support group participant), 194, 198, 200, 202, 203, 205, 208

Lacan, Jacques, 52, 54

Lacanian poetics, 72–73

Lacanian psychoanalytic theory, 8, 58–63
  and poems on Rodin and Claudel, 64–65, 73

Lack
  in Lacanian theory, 8, 63

  in relationship of Rodin and Claudel, 63

Language
  fugitive meanings in, 73
  of individualism, 43
  Lacan on, 58, 72–73
  and Morgan–Murray relationship, 22, 36, 37, 41, 44
  of relationship, 5, 46–48
  and self–other distinction, 5
  of therapy, 224

Lieblich, Amia, 4

Life-story construction, 230, 231

Liscomb, Jessie, 56, 57, 64
  in Rogers' poems on Rodin and Claudel, 66–69, 71, 73

Loevinger, Jane, 214

Loevinger's Sentence Completion Test, 217

Longitudinal study
  and Ann's life, 93–94, 97–98, 114
  changes for observers in, 94–95

"Looking glass self," 75–76

Lorenzo (case story), 78–80, 87–88
  holding and embeddedness of, 83–84
  life story of, 79, 82
  and role modeling, 84–87
  and schools, 87
  and sense of self, 80–82

Loss, and Ethiopian Israeli adolescents, 184

Love, 5–6, 47
  academic view of, 46, 47
  in Ann's story, 103–104, 106–107, 111, 112–113
  as being-with, 4
  caregiving as, 190
  and imagination, 39
  and Morgan–Murray relationship, 22, 35
  and subjectivity of another, 43

Love's Story Told (Robinson), 22n, 35. *See also* Robinson, Forrest

Love stories, taxonomy of, 244

Lucy (virtual support group participant), 194, 198–199, 200, 202–203, 203, 205, 208

MacKinnon, Donald, 44n14

Malakamo (Ethiopian Israeli study participant), 178, 179, 181, 182

Malka (Ethiopian Israeli study participant), 176, 179

Maya (participant in study on continuing bonds), 263, 270–273, 274, 276
McAdams, Dan, 4
Meaning(s)
    of caregiver words (researchers vs. caregivers), 207–208
    cultural, 144
    fugitive, 73
    in life story, 96
    as read into text, 72
    of relationships, 191
        difficulty in articulating, 47
    shared, 45
        through relationships, 144
    and Tolstoy's *Ivan Ilych*, 15
Meaning construction (meaning making)
    development of, 129
    and ego development, 214
    and identity formation, 138
    and therapy narratives, 225
Mellard, James, 54
Melville, Herman, and Murray–Morgan relationship, 23, 25, 27, 28, 30, 31, 32, 33, 41, 42
Message-board forums, 192–193, 193n1, 206. *See also* "Crisis—Not a Vent"
Mirror stage, for Lacan, 58–60
Missing out, in narrative of bonds with lost parents, 264, 265, 266
Mixed-race America, 144–145
Mixed-race identity
    of Rachel (interviewee), 149–150, 152, 160, 161
    See also Biracial identity
Moby Dick (Melville), 23. *See also* Melville, Herman
Modernism, and power of language, 47
Modernity, Western, 11. *See also* Western cultures
"Monoscene: Mother and Children" (Rogers), 67
Morgan, Christiana, 23, 33–34
    biography of, 22, 24–27, 28, 29, 31–32, 33, 34–36, 37, 38–39, 41–43, 44, 45
    childhood traumas of, 38
    and Mike Murray, 23, 24, 24–25n5
    relationship of with Henry Murray, 22–23, 28, 30, 33–34, 37, 47–48
    and agency, 29
    anima in, 24, 26, 27, 29, 30, 37, 41
    biographers' stances toward, 34–36

    in biography of Murray, 24, 27
    intersubjectivity in, 42–45
    and Jung, 26–27, 34, 35 (*see also* Anima; Jung, Carl)
    and love as central organizing force, 47
    as pathology, 38–40
    shared meanings in, 45
    as social critique, 40–42
    and the Tower, 30, 31–32, 33, 37, 41, 48
    on sick vs. ardent, 40
    trances of, 27, 28, 37
Morgan, Will (husband of Christiana Morgan), 27, 31, 36
Mourning
    and Ethiopian Israeli adolescents, 186
    and re-membering, 259
    See also Bereavement theory; Continuing bonds; Grief and grieving
Multiple reading method, 194, 195, 208
Multiracial identity, 145. *See also* Biracial identity
Mumford, Lewis, 33
Murray, Henry (Harry), 23, 33–34
    biography of, 22, 23–24, 25–26, 27–28, 29–31, 32–33, 34–37, 38, 39–40, 41, 44, 45
    childhood traumas of, 38
    relationship of to Morgan, 22–23, 28, 30, 33–34, 37, 47–48
    biographers' stances toward, 34–36
    intersubjectivity in, 42–45
    and Jung, 26, 26–27 (*see also* Jung, Carl)
    and love as central organizing force, 47
    as pathology, 38–40
    shared meanings in, 45
    as social critique, 40–42
    and the Tower, 30, 31–32, 33, 37, 41, 48
Murray, Jo (Mrs. Henry Murray). *See* Rantoul, Jo
Murray, Mike, 23, 24, 24–25n5
Mutuality, 77, 169

Nancy (virtual support group participant), 194, 197–198, 200, 201, 204, 208
Narcissism, and Morgan–Murray relationship, 25, 39n

Narrative(s)
American, 75
biographies of Christiana Morgan and
Henry Murray as, 22, 23–33, 34–37,
38–40, 41, 44, 45
and love, 47
and relationships, 4, 6, 11, 12, 21
as dialogic, 7
as difficult, 8
and understanding, 4
and self, 143
and Tolstoy's *Ivan Ilych*, 15
Narrative of attachment style development
(Ann), 97–114 (*see also* Ann)
Narrative contexts of relationship, 37
intersubjectivity as, 42–45, 48
pathology as, 38–40
social critique as, 40–42
Narrative identity construction, 216
Narrative inquiry
and relationships, 18
and spiritual sphere (Buber), 12
Narrative integrity, 15–18
Narrative material, presentation of, 7
Narrative psychology, 47–48, 72
Narrative research, and location of researcher, 6–7
Narratives of adolescence, 77, 78–79
Lorenzo's story as, 78–88
Narratives of biracial identity, 146, 159–161
of Jean, 146–147, 153–161
of Rachel, 146–153, 159–161
Narratives of bonds with lost parents, 256,
260–263
and choice not to re-member, 276–277
of Danny, 263, 264–267, 276
of Maya, 263, 270–273, 274, 276
of Niebal, 263, 273–276
of Sharon, 263, 267–270, 272–273, 276
Narratives of caregiver support group, 191,
195–196, 208–209
then-and-there level (level 1), 196–199
here-and-now level (level 2), 199–203
self-to-self level (level 3), 203–206
See also "Crisis—Not a Vent"
Narrative scripts, limited range of, 46
Narratives of Ethiopian immigrants to Israel,
166
Barahanu, 176
Haila, 173–176, 178, 181, 182
Malka, 176, 179
Zaudo, 176, 183

See also Ethiopian Israeli community,
adolescents of
Narratives of identity formation among Japanese women, 122–138. *See also* Identity formation for Japanese women,
cultural context of
Narratives of romantic-relationship difficulties, 240–241
of Itai, 244–249
methodological considerations in,
249–250
and open dialogue, 250
and positivistic view, 251
and safety margins, 251
and sensitivity to rejection, 251
of Tamar, 241–244
and testing situations, 242, 246, 250
Narratives of therapy. *See* Therapy narratives
Narrative Study of Lives, The, 4
Narrative theory, and psychotherapy, 213.
See also Therapy narratives
Narrative tradition of analysis, 77
"Narrative turn," 5
Negotiation, 121, 124, 137
Niebal (participant in study on continuing
bonds), 263, 273–276
Nietzsche, Friedrich, and Morgan–Murray
relationship, 31
Nora (therapy-narrative study participant),
218–220, 221, 222, 223, 224, 224–
225
Norms, cultural (Ethiopian Israeli adoles-
cents), 178–179

Object relations theory, in biographies of
Morgan and Murray, 38
Oedipal period, Lacan's revision of, 58, 62
and relationship of Rodin and Claudel,
58
Oneness, with lost parent, 260, 272–273
"Ongoing relationships," 277, 278. *See also*
Continuing bonds with lost parent
Open dialogue, and romantic relationships,
250
Other, the, 12
for Buber, 12, 13
and "devotional objects," 16–17
egos of (outerworld of the ego), 117
generalized, 75–76
in Lacanian psychoanalysis, 61, 72
and narrative, 18
and relationship, 18

in Rogers' poems on Rodin and Claudel, 66, 67, 69

and self, 3, 5

significant others (study of Japanese female adolescents), 118, 127, 128, 132, 134

trusted (Ann), 108

Outerworld of the ego, 117

Paranoiac knowledge, Lacan on, 60

Parenting

caregiving system in, 96

in collectivist vs. noncollectivist cultures, 180

and holding, 172

in study of Ethiopian Israeli adolescents, 174, 176–181, 182, 183, 184, 185

and loss in immigration experience (Ethiopian Israelis), 178–179, 183, 184

in story of Ann, 103–104, 105, 106–107

Participant observers, 94

Passion, 45, 77, 169

Paternal metaphor, Lacan on, 62

Pathology, as narrative context, 38–40

Pearlin, Leonard, 190

Performative means of presentation, 8

Performative texts, 53

Personal agency. *See* Agency, personal

Personality development

and longitudinal data, 93

See also Identity development

Personality style, attachment status as, 97

Personal narrative. *See* Narrative

Persons, Buber on, 17–18

Person, Ethel, 46

Perspective-taking

development of, 119, 121–121

in study on Japanese women, 125–139

Persuasion and Healing (Frank), 215

"Petersborough, England" (Rogers), 64, 69–70

Pilobus dance company, 46

Plato

on double creatures, 46

Symposium of, 5

Play, progression in, 244

Poetics, 53

Aristotelian, 53

Lacanian, 52, 54, 72–73

and psychology, 53–54

Poetry

and ambiguities, 65

as qualitative inquiry, 53

on Rodin and Claudel (Rogers), 64–72, 73

"Diptych: Father and Child," 67–68

"Double," 65–66

"The Farewell," 70–71

"Monoscene: Mother and Children," 67

"Petersborough, England," 69–70

"Sill, Montdevergues," 71–72

"Triptych: Mother-Child-Sculpting," 68–69

Positioning theory, 191, 194, 208

then-and-there level (Level 1), 196–199, 208

here-and-now level (Level 2), 199–203, 208

self-to-self level (Level 3), 203–206, 208

Positive and Negative Affect Schedule, 217

Postmodernism

and participant observers, 94

poetry and poetics in, 53

and power of language, 47

Poststructuralism, poetry and poetics in, 53

Powerlessness, and therapy narratives, 231, 233

Preoccupation with the deceased, 257

Preoccupied attachment style, 97, 114

Presence, in Ethiopian Israeli adolescents study, 176

Privatization, political push for, 88

Problems, in therapy narratives, 221–222, 227

Proposition (proposed Morgan–Murray manifesto), 29, 30, 31, 33, 37, 40–41, 41

Psychic structures, Lacan's theory of, 52

Psychoanalysis

and infantile or irrational roots of experience, 38

Lacanian, 8, 58–63

and poems on Rodin and Claudel, 64–65, 73

and love, 5

Psychological Well-Being Scales, 217

Psychology, and poetics, 53–54

Psychology class, and identity exploration of Jean (biracial interviewee), 154–155, 156, 157

Psychology and Culture (Lonner and Malpass), 155

Psychotherapy
    alternative self-stories from, 214, 215,
        217, 230, 233
    in life story of Ann, 104, 105, 106, 108,
        114
    and narrative theory, 213–215 (*see also*
        Therapy narratives)
    and romantic-relationship failure, 237
Psychotherapy relationship. *See* Therapeutic
    relationship or alliance

Qualitative inquiry, poetry as, 53

Race, definition of, 145
Race defilement laws, 145
Race relationships, and biracial individuals,
    145–146
Rachel (biracial interviewee), 146–153, 159–
    161
Racial identity, 9, 144–146
    ambiguity of, 144
    of biracial young women (Rachel), 147–
        153 (*see also* Biracial identity, nar-
        ratives of)
    need for, 146
Ragland-Sullivan, Ellie, 54
Rantoul, Jo (Mrs. Henry Murray), 24, 26, 27,
    33, 34, 36
RAP (Relationship Anecdotes Paradigm),
    240, 249
Real, in Lacanian theory, 62
    and Rogers' poems, 65, 67
Rebellion
    creative (Morgan–Murray relationship),
        40
    in narrative of bond with mother,
        268
Rejection, sensitivity to (romantic relation-
    ship), 251
Relatedness, 167
    and adolescents, 78, 88
        in Lorenzo's story, 78–79
    as basic need, 76
    as culturally dependent, 167
    dimensions of (Josselson), 77, 169–170
    in identity exploration (levels), 118–
        121, 139
        mechanisms of transition for (Japa-
            nese women), 124–138
    and spaces for Black individuals, 82
Relation, Buber on, 12
    three spheres of, 12–15

Relational experience, "scientific" knowledge
    of, 46
Relational identities, 159–161
    context in development of, 77
Relational learning, and Lorenzo as role
    model, 85
Relational space maps, 170–171
Relational space model, 169–170
Relational thinking, 11
"Relational turn," 5
Relationship(s), 3, 21, 190
    and autonomy, 76
    for biracial youth (parental), 161
    caregiving as, 190–191, 206–207, 209
        (*see also* Caregiving)
    and culture, 9, 46, 165
        cultural meanings, 144
        for Christiana Morgan and Henry
            Murray, 41
    with deceased, 277–278 (*see also* Con-
        tinuing bonds with lost parent)
    and development, 76–77
    as functional unit (nonwestern cul-
        tures), 167
    and identity, 8, 77, 159–161
        context in development of, 77
        cultural resources for, 143
        and story of Lorenzo, 78–88
    and immigration experience, 166
    language of, 5, 46–48
    and meanings, 191
        difficulty in articulating, 47
        shared, 144
    of mothers and daughters in *The Joy
        Luck Club*, 158
    and narrative, 4, 6, 11, 12, 21
        as dialogic, 7
        as difficult, 8
        and understanding, 4
    narrative context of, 37
        intersubjectivity as, 42–45, 48
        pathology as, 37–38
        social critique as, 40–42
    and Other, 16–17, 18 (*see also* Other,
        the)
    and self, 3, 76
    among series editors, 4
    Taylor on, 17
    virtual (Internet-based), 192
    and women, 76, 77, 161
    See also Dating; Friendships; Romantic
        relationships

Relationship, therapeutic. *See* Therapeutic relationship or alliance
Relationship Anecdotes Paradigm (RAP), 240, 249
Relationship maintenance, 238–239
Religion, and Morgan–Murray relationship, 43
Re-membering, 256, 258–259, 260, 270, 277
    and Danny, 266
    and Maya, 276
    and Niebal, 273, 275
    and Shannon, 269, 270
    and stage of life, 273
Repetition compulsion, in Morgan–Murray relationship, 38
Researcher
    location of, 6–7
    qualitative, 6
Responsibility
    individual (as American model), 88
    and Lorenzo, 80
        and father, 82
Revelation, in therapy narratives, 222–223
Rilke, Rainer, Maria, 255, 255n
Ritual, in Morgan–Murray relationship, 29–30, 40
Robinson, Forrest, 35
    Murray biography by, 22, 23–24, 25–26, 27–28, 29–31, 32–33, 34–35, 36–37, 38, 39, 41, 44, 45
Rodin, Auguste, 55–56, 57–58
    relationship of with Claudel, 56–57, 57–58, 63–64
    and Liscomb, 64
    in Rogers' poems, 63, 64, 69–71, 73
    sculptures of, 51
Rodin, Marie-Louise (Maria) (sister of Auguste), 55
Role, in "as-if" personality, 38
Role modeling, and Lorenzo, 81, 83, 84–87
Romanticism, and Morgan–Murray relationship, 42
Romantic relationship(s), 237–238
    avoidance in, 247
    difficulty in establishing
        good story about partner absent in, 249
    narratives on, 240–250
    and partner seen as rejecting, 248
    paucity of studies on, 238
    and positivistic view, 243, 251
    study on, 238–240

of Morgan and Murray, 22–37, 46–48
    narrative contexts of, 37–45
    (*see also* Morgan, Christiana; Murray, Henry)
as mutual story, 244, 251
prewritten scripts for, 243–244
and working models, 239
See also Morgan, Christiana; Murray, Henry; Significant others
Runyan, Mac, 39, 42

Sadomasochism, in Morgan–Murray relationship, 32, 38
Safety margins, in romantic relationships, 251
Sanford, Nevitt, 44n14
Satisfaction With Life Scale, 217
Schneidman, Edwin, 42
School, and Ethiopian Israeli adolescents, 181
    in Israel vs. in Ethiopia (Haila), 173–175
Secure attachment, 96, 97
    in story of Ann, 111–113
    and marriage, 108–109
Security, working model of, 104–105
Self, 3
    and attachment, 95
    and identity, 76
    for Lacan, 60
    of Lorenzo (case story), 79, 80–82
    and narratives, 18, 143, 144
    in non-Western cultures, 167
    and Other, 5, 12
    and relationships, 3, 76
    and social world, 75
    and story of Ann, 114
    Western conception of, 11
    See also Ego
Self, sense of
    and Lorenzo, 80–82
    and therapy problem, 227
Self-fulfilling prophecy, acute sensitivity as, 251
Self-narrative, of mourner, 261–262, 263, 269, 278
    Danny, 265–266
    See also Continuing bonds with lost parent
Self-in-relation, transformation of, 95
Self-silencing, 246–247, 250
Self-stories, 230–231

for Lorenzo, 83
in marriage and partnership of Ann,
108, 113
in Murray–Morgan relationship, 37

Unconscious
and Lacanian theory, 72–73
and Morgan–Murray relationship, 25,
28, 36
and Morgan's visions, 34
Murray's interest in, 30
Uri (Ethiopian Israeli study participant), 180,
181, 182
Using Lacan, Reading Fiction (Mellard), 54

Validation, 77, 169
and adolescents' conflicts with parents,
179
of Lorenzo, 79, 84–87
through meanings of relationships, 191
Venting (caregiver support group), 201. *See
also* "Crisis—Not a Vent"
"Vicissitudes of Creativity" (Murray), 36–37,
41
Virtual support groups, 192, 209. *See also*
"Crisis—Not a Vent"
Vocabulary
of caregiver, 208
See also Language

Weitzman, Chaim, 24
Well-being (WB), 214, 233. *See also* Therapy
narratives
Western cultures

independence of self in, 167
individualism and autonomy emphasized in, 11, 76, 166
and relational dimensions, 170
What Joy! (Morgan), 33, 37
White, Robert, 44n14
Whitehead, Alfred North, 33
Willy (therapy-narrative study participant),
225–227, 228
Wolff, Toni, 26, 27, 37
Women
relatedness in identity development of,
121
and relationships, 76, 77, 161
Women, Japanese. *See* Identity formation for
Japanese women, cultural context of
Working models, 239, 250
attachment status as, 96, 97
in Ann's life, 95, 101, 107, 111
and earned security, 95
and love, 5–6
as double-edged swords, 242
in romantic-relationship narratives, 242
and transference, 240
"Wrong answer," in romantic relationship
narrative, 241, 243, 244, 250
Wyatt, Fredrick, 44n14

Youth organizations, meaningful social role
in, 87

Zaudo (Ethiopian Israeli study participant),
176, 183

ABOUT THE EDITORS

Ruthellen Josselson, PhD, is professor of psychology at the Fielding Graduate University in Baltimore, Maryland. She was formerly professor of psychology at The Hebrew University of Jerusalem and has also been a visiting professor at the Harvard Graduate School of Education. A recipient of the 1994 Henry A. Murray Award from the American Psychological Association, she has published many scholarly articles and chapters on narrative and life-history research. She is the author of *Revising Herself: The Story of Women's Identity From College to Midlife*, which received the Delta Kappa Gamma International Educator's Award, and of *The Space Between Us: Exploring the Dimensions of Human Relationships*.

Amia Lieblich, PhD, is a professor of psychology at The Hebrew University of Jerusalem. Her books have presented an oral history of Israeli society and deal with war, military service, prisoners of war, and the kibbutz. She has written psychobiographies of the Israeli female author Dvora Baron (*Conversations With Dvora*, trans. by Naomi Seidman) and the Israeli female poet Lea Goldberg (*Learning About Lea*). She has also recently published (with Rivka Tuval-Mashiach and Tamar Zilber) *Narrative Research: Reading, Analysis, and Interpretation*, a book that presents her approach to narrative research. She has taught graduate courses on life stories and their use in research.

Dan P. McAdams, PhD, is professor of human development and social policy and of psychology as well as director of the Foley Center for the Study of Lives at Northwestern University. A fellow of the American Psychological Association and recipient of the 1989 Henry A. Murray Award, he has published widely on the topics of narrative identity and the self, generativity and adult development, and the role of life stories in personality development and in culture. His most recent work is *The Redemptive Self: Stories Americans Live By*.